Great Poetry of the English Language:
GEOFFREY CHAUCER TO EMILY DICKINSON

WATTS ULTRATYPE™ *Editions*

This is a series that includes the best of the world's literature in a superior format and design.

Selected Volumes

A WATTS ULTRATYPE ™ *Edition*

GREAT POETRY OF THE ENGLISH LANGUAGE:
Geoffrey Chaucer to Emily Dickinson

Selected and with an Introduction by
Henry B. Weisberg, B.S., M.Ed.

FRANKLIN WATTS, INC.

A DIVISION OF GROLIER INCORPORATED

575 Lexington Avenue

New York, New York 10022

Compilation and Introduction copyright © 1969 Henry B. Weisberg
Library of Congress Catalog Card Number: 74–79788

Printed in the United States of America

CONTENTS

INTRODUCTION

No anthology of English poetry is better known, more respected, more loved than Palgrave's *Golden Treasury*. In a simple chronological arrangement, without regard to theme or type, Palgrave collected for us the poems he loved best from the best loved poets in English and Scottish literature.

But Palgrave died nearly a hundred years ago, and, although four splendid revisions of the *Golden Treasury* have provided us with treasures by later poets, none have extended their selections to America. No criticism of these editions is intended as it may reasonably be considered that the inclusion of American poets would change the original intention and character of the first Palgrave. However, at this point in time who can draw a real distinction between English and American poetry? Which anthologist seeking to please a wide readership wherever poetry is loved would any longer exclude one or the other? Accordingly, I have deleted in this edition those poems I judge no longer likely to appeal to a contemporary reader, and I have added my own favorites in the public domain from the long chronology of distinguished American poets and a few poems by poets not yet distinguished.

HENRY B. WEISBERG, B.S., M.ED.
Head of the English Department
Central High School
Philadelphia, Pa.

BOOK FIRST

THE PROLOGUE TO
THE CANTERBURY TALES

WHEN April with his showers sweet with fruit
The drought of March has pierced unto the root
And bathed each vein with liquor that has power
To generate therein and sire the flower;
When Zephyr also has, with his sweet breath,
Quickened again, in every holt and heath,
The tender shoots and buds, and the young sun
Into the Ram one half his course has run,
And many little birds make melody
That sleep through all the night with open eye
(So Nature pricks them on to ramp and rage)—
Then do folk long to go on pilgrimage,
And palmers to go seeking out strange strands,
To distant shrines well known in sundry lands.
And specially from every shire's end
Of England they to Canterbury wend,
The holy blessed martyr there to seek
Who helped them when they lay so ill and weak.

    Befell that, in that season, on a day
In Southwark, at the Tabard, as I lay
Ready to start upon my pilgrimage

To Canterbury, full of devout homage,
There came at nightfall to that hostelry
Some nine and twenty in a company
Of sundry persons who had chanced to fall
In fellowship, and pilgrims were they all
That toward Canterbury town would ride.
The rooms and stables spacious were and wide,
And well we there were eased, and of the best.
And briefly, when the sun had gone to rest,
So had I spoken with them, every one,
That I was of their fellowship anon,
And made agreement that we'd early rise
To take the road, as you I will apprise.

But none the less, whilst I have time and space,
Before yet farther in this tale I pace,
It seems to me accordant with reason
To inform you of the state of every one
Of all of these, as it appeared to me,
And who they were, and what was their degree,
And even how arrayed there at the inn;
And with a knight thus will I first begin.

THE KNIGHT

A knight there was, and he a worthy man,
Who, from the moment that he first began
To ride about the world, loved chivalry,
Truth, honour, freedom and all courtesy.
Full worthy was he in his liege-lord's war,
And therein had he ridden (none more far)

As well in Christendom as heathenesse,
And honoured everywhere for worthiness.
    At Alexandria, he, when it was won;
Full oft the table's roster he'd begun
Above all nations' knights in Prussia.
In Latvia raided he, and Russia,
No christened man so oft of his degree.
In far Granada at the siege was he
Of Algeciras, and in Belmarie.
At Ayas was he and at Satalye
When they were won; and on the Middle Sea
At many a noble meeting chanced to be.
Of mortal battles he had fought fifteen,
And he'd fought for our faith at Tramissene
Three times in lists, and each time slain his foe.
This self-same worthy knight had been also
At one time with the lord of Palatye
Against another heathen in Turkey:
And always won he sovereign fame for prize.
Though so illustrious, he was very wise
And bore himself as meekly as a maid.
He never yet had any vileness said,
In all his life, to whatsoever wight.
He was a truly perfect, gentle knight.
But now, to tell you all of his array,
His steeds were good, but yet he was not gay.
Of simple fustian wore he a jupon
Sadly discoloured by his habergeon;
For he had lately come from his voyage
And now was going on this pilgrimage.

THE SQUIRE

With him there was his son, a youthful squire,
A lover and a lusty bachelor,
With locks well curled, as if they'd laid in press.
Some twenty years of age he was, I guess.
In stature he was of an average length,
Wondrously active, aye, and great of strength.
He'd ridden sometime with the cavalry
In Flanders, in Artois, and Picardy,
And borne him well within that little space
In hope to win thereby his lady's grace.
Prinked out he was, as if he were a mead,
All full of fresh-cut flowers white and red.
Singing he was, or fluting, all the day;
He was as fresh as is the month of May.
Short was his gown, with sleeves both long and wide.
Well could he sit on horse, and fairly ride.
He could make songs and words thereto indite,
Joust, and dance too, as well as sketch and write.
So hot he loved that, while night told her tale,
He slept no more than does a nightingale.
Courteous he, and humble, willing and able,
And carved before his father at the table.

THE YEOMAN

A yeoman had he, nor more servants, no,
At that time, for he chose to travel so;

And he was clad in coat and hood of green.
A sheaf of peacock arrows bright and keen
Under his belt he bore right carefully
(Well could he keep his tackle yeomanly:
His arrows had no draggled feathers low),
And in his hand he bore a mighty bow.
A cropped head had he and a sun-browned face.
Of woodcraft knew he all the useful ways.
Upon his arm he bore a bracer gay,
And at one side a sword and buckler, yea,
And at the other side a dagger bright,
Well sheathed and sharp as spear point in the light;
On breast a Christopher of silver sheen.
He bore a horn in baldric all of green;
A forester he truly was, I guess.

THE PRIORESS

There was also a nun, a prioress,
Who, in her smiling, modest was and coy;
Her greatest oath was but "By Saint Eloy!"
And she was known as Madam Eglantine.
Full well she sang the services divine,
Intoning through her nose, becomingly;
And fair she spoke her French, and fluently,
After the school of Stratford-at-the-Bow,
For French of Paris was not hers to know.
At table she had been well taught withal,
And never from her lips let morsels fall,
Nor dipped her fingers deep in sauce, but ate

With so much care the food upon her plate
That never driblet fell upon her breast.
In courtesy she had delight and zest.
Her upper lip was always wiped so clean
That in her cup was no iota seen
Of grease, when she had drunk her draught of wine.
Becomingly she reached for meat to dine.
And certainly delighting in good sport,
She was right pleasant, amiable—in short.
She was at pains to counterfeit the look
Of courtliness, and stately manners took,
And would be held worthy of reverence.
  But, to say something of her moral sense,
She was so charitable and piteous
That she would weep if she but saw a mouse
Caught in a trap, though it were dead or bled.
She had some little dogs, too, that she fed
On roasted flesh, or milk and fine white bread.
But sore she'd weep if one of them were dead,
Or if men smote it with a rod to smart:
For pity ruled her, and her tender heart.
Right decorous her pleated wimple was;
Her nose was fine; her eyes were blue as glass;
Her mouth was small and therewith soft and red;
But certainly she had a fair forehead;
It was almost a full span broad, I own,
For, truth to tell, she was not undergrown.
Neat was her cloak, as I was well aware.
Of coral small about her arm she'd bear
A string of beads and gauded all with green;

And therefrom hung a brooch of golden sheen
Whereon there was first written a crowned "A,"
And under, *Amor vincit omnia*.

THE NUN

Another little nun with her had she,

THE THREE PRIESTS

Who was her chaplain; and of priests she'd three.

THE MONK

A monk there was, one made for mastery,
An outrider, who loved his venery;
A manly man, to be an abbot able.
Full many a blooded horse had he in stable:
And when he rode men might his bridle hear
A-jingling in the whistling wind as clear,
Aye, and as loud as does the chapel bell
Where this brave monk was master of the cell.
The rule of Maurus or Saint Benedict,
By reason it was old and somewhat strict,
This said monk let such old things slowly pace
And followed new-world manners in their place.
He cared not for that text a clean-plucked hen
Which holds that hunters are not holy men;
Nor that a monk, when he is cloisterless,
Is like unto a fish that's waterless;

9

That is to say, a monk out of his cloister.
But this same text he held not worth an oyster;
And I said his opinion was right good.
What? Should he study as a madman would
Upon a book in cloister cell? Or yet
Go labour with his hands and swink and sweat,
As Austin bids? How shall the world be served?
Let Austin have his toil to him reserved.
Therefore he was a rider day and night;
Greyhounds he had, as swift as bird in flight.
Since riding and the hunting of the hare
Were all his love, for no cost would he spare.
I saw his sleeves were purfled at the hand
With fur of grey, the finest in the land;
Also, to fasten hood beneath his chin,
He had of good wrought gold a curious pin:
A love-knot in the larger end there was.
His head was bald and shone like any glass,
And smooth as one anointed was his face.
Fat was this lord, he stood in goodly case.
His bulging eyes he rolled about, and hot
They gleamed and red, like fire beneath a pot;
His boots were soft; his horse of great estate.
Now certainly he was a fine prelate:
He was not pale as some poor wasted ghost.
A fat swan loved he best of any roast.
His palfrey was as brown as is a berry.

THE FRIAR

A friar there was, a wanton and a merry,
A limiter, a very festive man.
In all the Orders Four is none that can
Equal his gossip and his fair language.
He had arranged full many a marriage
Of women young, and this at his own cost.
Unto his order he was a noble post.
Well liked by all and intimate was he
With franklins everywhere in his country,
And with the worthy women of the town:
For at confessing he'd more power in gown
(As he himself said) than a good curate,
For of his order he was licentiate.
He heard confession gently, it was said,
Gently absolved too, leaving naught of dread.
He was an easy man to give penance
When knowing he should gain a good pittance;
For to a begging friar, money given
Is sign that any man has been well shriven.
For if one gave (he dared to boast of this),
He took the man's repentance not amiss.
For many a man there is so hard of heart
He cannot weep however pains may smart.
Therefore, instead of weeping and of prayer,
Men should give silver to poor friars all bare.
His tippet was stuck always full of knives
And pins, to give to young and pleasing wives.

And certainly he kept a merry note:
Well could he sing and play upon the rote.
At balladry he bore the prize away.
His throat was white as lily of the May;
Yet strong he was as ever champion.
In towns he knew the taverns, every one,
And every good host and each barmaid too—
Better than begging lepers, these he knew.
For unto no such solid man as he
Accorded it, as far as he could see,
To have sick lepers for acquaintances.
There is no honest advantageousness
In dealing with such poverty-stricken curs;
It's with the rich and with big victuallers.
And so, wherever profit might arise,
Courteous he was and humble in men's eyes.
There was no other man so virtuous.
He was the finest beggar of his house;
A certain district being farmed to him,
None of his brethren dared approach its rim;
For though a widow had no shoes to show,
So pleasant was his *In principio*,
He always got a farthing ere he went.
He lived by pickings, it is evident.
And he could romp as well as any whelp.
On love days could he be of mickle help.
For there he was not like a cloisterer,
With threadbare cope as is the poor scholar,
But he was like a lord or like a pope.
Of double worsted was his semi-cope,

That rounded like a bell, as you may guess.
He lisped a little, out of wantonness,
To make his English soft upon his tongue;
And in his harping, after he had sung,
His two eyes twinkled in his head as bright
As do the stars within the frosty night.
This worthy limiter was named Hubert.

THE MERCHANT

There was a merchant with forked beard, and girt
In motley gown, and high on horse he sat,
Upon his head a Flemish beaver hat;
His boots were fastened rather elegantly.
He spoke his notions out right pompously,
Stressing the times when he had won, not lost.
He would the sea were held at any cost
Across from Middleburgh to Orwell town.
At money-changing he could make a crown.
This worthy man kept all his wits well set;
There was no one could say he was in debt,
So well he governed all his trade affairs
With bargains and with borrowings and with shares.
Indeed, he was a worthy man withal,
But, sooth to say, his name I can't recall.

THE CLERK

A clerk from Oxford was with us also,
Who'd turned to getting knowledge, long ago.

As meagre was his horse as is a rake,
Nor he himself too fat, I'll undertake,
But he looked hollow and went soberly.
Right threadbare was his overcoat; for he
Had got him yet no churchly benefice,
Nor was so worldly as to gain office.
For he would rather have at his bed's head
Some twenty books, all bound in black and red,
Of Aristotle and his philosophy
Than rich robes, fiddle, or gay psaltery.
Yet, and for all he was philosopher,
He had but little gold within his coffer;
But all that he might borrow from a friend
On books and learning he would swiftly spend,
And then he'd pray right busily for the souls
Of those who gave him wherewithal for schools.
Of study took he utmost care and heed.
Not one word spoke he more than was his need;
And that was said in fullest reverence
And short and quick and full of high good sense.
Pregnant of moral virtue was his speech;
And gladly would he learn and gladly teach.

THE LAWYER

A sergeant of the law, wary and wise,
Who'd often gone to Paul's walk to advise,
There was also, compact of excellence.
Discreet he was, and of great reverence;
At least he seemed so, his words were so wise.

Often he sat as justice in assize,
By patent or commission from the crown;
Because of learning and his high renown,
He took large fees and many robes could own.
So great a purchaser was never known.
All was fee simple to him, in effect,
Wherefore his claims could never be suspect.
Nowhere a man so busy of his class,
And yet he seemed much busier than he was.
All cases and all judgments could he cite
That from King William's time were apposite.
And he could draw a contract so explicit
Not any man could fault therefrom elicit;
And every statute he'd verbatim quote.
He rode but badly in a medley coat,
Belted in a silken sash, with little bars,
But of his dress no more particulars.

THE FRANKLIN

There was a franklin in his company;
White was his beard as is the white daisy.
Of sanguine temperament by every sign,
He loved right well his morning sop in wine.
Delightful living was the goal he'd won,
For he was Epicurus' very son,
That held opinion that a full delight
Was true felicity, perfect and right.
A householder, and that a great, was he;
Saint Julian he was in his own country.

His bread and ale were always right well done;
A man with better cellars there was none.
Baked meat was never wanting in his house,
Of fish and flesh, and that so plenteous
It seemed to snow therein both food and drink
Of every dainty that a man could think.
According to the season of the year
He changed his diet and his means of cheer.
Full many a fattened partridge did he mew,
And many a bream and pike in fish-pond too.
Woe to his cook, except the sauces were
Poignant and sharp, and ready all his gear.
His table, waiting in his hall alway,
Stood ready covered through the livelong day.
At county sessions was he lord and sire,
And often acted as a knight of shire.
A dagger and a trinket-bag of silk
Hung from his girdle, white as morning milk.
He had been sheriff and been auditor;
And nowhere was a worthier vavasor.

THE HABERDASHER AND THE CARPENTER

A haberdasher and a carpenter,

THE WEAVER, THE DYER,
AND THE ARRAS-MAKER

An arras-maker, dyer, and weaver
Were with us, clothed in similar livery,

All of one sober, great fraternity.
Their gear was new and well adorned it was;
Their weapons were not cheaply trimmed with brass,
But all with silver; chastely made and well
Their girdles and their pouches too, I tell.
Each man of them appeared a proper burgess
To sit in guildhall on a high dais.
And each of them, for wisdom he could span,
Was fitted to have been an alderman;
For chattels they'd enough, and, too, of rent;
To which their goodwives gave a free assent,
Or else for certain they had been to blame.
It's good to hear "Madam" before one's name,
And go to church when all the world may see,
Having one's mantle borne right royally.

THE COOK

A cook they had with them, just for the nonce,
To boil the chickens with the marrow-bones,
And flavour tartly and with galingale.
Well could he tell a draught of London ale.
And he could roast and seethe and broil and fry,
And make a good thick soup, and bake a pie.
But very ill it was, it seemed to me,
That on his shin a deadly sore had he;
For sweet blanc-mange, he made it with the best.

THE SAILOR

There was a sailor, living far out west;
For aught I know, he was of Dartmouth town.
He sadly rode a hackney, in a gown,
Of thick rough cloth falling to the knee.
A dagger hanging on a cord had he
About his neck, and under arm, and down.
The summer's heat had burned his visage brown;
And certainly he was a good fellow.
Full many a draught of wine he'd drawn, I trow,
Of Bordeaux vintage, while the trader slept.
Nice conscience was a thing he never kept.
If that he fought and got the upper hand,
By water he sent them home to every land.
But as for craft, to reckon well his tides,
His currents and the dangerous watersides,
His harbours, and his moon, his pilotage,
There was none such from Hull to far Carthage.
Hardy, and wise in all things undertaken,
By many a tempest had his beard been shaken.
He knew well all the havens, as they were,
From Gottland to the Cape of Finisterre,
And every creek in Brittany and Spain;
His vessel had been christened *Madeleine*.

THE PHYSICIAN

With us there was a doctor of physic;
In all this world was none like him to pick
For talk of medicine and surgery;
For he was grounded in astronomy.
He often kept a patient from the pall
By horoscopes and magic natural.
Well could he tell the fortune ascendent
Within the houses for his sick patient.
He knew the cause of every malady,
Were it of hot or cold, of moist or dry,
And where engendered, and of what humour;
He was a very good practitioner.
The cause being known, down to the deepest root
Anon he gave to the sick man his boot.
Ready he was, with his apothecaries,
To send him drugs and all electuaries;
By mutual aid much gold they'd always won—
Their friendship was a thing not new begun.
Well read was he in Esculapius,
And Deiscorides, and in Rufus,
Hippocrates, and Hali, and Galen,
Serapion, Rhazes, and Avicen,
Averrhoës, Gilbert, and Constantine,
Bernard, and Gatisden, and John Damascene.
In diet he was measured as could be,
Including naught of superfluity,
But nourishing and easy. It's no libel

19

To say he read but little in the Bible.
In blue and scarlet he went clad, withal,
Lined with a taffeta and with sendal;
And yet he was right chary of expense;
He kept the gold he gained from pestilence.
For gold in physic is a fine cordial,
And therefore loved he gold exceeding all.

THE WIFE OF BATH

There was a housewife come from Bath, or near,
Who—sad to say—was deaf in either ear.
At making cloth she had so great a bent
She bettered those of Ypres and even of Ghent.
In all the parish there was no goodwife
Should offering make before her, on my life;
And if one did, indeed, so wroth was she
It put her out of all her charity.
Her kerchiefs were of finest weave and ground;
I dare swear that they weighed a full ten pound
Which, of a Sunday, she wore on her head.
Her hose were of the choicest scarlet red,
Close gartered, and her shoes were soft and new.
Bold was her face, and fair, and red of hue.
She'd been respectable throughout her life,
With five churched husbands bringing joy and strife,
Not counting other company in youth;
But thereof there's no need to speak, in truth.
Three times she'd journeyed to Jerusalem;
And many a foreign stream she'd had to stem;

At Rome she'd been, and she'd been in Boulogne,
In Spain at Santiago, and at Cologne.
She could tell much of wandering by the way:
Gap-toothed was she, it is no lie to say.
Upon an ambler easily she sat,
Well wimpled, aye, and over all a hat
As broad as is a buckler or a targe;
A rug was tucked around her buttocks large,
And on her feet a pair of sharpened spurs.
In company well could she laugh her slurs.
The remedies of love she knew, perchance,
For of that art she'd learned the old, old dance.

THE PARSON

There was a good man of religion, too,
A country parson, poor, I warrant you;
But rich he was in holy thought and work.
He was a learned man also, a clerk,
Who Christ's own gospel truly sought to preach;
Devoutly his parishioners would he teach.
Benign he was and wondrous diligent.
Patient in adverse times and well content.
As he was ofttimes proven; always blithe,
He was right loath to curse to get a tithe,
But rather would he give, in case of doubt,
Unto those poor parishioners about,
Part of his income, even of his goods.
Enough with little, coloured all his moods.
Wide was his parish, houses far asunder,

But never did he fail, for rain or thunder,
In sickness, or in sin, or any state,
To visit to the farthest, small and great,
Going afoot, and in his hand a stave.
This fine example to his flock he gave,
That first he wrought and afterwards he taught;
Out of the gospel then that text he caught,
And this figure he added thereunto—
That, if gold rust, what shall poor iron do?
For if the priest be foul, in whom we trust,
What wonder if a layman yield to lust?
And shame it is, if priest take thought for keep,
A shitty shepherd, shepherding clean sheep.
Well ought a priest example good to give,
By his own cleanness, how his flock should live.
He never let his benefice for hire,
Leaving his flock to flounder in the mire,
And ran to London, up to old Saint Paul's
To get himself a chantry there for souls,
Nor in some brotherhood did he withhold;
But dwelt at home and kept so well the fold
That never wolf could make his plans miscarry;
He was a shepherd and not mercenary.
And holy though he was, and virtuous,
To sinners he was not impiteous,
Nor haughty in his speech, nor too divine,
But in all teaching prudent and benign.
To lead folk into Heaven but by stress
Of good example was his busyness.
But if some sinful one proved obstinate,

22

Be who it might, of high or low estate,
Him he reproved, and sharply, as I know.
There is nowhere a better priest, I trow.
He had no thirst for pomp or reverence,
Nor made himself a special, spiced conscience,
But Christ's own lore, and His apostles' twelve
He taught, but first he followed it himselve.

THE PLOWMAN

With him there was a plowman, was his brother,
That many a load of dung, and many another
Had scattered, for a good true toiler, he,
Living in peace and perfect charity.
He loved God most, and that with his whole heart
At all times, though he played or plied his art,
And next, his neighbour, even as himself.
He'd thresh and dig, with never thought of pelf,
For Christ's own sake, for every poor wight,
All without pay, if it lay in his might.
He paid his taxes, fully, fairly, well,
Both by his own toil and by stuff he'd sell.
In a tabard he rode upon a mare.
   There were also a reeve and miller there;
A summoner, manciple and pardoner,
And these, beside myself, made all there were.

THE MILLER

The miller was a stout churl, be it known,
Hardy and big of brawn and big of bone;

Which was well proved, for when he went on lam
At wrestling, never failed he of the ram.
He was a chunky fellow, broad of build;
He'd heave a door from hinges if he willed,
Or break it through, by running, with his head.
His beard, as any sow or fox, was red,
And broad it was as if it were a spade.
Upon the coping of his nose he had
A wart, and thereon stood a tuft of hairs,
Red as the bristles in an old sow's ears;
His nostrils they were black and very wide.
A sword and buckler bore he by his side.
His mouth was like a furnace door for size.
He was a jester and could poetize,
But mostly all of sin and ribaldries.
He could steal corn and full thrice charge his fees;
And yet he had a thumb of gold, begad.
A white coat and blue hood he wore, this lad.
A bagpipe he could blow well, be it known,
And with that same he brought us out of town.

THE MANCIPLE

There was a manciple from an inn of court,
To whom all buyers might quite well resort
To learn the art of buying food and drink;
For whether he paid cash or not, I think
That he so knew the markets, when to buy,
He never found himself left high and dry.
Now is it not of God a full fair grace

That such a vulgar man has wit to pace
The wisdom of a crowd of learned men?
Of masters had he more than three times ten,
Who were in law expert and curious;
Whereof there were a dozen in that house
Fit to be stewards of both rent and land
Of any lord in England who would stand
Upon his own and live in manner good,
In honour, debtless (save his head were wood),
Or live as frugally as he might desire;
These men were able to have helped a shire
In any case that ever might befall;
And yet this manciple outguessed them all.

THE REEVE

The reeve he was a slender, choleric man,
Who shaved his beard as close as razor can.
His hair was cut round even with his ears;
His top was tonsured like a pulpiteer's.
Long were his legs, and they were very lean,
And like a staff, with no calf to be seen.
Well could he manage granary and bin;
No auditor could ever on him win.
He could foretell, by drought and by the rain,
The yielding of his seed and of his grain.
His lord's sheep and his oxen and his dairy,
His swine and horses, all his stores, his poultry,
Were wholly in this steward's managing;
And, by agreement, he'd made reckoning

Since his young lord of age was twenty years;
Yet no man ever found him in arrears.
There was no agent, hind, or herd who'd cheat
But he knew well his cunning and deceit;
They were afraid of him as of the death.
His cottage was a good one, on a heath;
By green trees shaded with this dwelling-place.
Much better than his lord could he purchase.
Right rich he was in his own private right,
Seeing he'd pleased his lord, by day or night,
By giving him, or lending, of his goods,
And so got thanked—but yet got coats and hoods.
In youth he'd learned a good trade, and had been
A carpenter, as fine as could be seen.
This steward sat a horse that well could trot,
And was all dapple-grey, and was named Scot.
A long surcoat of blue did he parade,
And at his side he bore a rusty blade.
Of Norfolk was this reeve of whom I tell,
From near a town that men called Badeswell.
Bundled he was like friar from chin to croup,
And ever he rode hindmost of our troop.

THE SUMMONER

A summoner was with us in that place,
Who had a fiery-red, cherubic face,
For eczema he had; his eyes were narrow
As hot he was, and lecherous, as a sparrow;
With black and scabby brows and scanty beard;

26

He had a face that little children feared.
There was no mercury, sulphur, or litharge,
No borax, ceruse, tartar, could discharge,
Nor ointment that could cleanse enough, or bite,
To free him of his boils and pimples white,
Nor of the bosses resting on his cheeks.
Well loved he garlic, onions, aye and leeks,
And drinking of strong wine as red as blood.
Then would he talk and shout as madman would.
And when a deal of wine he'd poured within,
Then would he utter no word save Latin.
Some phrases had he learned, say two or three,
Which he had garnered out of some decree;
No wonder, for he'd heard it all the day;
And all you know right well that even a jay
Can call out "Wat" as well as can the pope.
But when, for aught else, into him you'd grope,
'Twas found he'd spent his whole philosophy;
Just *"Questio quid juris"* would he cry.
He was a noble rascal, and a kind;
A better comrade 'twould be hard to find.
Why, he would suffer, for a quart of wine,
Some good fellow to have his concubine
A twelve-month, and excuse him to the full
(Between ourselves, though, he could pluck a gull).
And if he chanced upon a good fellow,
He would instruct him never to have awe,
In such a case, of the archdeacon's curse,
Except a man's soul lie within his purse;
For in his purse the man should punished be.

"The purse is the archdeacon's Hell," said he.
But well I know he lied in what he said,
A curse ought every guilty man to dread
(For curse can kill, as absolution save),
And 'ware *significavit* to the grave.
In his own power had he, and at ease,
The boys and girls of all the diocese,
And knew their secrets, and by counsel led.
A garland had he set upon his head,
Large as a tavern's wine-bush on a stake;
A buckler had he made of bread they bake.

THE PARDONER

With him there rode a gentle pardoner
Of Rouncival, his friend and his compeer;
Straight from the court of Rome had journeyed he.
Loudly he sang "Come hither, love, to me,"
The summoner joining with a burden round;
Was never horn of half so great a sound.
This pardoner had hair as yellow as wax,
But lank it hung as does a strike of flax;
In wisps hung down such locks as he'd on head,
And with them he his shoulders overspread;
But thin they dropped, and stringy, one by one.
But as to hood, for sport of it, he'd none,
Though it was packed in wallet all the while.
It seemed to him he went in latest style,
Dishevelled, save for cap, his head all bare.
As shiny eyes he had as has a hare.

He had a fine veronica sewed to cap.
His wallet lay before him in his lap,
Stuffed full of pardons brought from Rome all hot.
A voice he had that bleated like a goat.
No beard had he, nor ever should he have,
For smooth his face as he'd just had a shave;
I think he was a gelding or a mare.
But in his craft, from Berwick unto Ware,
Was no such pardoner in any place.
For in his bag he had a pillowcase
The which, he said, was Our True Lady's veil:
He said he had a piece of the very sail
That good Saint Peter had, what time he went
Upon the sea, till Jesus changed his bent.
He had a latten cross set full of stones,
And in a bottle had he some pig's bones.
But with these relics, when he came upon
Some simple parson, then this paragon
In that one day more money stood to gain
Than the poor dupe in two months could attain.
And thus, with flattery and suchlike japes,
He made the parson and the rest his apes.
But yet, to tell the whole truth at the last,
He was, in church, a fine ecclesiast.
Well could he read a lesson or a story,
But best of all he sang an offertory;
For well he knew that when that song was sung,
Then might he preach, and all with polished tongue.
To win some silver, as he right well could;
Therefore he sang so merrily and so loud.

29

Now have I told you briefly, in a clause,
The state, the array, the number, and the cause
Of the assembling of this company
In Southwark, at this noble hostelry
Known as the Tabard Inn, hard by the Bell.
But now the time is come wherein to tell
How all we bore ourselves that very night
When at the hostelry we did alight.
And afterward the story I engage
To tell you of our common pilgrimage.
But first, I pray you, of your courtesy,
You'll not ascribe it to vulgarity
Though I speak plainly of this matter here,
Retailing you their words and means of cheer;
Nor though I use their very terms, nor lie.
For this thing do you know as well as I:
When one repeats a tale told by a man,
He must report, as nearly as he can,
Every least word, if he remember it,
However rude it be, or how unfit;
Or else he may be telling what's untrue,
Embellishing and fictionizing too.
He may not spare, although it were his brother;
He must as well say one word as another.
Christ spoke right broadly out, in holy writ,
And, you know well, there's nothing low in it.
And Plato says, to those able to read:
"The word should be the cousin to the deed."
Also, I pray that you'll forgive it me

If I have not set folk, in their degree
Here in this tale, by rank as they should stand.
My wits are not the best, you'll understand.

    Great cheer our host gave to us, every one,
And to the supper set us all anon;
And served us then with victuals of the best.
Strong was the wine and pleasant to each guest.
A seemly man our good host was, withal,
Fit to have been a marshal in some hall;
He was a large man, with protruding eyes,
As fine a burgher as in Cheapside lies;
Bold in his speech, and wise, and right well taught,
And as to manhood, lacking there in naught.
Also, he was a very merry man,
And after meat, at playing he began,
Speaking of mirth among some other things,
When all of us had paid our reckonings;
And saying thus: "Now masters, verily
You are all welcome here, and heartily:
For by my truth, and telling you no lie,
I have not seen, this year, a company
Here in this inn, fitter for sport than now.
Fain would I make you happy, knew I how.
And of a game have I this moment thought
To give you joy, and it shall cost you naught.
    "You go to Canterbury; may God speed
And the blest martyr soon requite your meed.
And well I know, as you go on your way,
You'll tell good tales and shape yourselves to play;

31

For truly there's no mirth nor comfort, none,
Riding the roads as dumb as is a stone;
And therefore will I furnish you a sport,
As I just said, to give you some comfort.
And if you like it, all, by one assent,
And will be ruled by me, of my judgment,
And will so do as I'll proceed to say,
Tomorrow, when you ride upon your way,
Then, by my father's spirit, who is dead,
If you're not gay, I'll give you up my head.
Hold up your hands, nor more about it speak."
　　Our full assenting was not far to seek;
We thought there was no reason to think twice,
And granted him his way without advice,
And bade him tell his verdict just and wise,
　　"Masters," quoth he, "here now is my advice;
But take it not, I pray you, in disdain;
This is the point, to put it short and plain,
That each of you, beguiling the long day,
Shall tell two stories as you wend your way
To Canterbury town; and each of you
On coming home, shall tell another two,
All of adventures he has known befall.
And he who plays his part the best of all,
That is to say, who tells upon the road
Tales of best sense, in most amusing mode,
Shall have a supper at the others' cost
Here in this room and sitting by this post,
When we come back again from Canterbury.
And now, the more to warrant you'll be merry,

32

I will myself, and gladly, with you ride
At my own cost, and I will be your guide.
But whosoever shall my rule gainsay
Shall pay for all that's bought along the way.
And if you are agreed that it be so,
Tell me at once, or if not, tell me no,
And I will act accordingly. No more."

This thing was granted, and our oaths we swore,
With right glad hearts, and prayed of him, also,
That he would take the office, nor forgo
The place of governor of all of us,
Judging our tales; and by his wisdom thus
Arrange that supper at a certain price,
We to be ruled, each one, by his advice
In things both great and small; by one assent,
We stood committed to his government.
And thereupon, the wine was fetched anon;
We drank, and then to rest went every one,
And that without a longer tarrying.

Next morning, when the day began to spring,
Up rose our host, and acting as our cock,
He gathered us together in a flock,
And forth we rode, a jog-trot being the pace,
Until we reached Saint Thomas' watering-place.
And there our host pulled horse up to a walk,
And said: "Now, masters, listen while I talk.
You know what you agreed at set of sun.
If even-song and morning-song are one,
Let's here decide who first shall tell a tale.
And as I hope to drink more wine and ale,

33

Whoso proves rebel to my government
Shall pay for all that by the way is spent.
Come now, draw cuts, before we farther win,
And he that draws the shortest shall begin.
Sir knight," said he, "my master and my lord,
You shall draw first as you have pledged your word.
Come near," quoth he, "my lady prioress:
And you, sir clerk, put by your bashfulness,
Nor ponder more; out hands, now, every man!"

At once to draw a cut each one began,
And, to make short the matter, as it was,
Whether by chance or whatsoever cause,
The truth is, that the cut fell to the knight,
At which right happy then was every wight.
Thus that his story first of all he'd tell,
According to the compact, it befell,
As you have heard. Why argue to and fro?
And when this good man saw that it was so,
Being a wise man and obedient
To plighted word, given by free assent,
He said: "Since I must then begin the game,
Why, welcome be the cut, and in God's name!
Now let us ride, and hearken what I say."

And at that word we rode forth on our way;
And he began to speak, with right good cheer,
His tale anon, as it is written here.

G. CHAUCER

TIME AND LOVE

I

WHEN I have seen by Time's fell hand defaced
The rich proud cost of out-worn buried age;
When sometime lofty towers I see down-razed,
And brass eternal slave to mortal rage;

When I have seen the hungry ocean gain
Advantage on the kingdom of the shore,
And the firm soil win of the watery main,
Increasing store with loss, and loss with store;

When I have seen such interchange of state,
Or state itself confounded to decay,
Ruin hath taught me thus to ruminate—
That Time will come and take my Love away:

—This thought is as a death, which cannot choose
But weep to have that which it fears to lose.

W. SHAKESPEARE

II

SINCE brass, nor stone, nor earth, nor boundless sea,
But sad mortality o'ersways their power,
How with this rage shall beauty hold a plea,
Whose action is no stronger than a flower?

O how shall summer's honey breath hold out
Against the wreckful siege of battering days,
When rocks impregnable are not so stout
Nor gates of steel so strong, but time decays?

O fearful meditation! where, alack!
Shall Time's best jewel from Time's chest lie hid?
Or what strong hand can hold his swift foot back,
Or who his spoil of beauty can forbid?

O! none, unless this miracle have might,
That in black ink my love may still shine bright.

W. SHAKESPEARE

THE PASSIONATE SHEPHERD TO HIS LOVE

Come live with me and be my Love,
And we will all the pleasures prove
That hills and valleys, dale and field,
And all the craggy mountains yield.

There will we sit upon the rocks
And see the shepherds feed their flocks,
By shallow rivers, to whose falls
Melodious birds sing madrigals.

There will I make thee beds of roses
And a thousand fragrant posies,
A cap of flowers, and a kirtle
Embroider'd all with leaves of myrtle.

A gown made of the finest wool,
Which from our pretty lambs we pull,
Fair linéd slippers for the cold,
With buckles of the purest gold.

A belt of straw and ivy buds
With coral clasps and amber studs:
And if these pleasures may thee move,
Come live with me and be my Love.

Thy silver dishes for thy meat

As precious as the gods do eat,
Shall on an ivory table be
Prepared each day for thee and me.

The shepherd swains shall dance and sing
For thy delight each May-morning:
If these delights thy mind may move,
Then live with me and be my Love.

C. MARLOWE

❧ 5 ❧

A MADRIGAL

CRABBED Age and Youth
Cannot live together:
Youth is full of pleasance,
Age is full of care;
Youth like summer morn,
Age like winter weather,
Youth like summer brave,
Age like winter bare:
Youth is full of sport,
Age's breath is short,
Youth is nimble, Age is lame:
Youth is hot and bold,
Age is weak and cold,
Youth is wild, and Age is tame:—
Age, I do abhor thee;
Youth, I do adore thee;

O! my Love, my Love is young!
Age, I do defy thee—
O sweet shepherd, hie thee,
For methinks thou stay'st too long.

W. SHAKESPEARE

○ 6 ○

UNDER the greenwood tree
Who loves to lie with me,
And tune his merry note
Unto the sweet bird's throat—
Come hither, come hither, come hither!
  Here shall he see
  No enemy
But winter and rough weather.

Who doth ambition shun
And loves to live i' the sun,
Seeking the food he eats
And pleased with what he gets—
Come hither, come hither, come hither!
  Here shall he see
  No enemy
But winter and rough weather.

W. SHAKESPEARE

❧ 7 ☙

ABSENCE

BEING your slave, what should I do but tend
Upon the hours and times of your desire?
I have no precious time at all to spend
Nor services to do, till you require:

Nor dare I chide the world-without-end hour
Whilst I, my sovereign, watch the clock for you,
Nor think the bitterness of absence sour
When you have bid your servant once adieu:

Nor dare I question with my jealous thought
Where you may be, or your affairs suppose,
But like a sad slave, stay and think of nought
Save, where you are, how happy you make those;—

So true a fool is love, that in your will
Though you do anything, he thinks no ill.

W. SHAKESPEARE

❧ 8 ☙

SONG

SWEETEST love, I do not go
For weariness of thee,

40

Nor in hope the world can show
    A fitter love for me;
        But since that I
Must die at last, 'tis best
To use myself in jest,
    Thus by feign'd deaths to die.

Yesternight the Sun went hence,
    And yet is here today;
He hath no desire nor sense,
    Nor half so short a way:
        Then fear not me,
But believe that I shall make
Speedier journeys, since I take
    More wings and spurs than he.

O how feeble is man's power,
    That if good fortune fall,
Cannot add another hour,
    Nor a lost hour recall!
        But come bad chance,
And we join to it our strength,
And we teach it art and length,
    Itself o'er us to advance.

When thou sigh'st, thou sigh'st not wind,
    But sigh'st my soul away;
When thou weep'st, unkindly kind,
    My life's blood doth decay.
        It cannot be
That thou lov'st me, as thou say'st,

If in thine my life thou waste,
　　Thou art the best of me.

Let not thy divining heart
　　Forethink me any ill;
Destiny may take thy part,
　　And may thy fears fulfill;
　　　　But think that we
Are but turn'd aside to sleep;
They who one another keep
　　Alive, ne'er parted be.

J. DONNE

❧ 9 ☙

How like a winter hath my absence been
From Thee, the pleasure of the fleeting year!
What freezing have I felt, what dark days seen,
What old December's bareness everywhere!

And yet this time removed was summer's time:
The teeming autumn, big with rich increase,
Bearing the wanton burden of the prime
Like widow'd wombs after their lords' decease:

Yet this abundant issue seem'd to me
But hope of orphans, and unfather'd fruit;
For summer and his pleasures wait on thee,
And, thou away, the very birds are mute;

Or if they sing, 'tis with so dull a cheer,
That leaves look pale, dreading the winter's near.

W. SHAKESPEARE

❧ 10 ☙

A CONSOLATION

WHEN in disgrace with fortune and men's eyes
I all alone beweep my outcast state,
And trouble deaf heaven with my bootless cries,
And look upon myself, and curse my fate;

Wishing me like to one more rich in hope,
Featured like him, like him with friends possest,
Desiring this man's art, and that man's scope,
With what I most enjoy contented least;

Yet in these thoughts myself almost despising,
Haply I think on Thee—and then my state,
Like to the lark at break of day arising
From sullen earth, sings hymns at heaven's gate;

For thy sweet love remember'd, such wealth brings,
That then I scorn to change my state with kings.

W. SHAKESPEARE

❧ 11 ❧

THE UNCHANGEABLE

O NEVER say that I was false of heart,
Though absence seem'd my flame to qualify:
As easy might I from myself depart
As from my soul, which in thy breast doth lie;

That is my home of love; if I have ranged,
Like him that travels, I return again,
Just to the time, not with the time exchanged,
So that myself bring water for my stain.

Never believe, though in my nature reign'd
All frailties that besiege all kinds of blood,
That it could so preposterously be stain'd
To leave for nothing all thy sum of good:

For nothing this wide universe I call,
Save thou, my rose: in it thou art my all.

W. SHAKESPEARE

❧ 12 ❧

COLIN

BEAUTY sat bathing by a spring
  Where fairest shades did hide her;
The winds blew calm, the birds did sing,

The cool streams ran beside her.
My wanton thoughts enticed mine eye
    To see what was forbidden:
But better memory said, fie!
    So vain desire was chidden:—
        Hey nonny nonny O!
        Hey nonny nonny!

Into a slumber then I fell,
    When fond imagination
Seeméd to see, but could not tell
    Her feature or her fashion.
But ev'n as babes in dreams do smile,
    And sometimes fall a-weeping,
So I awaked, as wise this while
    As when I fell a-sleeping:—
        Hey nonny nonny O!
        Hey nonny nonny!

THE SHEPHERD TONIE

13

TO HIS LOVE

SHALL I compare thee to a summer's day?
Thou art more lovely and more temperate:
Rough winds do shake the darling buds of May,
And summer's lease hath all too short a date:

Sometime too hot the eye of heaven shines,

And often is his gold complexion dimm'd:
And every fair from fair sometime declines,
By chance, or nature's changing course, untrimm'd.

But thy eternal summer shall not fade
Nor lose possession of that fair thou owest;
Nor shall death brag thou wanderest in his shade,
When in eternal lines to time thou growest;

So long as men can breathe, or eyes can see,
So long lives this, and this gives life to thee.

W. SHAKESPEARE

❧ 14 ☙

TO HIS LOVE

WHEN in the chronicle of wasted time
I see descriptions of the fairest wights,
And beauty making beautiful old rhyme
In praise of ladies dead, and lovely knights;

Then in the blazon of sweet beauty's best
Of hand, of foot, of lip, of eye, of brow,
I see their antique pen would have exprest
Ev'n such a beauty as you master now.

So all their praises are but prophecies
Of this our time, all, you prefiguring;
And for they look'd but with divining eyes,
They had not skill enough your worth to sing:

For we, which now behold these present days,
Have eyes to wonder, but lack tongues to praise.

W. SHAKESPEARE

❧ 15 ☙

LOVE'S PERJURIES

ON a day, alack the day!
Love, whose month is ever May,
Spied a blossom passing fair
Playing in the wanton air:
Through the velvet leaves the wind,
All unseen, 'gan passage find;
That the lover, sick to death,
Wish'd himself the heaven's breath.
Air, quoth he, thy cheeks may blow;
Air, would I might triumph so!
But, alack, my hand is sworn
Ne'er to pluck thee from thy thorn:
Vow, alack, for youth unmeet;
Youth so apt to pluck a sweet.
Do not call it sin in me
That I am forsworn for thee:
Thou for whom e'en Jove would swear
Juno but an Ethiope were,
And deny himself for Jove,
Turning mortal for thy love.

W. SHAKESPEARE

16

A SUPPLICATION

FORGET not yet the tried intent
Of such a truth as I have meant;
My great travail so gladly spent,
    Forget not yet!

Forget not yet when first began
The weary life ye know, since whan
The suit, the service none tell can;
    Forget not yet!

Forget not yet the great assays,
The cruel wrong, the scornful ways,
The painful patience in delays,
    Forget not yet!

Forget not! O, forget not this,
How long ago hath been, and is
The mind that never meant amiss—
    Forget not yet!

Forget not then thine own approved
The which so long hath thee so loved,
Whose steadfast faith yet never moved—
    Forget not this!
      SIR T. WYAT

❧ 17 ❧

TRUE LOVE

LET me not to the marriage of true minds
Admit impediments. Love is not love
Which alters when it alteration finds,
Or bends with the remover to remove:—

O no! it is an ever-fixéd mark
That looks on tempests, and is never shaken;
It is the star to every wandering bark,
Whose worth's unknown, although his height be taken.

Love's not Time's fool, though rosy lips and cheeks
Within his bending sickle's compass come;
Love alters not with his brief hours and weeks,
But bears it out ev'n to the edge of doom:—

If this be error, and upon me proved,
I never writ, nor no man ever loved.

W. SHAKESPEARE

THE ANNIVERSARY

ALL Kings, and all their favorites,
   All glory of honors, beauties, wits,
The Sun itself, which makes times, as they pass,
Is elder by a year, now, than it was
When thou and I first one another saw:
All other things, to their destruction draw,
   Only our love hath no decay;
This, no tomorrow hath, nor yesterday;
Running, it never runs from us away,
But truly keeps his first, last, everlasting day.

   Two graves must hide thine and my corse,
   If one might, death were no divorce;
Alas, as well as other Princes, we,
(Who Prince enough in one another be,)
Must leave at last in death, these eyes, and ears,
Oft fed with true oaths, and with sweet salt tears;
   But souls where nothing dwells but love
(All other thoughts being inmates) then shall prove
This, or a love increasèd there above,
When bodies to their graves, souls from their graves
   remove.

   And then we shall be throughly blest,
   But we no more, than all the rest;

Here upon earth, we are Kings, and none but we
Can be such Kings, nor of such subjects be;
Who is so safe as we? where none can do
Treason to us, except one of us two.
   True and false fears let us refrain,
Let us love nobly, and live, and add again
Years and years unto years, till we attain
To write threescore: this is the second of our reign.

J. DONNE

❧ 19 ❧

A DITTY

My true-love hath my heart, and I have his,
By just exchange one to the other given:
I hold his dear, and mine he cannot miss,
There never was a better bargain driven:
   My true-love hath my heart, and I have his.

His heart in me keeps him and me in one,
My heart in him his thoughts and senses guides:
He loves my heart, for once it was his own,
I cherish his because in me it bides:
   My true-love hath my heart, and I have his.

SIR P. SIDNEY

❧ 20 ☙

LOVE'S OMNIPRESENCE

WERE I as base as is the lowly plain,
And you, my Love, as high as heaven above,
Yet should the thoughts of me your humble swain
Ascend to heaven, in honour of my Love.

Were I as high as heaven above the plain,
And you, my Love, as humble and as low
As are the deepest bottoms of the main,
Whereso'er you were, with you my love should go.

Were you the earth, dear Love, and I the skies,
My love should shine on you like to the sun,
And look upon you with ten thousand eyes
Till heaven wax'd blind, and till the world were done.

Whereso'er I am, below, or else above you,
Whereso'er you are, my heart shall truly love you.

J. SYLVESTER

❧ 21 ☙

CARPE DIEM

O MISTRESS mine, where are you roaming?
O stay and hear! your true-love's coming

That can sing both high and low;
Trip no further, pretty sweeting,
Journeys end in lovers' meeting—
  Every wise man's son doth know.

What is love? 'tis not hereafter;
Present mirth hath present laughter;
  What's to come is still unsure:
In delay there lies no plenty,—
Then come kiss me, Sweet-and-twenty,
  Youth's a stuff will not endure.

      W. SHAKESPEARE

❧ 22 ❧

WINTER

WHEN icicles hang by the wall
 And Dick the shepherd blows his nail,
And Tom bears logs into the hall,
 And milk comes frozen home in pail;
When blood is nipt, and ways be foul,
Then nightly sings the staring owl
    Tuwhoo!
Tuwhit! tuwhoo! A merry note!
While greasy Joan doth keel the pot.

When all around the wind doth blow,
 And coughing drowns the parson's saw,
And birds sit brooding in the snow,

53

And Marian's nose looks red and raw;
When roasted crabs hiss in the bowl—
Then nightly sings the staring owl
        Tuwhoo!
Tuwhit! tuwhoo! A merry note!
While greasy Joan doth keel the pot.

W. SHAKESPEARE

❧ 23 ❧

THAT time of year thou may'st in me behold
When yellow leaves, or none, or few, do hang
Upon those boughs which shake against the cold,
Bare ruin'd choirs, where late the sweet birds sang.

In me thou see'st the twilight of such day
As after sunset fadeth in the west,
Which by and by black night doth take away,
Death's second self, that seals up all in rest.

In me thou see'st the glowing of such fire,
That on the ashes of his youth doth lie
As the death-bed whereon it must expire,
Consumed with that which it was nourish'd by:

—This thou perceiv'st, which makes thy love more strong,
To love that well which thou must leave ere long.

W. SHAKESPEARE

❧ 24 ❧

REMEMBRANCE

WHEN to the sessions of sweet silent thought
I summon up remembrance of things past,
I sigh the lack of many a thing I sought,
And with old woes new wail my dear time's waste:

Then can I drown an eye, unused to flow,
For precious friends hid in death's dateless night,
And weep afresh love's long-since-cancell'd woe,
And moan the expense of many a vanish'd sight.

Then can I grieve at grievances foregone,
And heavily from woe to woe tell o'er
The sad account of fore-bemoanéd moan,
Which I new pay as if not paid before:

—But if the while I think on thee, dear friend,
All losses are restored, and sorrows end.

W. SHAKESPEARE

❧ 25 ❧

FAREWELL! thou art too dear for my possessing,
And like enough thou know'st thy estimate:
The charter of thy worth gives thee releasing;
My bonds in thee are all determinate.

For how do I hold thee but by thy granting?
And for that riches where is my deserving?
The cause of this fair gift in me is wanting,
And so my patent back again is swerving.

Thyself thou gav'st, thy own worth then not knowing,
Or me, to whom thou gav'st it, else mistaking;
So thy great gift, upon misprision growing,
Comes home again, on better judgement making.

Thus have I had thee as a dream doth flatter;
In sleep, a king; but waking, no such matter.

W. SHAKESPEARE

✤ 26 ✤

THE LIFE WITHOUT PASSION

THEY that have power to hurt, and will do none,
That do not do the thing they most do show,
Who, moving others, are themselves as stone,
Unmovéd, cold, and to temptation slow,—

They rightly do inherit Heaven's graces,
And husband nature's riches from expense;
They are the lords and owners of their faces,
Others, but stewards of their excellence.

The summer's flower is to the summer sweet,
Though to itself it only live and die;
But if that flower with base infection meet,
The basest weed outbraves his dignity:

For sweetest things turn sourest by their deeds;
Lilies that fester smell far worse than weeds.

W. SHAKESPEARE

❧ 27 ☙

THE LOVER'S APPEAL

AND wilt thou leave me thus?
Say nay! say nay! for shame,
To save thee from the blame
Of all my grief and grame.
And wilt thou leave me thus?
Say nay! say nay!

And wilt thou leave me thus?
That hath loved thee so long
In wealth and woe among:
And is thy heart so strong
As for to leave me thus?
Say nay! say nay!

And wilt thou leave me thus,
That hath given thee my heart
Never for to depart
Neither for pain nor smart:
And wilt thou leave me thus?
Say nay! say nay!

And wilt thou leave me thus,
And have no more pity

Of him that loveth thee?
Alas! thy cruelty!
And wilt thou leave me thus?
Say nay! say nay!

SIR T. WYAT

28

THE NIGHTINGALE

As it fell upon a day
In the merry month of May,
Sitting in a pleasant shade
Which a grove of myrtles made,
Beasts did leap and birds did sing,
Trees did grow and plants did spring,
Everything did banish moan
Save the Nightingale alone.
She, poor bird, as all forlorn,
Lean'd her breast against a thorn,
And there sung the dolefull'st ditty
That to hear it was great pity.
Fie, fie, fie, now would she cry;
Tereu, tereu, by and by:
That to hear her so complain
Scarce I could from tears refrain;
For her griefs so lively shown
Made me think upon mine own.
—Ah, thought I, thou mourn'st in vain,

None takes pity on thy pain:
Senseless trees, they cannot hear thee,
Ruthless beasts, they will not cheer thee;
King Pandion, he is dead,
All thy friends are lapp'd in lead:
All thy fellow birds do sing
Careless of thy sorrowing:
Even so, poor bird, like thee
None alive will pity me.

R. BARNEFIELD

❧ 29 ❧

CARE-CHARMER Sleep, son of the sable Night,
Brother to Death, in silent darkness born,
Relieve my languish, and restore the light;
With dark forgetting of my care return.

And let the day be time enough to mourn
The shipwreck of my ill adventured youth:
Let waking eyes suffice to wail their scorn,
Without the torment of the night's untruth.

Cease, dreams, the images of day-desires,
To model forth the passions of the morrow;
Never let rising Sun approve you liars
To add more grief to aggravate my sorrow:

Still let me sleep, embracing clouds in vain,
And never wake to feel the day's disdain.

S. DANIEL

MADRIGAL

TAKE, O take those lips away
That so sweetly were forsworn,
And those eyes, the break of day,
Lights that do mislead the morn:
But my kisses bring again,
        Bring again—
Seals of love, but seal'd in vain,
        Seal'd in vain!

W. SKAKESPEARE

❦ 31 *❦*

LOVE'S FAREWELL

SINCE there's no help, come let us kiss and part,—
Nay I have done, you get no more of me;
And I am glad, yea, glad with all my heart,
That thus so cleanly I myself can free;

Shake hands for ever, cancel all our vows,
And when we meet at any time again,
Be it not seen in either of our brows
That we one jot of former love retain.

Now at the last gasp of love's latest breath,

When his pulse failing, passion speechless lies,
When faith is kneeling by his bed of death,
And innocence is closing up his eyes,

—Now if thou would'st, when all have given him over,
From death to life thou might'st him yet recover!

M. DRAYTON

❧ 32 ☙

TO HIS LUTE

My lute, be as thou wert when thou didst grow
With thy green mother in some shady grove,
When immelodious winds but made thee move,
And birds their ramage did on thee bestow.

Since that dear Voice which did thy sounds approve,
Which wont in such harmonious strains to flow,
Is reft from Earth to tune those spheres above,
What art thou but a harbinger of woe?

Thy pleasing notes be pleasing notes no more,
But orphans' wailings to the fainting ear;
Each stroke a sigh, each sound draws forth a tear;
For which be silent as in woods before:

Or if that any hand to touch thee deign,
Like widow'd turtle still her loss complain.

W. DRUMMOND

A RENUNCIATION

If women could be fair, and yet not fond,
Or that their love were firm, not fickle still,
I would not marvel that they make men bond
By service long to purchase their goodwill;
But when I see how frail those creatures are,
I muse that men forget themselves so far.

To mark the choice they make, and how they change,
How oft from Phoebus they do flee to Pan;
Unsettled still, like haggards wild they range,
These gentle birds that fly from man to man;
Who would not scorn and shake them from the fist,
And let them fly, fair fools, which way they list?

Yet for disport we fawn and flatter both,
To pass the time when nothing else can please,
And train them to our lure with subtle oath,
Till, weary of their wiles, ourselves we ease;
And then we say when we their fancy try,
To play with fools, O what a fool was I!

E. VERE, EARL OF OXFORD

BLOW, blow, thou winter wind,
Thou art not so unkind
As man's ingratitude;
Thy tooth is not so keen
Because thou art not seen
Although thy breath be rude.
Heigh ho! sing heigh ho! unto the green holly:
Most friendship is feigning, most loving mere folly:
Then, heigh ho! the holly!
This life is most jolly.

Freeze, freeze, thou bitter sky,
Thou dost not bite so nigh
As benefits forgot:
Though thou the waters warp,
Thy sting is not so sharp
As friend remember'd not.
Heigh ho! sing heigh ho! unto the green holly:
Most friendship is feigning, most loving mere folly:
Then, heigh ho! the holly!
This life is most jolly.

W. SHAKESPEARE

DIRGE OF LOVE

COME away, come away, Death,
And in sad cypres let me be laid;
　Fly away, fly away, breath;
I am slain by a fair cruel maid.
My shroud of white, stuck all with yew,
　　　O prepare it!
My part of death, no one so true
　　　Did share it.

　Not a flower, not a flower sweet
On my black coffin let there be strown;
　Not a friend, not a friend greet
My poor corpse, where my bones shall be thrown:
A thousand thousand sighs to save,
　　　Lay me, O where
Sad true lover never find my grave,
　　　To weep there.

W. SHAKESPEARE

FIDELE

FEAR no more the heat o' the sun
    Nor the furious winter's rages;
Thou thy worldly task hast done,
    Home art gone and ta'en thy wages:
Golden lads and girls all must,
As chimney-sweepers, come to dust.

Fear no more the frown o' the great,
    Thou art past the tyrant's stroke;
Care no more to clothe and eat;
    To thee the reed is as the oak:
The sceptre, learning, physic, must
All follow this, and come to dust.

Fear no more the lightning-flash
    Nor the all-dreaded thunder-stone;
Fear not slander, censure rash;
    Thou hast finish'd joy and moan:
All lovers young, all lovers must
Consign to thee, and come to dust.

W. SHAKESPEARE

A SEA DIRGE

FULL fathom five thy father lies:
    Of his bones are coral made;
Those are pearls that were his eyes:
    Nothing of him that doth fade,
But doth suffer a sea-change
Into something rich and strange.
Sea-nymphs hourly ring his knell:
Hark! now I hear them,—
    Ding, dong, bell.

W. SHAKESPEARE

38

A LAND DIRGE

CALL for the robin redbreast and the wren,
Since o'er shady groves they hover
And with leaves and flowers do cover
The friendless bodies of unburied men.
Call unto his funeral dole
The ant, the field-mouse, and the mole
To rear him hillocks that shall keep him warm
And (when gay tombs are robb'd) sustain no harm;

But keep the wolf far thence, that's foe to men,
For with his nails he'll dig them up again.

J. WEBSTER

❧ 39 ❧

POST MORTEM

IF thou survive my well-contented day
When that churl Death my bones with dust shall cover,
And shalt by fortune once more re-survey
These poor rude lines of thy deceaséd lover;

Compare them with the bettering of the time,
And though they be outstripp'd by every pen,
Reserve them for my love, not for their rhyme
Exceeded by the height of happier men.

O then vouchsafe me but this loving thought—
'Had my friend's muse grown with this growing age,
A dearer birth than this his love had brought,
To march in ranks of better equipage:

But since he died, and poets better prove,
Theirs for their style I'll read, his for his love.'

W. SHAKESPEARE

❧ 40 ❧

THE TRIUMPH OF DEATH

No longer mourn for me when I am dead
Than you shall hear the surly sullen bell
Give warning to the world, that I am fled
From this vile world, with vilest worms to dwell;

Nay, if you read this line, remember not
The hand that writ it; for I love you so,
That I in your sweet thoughts would be forgot,
If thinking on me then should make you woe.

O if, I say, you look upon this verse
When I perhaps compounded am with clay,
Do not so much as my poor name rehearse,
But let your love even with my life decay;

Lest the wise world should look into your moan,
And mock you with me after I am gone.

W. SHAKESPEARE

❧ 41 ❧

MADRIGAL

TELL me where is Fancy bred,
Or in the heart, or in the head?

How begot, how nourishéd?
    Reply, reply.

It is engender'd in the eyes,
With gazing fed; and Fancy dies
In the cradle where it lies:
Let us all ring Fancy's knell;
I'll begin it,—Ding, dong, bell.
    —Ding, dong, bell.
        W. SHAKESPEARE

❧ 42 ❦

CUPID AND CAMPASPE

CUPID and my Campaspe play'd
At cards for kisses; Cupid paid:
He stakes his quiver, bow, and arrows,
His mother's doves, and team of sparrows;
Loses them too; then down he throws
The coral of his lip, the rose
Growing on's cheek (but none knows how);
With these, the crystal of his brow,
And then the dimple on his chin;
All these did my Campaspe win:
At last he set her both his eyes—
She won, and Cupid blind did rise.
    O Love! has she done this to thee?
    What shall, alas! become of me?
        J. LYLY

PROTHALAMION

CALM was the day, and through the trembling air
Sweet-breathing Zephyrus did softly play—
A gentle spirit, that lightly did delay
Hot Titan's beams, which then did glister fair;
When I (whom sullen care,
Through discontent of my long fruitless stay
In princes' court, and expectation vain
Of idle hopes, which still do fly away
Like empty shadows, did afflict my brain),
Walk'd forth to ease my pain
Along the shore of silver-streaming Thames:
Whose rutty bank, the which his river hems,
Was painted all with variable flowers,
And all the meads adorn'd with dainty gems
Fit to deck maidens' bowers,
And crown their paramours
Against the bridal day, which is not long:
　　Sweet Thames! run softly, till I end my song.

There in a meadow by the river's side
A flock of nymphs I chancéd to espy,
All lovely daughters of the flood thereby,
With goodly greenish locks all loose untied
As each had been a bride;

And each one had a little wicker basket
Made of fine twigs, entrailéd curiously,
In which they gather'd flowers to fill their flasket,
And with fine fingers cropt full feateously
The tender stalks on high.
Of every sort which in that meadow grew
They gather'd some; the violet, pallid blue,
The little daisy that at evening closes,
The virgin lily and the primrose true:
With store of vermeil roses,
To deck their bridegrooms' posies
Against the bridal day, which was not long:
    Sweet Thames! run softly, till I end my song.

With that I saw two swans of goodly hue
Come softly swimming down along the lee;
Two fairer birds I yet did never see;
The snow which doth the top of Pindus strow
Did never whiter show,
Nor Jove himself, when he a swan would be
For love of Leda, whiter did appear;
Yet Leda was (they say) as white as he,
Yet not so white as these, nor nothing near;
So purely white they were
That even the gentle stream, the which them bare,
Seem'd foul to them, and bade his billows spare
To wet their silken feathers, lest they might
Soil their fair plumes with water not so fair,
And mar their beauties bright
That shone as Heaven's light

71

Against their bridal day, which was not long:
   Sweet Thames! run softly, till I end my song.

Eftsoons the nymphs, which now had flowers their fill,
Ran all in haste to see that silver brood
As they came floating on the crystal flood;
Whom when they saw, they stood amazéd still,
Their wondering eyes to fill;
Them seem'd they never saw a sight so fair
Of fowls, so lovely, that they sure did deem
Them heavenly born, or to be that same pair
Which through the sky draw Venus' silver team;
For sure they did not seem
To be begot of any earthly seed,
But rather angels, or of angels' breed;
Yet were they bred of summer's heat, they say,
In sweetest season, when each flower and weed
The earth did fresh array;
So fresh they seem'd as day,
Even as their bridal day, which was not long:
   Sweet Thames! run softly, till I end my song.

Then forth they all out of their baskets drew
Great store of flowers, the honour of the field,
That to the sense did fragrant odours yield,
All which upon those goodly birds they threw
And all the waves did strew,
That like old Peneus' waters they did seem
When down along by pleasant Tempe's shore
Scatter'd with flowers, through Thessaly they stream,

That they appear, through lilies' plenteous store,
Like a bride's chamber-floor.
Two of those nymphs meanwhile two garlands bound
Of freshest flowers which in that mead they found,
The which presenting all in trim array,
Their snowy foreheads therewithal they crown'd;
Whilst one did sing this lay
Prepared against that day,
Against their bridal day, which was not long:
   Sweet Thames! run softly, till I end my song.

'Ye gentle birds! the world's fair ornament,
And Heaven's glory, whom this happy hour
Doth lead unto your lovers' blissful bower,
Joy may you have, and gentle heart's content
Of your love's complement;
And let fair Venus, that is queen of love,
With her heart-quelling son upon you smile,
Whose smile, they say, hath virtue to remove
All love's dislike, and friendship's faulty guile
For ever to assoil.
Let endless peace your steadfast hearts accord,
And blessed plenty wait upon your board;
And let your bed with pleasures chaste abound,
That fruitful issue may to you afford
Which may your foes confound,
And make your joys redound
Upon your bridal day, which is not long:
   Sweet Thames! run softly, till I end my song.'

So ended she; and all the rest around

To her redoubled that her undersong,
Which said their bridal day should not be long:
And gentle Echo from the neighbour ground
Their accents did resound.
So forth those joyous birds did pass along
Adown the lee that to them murmur'd low,
As he would speak but that he lack'd a tongue,
Yet did by signs his glad affection show,
Making his stream run slow.
And all the fowl which in his flood did dwell
'Gan flock about these twain, that did excel
The rest, so far as Cynthia doth shend
The lesser stars. So they, enrangéd well,
Did on those two attend,
And their best service lend
Against their wedding day, which was not long:
    Sweet Thames! run softly, till I end my song.

At length they all to merry London came,
To merry London, my most kindly nurse,
That to me gave this life's first native source,
Though from another place I take my name,
An house of ancient fame:
There when they came whereas those bricky towers
The which on Thames' broad aged back do ride,
Where now the studious lawyers have their bowers,
There whilome wont the Templar-knights to bide,
Till they decay'd through pride;
Next whereunto there stands a stately place,
Where oft I gainéd gifts and goodly grace

Of that great lord, which therein wont to dwell,
Whose want too well now feels my friendless case;
But ah! here fits not well
Old woes, but joys to tell
Against the bridal day, which is not long:
    Sweet Thames! run softly, till I end my song.

Yet therein now doth lodge a noble peer,
Great England's glory and the world's wide wonder,
Whose dreadful name late thro' all Spain did thunder,
And Hercules' two pillars standing near
Did make to quake and fear:
Fair branch of honour, flower of chivalry!
That fillest England with thy triumphs' fame
Joy have thou of thy noble victory,
And endless happiness of thine own name
That promiseth the same;
That through thy prowess and victorious arms
Thy country may be freed from foreign harms,
And great Eliza's glorious name may ring
Through all the world, fill'd with thy wide alarms
Which some brave Muse may sing
To ages following,
Upon the bridal day, which is not long:
    Sweet Thames! run softly, till I end my song.

From those high towers this noble lord issúing
Like radiant Hesper, when his golden hair
In th' ocean billows he hath bathéd fair,
Descended to the river's open viewing
With a great train ensuing.

Above the rest were goodly to be seen
Two gentle knights of lovely face and feature,
Beseeming well the bower of any queen,
With gifts of wit and ornaments of nature,
Fit for so goodly stature,
That like the twins of Jove they seem'd in sight
Which deck the baldric of the Heavens bright;
They two, forth pacing to the river's side,
Received those two fair brides, their love's delight;
Which, at th' appointed tide,
Each one did make his bride
Against their bridal day, which is not long:
  Sweet Thames! run softly, till I end my song.

E. SPENSER

❧ 44 ❧

THE HAPPY HEART

ART thou poor, yet hast thou golden slumbers?
      O sweet content!
Art thou rich, yet is thy mind perplexéd?
      O punishment!
Dost thou laugh to see how fools are vexéd
To add to golden numbers, golden numbers?
O sweet content! O sweet, O sweet content!
  Work apace, apace, apace, apace;
  Honest labour bears a lovely face;
Then hey nonny nonny, hey nonny nonny!

Canst drink the waters of the crispéd spring?
     O sweet content!
Swimmin'st thou in wealth, yet sink'st in thine own tears?
     O punishment!
Then he that patiently want's burden bears
No burden bears, but is a king, a king!
O sweet content! O sweet, O sweet content!
  Work apace, apace, apace, apace;
  Honest labour bears a lovely face;
Then hey nonny nonny, hey nonny nonny!

                   T. DEKKER

❧ 45 ❧

THIS Life, which seems so fair,
Is like a bubble blown up in the air
By sporting children's breath,
Who chase it everywhere
And strive who can most motion it bequeath.
And though it sometimes seem of its own might
Like to an eye of gold to be fix'd there,
And firm to hover in that empty height,
That only is because it is so light.
—But in that pomp it doth not long appear;
For when 'tis most admired, in a thought,
Because it erst was nought, it turns to nought.

                W. DRUMMOND

✿ 46 ✿

SOUL AND BODY

Poor Soul, the centre of my sinful earth,
Fool'd by those rebel powers that thee array,
Why dost thou pine within, and suffer dearth,
Painting thy outward walls so costly gay?

Why so large cost, having so short a lease,
Dost thou upon thy fading mansion spend?
Shall worms, inheritors of this excess,
Eat up thy charge? is this thy body's end?

Then, Soul, live thou upon thy servant's loss,
And let that pine to aggravate thy store;
Buy terms divine in selling hours of dross;
Within be fed, without be rich no more:—

So shalt thou feed on death, that feeds on men,
And death once dead, there's no more dying then.

W. SHAKESPEARE

✿ 47 ✿

DEATH, BE NOT PROUD

Death, be not proud, though some have called thee
Mighty and dreadful, for thou are not so;
For those whom thou think'st thou dost overthrow

Die not, poor Death; nor yet canst thou kill me.
From rest and sleep, which but thy picture be,
Much pleasure; then from thee much more must flow;
And soonest our best men with thee do go—
Rest of their bones and souls' delivery!
Thou'rt slave to fate, chance, kings, and desperate men,
And dost with poison, war, and sickness dwell;
And poppy or charms can make us sleep as well
And better than thy stroke. Why swell'st thou then?
One short sleep past, we wake eternally,
And Death shall be no more: Death, thou shalt die.

J. DONNE

❧ 48 ❧

LIFE

THE World's a bubble, and the Life of Man
   Less than a span:
In his conception wretched, from the womb
   So to the tomb;
Curst from his cradle, and brought up to years
   With cares and fears.
Who then to frail mortality shall trust,
But limns on water, or but writes in dust.

Yet whilst with sorrow here we live opprest,
   What life is best?
Courts are but only superficial schools
   To dandle fools:

79

The rural parts are turn'd into a den
          Of savage men:
And where's a city from foul vice so free,
But may be term'd the worst of all the three?

Domestic cares afflict the husband's bed,
          Or pains his head:
Those that live single, take it for a curse,
          Or do things worse:
Some would have children: those that have them moan
          Or wish them gone:
What is it, then, to have, or have no wife,
But single thraldom, or a double strife?

Our own affections still at home to please
          Is a disease:
To cross the seas to any foreign soil,
          Peril and toil:
Wars with their noise affright us; when they cease,
          We are worse in peace;—
What then remains, but that we still should cry
For being born, or, being born, to die?

LORD BACON

✣ 49 ✣

THE LESSONS OF NATURE

Of this fair volume which we World do name
If we the sheets and leaves could turn with care,

Of Him who it corrects, and did it frame,
We clear might read the art and wisdom rare:

Find out His power which wildest powers doth tame,
His providence extending everywhere,
His justice which proud rebels doth not spare,
In every page, no period of the same,

But silly we, like foolish children, rest
Well pleased with colour'd vellum, leaves of gold,
Fair dangling ribbands, leaving what is best,
On the great Writer's sense ne'er taking hold;

Or if by chance we stay our minds on aught,
It is some picture on the margin wrought.

W. DRUMMOND

❧ 50 ☙

DOTH then the World go thus, doth all thus move?
Is this the justice which on Earth we find?
Is this that firm decree which all doth bind?
Are these your influences, Powers above?

Those souls which vice's moody mists doth blind,
Blind Fortune, blindly, most their friend doth prove;
And they who thee, poor idol Virtue! love,
Ply like a feather toss'd by storm and wind.

Ah! if a Providence doth sway this all
Why should best minds groan under most distress?

81

Or why should pride humility make thrall,
And injuries the innocent oppress?

Heavens! hinder, stop this fate; or grant a time
When good may have, as well as bad, their prime!

W. DRUMMOND

❧ 51 ☙

THE WORLD'S WAY

TIRED with all these, for restful death I cry—
As, to behold desert a beggar born
And needy nothing trimm'd in jollity,
And purest faith unhappily forsworn,

And gilded honour shamefully misplaced,
And maiden virtue rudely strumpeted,
And right perfection wrongfully disgraced,
And strength by limping sway disabled,

And art made tongue-tied by authority,
And folly, doctor-like, controlling skill,
And simple truth miscall'd simplicity,
And captive Good attending captain Ill:—

—Tired with all these, from these would I be gone,
Save that, to die, I leave my Love alone.

W. SHAKESPEARE

52

SAINT JOHN BAPTIST

THE last and greatest Herald of Heaven's King
Girt with rough skins, hies to the deserts wild,
Among that savage brood the woods forth bring,
Which he more harmless found than man, and mild.

His food was locusts, and what there doth spring,
With honey that from virgin hives distill'd;
Parch'd body, hollow eyes, some uncouth thing
Made him appear, long since from earth exiled.

There burst he forth: All ye whose hopes rely
On God, with me amidst these deserts mourn,
Repent, repent, and from old errors turn!
—Who listen'd to his voice, obey'd his cry?

Only the echoes, which he made relent,
Rung from their flinty caves, Repent! Repent!

W. DRUMMOND

BOOK SECOND

53

ODE ON THE
MORNING OF CHRIST'S NATIVITY

THIS is the month, and this the happy morn
Wherein the Son of Heaven's Eternal King
Of wedded maid and virgin mother born,
Our great redemption from above did bring;
For so the holy sages once did sing
That He our deadly forfeit should release,
And with His Father work us a perpetual peace.

That glorious Form, that Light unsufferable,
And that far-beaming blaze of Majesty
Wherewith He wont at Heaven's high council-table
To sit the midst of Trinal Unity,
He laid aside; and, here with us to be,
Forsook the courts of everlasting day,
And chose with us a darksome house of mortal clay.

Say, heavenly Muse, shall not thy sacred vein
Afford a present to the Infant God?
Hast thou no verse, no hymn, or solemn strain
To welcome Him to this His new abode,
Now while the heaven, by the sun's team untrod,

Hath took no print of the approaching light,
And all the spangled host keep watch in squadrons bright?

See how from far, upon the eastern road,
The star-led wizards haste with odours sweet:
O run, prevent them with thy humble ode
And lay it lowly at His blessed feet;
Have thou the honour first thy Lord to greet,
And join thy voice unto the angel quire
From out His secret altar touch'd with hallow'd fire.

THE HYMN

It was the winter wild
While the heaven-born Child
All meanly wrapt in the rude manger lies;
Nature in awe to Him
Had doff'd her gaudy trim,
With her great Master so to sympathize:
It was no season then for her
To wanton with the sun, her lusty paramour.

Only with speeches fair
She woos the gentle air
To hide her guilty front with innocent snow;
And on her naked shame,
Pollute with sinful blame,
The saintly veil of maiden white to throw;
Confounded, that her Maker's eyes
Should look so near upon her foul deformities.

But He, her fears to cease,

Sent down the meek-eyed Peace;
She, crown'd with olive green, came softly sliding
Down through the turning sphere,
His ready harbinger,
With turtle wing the amorous clouds dividing;
And waving wide her myrtle wand,
She strikes a universal peace through sea and land.

No war, or battle's sound
Was heard the world around:
The idle spear and shield were high uphung;
The hookéd chariot stood
Unstain'd with hostile blood;
The trumpet spake not to the arméd throng;
And kings sat still with awful eye,
As if they surely knew their sovran Lord was by.

But peaceful was the night
Wherein the Prince of Light
His reign of peace upon the earth began:
The winds, with wonder whist,
Smoothly the waters kist
Whispering new joys to the mild oceán—
Who now hath quite forgot to rave,
While birds of calm sit brooding on the charméd wave.

The stars, with deep amaze,
Stand fix'd in steadfast gaze,
Bending one way their precious influence;
And will not take their flight
For all the morning light,
Or Lucifer that often warn'd them thence;

But in their glimmering orbs did glow
Until their Lord Himself bespake, and bid them go.

And though the shady gloom
Had given day her room,
The sun himself withheld his wonted speed,
And hid his head for shame,
As his inferior flame
The new-enlighten'd world no more should need:
He saw a greater Sun appear
Than his bright throne, or burning axletree, could bear.

The shepherds on the lawn
Or ere the point of dawn
Sate simply chatting in a rustic row;
Full little thought they then
That the mighty Pan
Was kindly come to live with them below;
Perhaps their loves, or else their sheep
Was all that did their silly thoughts so busy keep.

When such music sweet
Their hearts and ears did greet
As never was by mortal finger strook—
Divinely-warbled voice
Answering the stringéd noise,
As all their souls in blissful rapture took:
The air, such pleasure loth to lose,
With thousand echoes still prolongs each heavenly close.

Nature that heard such sound
Beneath the hollow round

Of Cynthia's seat the airy region thrilling,
Now was almost won
To think her part was done,
And that her reign had here its last fulfilling;
She knew such harmony alone
Could hold all heaven and earth in happier union.

At last surrounds their sight
A globe of circular light
That with long beams the shamefaced night array'd;
The helméd Cherubim
And sworded Seraphim
Are seen in glittering ranks with wings display'd,
Harping in loud and solemn quire
With unexpressive notes, to Heaven's new-born Heir.

Such music (as 'tis said)
Before was never made
But when of old the sons of morning sung,
While the Creator great
His constellations set
And the well-balanced world on hinges hung;
And cast the dark foundations deep,
And bid the weltering waves their oozy channel keep.

Ring out, ye crystal spheres!
Once bless our human ears,
If ye have power to touch our senses so;
And let your silver chime
Move in melodious time;
And let the base of heaven's deep organ blow;

91

And with your ninefold harmony
Make up full consort to the angelic symphony.

For it such holy song
Enwrap our fancy long,
Time will run back, and fetch the age of gold;
And speckled vanity
Will sicken soon and die,
And leprous sin will melt from earthly mould;
And Hell itself will pass away,
And leave her dolorous mansions to the peering day.

Yea, Truth and Justice then
Will down return to men,
Orb'd in a rainbow; and, like glories wearing,
Mercy will sit between
Throned in celestial sheen,
With radiant feet the tissued clouds down steering;
And Heaven, as at some festival,
Will open wide the gates of her high palace hall.

But wisest Fate says No;
This must not yet be so;
The Babe yet lies in smiling infancy
That on the bitter cross
Must redeem our loss;
So both Himself and us to glorify:
Yet first, to those ychain'd in sleep
The wakeful trump of doom must thunder through the
    deep;

With such a horrid clang

As on mount Sinai rang
While the red fire and smouldering clouds outbrake:
The aged Earth aghast
With terror of that blast
Shall from the surface to the centre shake,
When, at the world's last sessión,
The dreadful Judge in middle air shall spread His throne.

And then at last our bliss
Full and perfect is,
But now begins; for from this happy day
The old Dragon under ground,
In straiter limits bound,
Not half so far casts his usurpéd sway;
And, wroth to see his kingdom fail,
Swinges the scaly horror of his folded tail.

The oracles are dumb;
No voice or hideous hum
Runs through the archéd roof in words deceiving:
Apollo from his shrine
Can no more divine,
With hollow shriek the steep of Delphos leaving:
No nightly trance or breathéd spell
Inspires the pale-eyed priest from the prophetic cell.

The lonely mountains o'er
And the resounding shore
A voice of weeping heard, and loud lament;
From haunted spring and dale
Edged with popular pale

The parting Genius is with sighing sent;
With flower-inwoven tresses torn
The nymphs in twilight shade of tangled thickets mourn.

In consecrated earth
And on the holy hearth
The Lars and Lemurés moan with midnight plaint;
In urns and altars round
A drear and dying sound
Affrights the Flamens at their service quaint;
And the chill marble seems to sweat,
While each peculiar Power forgoes his wonted seat.

Peor and Baalim
Forsake their temples dim,
With that twice-batter'd god of Palestine;
And moonéd Ashtaroth
Heaven's queen and mother both,
Now sits not girt with tapers' holy shine;
The Lybic Hammon shrinks his horn,
In vain the Tyrian maids their wounded Thammuz mourn.

And sullen Moloch, fled,
Hath left in shadows dread
His burning idol all of blackest hue;
In vain with cymbals' ring
They call the grisly king,
In dismal dance about the furnace blue;
The brutish gods of Nile as fast,
Isis, and Orus, and the dog Anubis, haste.

Nor is Osiris seen

94

In Memphian grove, or green,
Trampling the unshower'd grass with lowings loud:
Nor can he be at rest
Within his sacred chest;
Nought but profoundest hell can be his shroud;
In vain with timbrell'd anthems dark
The sable stoléd sorcerers bear his worshipt ark.

He feels from Juda's land
The dreaded infant's hand;
The rays of Bethlehem blind his dusky eyn;
Nor all the gods beside
Longer dare abide,
Nor Typhon huge ending in snaky twine:
Our Babe, to show his Godhead true,
Can in His swaddling bands control the damnéd crew.

So, when the sun in bed
Curtain'd with cloudy red
Pillows his chin upon an orient wave,
The flocking shadows pale
Troop to the infernal jail,
Each fetter'd ghost slips to his several grave;
And the yellow-skirted fays
Fly after the night-steeds, leaving their moon-loved maze.

But see, the Virgin blest
Hath laid her Babe to rest;
Time is, our tedious song should here have ending:
Heaven's youngest-teeméd star
Hath fix'd her polish'd car,

Her sleeping Lord with hand-maid lamp attending:
And all about the courtly stable
Bright-harness'd angels sit in order serviceable.

J. MILTON

54

SONG FOR SAINT CECILIA'S DAY, 1687

FROM Harmony, from heavenly Harmony
    This universal frame began:
  When Nature underneath a heap
    Of jarring atoms lay
  And could not heave her head,
The tuneful voice was heard from high
    Arise, ye more than dead!
Then cold, and hot, and moist, and dry
In order to their stations leap,
    And Music's power obey.
From harmony, from heavenly harmony
    This universal frame began:
    From harmony to harmony
Through all the compass of the notes it ran,
The diapason closing full in Man.

What passion cannot Music raise and quell?
    When Jubal struck the chorded shell
  His listening brethren stood around,
    And, wondering, on their faces fell
  To worship that celestial sound.

Less than a god they thought there could not dwell
    Within the hollow of that shell
    That spoke so sweetly and so well.
What passion cannot Music raise and quell?

    The trumpet's loud clangor
        Excites us to arms,
    With shrill notes of anger
        And mortal alarms.
    The double double double beat
        Of the thundering drum
Cries 'Hark! the foes come;
Charge, charge, 'tis too late to retreat!'

    The soft complaining flute
    In dying notes discovers
    The woes of hopeless lovers,
Whose dirge is whisper'd by the warbling lute.

    Sharp violins proclaim
    Their jealous pangs and desperation,
    Fury, frantic indignation,
    Depth of pains, and height of passion
        For the fair disdainful dame.

But oh! what art can teach,
What human voice can reach
    The sacred organ's praise?
Notes inspiring holy love,
Notes that wing their heavenly ways
    To mend the choirs above.

Orpheus could lead the savage race,
And trees uprooted left their place
   Sequacious of the lyre:
But bright Cecilia raised the wonder higher:
When to her Organ vocal breath was given
An Angel heard, and straight appear'd—
Mistaking Earth for Heaven!

Grand Chorus

As from the power of sacred lays
   The spheres began to move,
And sung the great Creator's praise
   To all the blest above;
So when the last and dreadful hour
This crumbling pageant shall devour,
The trumpet shall be heard on high,
The dead shall live, the living die,
And Music shall untune the sky.

J. DRYDEN

❧ 55 ❧

HORATIAN ODE UPON CROMWELL'S RETURN FROM IRELAND

THE forward youth that would appear,
Must now forsake his Muses dear,
   Nor in the shadows sing
   His numbers languishing.

'Tis time to leave the books in dust,
And oil the unused armour's rust,
    Removing from the wall
    The corslet of the hall.

So restless Cromwell could not cease
In the inglorious arts of peace,
    But through adventurous war
    Urgéd his active star:

And like the three-fork'd lightning first,
Breaking the clouds where it was nurst,
    Did thorough his own side
    His fiery way divide:

For 'tis all one to courage high
The emulous, or enemy;
    And with such, to enclose
    Is more than to oppose.

Then burning through the air he went
And palaces and temples rent;
    And Caesar's head at last
    Did through his laurels blast.

'Tis madness to resist or blame
The face of angry heaven's flame;
    And if we would speak true,
    Much to the Man is due

Who, from his private gardens, where
He lived reservéd and austere

(As if his highest plot
To plant the bergamot),

Could by industrious valour climb
To ruin the great work of time,
And cast the Kingdoms old
Into another mould.

Though Justice against Fate complain,
And plead the ancient Rights in vain—
But those do hold or break
As men are strong or weak.

Nature, that hateth emptiness,
Allows of penetration less,
And therefore must make room
Where greater spirits come.

What field of all the civil war
Where his were not the deepest scar?
And Hampton shows what part
He had of wiser art,

Where, twining subtle fears with hope,
He wove a net of such a scope
That Charles himself might chase
To Carisbrook's narrow case;

That thence the Royal actor borne
The tragic scaffold might adorn:
While round the arméd bands
Did clap their bloody hands;

He nothing common did or mean

Upon that memorable scene,
But with his keener eye
The axe's edge did try;

Nor call'd the Gods, with vulgar spite,
To vindicate his helpless right;
But bow'd his comely head
Down, as upon a bed.

—This was that memorable hour
Which first assured the forcéd power:
So when they did design
The Capitol's first line.

A Bleeding Head, where they begun,
Did fright the architects to run;
And yet in that the State
Foresaw its happy fate!

And now the Irish are ashamed
To see themselves in one year tamed:
So much one man can do
That does both act and know.

They can affirm his praises best,
And have, though overcome, confest
How good he is, how just
And fit for highest trust;

Nor yet grown stiffer with command,
But still in the Republic's hand—
How fit he is to sway
That can so well obey!

He to the Commons' feet presents
A Kingdom for his first year's rents.
    And (what he may) forbears
    His fame, to make it theirs:

And has his sword and spoils ungirt
To lay them at the Public's skirt.
    So when the falcon high
    Falls heavy from the sky,

She, having kill'd, no more does search
But on the next green bough to perch,
    Where, when he first does lure,
    The falconer has her sure.

—What may not then our Isle presume
While victory his crest does plume?
    What may not others fear
    If thus he crowns each year!

As Caesar he, ere long, to Gaul,
To Italy an Hannibal,
    And to all states not free
    Shall climacteric be.

The Pict no shelter now shall find
Within his parti-colour'd mind,
    But from this valour, sad
    Shrink underneath the plaid—

Happy, if in the tufted brake
The English hunter him mistake,

Nor lay his hounds in near
The Caledonian deer.

But Thou, the War's and Fortune's son,
March indefatigably on;
    And for the last effect
    Still keep the sword erect:

Besides the force it has to fright
The spirits of the shady night,
    The same arts that did gain
    A power, must it maintain.

A. MARVELL

❧ 56 ❧

LYCIDAS

Elegy on a Friend drowned in the Irish Channel

YET once more, O ye laurels, and once more
Ye myrtles brown, with ivy never sere,
I come to pluck your berries harsh and crude,
And with forced fingers rude
Shatter your leaves before the mellowing year.
Bitter constraint, and sad occasion dear
Compels me to disturb your season due,
For Lycidas is dead, dead ere his prime,
Young Lycidas, and hath not left his peer:
Who would not sing for Lycidas? he knew
Himself to sing, and build the lofty rhyme.

He must not float upon his watery bier
Unwept, and welter to the parching wind,
Without the meed of some melodious tear.

Begin then, Sisters of the sacred well
That from beneath the seat of Jove doth spring,
Begin, and somewhat loudly sweep the string.
Hence with denial vain and coy excuse:
So may some gentle Muse
With lucky words favour my destined urn;
And as he passes, turn
And bid fair peace be to my sable shroud.

For we were nursed upon the selfsame hill,
Fed the same flock by fountain, shade, and rill.
Together both, ere the high lawns appear'd
Under the opening eye-lids of the morn,
We drove a-field, and both together heard
What time the gray-fly winds her sultry horn,
Battening our flocks with the fresh dews of night,
Oft till the star, that rose at evening bright,
Towards heaven's descent had sloped his westering wheel.
Meanwhile the rural ditties were not mute,
Temper'd to the oaten flute;
Rough Satyrs danced, and Fauns with cloven heel
From the glad sound would not be absent long;
And old Damoetas loved to hear our song.

But, O the heavy change, now thou art gone,
Now thou art gone, and never must return!
Thee, Shepherd, thee the woods, and desert caves
With wild thyme and the gadding vine o'ergrown,

And all their echoes, mourn:
The willows and the hazel copses green
Shall now no more be seen
Fanning their joyous leaves to thy soft lays:—
As killing as the canker to the rose,
Or taint-worm to the weanling herds that graze,
Or frost to flowers, that their gay wardrobe wear
When first the white-thorn blows;
Such, Lycidas, thy loss to shepherd's ear.

Where were ye, Nymphs, when the remorseless deep
Closed o'er the head of your loved Lycidas?
For neither were ye playing on the steep
Where your old bards, the famous Druids, lie,
Nor on the shaggy top of Mona high,
Nor yet where Deva spreads her wizard stream:
Ay me! I fondly dream—
Had ye been there—for what could that have done?
What could the Muse herself that Orpheus bore,
The Muse herself, for her enchanting son,
Whom universal nature did lament,
When by the rout that made the hideous roar
His gory visage down the stream was sent,
Down the swift Hebrus to the Lesbian shore?

Alas! what boots it with uncessant care
To tend the homely, slighted, shepherd's trade
And strictly meditate the thankless Muse?
Were it not better done, as others use,
To sport with Amaryllis in the shade.
Or with the tangles of Neaera's hair?

Fame is the spur that the clear spirit doth raise
(That last infirmity of noble mind)
To scorn delights, and live laborious days:
But the fair guerdon when we hope to find,
And think to burst out into sudden blaze,
Comes the blind Fury with the abhorréd shears
And slits the thin-spun life. 'But not the praise'
Phoebus replied, and touch'd my trembling ears;
'Fame is no plant that grows on mortal soil,
Nor in the glistering foil
Set off to the world, nor in broad rumour lies:
But lives and spreads aloft by those pure eyes
And perfect witness of all-judging Jove;
As he pronounces lastly on each deed,
Of so much fame in heaven expect thy meed.

O fountain Arethuse, and thou honour'd flood,
Smooth-sliding Mincius, crown'd with vocal reeds,
That strain I heard was of a higher mood:
But now my oat proceeds,
And listens to the herald of the sea
That came in Neptune's plea:
He ask'd the waves, and ask'd the felon winds,
What hard mishap hath doom'd this gentle swain?
And question'd every gust of rugged wings
That blows from off each beakéd promontory:
They knew not of his story;
And sage Hippotadés their answer brings,
That not a blast was from his dungeon stray'd;
The air was calm, and on the level brine

Sleek Panopé with all her sisters play'd.
It was that fatal and perfidious bark
Built in the eclipse, and rigg'd with curses dark,
That sunk so low that sacred head of thine.

Next Camus, reverend sire, went footing slow,
His mantle hairy, and his bonnet sedge
Inwrought with figures dim, and on the edge
Like to that sanguine flower inscribed with woe:
'Ah! who hath reft,' quoth he, 'my dearest pledge!'
Last came, and last did go
The pilot of the Galilean lake;
Two massy keys he bore of metals twain
(The golden opes, the iron shuts amain);
He shook his mitred locks, and stern bespake:
'How well could I have spared for thee, young swain,
Enow of such, as for their bellies' sake
Creep and intrude and climb into the fold!
Of other care they little reckoning make
Than how to scramble at the shearers' feast,
And shove away the worthy bidden guest.
Blind mouths! that scarce themselves know how to hold
A sheep-hook, or have learn'd aught else the least
That to the faithful herdman's art belongs!
What recks it them? What need they? They are sped;
And when they list, their lean and flashy songs
Grate on their scrannel pipes of wretched straw:
The hungry sheep look up, and are not fed,
But swoln with wind and the rank mist they draw
Rot inwardly, and foul contagion spread:

Besides what the grim wolf with privy paw
Daily devours apace, and nothing said:
—But that two-handed engine at the door
Stands ready to smite once, and smite no more.'

Return, Alphéus, the dread voice is past
That shrunk thy streams; return, Sicilian Muse,
And call the vales, and bid them hither cast
Their bells and flowerets of a thousand hues.
Ye valleys low, where the mild whispers use
Of shades, and wanton winds, and gushing brooks
On whose fresh lap the swart star sparely looks;
Throw hither all your quaint enamell'd eyes
That on the green turf suck the honey'd showers
And purple all the ground with vernal flowers.
Bring the rathe primrose that forsaken dies,
The tufted crow-toe, and pale jessamine,
The white pink, and the pansy freak'd with jet,
The glowing violet,
The musk-rose, and the well-attired woodbine,
With cowslips wan that hang the pensive head,
And every flower that sad embroidery wears:
Bid Amaranthus all his beauty shed,
And daffodillies fill their cups with tears
To strew the laureat hearse where Lycid lies.
For so to interpose a little ease,
Let our frail thoughts dally with false surmise;
Ay me! whilst thee the shores and sounding seas
Wash far away,—where'er thy bones are hurl'd,
Whether beyond the stormy Hebrides

Where thou perhaps, under the whelming tide,
Visitest the bottom of the monstrous world;
Or whether thou, to our moist vows denied,
Sleep'st by the fable of Bellerus old,
Where the great Vision of the guarded mount
Looks towards Namancos and Bayona's hold,
—Look homeward, Angel, now, and melt with ruth:
—And, O ye dolphins, waft the hapless youth!

Weep no more, woful shepherds, weep no more,
For Lycidas, your sorrow, is not dead,
Sunk though he be beneath the watery floor;
So sinks the day-star in the ocean-bed,
And yet anon repairs his drooping head
And tricks his beams, and with new-spangled ore
Flames in the forehead of the morning sky:
So Lycidas sunk low, but mounted high
Through the dear might of Him that walk'd the waves;
Where, other groves and other streams along,
With nectar pure his oozy locks he laves,
And hears the unexpressive nuptial song
In the blest kingdoms meek of joy and love.
There entertain him all the saints above
In solemn troops, and sweet societies,
That sing, and singing, in their glory move,
And wipe the tears for ever from his eyes.
Now, Lycidas, the shepherds weep no more;
Henceforth thou art the Genius of the shore
In thy large recompense, and shalt be good
To all that wander in that perilous flood.

Thus sang the uncouth swain to the oaks and rills,
While the still morn went out with sandals grey;
He touch'd the tender stops of various quills,
With eager thought warbling his Doric lay:
And now the sun had stretch'd out all the hills,
    And now was dropt into the western bay:
    At last he rose, and twitch'd his mantle blue:
    Tomorrow to fresh woods, and pastures new.

J. MILTON

❧ 57 ❧

ON THE TOMBS IN WESTMINSTER ABBEY

MORTALITY, behold and fear
What a change of flesh is here!
Think how many royal bones
Sleep within these heaps of stones;
Here they lie, had realms and lands,
Who now want strength to stir their hands,
Where from their pulpits seal'd with dust
They preach, 'In greatness is no trust.'
Here's an acre sown indeed
With the richest royallest seed
That the earth did e'er suck in
Since the first man died for sin:
Here the bones of birth have cried
'Though gods they were, as men they died!'

Here are sands, ignoble things,
Dropt from the ruin'd sides of kings;
Here's a world of pomp and state
Buried in dust, once dead by fate.

F. BEAUMONT

❧ 58 ❧

THE LAST CONQUEROR

VICTORIOUS men of earth, no more
    Proclaim how wide your empires are;
Though you bind-in every shore
    And your triumphs reach as far
        As night or day,
    Yet you, proud monarchs, must obey
And mingle with forgotten ashes, when
Death calls ye to the crowd of common men.
Devouring Famine, Plague, and War,
    Each able to undo mankind,
Death's servile emissaries are;
    Nor to these alone confined,
        He hath at will
    More quaint and subtle ways to kill;
A smile or kiss, as he will use the art,
Shall have the cunning skill to break a heart.

J. SHIRLEY

DEATH THE LEVELLER

THE glories of our blood and state
    Are shadows, not substantial things;
There is no armour against fate;
    Death lays his icy hand on kings:
        Sceptre and Crown
        Must tumble down,
And in the dust be equal made
With the poor crooked scythe and spade.

Some men with swords may reap the field,
    And plant fresh laurels where they kill:
But their strong nerves at last must yield;
    They tame but one another still:
        Early or late
        They stoop to fate,
And must give up their murmuring breath
When they, pale captives, creep to death.

The garlands wither on your brow;
    Then boast no more your mighty deeds;
Upon Death's purple altar now
    See where the victor-victim bleeds:
        Your heads must come
        To the cold tomb;

Only the actions of the just
Smell sweet, and blossom in their dust.

J. SHIRLEY

❧ 60 ❧

WHEN THE ASSAULT WAS INTENDED
TO THE CITY

CAPTAIN, or Colonel, or Knight in arms,
Whose chance on these defenceless doors may seize,
If deed of honour did thee ever please,
Guard them, and him within protect from harms.

He can requite thee; for he knows the charms
That call fame on such gentle acts as these,
And he can spread thy name o'er lands and seas,
Whatever clime the sun's bright circle warms.

Lift not thy spear against the Muses' bower:
The great Emathian conqueror did spare
The house of Pindarus, when temple and tower
Went to the ground: and the repeated air
Of sad Electra's poet had the power
To save the Athenian walls from ruin bare.

J. MILTON

ON HIS BLINDNESS

WHEN I consider how my light is spent
Ere half my days, in this dark world and wide,
And that one talent which is death to hide
Lodged with me useless, though my soul more bent

To serve therewith my Maker, and present
My true account, lest He returning chide,—
Doth God exact day-labour, light denied?
I fondly ask:—But Patience, to prevent

That murmur, soon replies; God doth not need
Either man's work, or His own gifts: who best
Bear His mild yoke, they serve Him best: His state

Is kingly; thousands at His bidding speed
And post o'er land and ocean without rest:—
They also serve who only stand and wait.

J. MILTON

CHARACTER OF A HAPPY LIFE

How happy is he born and taught
That serveth not another's will:
Whose armour is his honest thought
And simple truth his utmost skill!

Whose passions not his masters are,
Whose soul is still prepared for death,
Not tied unto the world with care
Of public fame, or private breath;

Who envies none that chance doth raise
Or vice; Who never understood
How deepest wounds are given by praise;
Nor rules of state, but rules of good;

Who hath his life from rumours freed,
Whose conscience is his strong retreat;
Whose state can neither flatterers feed,
Nor ruin make accusers great;

Who God doth late and early pray
More of His grace than gifts to lend;
And entertains the harmless day
With a well-chosen book or friend;

—This man is freed from servile bands

Of hope to rise, or fear to fall;
Lord of himself, though not of lands;
And have nothing, yet hath all.

SIR H. WOTTON

❧ 63 ❧

THE NOBLE NATURE

IT is not growing like a tree
In bulk, doth make Man better be;
Or standing long an oak, three hundred year,
To fall a log at last, dry, bald, and sere:
A lily of a day
Is fairer far in May,
Although it fall and die that night—
It was the plant and flower of Light.
In small proportions we just beauties see:
And in short measures life may perfect be.

B. JONSON

❧ 64 ❧

THE GIFTS OF GOD

WHEN God at first made Man,
Having a glass of blessings standing by;
Let us (said He) pour on him all we can:

Let the world's riches, which dispersèd lie,
        Contract into a span.

        So strength first made a way;
Then beauty flow'd, then wisdom, honour, pleasure:
When almost all was out, God made a stay,
Perceiving that alone, of all His treasure,
        Rest in the bottom lay.

        For if I should (said He)
Bestow this jewel also on my creature,
He would adore My gifts instead of Me,
And rest in Nature, not the God of Nature:
        So both should losers be.

        Yet let him keep the rest,
But keep them with repining restlessness:
Let him be rich and weary, that at least,
If goodness lead him not, yet weariness
        May toss him to My breast.

                                        G. HERBERT

⚜ 65 ⚜

THE RETREAT

HAPPY those early days, when I
Shined in my Angel-infancy!
Before I understood this place
Appointed for my second race,
Or taught my soul to fancy aught

117

But a white, celestial thought;
When yet I had not walk'd above
A mile or two from my first Love,
And looking back, at that short space
Could see a glimpse of His bright face;
When on some gilded cloud or flower
My gazing soul would dwell an hour,
And in those weaker glories spy
Some shadows of eternity;
Before I taught my tongue to wound
My conscience with a sinful sound,
Or had the black art to dispense
A several sin to every sense,
But felt through all this fleshly dress
Bright shoots of everlastingness.

O how I long to travel back,
And tread again that ancient track!
That I once more might reach that plain,
Where first I left my glorious train;
From whence th' enlighten'd spirit sees
That shady City of Palm-trees!
But ah! my soul with too much stay
Is drunk, and staggers in the way:—
Some men a forward motion love,
But I by backward steps would move;
And when this dust falls to the urn,
In that state I came, return.

H. VAUGHAN

118

66

HYMN TO DIANA

QUEEN and Huntress, chaste and fair,
    Now the sun is laid to sleep,
Seated in thy silver chair
    State in wonted manner keep:
        Hesperus entreats thy light,
        Goddess excellently bright.

Earth, let not thy envious shade
    Dare itself to interpose;
Cynthia's shining orb was made
    Heaven to clear when day did close:
        Bless us then with wishéd sight,
        Goddess excellently bright.

Lay thy bow of pearl apart
    And thy crystal-shining quiver;
Give unto the flying hart
    Space to breathe, how short soever:
        Thou that mak'st a day of night,
        Goddess excellently bright!

B. JONSON

CHILD AND MAIDEN

Aн, Chloris! could I now but sit
   As unconcern'd as when
Your infant beauty could beget
   No happiness or pain!
When I the dawn used to admire,
   And praised the coming day,
I little thought the rising fire
   Would take my rest away.

Your charms in harmless childhood lay
   Like metals in a mine;
Age from no face takes more away
   Than youth conceal'd in thine.
But as your charms insensibly
   To their perfection prest,
So love as unperceived did fly,
   And center'd in my breast.

My passion with your beauty grew,
   While Cupid at my heart
Still as his mother favour'd you
   Threw a new flaming dart:
Each gloried in their wanton part;
   To make a lover, he

Employ'd the utmost of his art—
    To make a beauty, she.

SIR C. SEDLEY

❧ 68 ❧

COUNSEL TO GIRLS

GATHER ye rose-buds while ye may,
    Old Time is still a-flying:
And this same flower that smiles today,
    Tomorrow will be dying.

The glorious Lamp of Heaven, the Sun,
    The higher he's a-getting
The sooner will his race be run,
    And nearer he's to setting.

That age is best which is the first,
    When youth and blood are warmer:
But being spent, the worse, and worst
    Times, will succeed the former.

Then be not coy, but use your time;
    And while ye may, go marry:
For having lost but once your prime,
    You may for ever tarry.

R. HERRICK

TO LUCASTA, ON GOING TO THE WARS

TELL me not, Sweet, I am unkind
    That from the nunnery
Of thy chaste breast and quiet mind,
    To war and arms I fly.

True, a new mistress now I chase,
    The first foe in the field;
And with a stronger faith embrace
    A sword, a horse, a shield.

Yet this inconstancy is such
    As you too shall adore;
I could not love thee, Dear, so much,
    Loved I not Honour more.

COLONEL LOVELACE

70

ELIZABETH OF BOHEMIA

YOU meaner beauties of the night,
    Which poorly satisfy our eyes
More by your number than your light,
    You common people of the skies,

What are you, when the Moon shall rise?

Ye violets that first appear,
    By your pure purple mantles known
Like the proud virgins of the year
    As if the spring were all your own,—
What are you, when the Rose is blown?

Ye curious chanters of the wood
    That warble forth dame Nature's lays,
Thinking your passions understood
    By your weak accents; what's your praise
When Philomel her voice doth raise?

So when my Mistress shall be seen
    In sweetness of her looks and mind,
By virtue first, then choice, a Queen,
    Tell me, if she were not design'd
Th' eclipse and glory of her kind?

SIR H. WOTTON

❧ 71 ❧

THE LOVELINESS OF LOVE

IT is not Beauty I demand,
A crystal brow, the moon's despair,
Nor the snow's daughter, a white hand,
Nor mermaid's yellow pride of hair:

Tell me not of your starry eyes,
Your lips that seem on roses fed,

Your breasts, where Cupid tumbling lies
Nor sleeps for kissing of his bed:—

A bloomy pair of vermeil cheeks
Like Hebe's in her ruddiest hours,
A breath that softer music speaks
Than summer winds a-wooing flowers.

These are but gauds: nay what are lips?
Coral beneath the ocean-stream,
Whose brink when your adventurer slips
Full oft he perisheth on them.

And what are cheeks, but ensigns oft
That wave hot youth to fields of blood?
Did Helen's breast, though ne'er so soft,
Do Greece or Illium any good?

Eyes can with baleful ardour burn;
Poison can breath, that erst perfumed;
There's many a white hand holds an urn
With lovers' hearts to dust consumed.

For crystal brows there's nought within;
They are but empty cells for pride;
He who the Syren's hair would win
Is mostly strangled in the tide.

Give me, instead of Beauty's bust,
A tender heart, a loyal mind
Which with temptation I would trust,
Yet never link'd with error find,—

One in whose gentle bosom I

Could pour my secret heart of woes,
Like the care-burthen'd honey-fly
That hides his murmurs in the rose,—

My earthly Comforter! whose love
So indefeasible might be
That, when my spirit wonn'd above,
Hers could not stay, for sympathy.

G. DARLEY

✿ 72 ✿

THE TRUE BEAUTY

HE that loves a rosy cheek
   Or a coral lip admires,
Or from starlike eyes doth seek
   Fuel to maintain his fires;
As old Time makes these decay,
So his flames must waste away.

But a smooth and steadfast mind,
   Gentle thoughts, and calm desires,
Hearts with equal love combined,
   Kindle never-dying fires:—
Where these are not, I despise
Lovely cheeks or lips or eyes.

T. CAREW

❧ 73 ❧

TO DIANEME

SWEET, be not proud of those two eyes
Which starlike sparkle in their skies;
Nor be you proud, that you can see
All hearts your captives; yours yet free:
Be you not proud of that rich hair
Which wantons with the lovesick air;
Whenas that ruby which you wear,
Sunk from the tip of your soft ear,
Will last to be a precious stone
When all your world of beauty's gone.

R. HERRICK

❧ 74 ❧

TO CELIA

DRINK to me only with thine eyes,
    And I will pledge with mine;
Or leave a kiss but in the cup
    And I'll not look for wine.
The thirst that from the soul doth rise
    Doth ask a drink divine;
But might I of Jove's nectar sup,
    I would not change for thine.

126

I sent thee late a rosy wreath,
   Not so much honouring thee
As giving it a hope that there
   It could not wither'd be;
But thou thereon didst only breathe
   And sent'st it back to me;
Since when it grows, and smells, I swear,
   Not of itself but thee!

B. JONSON

❧ 75 ❧

CHERRY-RIPE

THERE is a garden in her face
   Where roses and white lilies blow;
A heavenly paradise is that place,
   Wherein all pleasant fruits do grow;
There cherries grow that none may buy,
Till Cherry-Ripe themselves do cry.

Those cherries fairly do enclose
   Of orient pearl a double row,
Which when her lovely laughter shows,
   They look like rose-buds fill'd with snow:
Yet them no peer nor prince may buy,
Till Cherry-Ripe themselves do cry.

Her eyes like angels watch them still;
   Her brows like bended bows do stand,

Threat'ning with piercing frowns to kill
   All that approach with eye or hand
These sacred cherries to come nigh,
—Till Cherry-Ripe themselves do cry!

T. CAMPION

❧ 76 ☙

THE POETRY OF DRESS

I

A SWEET disorder in the dress
Kindles in clothes a wantonness:—
A lawn about the shoulders thrown
Into a fine distractión,—
An erring lace, which here and there
Enthrals the crimson stomacher,—
A cuff neglectful, and thereby
Ribbands to flow confusedly,—
A winning wave, deserving note,
In the tempestuous petticoat,—
A careless shoe-string, in whose tie
I see a wild civility,—
Do more bewitch me, than when art
Is too precise in every part.

R. HERRICK

✤ 77 ✤

II

WHENAS in silks my Julia goes
Then, then (methinks) how sweetly flows
That liquefaction of her clothes.

Next, when I cast mine eyes and see
That brave vibration each way free;
O how that glittering taketh me!

R. HERRICK

✤ 78 ✤

III

MY Love in her attire doth shew her wit,
    It doth so well become her:
For every season she hath dressings fit,
    For Winter, Spring, and Summer.
    No beauty she doth miss
    When all her robes are on:
    But Beauty's self she is
    When all her robes are gone.

ANON.

ON A GIRDLE

THAT which her slender waist confined
Shall now my joyful temples bind:
No monarch but would give his crown
His arms might do what this has done.

It was my Heaven's extremest sphere,
The pale which held that lovely deer:
My joy, my grief, my hope, my love
Did all within this circle move.

A narrow compass! and yet there
Dwelt all that's good, and all that's fair:
Give me but what this ribband bound,
Take all the rest the Sun goes round.

                              E. WALLER

ॐ 80 ॐ

TO ANTHEA WHO MAY COMMAND
HIM ANY THING

BID me to live, and I will live,
    Thy Protestant to be:
Or bid me love, and I will give
    A loving heart to thee.

A heart as soft, a heart as kind,
    A heart as sound and free
As in the whole world thou canst find,
    That heart I'll give to thee.

Bid that heart stay, and it will stay,
    To honour thy decree:
Or bid it languish quite away,
    And't shall do so for thee.

Bid me to weep, and I will weep
    While I have eyes to see:
And having none, yet I will keep
    A heart to weep for thee.

Bid me despair, and I'll despair,
    Under that cypress tree:
Or bid me die, and I will dare
    E'en Death, to die for thee.

Thou art my life, my love, my heart,
    The very eyes of me,
And hast command of every part,
    To live and die for thee.

R. HERRICK

❧ 81 ❧

LOVE not me for comely grace,
For my pleasing eye or face,

Nor for any outward part,
No, nor for my constant heart,—
  For those may fail, or turn to ill,
  So thou and I shall sever:
Keep therefore a true woman's eye,
And love me still, but know not why—
  So hast thou the same reason still
  To doat upon me ever!

ANON.

❧ 82 ❧

Not, Celia, that I juster am
  Or better than the rest;
For I would change each hour, like them,
  Were not my heart at rest.

But I am tied to very thee
  By every thought I have;
Thy face I only care to see,
  Thy heart I only crave.

All that in woman is adored
  In thy dear self I find—
For the whole sex can but afford
  The handsome and the kind.

Why then should I seek further store,
  And still make love anew?
When change itself can give no more,
  'Tis easy to be true.

SIR C. SEDLEY

TO ALTHEA FROM PRISON

WHEN Love with unconfinéd wings
    Hovers within my gates,
And my divine Althea brings
    To whisper at the grates;
When I lie tangled in her hair
    And fetter'd to her eye,
The birds that wanton in the air
    Know no such liberty.

When flowing cups run swiftly round
    With no allaying Thames,
Our careless heads with roses crown'd,
    Our hearts with loyal flames;
When thirsty grief in wine we steep,
    When healths and draughts go free—
Fishes that tipple in the deep
    Know no such liberty.

When, linnet-like confinéd, I
    With shriller throat shall sing
The sweetness, mercy, majesty
    And glories of my King;
When I shall voice aloud how good
    He is, how great should be,
Enlargéd winds, that curl the flood,
    Know no such liberty.

Stone walls do not a prison make,
    Nor iron bars a cage;
Minds innocent and quiet take
    That for an hermitage:
If I have freedom in my love
    And in my soul am free,
Angels alone, that soar above,
    Enjoy such liberty.

COLONEL LOVELACE

✣ 84 ✣

ENCOURAGEMENTS TO A LOVER

WHY so pale and wan, fond lover?
    Prythee, why so pale?
Will, if looking well can't move her,
    Looking ill prevail?
    Prythee, why so pale?

Why so dull and mute, young sinner?
    Prythee, why so mute?
Will, when speaking well can't win her,
    Saying nothing do't?
    Prythee, why so mute?

Quit, quit, for shame! this will not move,
    This cannot take her;
If of herself she will not love,
    Nothing can make her:
    The D—l take her!

SIR J. SUCKLING

✣ 85 ✣

A SUPPLICATION

AWAKE, awake, my Lyre!
And tell thy silent master's humble tale
   In sounds that may prevail;
   Sounds that gentle thoughts inspire:
      Though so exalted she
      And I so lowly be
Tell her, such different notes make all thy harmony.

   Hark! how the strings awake:
And, though the moving hand approach not near,
      Themselves with awful fear
   A kind of numerous trembling make.
      Now all thy forces try.
      Now all thy charms apply;
Revenge upon her ear the conquests of her eye.

   Weak Lyre! thy virtue sure
Is useless here, since thou art only found
      To cure, but not to wound,
   And she to wound, but not to cure,
      Too weak too wilt thou prove
      My passion to remove;
Physic to other ills, thou'rt nourishment to love.

   Sleep, sleep again, my Lyre!
For thou canst never tell my humble tale

135

In sounds that will prevail,
Nor gentle thoughts in her inspire;
All thy vain mirth lay by,
Bid thy strings silent lie,
Sleep, sleep again, my Lyre, and let thy master die.

A. COWLEY

✤ 86 ✤

THE MANLY HEART

SHALL I, wasting in despair,
Die because a woman's fair?
Or my cheeks make pale with care
'Cause another's rosy are?
Be she fairer than the day
Or the flowery meads in May—
If she be not so to me
What care I how fair she be?

Shall my foolish heart be pined
'Cause I see a woman kind;
Or a well disposéd nature
Joinéd with a lovely feature?
Be she meeker, kinder, than
Turtle-dove or pelican,
If she be not so to me
What care I how kind she be?

Shall a woman's virtues move

136

Me to perish for her love?
Or her merit's value known
Make me quite forget mine own?
Be she with that goodness blest
Which may gain her name of Best;
 If she seem not such to me,
 What care I how good she be?

'Cause her fortune seems too high,
Shall I play the fool and die?
Those that bear a noble mind
Where they want of riches find,
Think what with them they would do
Who without them dare to woo;
 And unless that mind I see,
 What care I though great she be?

Great or good, or kind or fair,
I will ne'er the more despair;
If she love me, this believe,
I will die ere she shall grieve;
If she slight me when I woo,
I can scorn and let her go;
 For if she be not for me,
 What care I for whom she be?

G. WITHER

MELANCHOLY

HENCE, all you vain delights,
As short as are the nights
Wherein you spend your folly:
There's nought in this life sweet
If man were wise to see't,
But our melancholy,
O sweetest Melancholy!
Welcome, folded arms, and fixéd eyes,
A sigh that piercing mortifies,
A look that's fasten'd to the ground,
A tongue chain'd up without a sound!
Fountain heads and pathless groves,
Places which pale passion loves!
Moonlight walks, when all the fowls
Are warmly housed save bats and owls!
A midnight bell, a parting groan!
These are the sounds we feed upon;
Then stretch our bones in a still gloomy valley;
Nothing's so dainty sweet as lovely melancholy.

J. FLETCHER

TO A LOCK OF HAIR

THY hue, dear pledge, is pure and bright
As in that well-remember'd night
When first thy mystic braid was wove,
And first my Agnes whisper'd love.

Since then how often hast thou prest
The torrid zone of this wild breast,
Whose wrath and hate have sworn to dwell
With the first sin that peopled hell;
A breast whose blood's a troubled ocean,
Each throb the earthquake's wild commotion!
O if such clime thou canst endure
Yet keep thy hue unstain'd and pure,
What conquest o'er each erring thought
Of that fierce realm had Agnes wrought!
I had not wander'd far and wide
With such an angel for my guide;
Nor heaven nor earth could then reprove me
If she had lived, and lived to love me.

Not then this world's wild joys had been
To me one savage hunting scene,
My sole delight the headlong race
And frantic hurry of the chase;
To start, pursue, and bring to bay,

139

Rush in, drag down, and rend my prey,
Then—from the carcass turn away!
Mine ireful mood had sweetness tamed,
And soothed each wound which pride inflamed:—
Yes, God and man might now approve me
If thou hadst lived, and lived to love me!

SIR W. SCOTT

✤ 89 ✤

THE FORSAKEN BRIDE

O WALY waly up the bank,
    And waly waly down the brae,
And waly waly yon burn-side
    Where I and my Love wont to gae!
I leant my back unto an aik,
    I thought it was a trusty tree;
But first it bow'd, and syne it brak,
    Sae my true Love did lichtly me.

O waly waly, but love be bonny
    A little time while it is new;
But when 'tis auld, it waxeth cauld
    And fades awa' like morning dew.
O wherefore should I busk my head?
    Or wherefore should I kame my hair?
For my true Love has me forsook,
    And says he'll never loe me mair.

140

Now Authur-seat sall be my bed;
    The sheets shall ne'er be prest by me:
Saint Anton's well sall be my drink,
    Since my true Love has forsaken me.
Marti'mas wind, when wilt thou blaw
    And shake the green leaves aff the tree?
O gentle Death, when wilt thou come?
    For of my life I am wearíe.

'Tis not the frost, that freezes fell,
    Nor blawing snaw's inclemencie;
'Tis not sic cauld that makes me cry,
    But my Love's heart grown cauld to me.
When we came in by Glasgow town
    We were a comely sight to see;
My Love was clad in the black velvét,
    And I myself in cramasie.

But had I wist, before I kist,
    That love had been sae ill to win;
I had lockt my heart in a case of gowd
    And pinn'd it with a siller pin.
And, O! if my young babe were born,
    And set upon the nurse's knee.
And I mysell were dead and gane,
    And the green grass growning over me!

ANON.

141

FAIR HELEN

I WISH I were where Helen lies;
Night and day on me she cries;
O that I were where Helen lies
    On fair Kirconnell lea!

Curst be the heart that thought the thought,
And curst the hand that fired the shot,
When in my arms burd Helen dropt,
    And died to succour me!

O think na but my heart was sair
When my Love dropt down and spak nae mair!
I laid her down wi' meikle care
    On fair Kirconnell lea.

As I went down the water-side,
None but my foe to be my guide,
None but my foe to be my guide,
    On fair Kirconnell lea;

I lighted down my sword to draw,
I hackéd him in pieces sma',
I hackéd him in pieces sma',
    For her sake that died for me.

O Helen fair, beyond compare!
I'll make a garland of thy hair

Shall bind my heart for evermair
    Until the day I die.

O that I were where Helen lies!
Night and day on me she cries;
Out of my bed she bids me rise,
    Says, 'Haste and come to me!'

O Helen fair! O Helen chaste!
If I were with thee, I were blest,
Where thou lies low and takes thy rest
    On fair Kirconnell lea.

I wish my grave were growing green,
A winding-sheet drawn ower my een,
And I in Helen's arms lying,
    On fair Kirconnell lea.

I wish I were where Helen lies;
Night and day on me she cries;
And I am weary of the skies,
    Since my Love died for me.

ANON.

❧ 91 ❧

THE TWA CORBIES

As I was walking all alane
I heard twa corbies making a mane;
The tane unto the t'other say,
'Where sall we gang and dine today?'

'—In behint yon auld fail dyke,
I wot there lies a new-slain Knight;
And naebody kens that he lies there,
But his hawk, his hound, and lady fair.

'His hound is to the hunting gane,
His hawk to fetch the wild-fowl hame,
His lady's ta'en another mate,
So we may mak our dinner sweet.

'Ye'll sit on his white hause-bane,
And I'll pick out his bonny blue een:
Wi' ae lock o' his gowden hair
We'll theek our nest when it grows bare.

'Mony a one for him makes mane,
But nane sall ken where he is gane;
O'er his white banes, when they are bare,
The wind sall blaw for evermair.'

ANON.

❦ 92 ❧

TO BLOSSOMS

FAIR pledges of a fruitful tree,
    Why do ye fall so fast?
    Your date is not so past,
But you may stay yet here awhile
    To blush and gently smile,
        And go at last.

144

What, were ye born to be
　　An hour or half's delight,
　　　And so to bid good-night?
'Twas pity Nature brought ye forth
　　Merely to show your worth,
　　　And lose you quite.

But you are lovely leaves, where we
　　May read how soon things have
　　　Their end, though ne'er so brave:
And after they have shown their pride
　　Like you, awhile, they glide
　　　Into the grave.

R. HERRICK

93

TO DAFFODILS

Fair Daffodils, we weep to see
　　You haste away so soon:
As yet the early-rising Sun
　　Has not attain'd his noon.
　　　Stay, stay,
　　Until the hasting day
　　　Has run
　　But to the even-song;
And, having pray'd together, we
　　Will go with you along.

We have short time to stay, as you,
We have as short a Spring;
As quick a growth to meet decay
As you, or any thing.
We die,
As your hours do, and dry
Away
Like to the Summer's rain;
Or as the pearls of morning's dew
Ne'er to be found again.

R. HERRICK

❧ 94 ❧

THOUGHTS IN A GARDEN

How vainly men themselves amaze
To win the palm, the oak, or bays,
And their incessant labours see
Crown'd from some single herb or tree,
Whose short and narrow-vergéd shade
Does prudently their toils upbraid;
While all the flowers and trees do close
To weave the garlands of Repose.

Fair Quiet, have I found thee here,
And Innocence thy sister dear?
Mistaken long, I sought you then
In busy companies of men:
Your sacred plants, if here below,

146

Only among the plants will grow:
Society is all but rude
To this delicious solitude.

No white nor red was ever seen
So amorous as this lovely green.
Fond lovers, cruel as their flame,
Cut in these trees their mistress' name:
Little, alas, they know or heed
How far these beauties her exceed!
Fair trees! where'er your barks I wound,
No name shall but your own be found.

When we have run our passion's heat
Love hither makes his best retreat:
The gods, who mortal beauty chase,
Still in a tree did end their race:
Apollo hunted Daphne so
Only that she might laurel grow:
And Pan did after Syrinx speed
Not as a nymph, but for a reed.

What wondrous life is this I lead!
Ripe apples drop about my head;
The luscious clusters of the vine
Upon my mouth do crush their wine;
The nectarine and curious peach
Into my hands themselves do reach;
Stumbling on melons, as I pass,
Ensnared with flowers, I fall on grass.

Meanwhile the mind from pleasure less
Withdraws into its happiness;
The mind, that ocean where each kind
Does straight its own resemblance find;
Yet it creates, transcending these,
Far other worlds, and other seas;
Annihilating all that's made
To a green thought in a green shade.

Here at the fountain's sliding foot
Or at some fruit-tree's mossy root,
Casting the body's vest aside
My soul into the boughs does glide;
There, like a bird, it sits and sings,
Then whets and claps its silver wings,
And, till prepared for longer flight,
Waves in its plumes the various light.

Such was that happy Garden-state
While man there walk'd without a mate:
After a place so pure and sweet,
What other help could yet be meet!
But 'twas beyond a mortal's share
To wander solitary there:
Two paradises 'twere in one,
To live in Paradise alone.

How well the skilful gardener drew
Of flowers and herbs this dial new!
Where, from above, the milder sun
Does through a fragrant zodiac run:

And, as it works, th' industrious bee
Computes its time as well as we.
How could such sweet and wholesome hours
Be reckon'd, but with herbs and flowers!

A. MARVELL

❧ 95 ❧

L'ALLÉGRO

HENCE, loathéd Melancholy,
  Of Cerberus and blackest Midnight born
In Stygian cave forlorn
  'Mongst horrid shapes, and shrieks, and sights unholy!
Find out some uncouth cell
  Where brooding Darkness spreads his jealous wings
And the night-raven sings;
  There under ebon shades, and low-brow'd rocks
As ragged as thy locks,
  In dark Cimmerian desert ever dwell.

    But come, thou Goddess fair and free,
  In heaven yclep'd Euphrosyne,
  And by men, heart-easing Mirth,
  Whom lovely Venus at a birth
  With two sister Graces more
  To ivy-crownéd Bacchus bore

149

Or whether (as some sager sing)
The frolic wind that breathes the spring
Zephyr, with Aurora playing,
As he met her once a-Maying—
There on beds of violets blue
And fresh-blown roses wash'd in dew
Fill'd her with thee, a daughter fair,
So buxom, blithe, and debonair.

    Haste thee, Nymph, and bring with thee
Jest, and youthful jollity,
Quips, and cranks, and wanton wiles,
Nods, and becks, and wreathéd smiles
Such as hang on Hebe's cheek,
And love to live in dimple sleek;
Sport that wrinkled Care derides,
And Laughter holding both his sides:—
Come, and trip it as you go
On the light fantastic toe;
And in thy right hand lead with thee
The mountain nymph, sweet Liberty;
And if I give thee honour due
Mirth, admit me of thy crew,
To live with her, and live with thee
In unreprovéd pleasures free;
To hear the lark begin his flight
And singing startle the dull night
From his watch-tower in the skies,
Till the dappled dawn doth rise;
Then to come, in spite of sorrow,
And at my window bid good-morrow

Through the sweetbriar, or the vine,
Or the twisted eglantine:
While the cock with lively din
Scatters the rear of darkness thin,
And to the stack, or the barn-door,
Stoutly struts his dames before:
Oft listening how the hounds and horn
Cheerly rouse the slumbering morn,
From the side of some hoar hill,
Through the high wood echoing shrill.
Sometime walking, not unseen,
By hedge-row elms, on hillocks green,
Right against the eastern gate
Where the great Sun begins his state
Robed in flames and amber light,
The clouds in thousand liveries dight,
While the ploughman, near at hand,
Whistles o'er the furrow'd land,
And the milkmaid singeth blithe,
And the mower whets his scythe,
And every shepherd tells his tale
Under the hawthorn in the dale.
　　Straight mine eye hath caught new pleasures
Whilst the landscape round it measures;
Russet lawns, and fallows grey,
Where the nibbling flocks do stray;
Mountains, on whose barren breast
The labouring clouds do often rest;
Meadows trim with daisies pied,
Shallow brooks and rivers wide;

151

Towers and battlements it sees
Bosom'd high in tufted trees,
Where perhaps some Beauty lies,
The Cynosure of neighbouring eyes.
    Hard by, a cottage chimney smokes
From betwixt two aged oaks,
Where Corydon and Thyrsis, met,
Are at their savoury dinner set
Of herbs, and other country messes
Which the neat-handed Phillis dresses;
And then in haste her bower she leaves
With Thestylis to bind the sheaves;
Or, if the earlier season lead,
To the tann'd haycock in the mead.
    Sometimes with secure delight
The upland hamlets will invite,
When the merry bells ring round,
And the jocund rebecks sound
To many a youth and many a maid,
Dancing in the chequer'd shade;
And young and old come forth to play
On a sun-shine holy-day,
Till the live-long day-light fail:
Then to the spicy nut-brown ale,
With stories told of many a feat,
How Faery Mab the junkets eat;
She was pinch'd, and pull'd, she said;
And he, by Friar's lantern led;
Tells how the drudging Goblin sweat
To earn his cream-bowl duly set,

When in one night, ere glimpse of morn,
His shadowy flail hath thresh'd the corn
That ten day-labourers could not end;
Then lies him down the lubber fiend,
And, stretch'd out all the chimney's length,
Basks at the fire his hairy strength;
And crop-full out of doors he flings,
Ere the first cock his matin rings.
   Thus done the tales, to bed they creep,
By whispering winds soon lull'd asleep.
   Tower'd cities please us then
And the busy hum of men,
Where throngs of knights and barons bold,
In weeds of peace high triumphs hold,
With store of ladies, whose bright eyes
Rain influence, and judge the prize
Of wit or arms, while both contend
To win her grace, whom all commend.
There let Hymen oft appear
In saffron robe, with taper clear,
And pomp, and feast, and revelry,
With mask, and antique pageantry;
Such sights as youthful poets dream
On summer eves by haunted stream.
Then to the well-trod stage anon,
If Jonson's learned sock be on,
Or sweetest Shakespeare, Fancy's child,
Warble his native wood-notes wild.
   And ever against eating cares
Lap me in soft Lydian airs

Married to immortal verse,
Such as the meeting soul may pierce
In notes, with many a winding bout
Of linkéd sweetness long drawn out,
With wanton heed and giddy cunning,
The melting voice through mazes running,
Untwisting all the chains that tie
The hidden soul of harmony;
That Orpheus' self may heave his head
From golden slumber, on a bed
Of heap'd Elysian flowers, and hear
Such strains as would have won the ear
Of Pluto, to have quite set free
His half-regain'd Eurydice.

These delights if thou canst give,
Mirth, with thee I mean to live.

J. MILTON

✣ 96 ✣

IL PENSEROSO

HENCE, vain deluding Joys,
    The brood of Folly without father bred!
How little you bestead
    Or fill the fixéd mind with all your toys!
Dwell in some idle brain,
    And fancies fond with gaudy shapes possess

As thick and numberless
    As the gay motes that people the sunbeams,
Or likest hovering dreams,
    The fickle pensioners of Morpheus' train.
    But hail, thou goddess sage and holy,
Hail, divinest Melancholy!
Whose saintly visage is too bright
To hit the sense of human sight,
And therefore to our weaker view
O'erlaid with black, staid Wisdom's hue;
Black, but such as in esteem
Prince Memnon's sister might beseem,
Or that starr'd Ethiop queen that strove
To set her beauty's praise above
The sea-nymphs, and their powers offended:
Yet thou art higher far descended:
Thee bright-hair'd Vesta, long of yore,
To solitary Saturn bore;
His daughter she; in Saturn's reign
Such mixture was not held a stain:
Oft in glimmering bowers and glades
He met her, and in secret shades
Of woody Ida's inmost grove,
While yet there was no fear of Jove.
    Come, pensive nun, devout and pure,
Sober, steadfast, and demure,
All in a robe of darkest grain
Flowing with majestic train,
And sable stole of cypres lawn

Over thy decent shoulders drawn:
Come, but keep thy wonted state,
With even step, and musing gait,
And looks commercing with the skies,
Thy rapt soul sitting in thine eyes:
There, held in holy passion still,
Forget thyself to marble, till
With a sad leaden downward cast
Thou fix them on the earth as fast:
And join with thee calm Peace, and Quiet,
Spare Fast, that oft with gods doth diet,
And hears the Muses in a ring
Ay round about Jove's altar sing;
And add to these retired Leisure
That in trim gardens takes his pleasure:—
But first, and chiefest, with thee bring
Him that yon soars on golden wing
Guiding the fiery-wheeléd throne,
The cherub Contemplatión;
And the mute Silence hist along,
'Less Philomel will deign a song
In her sweetest saddest plight,
Smoothing the rugged brow of Night,
While Cynthia checks her dragon yoke
Gently o'er the accustom'd oak.
—Sweet bird, that shunn'st the noise of folly
Most musical, most melancholy!
Thee, chauntress, oft, the woods among
I woo, to hear thy even-song;
And missing thee, I walk unseen

On the dry smooth-shaven green,
To behold the wandering Moon
Riding near her highest noon,
Like one that had been led astray
Through the heaven's wide pathless way,
And oft, as if her head she bow'd,
Stooping through a fleecy cloud.

Oft, on a plat of rising ground
I hear the far-off curfeu sound
Over some wide-water'd shore,
Swinging slow with sullen roar:
Or, if the air will not permit,
Some still removéd place will fit,
Where glowing embers through the room
Teach light to counterfeit a gloom;
Far from all resort of mirth,
Save the cricket on the hearth,
Or the bellman's drowsy charm
To bless the doors from nightly harm.

Or let my lamp at midnight hour
Be seen in some high lonely tower,
Where I may oft out-watch the Bear
With thrice-great Hermes, or unsphere
The spirit of Plato, to unfold
What worlds or what vast regions hold
The immortal mind, that hath forsook
Her mansion in this fleshly nook:
And of those demons that are found
In fire, air, flood, or under ground,
Whose power hath a true consent

With planet, or with element.
Sometime let gorgeous Tragedy
In scepter'd pall come sweeping by,
Presenting Thebes, or Pelops' line,
Or the tale of Troy divine;
Or what (though rare) of later age
Ennobled hath the buskin'd stage.

But, O sad Virgin, that thy power
Might raise Musaeus from his bower,
Or bid the soul of Orpheus sing
Such notes as, warbled to the string,
Drew iron tears down Pluto's cheek
And made Hell grant what Love did seek!
Or call up him that left half-told
The story of Cambuscan bold,
Of camball, and of Algarsife,
And who had Canacé to wife,
That own'd the virtuous ring and glass,
And of the wondrous horse of brass
On which the Tartar king did ride:
And if aught else great bards beside
In sage and solemn tunes have sung
Of turneys, and of trophies hung,
Of forests and enchantments drear,
Where more is meant than meets the ear.

Thus, Night, oft see me in thy pale career,
Till civil-suited Morn appear,
Not trick'd and frounced as she was wont
With the Attic Boy to hunt,
But kercheft in a comely cloud

While rocking winds are piping loud,
Or usher'd with a shower still,
When the gust hath blown his fill,
Ending on the rustling leaves
With minute drops from off the eaves.
And when the sun begins to fling
His flaring beams, me, goddess, bring
To archéd walks of twilight groves,
And shadows brown, that Sylvan loves,
Of pine, or monumental oak,
Where the rude axe, with heavéd stroke,
Was never heard the nymphs to daunt
Or fright them from their hallow'd haunt.
There in close covert by some brook
Where no profaner eye may look,
Hide me from day's garish eye,
While the bee with honey'd thigh
That at her flowery work doth sing,
And the waters murmuring,
With such consort as they keep
Entice the dewy-feather'd Sleep;
And let some strange mysterious dream
Wave at his wings in airy stream
Of lively portraiture display'd,
Softly on my eyelids laid:
And, as I wake, sweet music breathe
Above, about, or underneath,
Sent by some Spirit to mortals good,
Or the unseen Genius of the wood.
  But let my due feet never fail

To walk the studious cloister's pale,
And love the high-embowéd roof,
With antique pillars massy proof,
And storied windows richly dight
Casting a dim religious light:
There let the pealing organ blow
To the full-voiced quire below
In service high and anthems clear,
As may with sweetness, through mine ear,
Dissolve me into ecstasies,
And bring all Heaven before mine eyes.
    And may at last my weary age
Find out the peaceful hermitage,
The hairy gown and mossy cell
Where I may sit and rightly spell
Of every star that heaven doth show,
And every herb that sips the dew:
Till old experience do attain
To something like prophetic strain.

    These pleasures, Melancholy, give,
And I with thee will choose to live.

J. MILTON

ALEXANDER'S FEAST; OR, THE POWER
OF MUSIC

'Twas at the royal feast for Persia won
   By Philip's warlike son—
   Aloft in awful state
   The godlike hero sate
   On his imperial throne;
   His valiant peers were placed around,
   Their brows with roses and with myrtles bound
   (So should desert in arms be crown'd);
   The lovely Thais by his side
   Sate like a blooming eastern bride
   In flower of youth and beauty's pride:—
   Happy, happy, happy pair!
   None but the brave
   None but the brave
   None but the brave deserves the fair!

   Timotheus placed on high
Amid the tuneful quire
With flying fingers touch'd the lyre:
The trembling notes ascend the sky
And heavenly joys inspire.
The song began from Jove
Who left his blissful seats above—

Such is the power of mighty love!
A dragon's fiery form belied the god;
Sublime on radiant spires he rode
When he to fair Olympia prest,
And while he sought her snowy breast,
Then round her slender waist he curl'd,
And stamp'd an image of himself, a sovereign of the world.
—The listening crowd admire the lofty sound!
A present deity! they shout around:
A present deity! the vaulted roofs rebound!
With ravish'd ears
The monarch hears,
Assumes the god;
Affects to nod
And seems to shake the spheres.

The praise of Bacchus then the sweet musician sung,
Of Bacchus ever fair and ever young:
The jolly god in triumph comes!
Sound the trumpets, beat the drums!
Flush'd with a purple grace
He shows his honest face:
Now give the hautboys breath; he comes, he comes!
Bacchus, ever fair and young,
Drinking joys did first ordain;
Bacchus' blessings are a treasure,
Drinking is the soldier's pleasure:
Rich the treasure,
Sweet the pleasure,
Sweet is pleasure after pain.

Soothed with the sound, the king grew vain;
Fought all his battles o'er again,
And thrice he routed all his foes, and thrice he slew the
    slain!
The master saw the madness rise,
His glowing cheeks, his ardent eyes;
And while he Heaven and Earth defied
Changed his hand and check'd his pride.
He chose a mournful Muse
Soft pity to infuse:
He sung Darius great and good,
By too severe a fate
Fallen, fallen, fallen, fallen,
Fallen from his high estate,
And weltering in his blood;
Deserted, at his utmost need,
By those his former bounty fed;
On the bare earth exposed he lies
With not a friend to close his eyes.
—With downcast looks the joyless victor sate,
Revolving in his alter'd soul
The various turns of Chance below;
And now and then a sigh he stole,
And tears began to flow.

The mighty master smiled to see
That love was in the next degree;
'Twas but a kindred sound to move,
For pity melts the mind to love.
Softly sweet, in Lydian measures

Soon he soothed his soul to pleasures.
War, he sung, is toil and trouble,
Honour but an empty bubble;
Never ending, still beginning,
Fighting still, and still destroying;
If the world be worth thy winning,
Think, O think, it worth enjoying:
Lovely Thais sits beside thee,
Take the good the gods provide thee!
—The many rend the skies with loud applause;
So Love was crown'd, but Music won the cause.
The prince, unable to conceal his pain,
Gazed on the fair
Who caused his care,
And sigh'd and look'd, sigh'd and look'd,
Sigh'd and look'd, and sigh'd again:
At length with love and wine at once opprest
The vanquish'd victor sunk upon her breast.

Now strike the golden lyre again:
A louder yet, and yet a louder strain
Break his bands of sleep asunder
And rouse him like a rattling peal of thunder.
Hark, hark! the horrid sound
Has raised up his head:
As awaked from the dead
And amazed he stares around.
Revenge, revenge, Timotheus cries,
See the Furies arise!
See the snakes that they rear

164

How they hiss in their hair,
And the sparkles that flash from their eyes!
Behold a ghastly band,
Each a torch in his hand!
Those are Grecian ghosts, that in battle were slain
And unburied remain
Inglorious on the plain:
Give the vengeance due
To the valiant crew!
Behold how they toss their torches on high
How they point to the Persian abodes
And glittering temples of their hostile gods.
—The princes applaud with a furious joy:
And the King seized a flambeau with zeal to destroy;
Thais led the way
To light him to his prey,
And like another Helen, fired another Troy!

—Thus, long ago,
Ere heaving bellows learn'd to blow
While organs yet were mute,
Timotheus, to his breathing flute
And sounding lyre
Could swell the soul to rage, or kindle soft desire.
At last divine Cecilia came,
Inventress of the vocal frame;
The sweet enthusiast from her sacred store
Enlarged the former narrow bounds,
And added length to solemn sounds,
With Nature's mother-wit, and arts unknown before.

—Let old Timotheus yield the prize
Or both divide the crown;
He raised a mortal to the skies;
She drew an angel down!

J. DRYDEN

BOOK THIRD

THE QUIET LIFE

HAPPY the man, whose wish and care
A few paternal acres bound,
Content to breathe his native air
      In his own ground.

Whose herds with milk, whose fields with bread,
Whose flocks supply him with attire;
Whose trees in summer yield him shade,
      In winter, fire.

Blest, who can unconcern'dly find
Hours, days, and years, slide soft away
In health of body, peace of mind,
      Quiet by day,

Sound sleep by night; study and ease
Together mix'd; sweet recreation,
And innocence, which most does please
      With meditation.

Thus let me live, unseen, unknown;
Thus unlamented let me die;
Steal from the world, and not a stone
      Tell where I lie.

A. POPE

THE BLIND BOY

O say what is that thing call'd Light,
    Which I must ne'er enjoy;
What are the blessings of the sight,
    O tell your poor blind boy!

You talk of wondrous things you see,
    You say the sun shines bright;
I feel him warm, but how can he
    Or make it day or night?

My day or night myself I make
    Whene'er I sleep or play;
And could I ever keep awake
    With me 'twere always day.

With heavy sighs I often hear
    You mourn my hapless woe;
But sure with patience I can bear
    A loss I ne'er can know.

Then let not what I cannot have
    My cheer of mind destroy:
Whilst thus I sing, I am a king,
    Although a poor blind boy.

C. CIBBER

ON A FAVOURITE CAT, DROWNED
IN A TUB OF GOLD FISHES

'Twas on a lofty vase's side
Where China's gayest art had dyed
The azure flowers that blow,
Demurest of the tabby kind
The pensive Selima, reclined,
Gazed on the lake below.

Her conscious tail her joy declared:
The fair round face, the snowy beard,
The velvet of her paws,
Her coat that with the tortoise vies,
Her ears of jet, and emerald eyes—
She saw, and purr'd applause.

Still had she gazed, but 'midst the tide
Two angel forms were seen to glide,
The Genii of the stream:
Their scaly armour's Tyrian hue
Through richest purple, to the view
Betray'd a golden gleam.

The hapless Nymph with wonder saw:
A whisker first, and then a claw
With many an ardent wish
She stretch'd, in vain, to reach the prize—

What female heart can gold despise?
What Cat's averse to Fish?

Presumptuous maid! with looks intent
Again she stretch'd, again she bent,
Nor knew the gulf between—
Malignant Fate sat by and smiled—
The slippery verge her feet beguiled;
She tumbled headlong in!

Eight times emerging from the flood
She mew'd to every watery God
Some speedy aid to send:—
No Dolphin came, no Nereid stirr'd,
Nor cruel Tom nor Susan heard—
A favourite has no friend!

From hence, ye Beauties! undeceived
Know one false step is ne'er retrieved,
And be with caution bold:
Not all that tempts your wandering eyes
And heedless hearts, is lawful prize,
Not all that glisters, gold!

T. GRAY

❧ 101 ❧

RULE, BRITANNIA

WHEN Britain first at Heaven's command
Arose from out the azure main,

This was the charter of her land,
    And guardian angels sung the strain:
Rule, Britannia! Britannia, rule the waves!
    Britons never shall be slaves.

The nations not so blest as thee
    Must in their turn to tyrants fall,
Whilst thou shalt flourish great and free,
    The dread and envy of them all.

Still more majestic shalt thou rise,
    More dreadful from each foreign stroke;
As the loud blast that tears the skies
    Serves but to root thy native oak.

Thee haughty tyrants ne'er shall tame;
    All their attempts to bend thee down
Will but arouse thy generous flame,
    And work their woe and thy renown.

To thee belongs the rural reign;
    Thy cities shall with commerce shine;
All thine shall be the subject main,
    And every shore it circles thine!

The Muses, still with Freedom found,
    Shall to thy happy coast repair;
Blest Isle, with matchless beauty crown'd,
    And manly hearts to guard the fair:—
Rule, Britannia! Britannia, rule the waves!
    Britons never shall be slaves.

                              J. THOMSON

THE BARD

Pindaric Ode

'RUIN seize thee, ruthless King!
Confusion on thy banners wait!
Tho' fann'd by Conquest's crimson wing
   They mock the air with idle state.
Helm, nor hauberk's twisted mail,
Nor e'en thy virtues, tyrant, shall avail
To save thy secret soul from nightly fears,
From Cambria's curse, from Cambria's tears!'
—Such were the sounds that o'er the crested pride
   Of the first Edward scatter'd wild dismay,
As down the steep of Snowdon's shaggy side
   He wound with toilsome march his long array:—
Stout Glo'ster stood aghast in speechless trance;
'To arms!' cried Mortimer, and couch'd his quivering lance.

   On a rock, whose haughty brow
Frowns o'er old Conway's foaming flood,
   Robed in the sable garb of woe
With haggard eyes the Poet stood;
(Loose his beard and hoary hair
Stream'd like a meteor to the troubled air)
And with a master's hand and prophet's fire
Struck the deep sorrows of his lyre:
   'Hark, how each giant oak and desert-cave

Sighs to the torrent's awful voice beneath!
O'er thee, O King! their hundred arms they wave,
   Revenge on thee in hoarser murmurs breathe:
Vocal no more, since Cambria's fatal day,
To high-born Hoel's harp, or soft Llewellyn's lay.

   'Cold is Cadwallo's tongue,
     That hush'd the stormy main:
Brave Urien sleeps upon his craggy bed:
     Mountains, ye mourn in vain
     Modred, whose magic song
Made huge Plinlimmon bow his cloud-topt head.
   On dreary Arvon's shore they lie
Smear'd with gore and ghastly pale:
   Far, far aloof the affrighted ravens sail;
     The famish'd eagle screams, and passes by.
Dear lost companions of my tuneful art,
     Dear as the light that visits these sad eyes,
Dear as the ruddy drops that warm my heart,
     Ye died amidst your dying country's cries—
No more I weep; They do not sleep;
     On yonder cliffs, a griesly band,
I see them sit; They linger yet,
     Avengers of their native land:
With me in dreadful harmony they join,
And weave with bloody hands the tissue of thy line.

'Weave the warp and weave the woof
   The winding sheet of Edward's race:
Give ample room and verge enough
   The characters of hell to trace.

Mark the year and mark the night
When Severn shall re-echo with affright
The shrieks of death thro' Berkley's roof that ring,
Shrieks of an agonizing king!
    She-wolf of France, with unrelenting fangs
That tear'st the bowels of thy mangled mate,
    From thee be born, who o'er thy country hangs
The scourge of Heaven! What terrors round him wait!
Amazement in his van, with Flight combined,
And Sorrow's faded form, and Solitude behind.

'Mighty victor, mighty lord,
    Low on his funeral couch he lies!
No pitying heart, no eye, afford
    A tear to grace his obsequies.
Is the sable warrior fled?
Thy son is gone. He rests among the dead.
The swarm that in thy noon-tide beam were born?
—Gone to salute the rising morn.
Fair laughs the Morn, and soft the zephyr blows,
    While proudly riding o'er the azure realm
In gallant trim the gilded Vessel goes:
    Youth on the prow, and Pleasure at the helm:
Regardless of the sweeping Whirlwind's sway,
That hush'd in grim repose expects his evening prey.

    'Fill high the sparkling bowl,
The rich repast prepare;
    Reft of a crown, he yet may share the feast:
Close by the regal chair
    Fell Thirst and Famine scowl

176

A baleful smile upon their baffled guest.
Heard ye the din of battle bray,
　　Lance to lance, and horse to horse?
　　Long years of havoc urge their destined course,
And thro' the kindred squadrons mow their way.
　　Ye towers of Julius, London's lasting shame,
With many a foul and midnight murder fed,
　　Revere his Consort's faith, his Father's fame,
And spare the meek usurper's holy head!
Above, below, the rose of snow,
　　Twined with her blushing foe, we spread:
The bristled boar in infant-gore
　　Wallows beneath the thorny shade.
Now, brothers, bending o'er the accurséd loom,
Stamp we our vengeance deep, and ratify his doom.

'Edward, lo! to sudden fate
　　(Weave we the woof; The thread is spun;)
Half of thy heart we consecrate.
　　(The web is wove; The work is done;)
Stay, O stay! nor thus forlorn
Leave me unbless'd, unpitied, here to mourn:
In yon bright track that fires the western skies
They melt, they vanish from my eyes.
But O! what solemn scenes on Snowdon's height
　　Descending slow their glittering skirts unroll?
Visions of glory, spare my aching sight,
　　Ye unborn ages, crowd not on my soul
No more our long-lost Arthur we bewail:—
All hail, ye genuine kings! Britannia's issue, hail!

'Girt with many a baron bold
Sublime their starry fronts they rear;
    And gorgeous dames, and statesmen old
In bearded majesty, appear.
In the midst a form divine!
Her eye proclaims her of the Briton-Line:
Her lion-port, her awe-commanding face
Attemper'd sweet to virgin grace.
What strings symphonious tremble in the air,
    What strains of vocal transport round her play?
Hear from the grave, great Taliessin, hear;
    They breathe a soul to animate thy clay.
Bright Rapture calls, and soaring as she sings,
Waves in the eye of Heaven her many-colour'd wings.

'The verse adorn again
    Fierce War, and faithful Love,
And Truth severe, by fairy Fiction drest.
    In buskin'd measures move
Pale Grief, and pleasing Pain,
With Horror, tyrant of the throbbing breast.
A voice as of the cherub-choir
    Gales from blooming Eden bear,
    And distant warblings lessen on my ear
That lost in long futurity expire.
Fond impious man, think'st thou yon sanguine cloud
    Raised by thy breath, has quench'd the orb of day?
Tomorrow he repairs the golden flood
    And warms the nations with redoubled ray.
Enough for me: with joy I see

The different doom our fates assign:
Be thine Despair and sceptred Care;
  To triumph and to die are mine.'
—He spoke, and headlong from the mountain's height
Deep in the roaring tide he plunged to endless night.

T. GRAY

❧ 103 ❧

ODE WRITTEN IN MDCCXLVI

How sleep the Brave who sink to rest
By all their Country's wishes blest!
When Spring, with dewy fingers cold,
Returns to deck their hallow'd mould,
She there shall dress a sweeter sod
Than Fancy's feet have ever trod.

By fairy hands their knell is rung,
By forms unseen their dirge is sung:
There Honour comes, a pilgrim grey,
To bless the turf that wraps their clay;
And Freedom shall awhile repair
To dwell a weeping hermit there!

W. COLLINS

104

LAMENT FOR CULLODEN

THE lovely lass o' Inverness,
Nae joy nor pleasure can she see;
For e'en and morn she cries, Alas!
And ay the saut tear blin's her e'e:
Drumossie moor—Drumossie day—
A waefu' day it was to me!
For there I lost my father dear,
My father dear, and brethren three.

Their winding-sheet the bluidy clay,
Their graves are growing green to see:
And by them lies the dearest lad
That ever blest a woman's e'e!
Now wae to thee, thou cruel lord,
A bluidy man I trow thou be;
For mony a heart thou hast made sair
That ne'er did wrong to thine or thee.

R. BURNS

105

WILLY DROWNED IN YARROW

Down in yon garden sweet and gay
   Where bonnie grows the lily,
I heard a fair maid sighing say,
   'My wish be wi' sweet Willie!

'Willie's rare, and Willie's fair,
   And Willie's wondrous bonny;
And Willie hecht to marry me
   Gin e'er he married ony.

'O gentle wind, that bloweth south
   From where my Love repaireth,
Convey a kiss frae his dear mouth
   And tell me how he fareth!

'O tell sweet Willie to come doun
   And hear the mavis singing,
And see the birds on ilka bush
   And leaves around them hinging.

'The lav'rock there, wi' her white breast
   And gentle throat sae narrow;
There's sport eneuch for gentlemen
   On Leader haughs and Yarrow.

'O Leader haughs are wide and braid
   And Yarrow haughs are bonny;

There Willie hecht to marry me
    If e'er he married ony.

'But Willie's gone, whom I thought on,
    And does not hear me weeping;
Draws many a tear frae true love's e'e
    When other maids are sleeping.

'Yestreen I made my bed fu' braid,
    The night I'll mak' it narrow,
For a' the live-lang winter night
    I lie twined o' my marrow.

'O came ye by yon water-side?
    Pou'd you the rose or lily?
Or came you by yon meadow green,
    Or saw you my sweet Willie?'

She sought him up, she sought him down,
    She sought him braid and narrow;
Syne, in the cleaving of a craig,
    She found him drown'd in Yarrow!

ANON.

❧ 106 ☙

LOSS OF THE ROYAL GEORGE

Toll for the Brave!
The brave that are no more!
All sunk beneath the wave
Fast by their native shore!

Eight hundred of the brave
Whose courage well was tried,
Had made the vessel heel
And laid her on her side.
A land-breeze shook the shrouds
And she was overset;
Down went the Royal George,
With all her crew complete.

Toll for the brave!
Brave Kempenfelt is gone;
His last sea-fight is fought,
His work of glory done.
It was not in the battle;
No tempest gave the shock;
She sprang no fatal leak,
She ran upon no rock.
His sword was in its sheath,
His fingers held the pen,
When Kempenfelt went down
With twice four hundred men.

Weigh the vessel up
Once dreaded by our foes!
And mingle with our cup
The tears that England owes.
Her timbers yet are sound,
And she may float again
Full charged with England's thunder,
And plough the distant main:

But Kempenfelt is gone,
His victories are o'er;
And he and his eight hundred
Shall plough the wave no more.

W. COWPER

❧ 107 ☙

BLACK-EYED SUSAN

ALL in the Downs the fleet was moor'd,
  The streamers waving in the wind,
When black-eyed Susan came aboard;
  'O! where shall I my true-love find?
Tell me, ye jovial sailors, tell me true
If my sweet William sails among the crew.'

William, who high upon the yard
  Rock'd with the billow to and fro,
Soon as her well-known voice he heard
  He sigh'd, and cast his eyes below:
The cord slides swiftly through his glowing hands,
And quick as lightning on the deck he stands.

So the sweet lark, high poised in air,
  Shuts close his pinions to his breast
If chance his mate's shrill call he hear,
  And drops at once into her nest:—
The noblest captain in the British fleet
Might envy William's lip those kisses sweet.

'O Susan, Susan, lovely dear,
    My vows shall ever true remain;
Let me kiss off that falling tear;
    We only part to meet again.
Change as ye list, ye winds; my heart shall be
The faithful compass that still points to thee.

'Believe not what the landmen say
    Who tempt with doubts thy constant mind:
They'll tell thee, sailors, when away,
    In every port a mistress find:
Yes, yes, believe them when they tell thee so,
For Thou art present wheresoe'er I go.

'If to fair India's coast we sail,
    Thy eyes are seen in diamonds bright,
Thy breath is Afric's spicy gale,
    Thy skin is ivory so white.
Thus every beauteous object that I view
Wakes in my soul some charm of lovely Sue.

'Though battle call me from thy arms
    Let not my pretty Susan mourn;
Though cannons roar, yet safe from harms
    William shall to his Dear return.
Love turns aside the balls that round me fly,
Lest precious tears should drop from Susan's eye.'

The boatswain gave the dreadful word,
    The sails their swelling bosom spread;
No longer must she stay aboard;
    They kiss'd, she sigh'd, he hung his head.

Her lessening boat unwilling rows to land;
'Adieu!' she cries; and waved her lily hand.

J. GAY

❧ 108 ☙

SALLY IN OUR ALLEY

OF all the girls that are so smart
   There's none like pretty Sally;
She is the darling of my heart,
   And she lives in our alley.
There is no lady in the land
   Is half so sweet as Sally;
She is the darling of my heart,
   And she lives in our alley.

Her father he makes cabbage-nets
   And through the streets does cry 'em;
Her mother she sells laces long
   To such as please to buy 'em:
But sure such folks could ne'er beget
   So sweet a girl as Sally!
She is the darling of my heart,
   And she lives in our alley.

When she is by, I leave my work,
   I love her so sincerely;
My master comes like any Turk,
   And bangs me most severely—

186

But let him bang his bellyful,
   I'll bear it all for Sally;
She is the darling of my heart,
   And she lives in our alley.

Of all the days that's in the week
   I dearly love but one day—
And that's the day that comes betwixt
   A Saturday and Monday;
For then I'm drest all in my best
   To walk abroad with Sally;
She is the darling of my heart,
   And she lives in our alley.

My master carries me to church,
   And often am I blamed
Because I leave him in the lurch
   As soon as text is named;
I leave the church in sermon-time
   And slink away to Sally;
She is the darling of my heart,
   And she lives in our alley.

When Christmas comes about again
   O then I shall have money;
I'll hoard it up, and box it all,
   I'll give it to my honey:
I would it were ten thousand pound,
   I'd give it all to Sally;
She is the darling of my heart,
   And she lives in our alley.

My master and the neighbours all
    Make game of me and Sally,
And, but for her, I'd better be
    A slave and row a galley;
But when my seven long years are out
    O then I'll marry Sally,—
O then we'll wed, and then we'll bed,
    But not in our alley!

H. CAREY

❧ 109 ☙

A FAREWELL

Go fetch to me a pint o' wine,
    An' fill it in a silver tassie;
That I may drink before I go
    A service to my bonnie lassie;
The boat rocks at the pier o' Leith,
    Fu' loud the wind blaws frae the Ferry,
The ship rides by the Berwick-law,
    And I maun leave my bonnie Mary.

The trumpets sound, the banners fly,
    The glittering spears are rankéd ready;
The shouts o' war are heard afar,
    The battle closes thick and bloody;
But it's not the roar o' sea or shore
    Wad make me langer wish to tarry;

Nor shout o' war that's heard afar—
   It's leaving thee, my bonnie Mary.

R. BURNS

❧ 110 ☙

IF doughty deeds my lady please
   Right soon I'll mount my steed;
And strong his arm, and fast his seat
   That bears frae me the meed.
I'll wear thy colours in my cap,
   Thy picture at my heart;
And he that bends not to thine eye
   Shall rue it to his smart!
      Then tell me how to woo thee, Love;
        O tell me how to woo thee!
      For thy dear sake, nae care I'll take
        Tho' ne'er another trow me.

If gay attire delight thine eye
   I'll dight me in array;
I'll tend thy chamber door all night,
   And squire thee all the day.
If sweetest sounds can win thine ear,
   These sounds I'll strive to catch;
Thy voice I'll steal to woo thysell,
   That voice that nane can match.

But if fond love thy heart can gain,
    I never broke a vow;
Nae maiden lays her skaith to me,
    I never loved but you.
For you alone I ride the ring,
    For you I wear the blue;
For you alone I strive to sing,
    O tell me how to woo!
        Then tell me how to woo thee, Love;
          O tell me how to woo thee!
        For thy dear sake, nae care I'll take,
          Tho' ne'er another trow me.

GRAHAM OF GARTMORE

❧ 111 ☙

TO A YOUNG LADY

SWEET stream, that winds through yonder glade,
Apt emblem of a virtuous maid—
Silent and chaste she steals along,
Far from the world's gay busy throng:
With gentle yet prevailing force,
Intent upon her destined course;
Graceful and useful all she does,
Blessing and blest where'er she goes;
Pure-bosom'd as that watery glass,
And Heaven reflected in her face.

W. COWPER

THE SLEEPING BEAUTY

SLEEP on, and dream of Heaven awhile—
Tho' shut so close thy laughing eyes,
Thy rosy lips still wear a smile
And move, and breathe delicious sighs!

Ah, now soft blushes tinge her cheeks
And mantle o'er her neck of snow:
Ah, now she murmurs, now she speaks
What most I wish—and fear to know!

She starts, she trembles, and she weeps!
Her fair hands folded on her breast:
—And now, how like a saint she sleeps!
A seraph in the realms of rest!

Sleep on secure! Above control
Thy thoughts belong to Heaven and thee:
And may the secret of thy soul
Remain within its sanctuary!

S. ROGERS

FOR ever, Fortune, wilt thou prove
An unrelenting foe to Love,
And when we meet a mutual heart
Come in between, and bid us part?

Bid us sigh on from day to day,
And wish and wish the soul away;
Till youth and genial years are flown,
And all the life of life is gone?

But busy, busy, still art thou,
To bind the loveless joyless vow,
The heart from pleasure to delude,
To join the gentle to the rude.

For once, O Fortune, hear my prayer,
And I absolve thy future care;
All other blessings I resign,
Make but the dear Amanda mine.

J. THOMSON

✣ 114 ✤

THE merchant, to secure his treasure,
Conveys it in a borrow'd name:
Euphelia serves to grace my measure,
But Cloe is my real flame.

My softest verse, my darling lyre
Upon Euphelia's toilet lay—
When Cloe noted her desire
That I should sing, that I should play.

My lyre I tune, my voice I raise,
But with my numbers mix my sighs;
And whilst I sing Euphelia's praise,
I fix my soul on Cloe's eyes.

Fair Cloe blush'd: Euphelia frown'd:
I sung, and gazed; I play'd, and trembled:
And Venus to the Loves around
Remark'd how ill we all dissembled.

M. PRIOR

❧ 115 ❧

WHEN lovely woman stoops to folly
And finds too late that men betray,—
What charm can soothe her melancholy,
What art can wash her guilt away?

The only art her guilt to cover,
To hide her shame from every eye
To give repentance to her lover
And wring his bosom, is—to die.

O. GOLDSMITH

Yᴇ banks and braes o' bonnie Doon
   How can ye bloom sae fair!
How can ye chant, ye little birds,
   And I sae fu' o' care!

Thou'll break my heart, thou bonnie bird
   That sings upon the bough;
Thou minds me o' the happy days
   When my fause Luve was true.

Thou'll break my heart, thou bonnie bird
   That sings beside thy mate;
For sae I sat, and sae I sang,
   And wist na o' my fate.

Aft hae I roved by bonnie Doon
   To see the woodbine twine,
And ilka bird sang o' its love;
   And sae did I o' mine.

Wi' lightsome heart I pu'd a rose,
   Frae aff its thorny tree;
And my fause luver staw the rose,
   But left the thorn wi' me.

R. BURNS

194

THE POPLAR FIELD

THE poplars are fell'd, farewell to the shade
And the whispering sound of the cool colonnade:
The winds play no longer and sing in the leaves,
Nor Ouse on his bosom their image receives.

Twelve years have elapsed since I first took a view
Of my favourite field, and the bank where they grew:
And now in the grass behold they are laid,
And the tree is my seat that once lent me a shade.

The blackbird has fled to another retreat
Where the hazels afford him a screen from the heat;
And the scene where his melody charm'd me before
Resounds with his sweet-flowing ditty no more.

My fugitive years are all hasting away,
And I must ere long lie as lowly as they,
With a turf on my breast and a stone at my head,
Ere another such grove shall arise in its stead.

'Tis a sight to engage me, if anything can,
To muse on the perishing pleasures of man;
Short-lived as we are, our enjoyments, I see,
Have a still shorter date, and die sooner than we.

W. COWPER

TO A FIELD MOUSE

WEE, sleekit, cow'rin', tim'rous beastie,
O what a panic's in thy breastie!
Thou need na start awa sae hasty,
Wi, bickering brattle!
I wad be laith to rin an' chase thee
Wi' murd'ring pattle!

I'm truly sorry man's dominion
Has broken nature's social union,
An' justifies that ill opinion
Which makes thee startle
At me, thy poor earth-born companion,
An' fellow-mortal!

I doubt na, whiles, but thou may thieve;
What then? poor beastie, thou maun live!
A daimen-icker in a thrave
'S a sma' request:
I'll get a blessin' wi' the lave,
And never miss't!

Thy wee bit housie, too, in ruin!
Its silly wa's the win's are strewin':
And naething, now, to big a new ane,
O' foggage green!

An' bleak December's winds ensuin'
Baith snell an' keen!

Thou saw the fields laid bare and waste
An' weary winter comin' fast,
An' cozie here, beneath the blast,
Thou thought to dwell,
Till, crash! the cruel coulter past
Out thro' thy cell.

That wee bit heap o' leaves an' stibble
Has cost thee mony a weary nibble!
Now thou's turn'd out, for a' thy trouble,
But house or hald,
To thole the winter's sleety dribble
An' cranreuch cauld!

But, Mousie, thou art no thy lane
In proving foresight may be vain:
The best laid schemes o' mice an' men
Gang aft a-gley,
An' lea'e us nought but grief an' pain,
For promised joy.

Still thou art blest, compared wi' me!
The present only toucheth thee:
But, oh! I backward cast my e'e
On prospects drear!
An' forward, tho' I canna see,
I guess an' fear!

R. BURNS

A WISH

MINE be a cot beside the hill;
A bee-hive's hum shall soothe my ear;
A willowy brook that turns a mill,
With many a fall shall linger near.

The swallow, oft, beneath my thatch
Shall twitter from her clay-built nest;
Oft shall the pilgrim lift the latch,
And share my meal, a welcome guest.

Around my ivied porch shall spring
Each fragrant flower that drinks the dew;
And Lucy, at her wheel, shall sing
In russet-gown and apron blue.

The village-church among the trees,
Where first our marriage-vows were given,
With merry peals shall swell the breeze
And point with taper spire to Heaven.

S. ROGERS

❧ 120 ☙

ELEGY
WRITTEN IN A COUNTRY CHURCH-YARD

THE curfew tolls the knell of parting day,
The lowing herd wind slowly o'er the lea,
The ploughman homeward plods his weary way,
And leaves the world to darkness and to me.

Now fades the glimmering landscape on the sight,
And all the air a solemn stillness holds,
Save where the beetle wheels his droning flight,
And drowsy tinklings lull the distant folds:

Save that from yonder ivy-mantled tower
The moping owl does to the moon complain
Of such as, wandering near her secret bower,
Molest her ancient solitary reign.

Beneath those rugged elms, that yew-tree's shade
Where heaves the turf in many a mouldering heap,
Each in his narrow cell for ever laid,
The rude Forefathers of the hamlet sleep.

The breezy call of incense-breathing morn,
The swallow twittering from the straw-built shed,
The cock's shrill clarion, or the echoing horn,
No more shall rouse them from their lowly bed.

For them no more the blazing hearth shall burn
Or busy housewife ply her evening care:
No children run to lisp their sire's return,
Or climb his knees the envied kiss to share.

Oft did the harvest to their sickle yield,
Their furrow oft the stubborn glebe has broke;
How jocund did they drive their team afield!
How bow'd the woods beneath their sturdy stroke!

Let not Ambition mock their useful toil,
Their homely joys, and destiny obscure;
Nor Grandeur hear with a disdainful smile
The short and simple annals of the Poor.

The boast of heraldry, the pomp of power,
And all that beauty, all that wealth e'er gave,
Awaits alike th' inevitable hour:—
The paths of glory lead but to the grave.

Nor you, ye Proud, impute to these the fault
If Memory o'er their tomb no trophies raise,
Where through the long-drawn aisle and fretted vault
The pealing anthem swells the note of praise.

Can storied urn or animated bust
Back to its mansion call the fleeting breath?
Can Honour's voice provoke the silent dust,
Or Flattery soothe the dull cold ear of Death?

Perhaps in this neglected spot is laid
Some heart once pregnant with celestial fire;

Hands, that the rod of empire might have sway'd,
Or waked to ecstasy the living lyre:

But Knowledge to their eyes her ample page
Rich with the spoils of time, did ne'er unroll;
Chill Penury repress'd their noble rage,
And froze the genial current of the soul.

Full many a gem of purest ray serene
The dark unfathom'd caves of ocean bear:
Full many a flower is born to blush unseen,
And waste its sweetness on the desert air.

Some village-Hampden, that with dauntless breast
The little tyrant of his fields withstood,
Some mute inglorious Milton here may rest,
Some Cromwell, guiltless of his country's blood.

Th' applause of list'ning senates to command,
The threats of pain and ruin to despise,
To scatter plenty o'er a smiling land,
And read their history in a nation's eyes

Their lot forbade: nor circumscribed alone
Their growing virtues, but their crimes confined;
Forbade to wade through slaughter to a throne,
And shut the gates of mercy on mankind;

The struggling pangs of conscious truth to hide,
To quench the blushes of ingenuous shame,
Or heap the shrine of Luxury and Pride
With incense kindled at the Muse's flame.

Far from the madding crowd's ignoble strife
Their sober wishes never learn'd to stray;
Along the cool sequester'd vale of life
They kept the noiseless tenor of their way.

Yet e'en these bones from insult to protect
Some frail memorial still erected nigh,
With uncouth rhymes and shapeless sculpture deck'd,
Implores the passing tribute of a sigh.

Their name, their years, spelt by th' unletter'd Muse,
The place of fame and elegy supply:
And many a holy text around she strews
That teach the rustic moralist to die.

For who, to dumb forgetfulness a prey,
This pleasing anxious being e'er resign'd,
Left the warm precincts of the cheerful day,
Nor cast one longing lingering look behind?

On some fond breast the parting soul relies,
Some pious drops the closing eye requires;
E'en from the tomb the voice of Nature cries,
E'en in our ashes live their wonted fires.

For thee, who, mindful of th' unhonour'd dead,
Dost in these lines their artless tale relate;
If chance, by lonely Contemplation led,
Some kindred spirit shall inquire thy fate,—

Haply some hoary-headed swain may say,
Oft have we seen him at the peep of dawn

Brushing with hasty steps the dews away,
To meet the sun upon the upland lawn;

There at the foot of yonder nodding beech
That wreathes its old fantastic roots so high,
His listless length at noon-tide would he stretch,
And pore upon the brook that babbles by.

Hard by yon wood, now smiling as in scorn,
Muttering his wayward fancies he would rove;
Now drooping, woful-wan, like one forlorn,
Or crazed with care, or cross'd in hopeless love.

One morn I miss'd him on the custom'd hill,
Along the heath, and near his favourite tree;
Another came; nor yet beside the rill,
Nor up the lawn, nor at the wood was he;

The next with dirges due in sad array
Slow through the church-way path we saw him borne,—
Approach and read (for thou canst read) the lay
Graved on the stone beneath yon aged thorn.

THE EPITAPH

Here rests his head upon the lap of Earth
A Youth, to Fortune and to Fame unknown;
Fair Science frown'd not on his humble birth,
And Melancholy mark'd him for her own.

Large was his bounty, and his soul sincere;
Heaven did a recompense as largely send:

203

He gave to Misery all he had, a tear,
He gain'd from Heaven, 'twas all he wish'd, a friend.

No farther seek his merits to disclose,
Or draw his frailties from their dread abode,
(There they alike in trembling hope repose,)
The bosom of his Father and his God.

T. GRAY

❧ 121 ❧

MARY MORISON

O MARY, at thy window be,
It is the wish'd, the trysted hour!
Those smiles and glances let me see
That make the miser's treasure poor:
How blythely wad I bide the stoure,
A weary slave frae sun to sun,
Could I the rich reward secure,
The lovely Mary Morison.

Yestreen when to the trembling string
The dance gaed thro' the lighted ha',
To thee my fancy took its wing,—
I sat, but neither heard nor saw:
Tho' this was fair, and that was braw,
And yon the toast of a' the town,
I sigh'd, and said amang them a',
'Ye are na Mary Morison.'

O Mary, canst thou wreck his peace
Wha for thy sake wad gladly dee?
Or canst thou break that heart of his,
Whase only faut is loving thee?
If love for love thou wilt na gie,
At least be pity to me shown;
A thought ungentle canna be
The thought o' Mary Morison.

R. BURNS

❧ 122 ❧

BONNIE LESLEY

O SAW ye bonnie Lesley
    As she gaed o'er the border?
She's gane, like Alexander,
    To spread her conquests farther.

To see her is to love her,
    And love but her for ever;
For nature made her what she is,
    And ne'er made sic anither!

Thou art a queen, fair Lesley,
    Thy subjects we, before thee;
Thou art divine, fair Lesley,
    The hearts o' men adore thee.

The deil he could na scaith thee,
    Or aught that wad belang thee;

He'd look into thy bonnie face,
  And say 'I canna wrang thee!'

The Powers aboon will tent thee;
  Misfortune sha' na steer thee;
Thou'rt like themselves sae lovely
  That ill they'll ne'er let near thee.

Return again, fair Lesley,
  Return to Caledonie!
That we may brag we hae a lass
  There's nane again sea bonnie.

R. BURNS

❧ 123 ❧

O MY Luve's like a red, red rose
  That's newly sprung in June:
O my Luve's like the melodie
  That's sweetly play'd in tune.

As fair art thou, my bonnie lass,
  So deep in luve am I:
And I will luve thee still, my dear,
  Till a' the seas gang dry:

Till a' the seas gang dry, my dear,
  And the rocks melt wi' the sun;
I will luve thee still, my dear,
  While the sands o' life shall run.

And fare thee weel, my only Luve
And fare thee weel awhile!
And I will come again, my Luve,
Tho' it were ten thousand mile.

R. BURNS

❧ 124 ❧

HIGHLAND MARY

Y<small>E</small> banks and braes and streams around
  The castle o' Montgomery,
Green be your woods, and fair your flowers,
  Your waters never drumlie!
There simmer first unfauld her robes,
  And there the langest tarry;
For there I took the last fareweel
  O' my sweet Highland Mary.

How sweetly bloom'd the gay green birk,
  How rich the hawthorn's blossom,
As underneath their fragrant shade
  I clasp'd her to my bosom!
The golden hours on angel wings
  Flew o'er me and my dearie;
For dear to me as light and life
  Was my sweet Highland Mary.

Wi' mony a vow and lock'd embrace
  Our parting was fu' tender;

And pledging aft to meet again,
 We tore oursels asunder;
But, O! fell Death's untimely frost,
 That nipt my flower sae early!
Now green's the sod, and cauld's the clay,
 That wraps my Highland Mary!

O pale, pale now, those rosy lips,
 I aft hae kiss'd sae fondly!
And closed for ay the sparkling glance
 That dwelt on me sae kindly;
And mouldering now in silent dust
 That heart that lo'ed me dearly;
But still within my bosom's core
 Shall live my Highland Mary.

R. BURNS

❧ 125 ❧

AULD ROBIN GRAY

WHEN the sheep are in the fauld, and the kye at hame,
And a' the warld to rest are gane,
The waes o' my heart fa' in showers frae my e'e,
While my gudeman lies sound by me.

Young Jamie lo'ed me weel, and sought me for his bride;
But saving a croun he had naething else beside:
To make the croun a pund, young Jamie gaed to sea;
And the croun and the pund were baith for me.

He hadna been awa' a week but only twa,

When my father brak his arm, and the cow was stown awa;
My mother she fell sick, and my Jamie at the sea—
And auld Robin Gray came a-courtin' me.

My father couldna work, and my mother couldna spin;
I toil'd day and night, but their bread I couldna win;
Auld Rob maintain'd them baith, and wi' tears in his e'e
Said, Jennie, for their sakes, O, marry me!

My heart it said nay; I look'd for Jamie back;
But the wind it blew high, and the ship it was a wrack;
His ship it was a wrack—why didna Jamie dee?
Or why do I live to cry, Wae's me?

My father urgit sair: my mother didna speak;
But she look'd in my face till my heart was like to break:
They gi'ed him my hand, but my heart was at the sea,
Sae auld Robin Gray he was gudeman to me.

I hadna been a wife a week but only four,
When mournfu' as I sat on the stane at the door,
I saw my Jamie's wraith, for I couldna think it he—
Till he said, I'm come hame to marry thee.

O sair, sair did we greet, and muckle did we say;
We took but ae kiss, and I bade him gang away:
I wish that I were dead, but I'm no like to dee;
And why was I born to say, Wae's me!

I gang like a ghaist, and I carena to spin;
I daurna think on Jamie, for that wad be a sin;
But I'll do my best a gude wife ay to be,
For auld Robin Gray he is kind unto me.

LADY A. LINDSAY

DUNCAN GRAY

DUNCAN Gray cam here to woo,
    Ha, ha, the wooing o't;
On blythe Yule night when we were fou,
    Ha, ha, the wooing o't:
Maggie coost her head fu' high,
Look'd asklent and unco skeigh,
Gart poor Duncan stand abeigh;
    Ha, ha, the wooing o't!

Duncan fleech'd, and Duncan pray'd;
Meg was deaf as Ailsa Craig;
Duncan sigh'd baith out and in,
Grat his een baith bleer't and blin',
Spak o' lowpin ower a linn!

Time and chance are but a tide,
Slighted love is sair to bide;
Shall I, like a fool, quoth he,
For a haughty hizzie dee?
She may gae to—France for me!

How it comes let doctors tell,
Meg grew sick—as he grew haill;
Something in her bosom wrings,
For relief a sigh she brings;
And O, her een, they spak sic things!

Duncan was a lad o' grace;
Maggie's was a piteous case;
Duncan couldna be her death,
Swelling pity smoor'd his wrath;
Now they're crouse and canty baith:
    Ha, ha, the wooing o't!

R. BURNS

❧ 127 ❧

THE SAILOR'S WIFE

AND are ye sure the news is true?
    And are ye sure he's weel?
Is this a time to think o' wark?
    Ye jades, lay by your wheel;
Is this the time to spin a thread,
    When Colin's at the door?
Reach down my cloak, I'll to the quay,
    And see him come ashore.
For there's nae luck about the house,
    There's nae luck at a';
There's little pleasure in the house
    When our gudeman's awa'.

And gie to me my bigonet,
    My bishop's satin gown;
For I maun tell the baillie's wife
    That Colin's in the town.
My Turkey slippers maun gae on,

My stockins pearly blue;
It's a' to pleasure our gudeman,
For he's baith leal and true.

Rise, lass, and mak a clean fireside,
Put on the muckle pot;
Gie little Kate her button gown
And Jock his Sunday coat;
And mak their shoon as black as slaes,
Their hose as white as snaw;
It's a' to please my ain gudeman,
For he's been long awa'.

There's twa fat hens upo' the coop
Been fed this month and mair;
Mak haste and thraw their necks about,
That Colin weel may fare;
And spread the table neat and clean,
Gar ilka thing look braw,
For wha can tell how Colin fared
When he was far awa'?

Sae true his heart, sae smooth his speech,
His breath like caller air;
His very foot has music in't
As he comes up the stair—
And will I see his face again?
And will I hear him speak?
I'm downright dizzy wi' the thought,
In troth I'm like to greet!

If Colin's weel, and weel content,

I hae nae mair to crave:
And gin I live to keep him sae,
    I'm blest aboon the lave:
And will I see his face again,
    And will I hear him speak?
I'm downright dizzy wi' the thought,
    In troth I'm like to greet.
For there's nae luck about the house,
    There's nae luck at a';
There's little pleasure in the house
    When our gudeman's awa'.

                      W. J. MICKLE

❧ 128 ❧

JEAN

OF a' the airts the wind can blaw
    I dearly like the West,
For there the bonnie lassie lives,
    The lassie I lo'e best:
There wild woods grow, and rivers row,
    And mony a hill between;
But day and night my fancy's flight
    Is ever wi' my Jean.

I see her in the dewy flowers,
    I see her sweet and fair:
I hear her in the tunefu' birds,
    I hear her charm the air:

There's not a bonnie flower that springs
    By fountain, shaw, or green,
There's not a bonnie bird that sings
    But minds me o' my Jean.

O blaw ye westlin winds, blaw saft
    Amang the leafy trees;
Wi' balmy gale, frae hill and dale
    Bring hame the laden bees;
And bring the lassie back to me
    That's ay sae neat and clean;
Ae smile o' her wad banish care,
    Sae charming is my Jean.

What sighs and vows amang the knowes
    Hae pass'd atween us twa!
How fond to meet, how wae to part
    That night she gaed awa!
The Powers aboon can only ken,
    To whom the heart is seen,
That nane can be sae dear to me
    As my sweet lovely Jean!

R. BURNS

❧ 129 ❧

JOHN ANDERSON

JOHN Anderson my jo, John,
When we were first acquent

Your locks were like the raven,
Your bonnie brow was brent;
But now your brow is bald, John,
Your locks are like the snow;
But blessings on your frosty pow,
John Anderson my jo.

John Anderson my jo, John,
We clamb the hill thegither,
And mony a canty day, John,
We've had wi' ane anither:
Now we maun totter down, John,
But hand in hand we'll go,
And sleep thegither at the foot,
John Anderson my jo.

R. BURNS

❧ 130 ☙

THE LAND O' THE LEAL

I'M wearing awa', Jean,
Like snaw when its thaw, Jean,
I'm wearing awa'
    To the land o' the leal.
There's nae sorrow there, Jean,
There's neither cauld nor care, Jean,
The day is ay fair
    In the land o' the leal.

Ye were ay leal and true, Jean,
Your task's ended noo, Jean,
And I'll welcome you
    To the land o' the leal.
Our bonnie bairn's there, Jean,
She was baith guid and fair, Jean;
O we grudged her right sair
    To the land o' the leal!

Then dry that tearfu' e'e, Jean,
My soul langs to be free, Jean,
And angels wait on me
    To the land o' the leal.
Now fare ye weel, my ain Jean,
This warld's care is vain, Jean;
We'll meet and ay be fain
    In the land o' the leal.

LADY NAIRNE

❦ 131 ❧

ODE ON A DISTANT PROSPECT OF ETON COLLEGE

YE distant spires, ye antique towers
    That crown the watery glade,
Where grateful Science still adores
    Her Henry's holy shade;
And ye, that from the stately brow
Of Windsor's heights th' expanse below

Of grove, of lawn, of mead survey,
Whose turf, whose shade, whose flowers among
Wanders the hoary Thames along
   His silver-winding way:

Ah happy hills! ah pleasing shade!
   Ah fields beloved in vain!
Where once my careless childhood stray'd,
   A stranger yet to pain!
I feel the gales that from ye blow
A momentary bliss bestow,
As waving fresh their gladsome wing
My weary soul they seem to soothe,
And, redolent of joy and youth,
   To breathe a second spring.

Say, Father Thames, for thou hast seen
   Full many a sprightly race
Disporting on thy margent green
   The paths of pleasure trace;
Who foremost now delight to cleave
With pliant arm, thy glassy wave
The captive linnet which enthral?
What idle progeny succeed
To chase the rolling circle's speed
   Or urge the flying ball?

While some on earnest business bent
   Their murmuring labours ply
'Gainst graver hours, that bring constraint
   To sweeten liberty:
Some bold adventurers disdain

The limits of their little reign
And unknown regions dare descry:
Still as they run they look behind,
They hear a voice in every wind
    And snatch a fearful joy.

Gay Hope is theirs by fancy fed,
    Less pleasing when possest;
The tear forgot as soon as shed,
    The sunshine of the breast:
Theirs buxom Health, of rosy hue,
Wild Wit, Invention ever new,
And lively Cheer, of Vigour born;
The thoughtless day, the easy night,
The spirits pure, the slumbers light
    That fly th' approach of morn.

Alas! regardless of their doom
    The little victims play!
No sense have they of ills to come
    Nor care beyond today:
Yet see how all around them wait
The ministers of human fate
And black Misfortune's baleful train!
Ah show them where in ambush stand
To seize their prey, the murderous band!
    Ah, tell them they are men!

These shall the fury Passions tear,
    The vultures of the mind,
Disdainful Anger, pallid Fear,

And Shame that skulks behind;
Or pining Love shall waste their youth,
Or Jealousy with rankling tooth
That inly gnaws the secret heart,
And Envy wan, and faded Care,
Grim-visaged comfortless Despair,
    And Sorrow's piercing dart.

Ambition this shall tempt to rise,
    Then whirl the wretch from high
To bitter Scorn a sacrifice
    And grinning Infamy.
The stings of Falsehood those shall try,
And hard Unkindness' alter'd eye,
That mocks the tear it forced to flow;
And keen Remorse with blood defiled,
And moody Madness laughing wild
    Amid severest woe.

Lo, in the Vale of Years beneath
    A griesly troop are seen,
The painful family of Death
    More hideous than their Queen:
This racks the joints, this fires the veins,
That every labouring sinew strains,
Those in the deeper vitals rage:
Lo, Poverty, to fill the band,
That numbs the soul with icy hand,
    And slow-consuming Age.

To each his sufferings: all are men,

Condemn'd alike to groan;
The tender for another's pain,
   Th' unfeeling for his own.
Yet, ah! why should they know their fate,
Since sorrow never comes too late,
And happiness too swiftly flies?
Thought would destroy their paradise!
No more;—where ignorance is bliss,
   'Tis folly to be wise.

T. GRAY

✿132 ✿

HYMN TO ADVERSITY

DAUGHTER of Jove, relentless power,
   Thou tamer of the human breast,
Whose iron scourge and torturing hour
   The bad affright, afflict the best!
Bound in thy adamantine chain
The proud are taught to taste of pain,
And purple tyrants vainly groan
With pangs unfelt before, unpitied and alone.

When first thy Sire to send on earth
   Virtue, his darling child, design'd,
To thee he gave the heavenly birth
   And bade to form her infant mind.
Stern, rugged Nurse! thy rigid lore
With patience many a year she bore:

220

What sorrow was, thou bad'st her know,
And from her own she learn'd to melt at others' woe.

Scared at thy frown terrific, fly
    Self-pleasing Folly's idle brood,
Wild Laughter, Noise, and thoughtless Joy,
    And leave us leisure to be good.
Light they disperse, and with them go
The summer Friend, the flattering Foe;
By vain Prosperity received,
To her they vow their truth, and are again believed.

Wisdom in sable garb array'd
    Immersed in rapturous thought profound,
And Melancholy, silent maid,
    With leaden eye, that loves the ground,
Still on thy solemn steps attend:
Warm Charity, the general friend,
With Justice, to herself severe,
And Pity dropping soft the sadly-pleasing tear.

O, gently on thy suppliant's head
    Dread Goddess, lay thy chastening hand!
Not in thy Gorgon terrors clad,
    Not circled with the vengeful band
(As by the impious thou art seen)
With thundering voice, and threatening mien,
With screaming Horror's funeral cry,
Despair, and fell Disease, and ghastly Poverty:

Thy form benign, O Goddess, wear,
    Thy milder influence impart,

Thy philosophic train be there
To soften, not to wound my heart.
The generous spark extinct revive,
Teach me to love and to forgive,
Exact my own defects to scan,
What others are to feel, and know myself a Man.

T. GRAY

❧ 133 ❦

THE SOLITUDE OF
ALEXANDER SELKIRK

I AM monarch of all I survey;
My right there is none to dispute;
From the centre all round to the sea
I am lord of the fowl and the brute.
O Solitude! where are the charms
That sages have seen in thy face?
Better dwell in the midst of alarms
Than reign in this horrible place.

I am out of humanity's reach,
I must finish my journey alone,
Never hear the sweet music of speech;
I start at the sound of my own.
The beasts that roam over the plain
My form with indifference see;
They are so unacquainted with man,
Their tameness is shocking to me.

Society, Friendship, and Love
Divinely bestow'd upon man,
O had I the wings of a dove
How soon would I taste you again!
My sorrows I then might assuage
In the ways of religion and truth,
Might learn from the wisdom of age,
And be cheer'd by the sallies of youth.

Ye winds that have made me your sport,
Convey to this desolate shore
Some cordial endearing report
Of a land I shall visit no more:
My friends, do they now and then send
A wish or a thought after me?
O tell me I yet have a friend,
Though a friend I am never to see.

How fleet is a glance of the mind!
Compared with the speed of its flight,
The tempest itself lags behind,
And the swift-wingéd arrows of light.
When I think of my own native land
In a moment I seem to be there;
But alas! recollection at hand
Soon hurries me back to despair.

But the seafowl is gone to her nest,
The beast is laid down in his lair;
Even here is a season of rest,
And I to my cabin repair.

There's mercy in every place,
And mercy, encouraging thought!
Gives even affliction a grace
And reconciles man to his lot.

W. COWPER

134

TO MARY UNWIN

THE twentieth year is wellnigh past
Since first our sky was overcast;
Ah would that this might be the last!
 My Mary!

Thy spirits have a fainter flow,
I see thee daily weaker grow—
'Twas my distress that brought thee low,
 My Mary!

Thy needles, once a shining store,
For my sake restless heretofore,
Now rust disused, and shine no more;
 My Mary!

For though thou gladly wouldst fulfil
The same kind office for me still,
Thy sight now seconds not thy will,
 My Mary!

But well thou play'dst the housewife's part,
And all thy threads with magic art

Have wound themselves about this heart,
    My Mary!

Thy indistinct expressions seem
Like language utter'd in a dream;
Yet me they charm, whate'er the theme,
    My Mary!

Thy silver locks, once auburn bright,
Are still more lovely in my sight
Than golden beams of orient light,
    My Mary!

For could I view nor them nor thee,
What sight worth seeing could I see?
The sun would rise in vain for me,
    My Mary!

Partakers of thy sad decline
Thy hands their little force resign;
Yet gently press'd, press gently mine,
    My Mary!

Such feebleness of limbs thou prov'st
That now at every step thou mov'st
Upheld by two; yet still thou lov'st,
    My Mary!

And still to love, though press'd with ill,
In wintry age to feel no chill,
With me is to be lovely still,
    My Mary!

But ah! by constant heed I know
How oft the sadness that I show
Transforms thy smiles to looks of woe,
    My Mary!

And should my future lot be cast
With much resemblance of the past,
Thy worn-out heart will break at last—
    My Mary!

W. COWPER

✤ 135 ✤

TOMORROW

IN the downhill of life, when I find I'm declining,
    May my lot no less fortunate be
Than a snug elbow-chair can afford for reclining,
    And a cot that o'erlooks the wide sea;
With an ambling pad-pony to pace o'er the lawn,
    While I carol away idle sorrow,
And blithe as the lark that each day hails the dawn
    Look forward with hope for tomorrow.

With a porch at my door, both for shelter and shade too,
    As the sunshine or rain may prevail;
And a small spot of ground for the use of the spade too,
    With a barn for the use of the flail:
A cow for my dairy, a dog for my game,
    And a purse when a friend wants to borrow;

I'll envy no nabob his riches or fame,
   Nor what honours await him tomorrow.

From the bleak northern blast may my cot be completely
   Secured by a neighbouring hill;
And at night may repose steal upon me more sweetly
   By the sound of a murmuring rill:
And while peace and plenty I find at my board,
   With a heart free from sickness and sorrow,
With my friends may I share what today may afford,
   And let them spread the table tomorrow.

And when I at last must throw off this frail covering
   Which I've worn for threescore years and ten,
On the brink of the grave I'll not seek to keep hovering,
   Nor my thread wish to spin o'er again:
But my face in the glass I'll serenely survey,
   And with smiles count each wrinkle and furrow;
As this old worn-out stuff, which is threadbare today,
   May become everlasting tomorrow.

                   J. COLLINS

136

Life! I know not what thou art,
But know that thou and I must part;
And when, or how, or where we met
I own to me's a secret yet.

Life! we've been long together

Through pleasant and through cloudy weather;
'Tis hard to part when friends are dear—
Perhaps 'twill cost a sigh, a tear;
—Then steal away, give little warning,
   Choose thine own time;
Say not Good Night,—but in some brighter clime
   Bid me Good Morning.

A. L. BARBAULD

BOOK FOURTH

ON FIRST LOOKING INTO CHAPMAN'S HOMER

MUCH have I travell'd in the realms of gold
And many goodly states and kingdoms seen;
Round many western islands have I been
Which bards in fealty to Apollo hold.

Oft of one wide expanse had I been told
That deep-brow'd Homer ruled as his demesne:
Yet did I never breathe its pure serene
Till I heard Chapman speak out loud and bold:

—Then felt I like some watcher of the skies
When a new planet swims into his ken;
Or like stout Cortez—when with eagle eyes

He stared at the Pacific, and all his men
Look'd at each other with a wild surmise—
Silent, upon a peak in Darien.

J. KEATS

ODE ON THE POETS

BARDS of Passion and of Mirth
Ye have left your souls on earth!
Have ye souls in heaven too,
Double-lived in regions new?

—Yes, and those of heaven commune
With the spheres of sun and moon;
With the noise of fountains wonderous
And the parle of voices thunderous;
With the whisper of heaven's trees
And one another, in soft ease
Seated on Elysian lawns
Browsed by none but Dian's fawns;
Underneath large blue bells tented,
Where the daisies are rose-scented,
And the rose herself has got
Perfume which on earth is not;
Where the nightingale doth sing
Not a senseless, trancéd thing,
But divine melodious truth;
Philosophic numbers smooth;
Tales and golden histories
Of heaven and its mysteries.

Thus ye live on high, and then

On the earth ye live again;
And the souls ye left behind you
Teach us, here, the way to find you,
Where your other souls are joying,
Never slumber'd, never cloying.
Here, your earth-born souls still speak
To mortals, of their little week;
Of their sorrows and delights;
Of their passions and their spites;
Of their glory and their shame;
What doth strengthen and what maim:—
Thus ye teach us, everyday,
Wisdom, though fled far away.

   Bards of Passion and of Mirth
Ye have left your souls on earth!
Ye have souls in heaven too,
Double-lived in regions new!

J. KEATS

❧ 139 ☙

LOVE

ALL thoughts, all passions, all delights,
Whatever stirs this mortal frame,
Are all but ministers of Love,
   And feed his sacred flame.

Oft in my waking dreams do I

233

Live o'er again that happy hour,
When midway on the mount I lay
    Beside the ruin'd tower.

The moonshine stealing o'er the scene
Had blended with the lights of eve;
And she was there, my hope, my joy,
    My own dear Genevieve!

She lean'd against the arméd man,
The statue of the arméd knight;
She stood and listen'd to my lay,
    Amid the lingering light.

Few sorrows hath she of her own,
My hope! my joy! my Genevieve!
She loves me best, whene'er I sing
    The songs that make her grieve.

I play'd a soft and doleful air,
I sang an old and moving story—
An old rude song, that suited well
    That ruin wild and hoary.

She listen'd with a flitting blush,
With downcast eyes and modest grace;
For well she knew, I could not choose
    But gaze upon her face.

I told her of the Knight that wore
Upon his shield a burning brand;
And that for ten long years he woo'd
    The Lady of the Land.

I told her how he pined: and ah!
The deep, the low, the pleading tone
With which I sang another's love
    Interpreted my own.

She listen'd with a flitting blush,
With downcast eyes, and modest grace;
And she forgave me, that I gazed
    Too fondly on her face.

But when I told the cruel scorn
That crazed that bold and lovely Knight,
And that he cross'd the mountain-woods,
    Nor rested day nor night;

That sometimes from the savage den,
And sometimes from the darksome shade,
And sometimes starting up at once
    In green and sunny glade

There came and look'd him in the face
An angel beautiful and bright;
And that he knew it was a Fiend,
    This miserable Knight!

And that unknowing what he did,
He leap'd amid a murderous band,
And saved from outrage worse than death
    The Lady of the Land;

And how she wept, and clasp'd his knees
And how she tended him in vain;
And ever strove to expiate
    The scorn that crazed his brain:

And that she nursed him in a cave,
And how his madness went away,
When on the yellow forest-leaves
 A dying man he lay;

—His dying words—but when I reach'd
That tenderest strain of all the ditty,
My faltering voice and pausing harp
 Disturb'd her soul with pity!

All impulses of soul and sense
Had thrill'd my guileless Genevieve;
The music and the doleful tale,
 The rich and balmy eve;

And hopes, and fears that kindle hope,
An undistinguishable throng,
And gentle wishes long subdued,
 Subdued and cherish'd long!

She wept with pity and delight,
She blush'd with love, and virgin shame;
And like the murmur of a dream,
 I heard her breathe my name.

Her bosom heaved—she stepp'd aside,
As conscious of my look she stept—
Then suddenly, with timorous eye
 She fled to me and wept.

She half enclosed me with her arms,
She press'd me with a meek embrace;

And bending back her head, look'd up,
　　And gazed upon my face.

'Twas partly love, and partly fear,
And partly 'twas a bashful art
That I might rather feel, than see,
　　The swelling of her heart.

I calm'd her fears, and she was calm
And told her love with virgin pride;
And so I won my Genevieve,
　　My bright and beauteous Bride.

S. T. COLERIDGE

❦ 140 ❧

ALL FOR LOVE

O TALK not to me of a name great in story;
The days of our youth are the days of our glory;
And the myrtle and ivy of sweet two-and-twenty
Are worth all your laurels, though ever so plenty.

What are garlands and crowns to the brow that is wrinkled?
'Tis but as a dead flower with May-dew besprinkled:
Then away with all such from the head that is hoary—
What care I for the wreaths that can only give glory?

O Fame!—if I e'er took delight in my praises,
'Twas less for the sake of thy high-sounding phrases,

Than to see the bright eyes of the dear one discover
She thought that I was not unworthy to love her.

There chiefly I sought thee, there only I found thee;
Her glance was the best of the rays that surround thee;
When it sparkled o'er aught that was bright in my story,
I knew it was love, and I felt it was glory.

LORD BYRON

✤ 141 ✤

THE OUTLAW

O BRIGNALL banks are wild and fair,
    And Greta woods are green,
And you may gather garlands there
    Would grace a summer-queen.
And as I rode by Dalton-Hall
    Beneath the turrets high,
A Maiden on the castle-wall
    Was singing merrily:
'O Brignall Banks are fresh and fair,
    And Greta woods are green;
I'd rather rove with Edmund there
    Than reign our English queen.'

'If, Maiden, thou wouldst wend with me,
    To leave both tower and town,
Thou first must guess what life lead we
    That dwell by dale and down.

And if thou canst that riddle read,
    As read full well you may,
Then to the greenwood shalt thou speed
    As blithe as Queen of May.'
Yet sung she, 'Brignall banks are fair,
    And Greta woods are green;
I'd rather rove with Edmund there
    Than reign our English queen.

'I read you by your bugle-horn
    And by your palfrey good,
I read you for a ranger sworn
    To keep the king's greenwood.'
'A Ranger, lady, winds his horn,
    And 'tis at peep of light;
His blast is heard at merry morn,
    And mine at dead of night.'
Yet sung she, 'Brignall banks are fair,
    And Greta woods are gay;
I would I were with Edmund there
    To reign his Queen of May!

'With burnish'd brand and musketoon
    So gallantly you come,
I read you for a bold Dragoon,
    That lists the tuck of drum.'
'I list no more the tuck of drum,
    No more the trumpet hear;
But when the beetle sounds his hum
    My comrades take the spear.
And O! though Brignall banks be fair

And Greta woods be gay,
Yet mickle must the maiden dare
    Would reign my Queen of May!

'Maiden! a nameless life I lead,
    A nameless death I'll die!
The fiend whose lantern lights the mead
    Were better mate than I!
And when I'm with my comrades met
    Beneath the greenwood bough,—
What once we were we all forget,
    Nor think what we are now.'

Chorus

Yet Brignall banks are fresh and fair,
    And Greta woods are green,
And you may gather garlands there
    Would grace a summer-queen.

SIR W. SCOTT

✣ 142 ✣

THERE be none of Beauty's daughters
    With a magic like Thee;
And like music on the waters
    Is thy sweet voice to me:
When, as if its sound were causing
The charméd ocean's pausing,

The waves lie still and gleaming,
And the lull'd winds seem dreaming:

And the midnight moon is weaving
　　Her bright chain o'er the deep,
Whose breast is gently heaving
　　As an infant's asleep:
So the spirit bows before thee
To listen and adore thee;
With a full but soft emotion,
Like the swell of Summer's ocean.

LORD BYRON

❧ 143 ❧

LINES TO AN INDIAN AIR

I ARISE from dreams of Thee
In the first sweet sleep of night,
When the winds are breathing low
And the stars are shining bright:
I arise from dreams of thee,
And a spirit in my feet
Has led me—who knows how?
To thy chamber-window, Sweet!

The wandering airs they faint
On the dark, the silent stream—
The champak odours fail
Like sweet thoughts in a dream;

The nightingale's complaint
It dies upon her heart,
As I must die on thine
O belovéd as thou art!

O lift me from the grass!
I die, I faint, I fail!
Let thy love in kisses rain
On my lips and eyelids pale.
My cheek is cold and white, alas!
My heart beats loud and fast;
O! press it close to thine again
Where it will break at last.

P. B. SHELLEY

✣ 144 ✣

SHE walks in beauty, like the night
Of cloudless climes and starry skies,
And all that's best of dark and bright
Meets in her aspect and her eyes,
Thus mellow'd to that tender light
Which heaven to gaudy day denies.

One shade the more, one ray the less
Had half impair'd the nameless grace
Which waves in every raven tress
Or softly lightens o'er her face,
Where thoughts serenely sweet express
How pure, how dear their dwelling-place.

And on that cheek and o'er that brow
So soft, so calm, yet eloquent,
The smiles that win, the tints that glow
But tell of days in goodness spent,—
A mind at peace with all below,
A heart whose love is innocent.

LORD BYRON

❧ 145 ❧

SHE was a phantom of delight
When first she gleam'd upon my sight:
A lovely apparition, sent
To be a moment's ornament;
Her eyes as stars of twilight fair;
Like Twilight's, too, her dusky hair;
But all things else about her drawn
From May-time and the cheerful dawn;
A dancing shape, an image gay,
To haunt, to startle, and waylay.

I saw her upon nearer view,
A spirit, yet a woman too!
Her household motions light and free,
And steps of virgin-liberty;
A countenance in which did meet
Sweet records, promises as sweet;
A creature not too bright or good
For human nature's daily food,

For transient sorrows, simple wiles,
Praise, blame, love, kisses, tears, and smiles.

And now I see with eye serene
The very pulse of the machine;
A being breathing thoughtful breath,
A traveller between life and death:
The reason firm, the temperate will,
Endurance, foresight, strength, and skill;
A perfect woman, nobly plann'd
To warn, to comfort, and command;
And yet a Spirit still, and bright
With something of an angel-light.

W. WORDSWORTH

❧ 146 ❧

SHE is not fair to outward view
    As many maidens be;
Her loveliness I never knew
    Until she smiled on me.
O then I saw her eye was bright,
A well of love, a spring of light.

But now her looks are coy and cold,
    To mine they ne'er reply,
And yet I cease not to behold
    The love-light in her eye:
Her very frowns are fairer far
Than smiles of other maidens are.

H. COLERIDGE

244

❧ 147 ☙

I FEAR thy kisses, gentle maiden;
Thou needest not fear mine;
My spirit is too deeply laden
Ever to burthen thine.

I fear thy mien, thy tones, thy motion;
Thou needest not fear mine;
Innocent is the heart's devotion
With which I worship thine.

P. B. SHELLEY

❧ 148 ☙

THE LOST LOVE

SHE dwelt among the untrodden ways
  Beside the springs of Dove;
A maid whom there were none to praise,
  And very few to love.

A violet by a mossy stone
  Half-hidden from the eye!
—Fair as a star, when only one
  Is shining in the sky.

She lived unknown, and few could know
  When Lucy ceased to be;
But she is in her grave, and O!
  The difference to me!

W. WORDSWORTH

I TRAVELL'D among unknown men
   In lands beyond the sea;
Nor, England! did I know till then
   What love I bore to thee.

'Tis past, that melancholy dream!
   Nor will I quit thy shore
A second time, for still I seem
   To love thee more and more.

Among thy mountains did I feel
   The joy of my desire;
And she I cherish'd turn'd her wheel
   Beside an English fire.

Thy mornings show'd, thy nights conceal'd
   The bowers where Lucy play'd;
And thine too is the last green field
   That Lucy's eyes survey'd.

                W. WORDSWORTH

THE EDUCATION OF NATURE

THREE years she grew in sun and shower;
Then Nature said, 'A lovelier flower

On earth was never sown:
This child I to myself will take;
She shall be mine, and I will make
A lady of my own.

'Myself will to my darling be
Both law and impulse: and with me
The girl, in rock and plain,
In earth and heaven, in glade and bower,
Shall feel an overseeing power
To kindle or restrain.

'She shall be sportive as the fawn
That wild with glee across the lawn
Or up the mountain springs;
And her's shall be the breathing balm,
And her's the silence and the calm
Of mute insensate things.

'The floating clouds their state shall lend
To her; for her the willow bend;
Nor shall she fail to see
E'en in the motions of the storm
Grace that shall mould the maiden's form
By silent sympathy.

'The stars of midnight shall be dear
To her; and she shall lean her ear
In many a secret place
Where rivulets dance their wayward round,
And beauty born of murmuring sound
Shall pass into her face.

247

'And vital feelings of delight
Shall rear her form to stately height,
Her virgin bosom swell;
Such thoughts to Lucy I will give
While she and I together live
Here in this happy dell.'

Thus Nature spake—The work was done--
How soon my Lucy's race was run!
She died, and left to me
This heath, this calm and quiet scene;
The memory of what has been,
And never more will be.

W. WORDSWORTH

151

A SLUMBER did my spirit seal;
   I had no human fears:
She seem'd a thing that could not feel
   The touch of earthly years.

No motion has she now, no force;
   She neither hears nor sees;
Roll'd round in earth's diurnal course
   With rocks, and stones, and trees!

W. WORDSWORTH

LORD ULLIN'S DAUGHTER

A CHIEFTAIN to the Highlands bound
Cries 'Boatman, do not tarry!
And I'll give thee a silver pound
To row us o'er the ferry!'

'Now who be ye, would cross Lochgyle
This dark and stormy water?'
'O I'm the chief of Ulva's isle,
And this, Lord Ullin's daughter.

'And fast before her father's men
Three days we've fled together,
For should he find us in the glen,
My blood would stain the heather.

'His horsemen hard behind us ride—
Should they our steps discover,
Then who will cheer my bonny bride
When they have slain her lover?'

Out spoke the hardy Highland wight,
'I'll go, my chief, I'm ready:
It is not for your silver bright,
But for your winsome lady:—

'And by my word! the bonny bird

In danger shall not tarry;
So though the waves are raging white
I'll row you o'er the ferry.'

By this the storm grew loud apace,
The water-wraith was shrieking;
And in the scowl of heaven each face
Grew dark as they were speaking.

But still as wilder blew the wind
And as the night grew drearer,
Adown the glen rode arméd men,
Their trampling sounded nearer.

'O haste thee, haste!' the lady cries,
'Though tempests round us gather;
I'll meet the raging of the skies,
But not an angry father.'

The boat has left a stormy land,
A stormy sea before her,—
When, O! too strong for human hand
The tempest gather'd o'er her.

And still they row'd amidst the roar
Of waters fast prevailing:
Lord Ullin reach'd that fatal shore,—
His wrath was changed to wailing.

For, sore dismay'd, through storm and shade
His child he did discover:—
One lovely hand she stretch'd for aid,
And one was round her lover.

'Come back! come back!' he cried in grief
'Across this stormy water:
And I'll forgive your Highland chief,
My daughter!—O my daughter!'

'Twas vain: the loud waves lash'd the shore,
Return or aid preventing:
The waters wild went o'er his child,
And he was left lamenting.

T. CAMPBELL

❦ 153 ❧

JOCK O' HAZELDEAN

'WHY weep ye by the tide, ladie?
    Why weep ye by the tide?
I'll wed ye to my youngest son,
    And ye sall be his bride:
And ye sall be his bride, ladie,
    Sae comely to be seen'—
But ay she loot the tears down fa'
    For Jock of Hazeldean.

'Now let this wilfu' grief be done,
    And dry that cheek so pale;
Young Frank is chief of Errington
    And lord of Langley-dale;
His step is first in peaceful ha',
    His sword in battle keen'—

But ay she loot the tears down fa'
    For Jock of Hazeldean.

'A chain of gold ye sall not lack,
    Nor braid to bind your hair,
Nor mettled hound, nor managed hawk,
    Nor palfrey fresh and fair;
And you the foremost o' them a'
    Shall ride our forest-queen'—
But ay she loot the tears down fa'
    For Jock of Hazeldean.

The kirk was deck'd at morning tide,
    The tapers glimmer'd fair;
The priest and bridegroom wait the bride,
    And dame and knight are there:
They sought her baith by bower and ha':
    The ladie was not seen!
She's o'er the Border, and awa'
    Wi' Jock of Hazeldean.

SIR W. SCOTT

❧ 154 ❧

FREEDOM AND LOVE

How delicious is the winning
Of a kiss at love's beginning,
When two mutual hearts are sighing
For the knot there's no untying!

252

Yet remember, 'midst our wooing,
Love has bliss, but Love has ruing;
Other smiles may make you fickle,
Tears for other charms may trickle.

Love he comes, and Love he tarries,
Just as fate or fancy carries;
Longest stays, when sorest chidden;
Laughs and flies, when press'd and bidden.

Bind the sea to slumber stilly,
Bind its odour to the lily,
Bind the aspen ne'er to quiver,
Then bind Love to last for ever.

Love's a fire that needs renewal
Of fresh beauty for its fuel:
Love's wing moults when caged and captured,
Only free, he soars enraptured.

Can you keep the bee from ranging
Or the ringdove's neck from changing?
No! nor fetter'd Love from dying
In the knot there's no untying.

T. CAMPBELL

❦ 155 ❧

LOVE'S PHILOSOPHY

THE fountains mingle with the river
And the rivers with the ocean,

The winds of heaven mix for ever
With a sweet emotion;
Nothing in the world is single,
All things by a law divine
In one another's being mingle—
Why not I with thine?

See the mountains kiss high heaven
And the waves clasp one another;
No sister-flower would be forgiven
If it disdain'd its brother:
And the sunlight clasps the earth,
And the moonbeams kiss the sea—
What are all these kissings worth,
If thou kiss not me?

P. B. SHELLEY

❧ 156 ❧

ECHOES

How sweet the answer Echo makes
To Music at night
When, roused by lute or horn, she wakes,
And far away o'er lawns and lakes
Goes answering light!

Yet Love hath echoes truer far
And far more sweet
Than e'er, beneath the moonlight's star,

Of horn or lute or soft guitar
The songs repeat.

'Tis when the sigh,—in youth sincere
And only then,
The sigh that's breathed for one to hear—
Is by that one, that only Dear
Breathed back again.

T. MOORE

❧157☙

A SERENADE

Ah! County Guy, the hour is nigh,
　　The sun has left the lea,
The orange-flower perfumes the bower,
　　The breeze is on the sea.
The lark, his lay who trill'd all day,
　　Sits hush'd his partner nigh;
Breeze, bird, and flower confess the hour,
　　But where is County Guy?

The village maid steals through the shade
　　Her shepherd's suit to hear;
To Beauty shy, by lattice high,
　　Sings high-born Cavalier.
The star of Love, all stars above,
　　Now reigns o'er earth and sky,
And high and low the influence know—
　　But where is County Guy?

SIR W. SCOTT

TO A DISTANT FRIEND

WHY art thou silent! Is thy love a plant
Of such weak fibre that the treacherous air
Of absence withers what was once so fair?
Is there no debt to pay, no boon to grant?

Yet have my thoughts for thee been vigilant,
Bound to thy service with unceasing care—
The mind's least generous wish a mendicant
For nought but what thy happiness could spare.

Speak!—though this soft warm heart, once free to hold
A thousand tender pleasures, thine and mine,
Be left more desolate, more dreary cold
Than a forsaken bird's-nest fill'd with snow
'Mid its own bush of leafless eglantine—
Speak, that my torturing doubts their end may know!

W. WORDSWORTH

WHEN we two parted
In silence and tears,
Half broken-hearted,
To sever for years,

Pale grew thy cheek and cold,
Colder thy kiss;
Truly that hour foretold
Sorrow to this!

The dew of the morning
Sunk chill on my brow;
It felt like the warning
Of what I feel now.
Thy vows are all broken,
And light is thy fame:
I hear thy name spoken
And share in its shame.

They name thee before me,
A knell to mine ear;
A shudder comes o'er me—
Why wert thou so dear?
They know not I knew thee
Who knew thee too well:
Long, long shall I rue thee
Too deeply to tell.

In secret we met:
In silence I grieve
That thy heart could forget,
Thy spirit deceive.
If I should meet thee
After long years,
How should I greet thee?—
With silence and tears.

LORD BYRON

THE RIME OF THE ANCIENT MARINER

IN SEVEN PARTS

ARGUMENT

How a Ship having passed the Line was driven by storms to the cold Country towards the South Pole; and how from thence she made her course to the tropical Latitude of the Great Pacific Ocean; and of the strange things that befell; and in what manner the Ancyent Marinere came back to his own Country.

PART I

An ancient Mariner meeteth three Gallants bidden to a wedding-feast, and detaineth one.

IT IS AN ancient Mariner,
And he stoppeth one of three.
"By thy long grey beard and glittering
    eye,
Now wherefore stopp'st thou me?

The Bridegroom's doors are opened
    wide,
And I am next of kin;
The guests are met, the feast is set:
May'st hear the merry din."

He holds him with his skinny hand,
"There was a ship," quoth he.

"Hold off! unhand me, grey-beard loon!"
Eftsoons his hand dropt he.

The Wedding-Guest is spellbound by the eye of the old seafaring man, and constrained to hear his tale.

He holds him with his glittering eye—
The Wedding-Guest stood still,
And listens like a three years' child:
The Mariner hath his will.

The Wedding-Guest sat on a stone:
He cannot choose but hear;
And thus spake on that ancient man,
The bright-eyed Mariner.

"The ship was cheered, the harbour
   cleared,
Merrily did we drop
Below the kirk, below the hill,
The Mariner tells how the ship sailed southward with a good wind and fair weather, till it reached the Line.
Below the lighthouse top.

The Sun came up upon the left,
Out of the sea came he!
And he shone bright, and on the right
Went down into the sea.

Higher and higher every day,
Till over the mast at noon—"
The Wedding-Guest here beat his breast,
For he heard the loud bassoon.

The Wedding-Guest heareth the bridal music; but the Mariner continueth his tale.

The bride hath paced into the hall,
Red as a rose is she;
Nodding their heads before her goes
The merry minstrelsy.

The Wedding-Guest he beat his breast,
Yet he cannot choose but hear;
And thus spake on that ancient man,
The bright-eyed Mariner.

The ship driven by a storm toward the south pole.

"And now the STORM-BLAST came, and he
Was tyrannous and strong;
He struck with his o'ertaking wings,
And chased us south along.

With sloping masts and dipping
      prow,
As who pursued with yell and blow
Still treads the shadow of his foe,
And forward bends his head,
The ship drove fast, loud roared the blast,
And southward aye we fled.

And now there came both mist and snow,
And it grew wondrous cold:
And ice, mast-high, came floating by,
As green as emerald.

The land of ice, and of fearful sounds where no living thing was to be seen.

And through the drifts the snowy
      clifts
Did send a dismal sheen:
Nor shapes of men nor beasts we ken—
The ice was all between.

The ice was here, the ice was there,
The ice was all around:
It cracked and growled, and roared and
      howled,

Like noises in a swound!

At length did cross an Albatross,
Thorough the fog it came;
As if it had been a Christian soul,
We hailed it in God's name.

It ate the food it ne'er had eat,
And round and round it flew.
The ice did split with a thunder-fit;
The helmsman steered us through!

And a good south wind sprung up be-
  hind;
The Albatross did follow,
And every day, for food or play,
Came to the mariners' hollo!

In mist or cloud, on mast or shroud,
It perched for vespers nine;
Whiles all the night, through fog-smoke
  white,
Glimmered the white Moon-shine."

"God save thee, ancient Mariner!
From the fiends, that plague thee
  thus!—
Why look'st thou so?"—"With my cross-
  bow
I shot the ALBATROSS.

PART II

The Sun now rose upon the right:
Out of the sea came he,
Still hid in mist, and on the left
Went down into the sea.

And the good south wind still blew be-
  hind,
But no sweet bird did follow,
Nor any day for food or play
Came to the mariners' hollo!

*His shipmates
cry out against
the ancient Mar-
iner, for killing
the bird of good
luck.*

And I had done a hellish thing,
And it would work 'em woe:
For all averred, I had killed the bird
That made the breeze to blow.
Ah wretch! said they, the bird to slay,
That made the breeze to blow!

*But when the
fog cleared off,
they justify the
same, and thus
make themselves
accomplices in
the crime.*

Nor dim nor red, like God's own head,
The glorious Sun uprist:
Then all averred, I had killed the bird
That brought the fog and mist.
'Twas right, said they, such birds to slay,
That bring the fog and mist.

*The fair breeze
continues; the
ship enters the
Pacific Ocean,
and sails north-
ward, even till it
reaches the Line.*

The fair breeze blew, the white foam
  flew,
The furrow followed free;
We were the first that ever burst
Into that silent sea.

262

The ship hath been suddenly becalmed.

Down dropt the breeze, the sails dropt
    down,
'Twas sad as sad could be;
And we did speak only to break
The silence of the sea!

All in a hot and copper sky,
The bloody Sun, at noon,
Right up above the mast did stand,
No bigger than the Moon.

Day after day, day after day,
We stuck, nor breath nor motion;
As idle as a painted ship
Upon a painted ocean.

And the Albatross begins to be avenged.

Water, water, every where,
And all the boards did shrink;
Water, water, every where,
Nor any drop to drink.

The very deep did rot: O Christ!
That ever this should be!
Yea, slimy things did crawl with legs
Upon the slimy sea.

About, about, in reel and rout
The death-fires danced at night;
The water, like a witch's oils,
Burnt green, and blue and white.

And some in dreams assuréd were
Of the Spirit that plagued us so;

A Spirit had followed them; one of the invisible inhabitants of this planet,
Nine fathom deep he had followed us
From the land of mist and snow.

neither departed souls nor angels; concerning whom the learned Jew, Josephus and the Platonic Constantinopolitan, Michael Psellus, may be consulted. They are very numerous, and there is no climate or element without one or more.

And every tongue, through utter
    drought,
Was withered at the root;
We could not speak, no more than if
We had been choked with soot.

Ah! well a-day! what evil looks
Had I from old and young!
The shipmates, in their sore distress, would fain throw the whole guilt on the ancient Mariner: in
Instead of the cross, the Albatross
About my neck was hung.

sign whereof they hang the dead sea-bird round his neck.

PART III

There passed a weary time. Each throat
Was parched, and glazed each eye.
A weary time! a weary time!
How glazed each weary eye,
The ancient Mariner beholdeth a sign in the element afar off.
When looking westward, I beheld
A something in the sky.

At first it seemed a little speck,
And then it seemed a mist;
It moved and moved, and took at last
A certain shape, I wist.

A speck, a mist, a shape, I wist!

264

And still it neared and neared:
As if it dodged a water-sprite,
It plunged and tacked and veered.

*At its nearer ap-
proach, it seem-
eth him to be a
ship; and at a
dear ransom he
freeth his speech
from the bonds
of thirst.*

With throats unslaked, with black lips
    baked,
We could nor laugh nor wail;
Through utter drought all dumb we
    stood!
I bit my arm, I sucked the blood,
And cried, A sail! a sail!

With throats unslaked, with black lips
    baked,
Agape they heard me call:

A flash of joy;

Gramercy! they for joy did grin,
And all at once their breath drew in,
As they were drinking all.

*And horror fol-
lows. For can it
be a ship that
comes onward
without wind or
tide?*

See! see! (I cried) she tacks no more!
Hither to work us weal;
Without a breeze, without a tide,
She steadies with upright keel!

The western wave was all a-flame.
The day was well nigh done!
Almost upon the western wave
Rested the broad bright Sun;
When that strange shape drove sud-
    denly
Betwixt us and the Sun.

*It seemeth him
but the skeleton
of a ship.*

And straight the Sun was flecked with
    bars,

(Heaven's Mother send us grace!)
As if through a dungeon-grate he peered
With broad and burning face.

Alas! (thought I, and my heart beat loud)
How fast she nears and nears!
Are those *her* sails that glance in the Sun,
Like the restless gossameres?

Are those *her* ribs through which the
    Sun
Did peer, as through a grate?
And is that Woman all her crew?
Is that a DEATH? and are there two?
Is DEATH that woman's mate?

Her lips were red, *her* looks were
    free,
Her locks were yellow as gold:
Her skin was as white as leprosy,
The Night-mare LIFE-IN-DEATH was she,
Who thicks man's blood with cold.

The naked hulk alongside came,
And the twain were casting dice;
'The game is done! I've won! I've won!'
Quoth she, and whistles thrice.

The Sun's rim dips; the stars rush out:
At one stride comes the dark;
With far-heard whisper, o'er the sea,
Off shot the spectre-bark.

*And its ribs are
seen as bars on
the face of the
setting Sun.*

*The Spectre-
Woman and her
Deathmate, and
no other on
board the skele-
ton ship.
Like vessel, like
crew!*

*Death and Life-
in-Death have
diced for the
ship's crew, and
she (the latter)
winneth the an-
cient Mariner.*

*No twilight
within the courts
of the Sun.*

266

At the rising of
the Moon,

We listened and looked sideways up!
Fear at my heart, as at a cup,
My life-blood seemed to sip!
The stars were dim, and thick the night,
The steersman's face by his lamp gleamed
    white;
From the sails the dew did drip—
Till clomb above the eastern bar
The hornéd Moon, with one bright
    star
Within the nether tip.

One after an-
other,

One after one, by the star-dogged Moon,
Too quick for groan or sigh,
Each turned his face with ghastly pang,
And cursed me with his eye.

His shipmates
drop down dead.

Four times fifty living men,
(And I heard nor sigh nor groan)
With heavy thump, a lifeless lump,
They dropped down one by one.

But Life-in-
Death begins her
work on the an-
cient Mariner.

The souls did from their bodies
    fly,—
They fled to bliss or woe!
And every soul, it passed me by,
Like the whizz of my cross-bow!"

PART IV

The Wedding-
Guest feareth
that a Spirit is
talking to him;

"I fear thee, ancient Mariner!
I fear thy skinny hand!

267

And thou art long, and lank, and brown,
As is the ribbed sea-sand.

I fear thee and thy glittering eye,
And thy skinny hand, so brown."—
"Fear not, fear not, thou Wedding-
    Guest!
This body dropt not down.

Alone, alone, all, all alone,
Alone on a wide wide sea!
And never a saint took pity on
My soul in agony.

The many men, so beautiful!
And they all dead did lie:
And a thousand thousand slimy things
Lived on; and so did I.

I looked upon the rotting sea,
And drew my eyes away;
I looked upon the rotting deck,
And there the dead men lay.

I looked to heaven, and tried to pray;
But or ever a prayer had gusht,
A wicked whisper came, and made
My heart as dry as dust.

I closed my lids, and kept them close,
And the balls like pulses beat;
For the sky and the sea, and the sea and
    the sky

Lay like a load on my weary eye,
And the dead were at my feet.

*But the curse
liveth for him in
the eye of the
dead men.*

The cold sweat melted from their limbs,
Nor rot nor reek did they:
The look with which they looked on
    me
Had never passed away.

An orphan's curse would drag to hell
A spirit from on high;
But oh! more horrible than that
Is the curse in a dead man's eye!
Seven days, seven nights, I saw that curse,
And yet I could not die.

The moving Moon went up the sky,
And no where did abide:
Softly she was going up,

*In his loneliness
and fixedness he
yearneth towards
the journeying
Moon, and the
stars that still
sojourn, yet still
move onward;
and everywhere
the blue sky be-
longs to them,
and is their ap-
pointed rest, and
their native
country and their own natural homes, which they enter unannounced, as lords that are
certainly expected and yet there is a silent joy at their arrival.*

And a star or two beside—

Her beams bemocked the sultry main,
Like April hoar-frost spread;
But where the ship's huge shadow lay,
The charméd water burnt alway
A still and awful red.

*By the light of
the Moon he be-
holdeth God's
creatures of the
great calm.*

Beyond the shadow of the ship,
I watched the water-snakes:
They moved in tracks of shining white,
And when they reared, the elfish
    light
Fell off in hoary flakes.

269

Within the shadow of the ship
I watched their rich attire:
Blue, glossy green, and velvet black,
They coiled and swam; and every
    track
Was a flash of golden fire.

O happy living things! no tongue
Their beauty might declare:
A spring of love gushed from my heart,

And I blessed them unaware:
Sure my kind saint took pity on me,
And I blessed them unaware.

The self-same moment I could pray;
And from my neck so free
The Albatross fell off, and sank
Like lead into the sea.

PART V

Oh sleep! it is a gentle thing,
Beloved from pole to pole!
To Mary Queen the praise be given!
She sent the gentle sleep from
    Heaven,
That slid into my soul.

The silly buckets on the deck,
That had so long remained,
I dreamt that they were filled with dew;
And when I awoke, it rained.

270

My lips were wet, my throat was cold,
My garments all were dank;
Sure I had drunken in my dreams,
And still my body drank.

I moved, and could not feel my
      limbs:
I was so light—almost
I thought that I had died in sleep,
And was a blesséd ghost.

*He heareth
sounds and seeth
strange sights
and commotions
in the sky and
the element.*
And soon I heard a roaring wind:
It did not come anear;
But with its sound it shook the sails,
That were so thin and sere.

The upper air burst into life!
And a hundred fire-flags sheen,
To and fro they were hurried about!
And to and fro, and in and out,
The wan stars danced between.

And the coming wind did roar more loud,
And the sails did sigh like sedge;
And the rain poured down from one black
      cloud;
The Moon was at its edge.

The thick black cloud was cleft, and still
The Moon was at its side:
Like waters shot from some high crag,
The lightning fell with never a jag,
A river steep and wide.

271

The bodies of
the ship's crew
are inspirited,
and the ship
moves on;

The loud wind never reached the ship,
Yet now the ship moved on!
Beneath the lightning and the Moon
The dead men gave a groan.

They groaned, they stirred, they all up-
rose,
Nor spake, nor moved their eyes;
It had been strange, even in a dream,
To have seen those dead men rise.

The helmsman steered, the ship moved
on;
Yet never a breeze up-blew;
The mariners all 'gan work the ropes,
Where they were wont to do;
They raised their limbs like lifeless tools—
We were a ghastly crew.

The body of my brother's son
Stood by me, knee to knee:
The body and I pulled at one rope,
But he said nought to me."

"I fear thee, ancient Mariner!"
"Be calm, thou Wedding-Guest!
'Twas not those souls that fled in pain,
Which to their corses came again,
But a troop of spirits blest:

But not by the
souls of the men,
nor by dæmons
of earth or mid-
dle air, but by a
blessed troop of
angelic spirits,
sent down by
the invocation of
the guardian
saint.

For when it dawned—they dropped their
arms,

And clustered round the mast;
Sweet sounds rose slowly through their
     mouths,
And from their bodies passed.

Around, around, flew each sweet sound,
Then darted to the Sun;
Slowly the sounds came back again,
Now mixed, now one by one.

Sometimes a-dropping from the sky
I heard the sky-lark sing;
Sometimes all little birds that are,
How they seemed to fill the sea and air
With their sweet jargoning!

And now 'twas like all instruments,
Now like a lonely flute;
And now it is an angel's song,
That makes the heavens be mute.

It ceased; yet still the sails made on
A pleasant noise till noon,
A noise like of a hidden brook
In the leafy month of June,
That to the sleeping woods all night
Singeth a quiet tune.

Till noon we quietly sailed on,
Yet never a breeze did breathe:
Slowly and smoothly went the ship,
Moved onward from beneath.

The lonesome
Spirit from the
south-pole car-
ries on the ship
as far as the
Line, in obedi-
ence to the an-
gelic troop, but
still requireth
vengeance.

Under the keel nine fathom deep,
From the land of mist and snow,
The spirit slid: and it was he
That made the ship to go.
The sails at noon left off their tune,
And the ship stood still also.

The Sun, right up above the mast,
Had fixed her to the ocean:
But in a minute she 'gan stir,
With a short uneasy motion—
Backwards and forwards half her length
With a short uneasy motion.

Then like a pawing horse let go,
She made a sudden bound:
It flung the blood into my head,
And I fell down in a swound.

The Polar
Spirit's fellow-
dæmons, the in-
visible inhabit-
ants of the ele-
ment, take part
in his wrong;
and two of them
relate, one to the
other, that pen-
ance long and
heavy for the
ancient Mariner
hath been ac-
corded to the
Polar Spirit, who
returneth south-
ward.

How long in that same fit I lay,
I have not to declare;
But ere my living life returned,
I heard and in my soul discerned
Two voices in the air.

'Is it he?' quoth one, 'Is this the man?
By him who died on cross,
With his cruel bow he laid full low
The harmless Albatross.

274

The spirit who bideth by himself
In the land of mist and snow,
He loved the bird that loved the man
Who shot him with his bow.'

The other was a softer voice,
As soft as honey-dew:
Quoth he, 'The man hath penance done,
And penance more will do.'

PART VI

FIRST VOICE

'But tell me, tell me! speak again,
Thy soft response renewing—
What makes that ship drive on so fast?
What is the ocean doing?'

SECOND VOICE

'Still as a slave before his lord,
The ocean hath no blast;
His great bright eye most silently
Up to the Moon is cast—

If he may know which way to go;
For she guides him smooth or grim.
See, brother, see! how graciously
She looketh down on him.'

The Mariner hath been cast into a trance; for the angelic power causeth the vessel to drive northward faster than human life could endure.

'But why drives on that ship so fast,
Without or wave or wind?'

SECOND VOICE

'The air is cut away before,
And closes from behind.

Fly, brother, fly! more high, more high!
Or we shall be belated:
For slow and slow that ship will go,
When the Mariner's trance is abated.'

The supernatural motion is retarded; the Mariner awakes, and his penance begins anew.

I woke, and we were sailing on
As in a gentle weather:
'Twas night, calm night, the moon was
    high;
The dead men stood together.

All stood together on the deck,
For a charnel-dungeon fitter:
All fixed on me their stony eyes,
That in the Moon did glitter.

The pang, the curse, with which they
    died,
Had never passed away:
I could not draw my eyes from
    theirs,
Nor turn them up to pray.

The curse is finally expiated.

And now this spell was snapt: once more

I viewed the ocean green,
And looked far forth, yet little saw
Of what had else been seen—

Like one, that on a lonesome road
Doth walk in fear and dread,
And having once turned round walks on,
And turns no more his head;
Because he knows, a frightful fiend
Doth close behind him tread.

But soon there breathed a wind on me,
Nor sound nor motion made:
Its path was not upon the sea,
In ripple or in shade.

It raised my hair, it fanned my cheek
Like a meadow-gale of spring—
It mingled strangely with my fears,
Yet it felt like a welcoming.

Swiftly, swiftly flew the ship,
Yet she sailed softly too:
Sweetly, sweetly blew the breeze—
On me alone it blew.

*And the ancient
Mariner behold-
eth his native
country.*

Oh! dream of joy! is this indeed
The light-house top I see?
Is this the hill? is this the kirk?
Is this mine own countree?

We drifted o'er the harbour-bar,
And I with sobs did pray—

O let me be awake, my God!
Or let me sleep alway.

The harbour-bay was clear as glass,
So smoothly it was strewn!
And on the bay the moonlight lay,
And the shadow of the Moon.

The rock shone bright, the kirk no less,
That stands above the rock:
The moonlight steeped in silentness
The steady weathercock.

And the bay was white with silent
    light,
Till rising from the same,
The angelic spirits leave the dead bodies, Full many shapes, that shadows were,
In crimson colours came.

A little distance from the prow
And appear in their own forms of light. Those crimson shadows were:
I turned my eyes upon the deck—
Oh, Christ! what saw I there!

Each corse lay flat, lifeless and flat,
And, by the holy rood!
A man all light, a seraph-man,
On every corse there stood.

This seraph-band, each waved his hand:
It was a heavenly sight!
They stood as signals to the land,
Each one a lovely light;

This seraph-band, each waved his hand
No voice did they impart—
No voice; but oh! the silence sank
Like music on my heart.

But soon I heard the dash of oars,
I heard the Pilot's cheer;
My head was turned perforce away
And I saw a boat appear.

The Pilot and the Pilot's boy,
I heard them coming fast:
Dear Lord in Heaven! it was a joy
The dead men could not blast.

I saw a third—I heard his voice:
It is the Hermit good!
He singeth loud his godly hymns
That he makes in the wood.
He'll shrieve my soul, he'll wash away
The Albatross's blood.

PART VII

The Hermit of
the Wood,

This Hermit good lives in that wood
Which slopes down to the sea.
How loudly his sweet voice he rears!
He loves to talk with marineres
That come from a far countree.

He kneels at morn, and noon, and eve—
He hath a cushion plump:

279

It is the moss that wholly hides
The rotted old oak-stump.

The skiff-boat neared: I heard them talk,
'Why, this is strange, I trow!
Where are those lights so many and
    fair,
That signal made but now?'

'Strange, by my faith!' the Hermit said—
'And they answered not our cheer!
The planks looked warped! and see those
    sails,
How thin they are and sere!
I never saw aught like to them,
Unless perchance it were

Brown skeletons of leaves that lag
My forest-brook along;
When the ivy-tod is heavy with
    snow,
And the owlet whoops to the wolf below,
That eats the she-wolf's young.'

'Dear Lord! it hath a fiendish look—
(The Pilot made reply)
I am a-feared'—'Push on, push on!'
Said the Hermit cheerily.

The boat came closer to the ship,
But I nor spake nor stirred;
The boat came close beneath the ship,
And straight a sound was heard.

The ship sud-
denly sinketh.

Under the water it rumbled on,
Still louder and more dread:
It reached the ship, it split the bay;
The ship went down like lead.

The ancient
Mariner is saved
in the Pilot's
boat.

Stunned by that loud and dreadful
    sound,
Which sky and ocean smote,
Like one that hath been seven days
    drowned
My body lay afloat;
But swift as dreams, myself I found
Within the Pilot's boat:

Upon the whirl, where sank the ship,
The boat spun round and round;
And all was still, save that the hill
Was telling of the sound.

I moved my lips—the Pilot shrieked
And fell down in a fit;
The holy Hermit raised his eyes,
And prayed where he did sit.

I took the oars: the Pilot's boy,
Who now doth crazy go,
Laughed loud and long, and all the while
His eyes went to and fro.
'Ha! ha!' quoth he, 'full plain I see
The Devil knows how to row.'

And now, all in my own countree,
I stood on the firm land!

281

The Hermit stepped forth from the boat,
And scarcely he could stand.

'O shrieve me, shrieve me, holy man!'
The Hermit crossed his brow.
'Say quick,' quoth he, 'I bid thee say—
What manner of man art thou?'

Forthwith this frame of mine was
    wrenched
With a woful agony,
Which forced me to begin my tale;
And then it left me free.

Since then, at an uncertain hour,
That agony returns:
And till my ghastly tale is told,
This heart within me burns.

I pass, like night, from land to land;
I have strange power of speech;
That moment that his face I see,
I know the man that must hear me:
To him my tale I teach.

What loud uproar bursts from that door!
The wedding-guests are there:
But in the garden-bower the bride
And bride-maids singing are:
And hark the little vesper bell,
Which biddeth me to prayer!

O Wedding-Guest! this soul hath been
Alone on a wide wide sea:
So lonely 'twas, that God himself
Scarce seeméd there to be.

O sweeter than the marriage-feast,
'Tis sweeter far to me,
To walk together to the kirk
With a goodly company!—

To walk together to the kirk,
And all together pray,
While each to his great Father bends,
Old men, and babes, and loving friends
And youths and maidens gay!

And to teach, by his own example, love and reverence to all things that God made and loveth.

Farewell, farewell! but this I tell
To thee, thou Wedding-Guest!
He prayeth well, who loveth well
Both man and bird and beast.

He prayeth best, who loveth best
All things both great and small;
For the dear God who loveth us,
He made and loveth all."

The Mariner, whose eye is bright,
Whose beard with age is hoar,
Is gone: and now the Wedding-
    Guest
Turned from the bridegroom's door.

He went like one that hath been stunned,
And is of sense forlorn:
A sadder and a wiser man,
He rose the morrow morn.

S. T. COLERIDGE

❧ 161 ❦

LA BELLE DAME SANS MERCI

'O WHAT can ail thee, knight-at-arms,
  Alone and palely loitering?
The sedge has wither'd from the lake,
  And no birds sing.

'O what can ail thee, knight-at-arms!
  So haggard and so woebegone?
The squirrel's granary is full,
  And the harvest's done.

'I see a lily on thy brow
  With anguish moist and fever-dew,
And on thy cheeks a fading rose
  Fast withereth too.'

'I met a lady in the meads,
  Full beautiful—a fairy's child,
Her hair was long, her foot was light,
  And her eyes were wild.

'I made a garland for her head,

And bracelets too, and fragrant zone;
She look'd at me as she did love,
   And made sweet moan.

'I set her on my pacing steed
   And nothing else saw all day long,
For sidelong would she bend, and sing
   A fairy's song.

'She found me roots of relish sweet,
   And honey wild and manna-dew,
And sure in language strange she said
   "I love thee true."

'She took me to her elfin grot,
   And there she wept, and sigh'd full sore,
And there I shut her wild wild eyes
   With kisses four.

'And there she lullèd me asleep,
   And there I dream'd—Ah! woe betide!
The latest dream I ever dream'd
   On the cold hill's side.

'I saw pale kings and princes too,
   Pale warriors, death-pale were they all;
They cried—"La belle Dame sans Merci
   Hath thee in thrall!"

'I saw their starved lips in the gloam
   With horrid warning gapèd wide,
And I awoke and found me here
   On the cold hill's side.

'And this is why I sojourn here
   Alone and palely loitering,
Though the sedge is wither'd from the lake
   And no birds sing.'

J. KEATS

⚶162 ❧

THE ROVER

'A WEARY lot is thine, fair maid,
   A weary lot is thine!
To pull the thorn thy brow to braid,
   And press the rue for wine.
A lightsome eye, a soldier's mien,
   A feather of the blue,
A doublet of the Lincoln green—
   No more of me you knew
         My Love!
No more of me you knew.

'This morn is merry June, I trow,
   The rose is budding fain;
But she shall bloom in winter snow
   Ere we two meet again.'
He turn'd his charger as he spake
   Upon the river shore,
He gave the bridle-reins a shake,
   Said 'Adieu for evermore
         My Love!
And adieu for evermore.'

SIR W. SCOTT

THE FLIGHT OF LOVE

WHEN the lamp is shatter'd
The light in the dust lies dead—
When the cloud is scatter'd,
The rainbow's glory is shed.
When the lute is broken,
Sweet tones are remember'd not;
When the lips have spoken,
Loved accents are soon forgot.

As music and splendour
Survive not the lamp and the lute,
The heart's echoes render
No song when the spirit is mute—
No song but sad dirges,
Like the wind through a ruin'd cell,
Or the mournful surges
That ring the dead seaman's knell.

When hearts have once mingled,
Love first leaves the well-built nest;
The weak one is singled
To endure what it once possess'd.
O Love! who bewailest
The frailty of all things here,

Why choose you the frailest
For your cradle, your home, and your bier?

Its passions will rock thee
As the storms rock the ravens on high;
Bright reason will mock thee
Like the sun from a wintry sky.
From thy nest every rafter
Will rot, and thine eagle home
Leave thee naked to laughter,
When leaves fall and cold winds come.

P. B. SHELLEY

❧ 164 ☙

THE MAID OF NEIDPATH

O LOVERS' eyes are sharp to see,
    And lovers' ears in hearing;
And love, in life's extremity,
    Can lend an hour of cheering.
Disease had been in Mary's bower
    And slow decay from mourning,
Though now she sits on Neidpath's tower
    To watch her Love's returning.

All sunk and dim her eyes so bright,
    Her form decay'd by pining,
Till through her wasted hand, at night,
    You saw the taper shining.

By fits a sultry hectic hue
    Across her cheek was flying;
By fits so ashy pale she grew
    Her maidens thought her dying.

Yet keenest powers to see and hear
    Seem'd in her frame residing;
Before the watch-dog prick'd his ear
    She heard her lover's riding;
Ere scarce a distant form was kenn'd
    She knew and waved to greet him,
And o'er the battlement did bend
    As on the wing to meet him.

He came—he pass'd—an heedless gaze
    As o'er some stranger glancing;
Her welcome, spoke in faltering phrase,
    Lost in his courser's prancing—
The castle-arch, whose hollow tone
    Returns each whisper spoken,
Could scarcely catch the feeble moan
    Which told her heart was broken.

SIR W. SCOTT

❧ 165 ☙

THE MAID OF NEIDPATH

EARL March look'd on his dying child,
    And, smit with grief to view her—

The youth, he cried, whom I exiled
    Shall be restored to woo her.

She's at the window many an hour
    His coming to discover:
And he look'd up to Ellen's bower
    And she look'd on her lover—

But ah! so pale, he knew her not,
    Though her smile on him was dwelling—
And am I then forgot—forgot?
    It broke the heart of Ellen.

In vain he weeps, in vain he sighs,
    Her cheek is cold as ashes;
Nor love's own kiss shall wake those eyes
    To lift their silken lashes.

T. CAMPBELL

❦ 166 ❧

BRIGHT Star! would I were steadfast as thou art—
Not in lone splendour hung aloft the night,
And watching, with eternal lids apart,
Like nature's patient sleepless Eremite,

The moving waters at their priestlike task
Of pure ablution round earth's human shores,
Or gazing on the new soft fallen mask
Of snow upon the mountains and the moors:—

No—yet still steadfast, still unchangeable,
Pillow'd upon my fair Love's ripening breast
To feel for ever its soft fall and swell,
Awake for ever in a sweet unrest;

Still, still to hear her tender-taken breath,
And so live ever,—or else swoon to death.

J. KEATS

❧ 167 ☙

THE TERROR OF DEATH

WHEN I have fears that I may cease to be
Before my pen has glean'd my teeming brain,
Before high-piléd books, in charact'ry
Hold like rich garners the full-ripen'd grain;

When I behold, upon the night's starr'd face,
Huge cloudy symbols of a high romance,
And think that I may never live to trace
Their shadows, with the magic hand of chance;

And when I feel, fair Creature of an hour!
That I shall never look upon thee more,
Never have relish in the fairy power
Of unreflecting love—then on the shore

Of the wide world I stand alone, and think
Till Love and Fame to nothingness do sink.

J. KEATS

THE INDIAN BURYING-GROUND

In spite of all the learned have said,
    I still my old opinion keep;
The posture that we give the dead
    Points out the soul's eternal sleep.

Not so the ancients of these lands;—
    The Indian, when from life released,
Again is seated with his friends,
    And shares again the joyous feast.

His imaged birds, and painted bowl,
    And venison, for a journey dressed,
Bespeak the nature of the soul,
    Activity, that wants no rest.

His bow for action ready bent,
    And arrows with a head of stone,
Can only mean that life is spent,
    And not the old ideas gone.

Thou, stranger, that shalt come this way,
    No fraud upon the dead commit,—
Observe the swelling turf, and say,
    They do not lie, but here they sit.

Here still a lofty rock remains,
    On which the curious eye may trace

(Now wasted half by wearing rains)
　　The fancies of a ruder race.

Here still an aged elm aspires,
　　Beneath whose far projecting shade
(And which the shepherd still admires)
　　The children of the forest played.

There oft a restless Indian queen
　　(Pale Shebah with her braided hair),
And many a barbarous form is seen
　　To chide the man that lingers there.

By midnight moons, o'er moistening dews,
　　In habit for the chase arrayed,
The hunter still the deer pursues,
　　The hunter and the deer—a shade!

And long shall timorous Fancy see
　　The painted chief, and pointed spear,
And Reason's self shall bow the knee
　　To shadows and delusions here.

P. FRENEAU

❧ 169 ☙

ELEGY ON THYRZA

AND thou art dead, as young and fair
　　As aught of mortal birth;
And forms so soft and charms so rare

293

Too soon return'd to Earth!
Though Earth received them in her bed,
And o'er the spot the crowd may tread
    In carelessness or mirth,
There is an eye which could not brook
A moment on that grave to look.

I will not ask where thou liest low
    Nor gaze upon the spot;
There flowers or weeds at will may grow
    So I behold them not:
It is enough for me to prove
That what I loved and long must love
    Like common earth can rot;
To me there needs no stone to tell
'Tis Nothing that I loved so well.

Yet did I love thee to the last,
    As fervently as thou
Who didst not change through all the past
    And canst not alter now.
The love where Death has set his seal
Nor age can chill, nor rival steal,
    Nor falsehood disavow:
And, what were worse, thou canst not see
Or wrong, or change, or fault in me.

The better days of life were ours;
    The worst can be but mine:
The sun that cheers, the storm that lours,
    Shall never more be thine.

The silence of that dreamless sleep
I envy now too much to weep;
   Nor need I to repine
That all those charms have pass'd away
I might have watch'd through long decay.

The flower in ripen'd bloom unmatch'd
   Must fall the earliest prey;
Though by no hand untimely snatch'd,
   The leaves must drop away.
And yet it were a greater grief
To watch it withering, leaf by leaf,
   Than see it pluck'd today;
Since earthly eye but ill can bear
To trace the change to foul from fair.

I know not if I could have borne
   To see thy beauties fade;
The night that follow'd such a morn
   Had worn a deeper shade:
Thy day without a cloud hath past,
And thou wert lovely to the last,
   Extinguish'd, not decay'd;
As stars that shoot along the sky
Shine brightest as they fall from high.

As once I wept, if I could weep,
   My tears might well be shed
To think I was not near, to keep
   One vigil o'er thy bed:
To gaze, how fondly! on thy face,

To fold thee in a faint embrace,
    Uphold thy drooping head;
And show that love, however vain,
Nor thou nor I can feel again.

Yet how much less it were to gain,
    Though thou hast left me free,
The loveliest things that still remain
    Than thus remember thee!
The all of thine that cannot die
Through dark and dread Eternity
    Returns again to me,
And more thy buried love endears
Than aught except its living years.

                              LORD BYRON

✣ 170 ✣

ONE word is too often profaned
    For me to profane it,
One feeling too falsely disdain'd
    For thee to disdain it.
One hope it too like despair
    For prudence to smother,
And Pity from thee more dear
    Than that from another.

I can give not what men call love;
    But wilt thou accept not
The worship the heart lifts above
    And the Heavens reject not:

The desire of the moth for the star,
    Of the night for the morrow,
The devotion to something afar
    From the sphere of our sorrow?

P. B. SHELLEY

❦ 171 ❧

GATHERING SONG OF DONALD
THE BLACK

PIBROCH of Donuil Dhu
    Pibroch of Donuil
Wake thy wild voice anew,
    Summon Clan Conuil.
Come away, come away,
    Hark to the summons!
Come in your war-array,
    Gentles and commons.

Come from deep glen, and
    From mountain so rocky;
The war-pipe and pennon
    Are at Inverlocky.
Come every hill-plaid, and
    True heart that wears one,
Come every steel blade, and
    Strong hand that bears one.

Leave untended the herd,

The flock without shelter;
Leave the corpse uninterr'd,
The bride at the altar;
Leave the deer, leave the steer,
Leave nets and barges:
Come with your fighting gear,
Broadswords and targes.

Come as the winds come, when
Forests are rended,
Come as the waves come, when
Navies are stranded:
Faster come, faster come,
Faster and faster,
Chief, vassal, page and groom,
Tenant and master.

Fast they come, fast they come;
See how they gather!
Wide waves the eagle plume
Blended with heather.
Cast your plaids, draw your blades,
Forward each man set!
Pibroch of Donuil Dhu
Knell for the onset!

SIR W. SCOTT

A WET sheet and a flowing sea,
   A wind that follows fast
And fills the white and rustling sail
   And bends the gallant mast;
And bends the gallant mast, my boys,
   While like the eagle free
Away the good ship flies and leaves
   Old England on the lee.

O for a soft and gentle wind!
   I heard a fair one cry;
But give to me the snoring breeze
   And white waves heaving high;
And white waves heaving high, my lads,
   The good ship tight and free—
The world of waters is our home,
   And merry men are we.

There's tempest in yon hornéd moon,
   And lightning in yon cloud;
But hark the music, mariners!
   The wind is piping loud;
The wind is piping loud, my boys,
   The lightning flashes free—
While the hollow oak our palace is,
   Our heritage the sea.

A. CUNNINGHAM

BATTLE OF THE BALTIC

OF Nelson and the North
Sing the glorious day's renown,
When to battle fierce came forth
All the might of Denmark's crown,
And her arms along the deep proudly shone;
By each gun the lighted brand
In a bold determined hand,
And the Prince of all the land
Led them on.

Like leviathans afloat
Lay their bulwarks on the brine;
While the sign of the battle flew
On the lofty British line:
It was ten of April morn by the chime:
As they drifted on their path
There was silence deep as death;
And the boldest held his breath
For a time.

But the might of England flush'd
To anticipate the scene;
And her van the fleeter rush'd
O'er the deadly space between.

'Hearts of oak!' our captains cried, when each gun
From its adamantine lips
Spread a death-shade round the ships,
Like the hurricane eclipse
Of the sun.

Again! again! again!
And the havoc did not slack,
Till a feeble cheer the Dane
To our cheering sent us back;—
Their shots along the deep slowly boom:—
Then ceased—and all is wail,
As they strike the shatter'd sail;
Or in conflagration pale
Light the gloom.

Out spoke the victor then
As he hail'd them o'er the wave,
'Ye are brothers! ye are men!
And we conquer but to save:—
So peace instead of death let us bring:
But yield, proud foe, thy fleet
With the crews, at England's feet,
And make submission meet
To our King.'

Then Denmark blest our chief
That he gave her wounds repose;
And the sounds of joy and grief
From her people wildly rose,
As death withdrew his shades from the day:

While the sun look'd smiling bright
O'er a wide and woful sight,
Where the fires of funeral light
Died away.

Now joy, old England, raise!
For the tidings of thy might,
By the festal cities' blaze,
Whilst the wine-cup shines in light;
And yet amidst that joy and uproar,
Let us think of them that sleep
Full many a fathom deep
By thy wild and stormy steep,
Elsinore!

Brave hearts! to Britain's pride
Once so faithful and so true,
On the deck of fame they died
With the gallant good Riou:
Soft sigh the winds of Heaven o'er their grave!
While the billow mournful rolls
And the mermaid's song condoles
Singing glory to the souls
Of the brave!

T. CAMPBELL

ODE TO DUTY

STERN Daughter of the Voice of God!
O Duty! if that name you love
Who art a light to guide, a rod
To check the erring, and reprove;
Thou who art victory and law
When empty terrors overawe;
From vain temptations dost set free,
And calm'st the weary strife of frail humanity!

There are who ask not if thine eye
Be on them; who, in love and truth
Where no misgiving is, rely
Upon the genial sense of youth:
Glad hearts! without reproach or blot,
Who do thy work, and know it not:
O! if through confidence misplaced
They fail, thy saving arms, dread Power! around them cast.

Serene will be our days and bright
And happy will our nature be
When love is an unerring light,
And joy its own security.
And they a blissful course may hold
Ev'n now who, not unwisely bold,

Live in the spirit of this creed;
Yet seek thy firm support, according to their need.

I, loving freedom, and untried,
No sport of every random gust,
Yet being to myself a guide,
Too blindly have reposed my trust:
And oft, when in my heart was heard
Thy timely mandate, I deferr'd
The task, in smoother walks to stray;
But thee I now would serve more strictly, if I may.

Through no disturbance of my soul
Or strong compunction in me wrought,
I supplicate for thy control,
But in the quietness of thought:
Me this uncharter'd freedom tires;
I feel the weight of chance desires:
My hopes no more must change their name;
I long for a repose that ever is the same.

Stern Lawgiver! yet thou dost wear
The Godhead's most benignant grace;
Nor know we anything so fair
As is the smile upon thy face:
Flowers laugh before thee on their beds,
And fragrance in thy footing treads;
Thou dost preserve the Stars from wrong;
And the most ancient Heavens, through Thee, are fresh
and strong.

To humbler functions, awful Power!

I call thee: I myself commend
Unto thy guidance from this hour;
O let my weakness have an end!
Give unto me, made lowly wise,
The spirit of self-sacrifice;
The confidence of reason give;
And in the light of truth thy Bondman let me live.

W. WORDSWORTH

❧ 175 ❧

ON THE CASTLE OF CHILLON

ETERNAL Spirit of the chainless Mind!
Brightest in dungeons, Liberty, thou art—
For there thy habitation is the heart—
The heart which love of Thee alone can bind;

And when thy sons to fetters are consign'd,
To fetters, and the damp vault's dayless gloom,
Their country conquers with their martyrdom,
And Freedom's fame finds wings on every wind.

Chillon! thy prison is a holy place
And thy sad floor an altar, for 'twas trod,
Until his very steps have left a trace

Worn as if thy cold pavement were a sod,
By Bonnivard! May none those marks efface!
For they appeal from tyranny to God.

LORD BYRON

❧ 176 ❧

ENGLAND AND SWITZERLAND

1802

Two Voices are there, one is of the Sea,
One of the Mountains, each a mighty voice:
In both from age to age thou didst rejoice,
They were thy chosen music, Liberty!

There came a tyrant, and with holy glee
Thou fought'st against him,—but hast vainly striven:
Thou from thy Alpine holds at length art driven
Where not a torrent murmurs heard by thee.

—Of one deep bliss thine ear hath been bereft;
Then cleave, O cleave to that which still is left—
For, high-soul'd Maid, what sorrow would it be

That Mountain floods should thunder as before,
And Ocean bellow from his rocky shore,
And neither awful Voice be heard by Thee!

W. WORDSWORTH

177

ON THE EXTINCTION OF THE VENETIAN REPUBLIC

ONCE did She hold the gorgeous East in fee
And was the safeguard of the West; the worth
Of Venice did not fall below her birth,
Venice, the eldest child of liberty.

She was a maiden city, bright and free;
No guile seduced, no force could violate;
And when she took unto herself a mate,
She must espouse the everlasting Sea.

And what if she had seen those glories fade,
Those titles vanish, and that strength decay,—
Yet shall some tribute of regret be paid

When her long life hath reach'd its final day:
Men are we, and must grieve when even the shade
Of that which once was great has pass'd away.

W. WORDSWORTH

178

LONDON, MDCCCII

O FRIEND! I know not which way I must look
For comfort, being, as I am, opprest
To think that now our life is only drest
For show; mean handiwork of craftsman, cook,

Or groom!—We must run glittering like a brook
In the open sunshine, or we are unblest;
The wealthiest man among us is the best:
No grandeur now in Nature or in book

Delights us. Rapine, avarice, expense,
This is idolatry; and these we adore:
Plain living and high thinking are no more:

The homely beauty of the good old cause
Is gone; our peace, our fearful innocence,
And pure religion breathing household laws.

W. WORDSWORTH

179

LONDON, MDCCCII

MILTON! thou shouldst be living at this hour:
England hath need of thee: she is a fen

Of stagnant waters: altar, sword, and pen,
Fireside, the heroic wealth of hall and bower,

Have forfeited their ancient English dower
Of inward happiness. We are selfish men:
O! raise us up, return to us again;
And give us manners, virtue, freedom, power.

Thy soul was like a Star, and dwelt apart:
Thou hadst a voice whose sound was like the sea,
Pure as the naked heavens, majestic, free;

So didst thou travel on life's common way
In cheerful godliness; and yet thy heart
The lowliest duties on herself did lay.

W. WORDSWORTH

❧ 180 ❧

WHEN I have borne in memory what has tamed
Great nations; how ennobling thoughts depart
When men change swords for ledgers, and desert
The student's bower for gold,—some fears unnamed

I had, my Country!—am I to be blamed?
Now, when I think of thee, and what thou art,
Verily, in the bottom of my heart,
Of those unfilial fears I am ashamed.

For dearly must we prize thee; we who find

In thee a bulwark for the cause of men;
And I by my affection was beguiled:

What wonder if a Poet now and then,
Among the many movements of his mind,
Felt for thee as a lover or a child!

W. WORDSWORTH

❧ 181 ☙

AFTER BLENHEIM

It was a summer evening,
   Old Kaspar's work was done,
And he before his cottage door
   Was sitting in the sun;
And by him sported on the green
His little grandchild Wilhelmine.

She saw her brother Peterkin
   Roll something large and round
Which he beside the rivulet
   In playing there had found;
He came to ask what he had found
That was so large and smooth and round.

Old Kaspar took it from the boy
   Who stood expectant by;
And then the old man shook his head,
   And with a natural sigh
' 'Tis some poor fellow's skull,' said he,
'Who fell in the great victory.'

'I find them in the garden,
    For there's many here about;
And often when I go to plough
    The ploughshare turns them out.
For many thousand men,' said he,
'Were slain in that great victory.'

'Now tell us what 'twas all about,'
    Young Peterkin he cries;
And little Wilhelmine looks up
    With wonder-waiting eyes;
'Now tell us all about the war,
And what they fought each other for.'

'It was the English,' Kaspar cried,
    'Who put the French to rout;
But what they fought each other for
    I could not well make out.
But everybody said,' quoth he,
'That 'twas a famous victory.

'My father lived at Blenheim then,
    Yon little stream hard by;
They burnt his dwelling to the ground,
    And he was forced to fly:
So with his wife and child he fled,
Nor had he where to rest his head.

'With fire and sword the country round
    Was wasted far and wide,
And many a childing mother then
    And newborn baby died:

But things like that, you know, must be
At every famous victory.

'They say it was a shocking sight
    After the field was won;
For many thousand bodies here
    Lay rotting in the sun:
But things like that, you know, must be
After a famous victory.

'Great praise the Duke of Marlbro' won
    And our good Prince Eugene;'
'Why, 'twas a very wicked thing!'
    Said little Wilhelmine;
'Nay . . nay . . my little girl,' quoth he,
'It was a famous victory.

'And everybody praised the Duke
    Who this great fight did win.'
'But what good came of it at last?'
    Quoth little Peterkin:—
'Why that I cannot tell,' said he,
'But 'twas a famous victory.'

R. SOUTHEY

182

PRO PATRIA MORI

WHEN he who adores thee has left but the name
Of his fault and his sorrows behind,

O! say wilt thou weep, when they darken the fame
  Of a life that for thee was resign'd!
Yes, weep, and however my foes may condemn,
  Thy tears shall efface their decree;
For, Heaven can witness, though guilty to them,
  I have been but too faithful to thee.

With thee were the dreams of my earliest love;
  Every thought of my reason was thine:
In my last humble prayer to the Spirit above
  Thy name shall be mingled with mine!
O! blest are the lovers and friends who shall live
  The days of thy glory to see;
But the next dearest blessing that Heaven can give
  Is the pride of thus dying for thee.

T. MOORE

❧ 183 ☙

THE BURIAL OF SIR JOHN MOORE
AT CORUNNA

Not a drum was heard, not a funeral note,
  As his corpse to the rampart we hurried;
Not a soldier discharged his farewell shot
  O'er the grave where our hero we buried.

We buried him darkly at dead of night,
  The sods with our bayonets turning;
By the struggling moonbeam's misty light
  And the lantern dimly burning.

No useless coffin enclosed his breast,
    Not in sheet nor in shroud we wound him;
But he lay like a warrior taking his rest
    With his martial cloak around him.

Few and short were the prayers we said,
    And we spoke not a word of sorrow;
But we steadfastly gazed on the face that was dead,
    And we bitterly thought of the morrow.

We thought, as we hollow'd his narrow bed
    And smoothed down his lonely pillow,
That the foe and the stranger would tread o'er his head,
    And we far away on the billow!

Lightly they'll talk of the spirit that's gone
    And o'er his cold ashes upbraid him,—
But little he'll reck, if they let him sleep on
    In the grave where a Briton has laid him.

But half of our heavy task was done
    When the clock struck the hour for retiring:
And we heard the distant and random gun
    That the foe was sullenly firing.

Slowly and sadly we laid him down,
    From the field of his fame fresh and gory;
We carved not a line, and we raised not a stone—
    But we left him alone with his glory.

C. WOLFE

THE OLD FAMILIAR FACES

I HAVE had playmates, I have had companions
In my days of childhood, in my joyful school-days;
All, all are gone, the old familiar faces.

I have been laughing, I have been carousing,
Drinking late, sitting late, with my bosom cronies;
All, all are gone, the old familiar faces.

I loved a Love once, fairest among women:
Closed are her doors on me, I must not see her—
All, all are gone, the old familiar faces.

I have a friend, a kinder friend has no man:
Like an ingrate, I left my friend abruptly;
Left him, to muse on the old familiar faces,

Ghost-like I paced round the haunts of my childhood,
Earth seem'd a desert I was bound to traverse,
Seeking to find the old familiar faces.

Friend of my bosom, thou more than a brother,
Why wert not thou born in my father's dwelling?
So might we talk of the old familiar faces,

How some they have died, and some they have left me,
And some are taken from me; all are departed;
All, all are gone, the old familiar faces.

C. LAMB

THE JOURNEY ONWARDS

As slow our ship her foamy track
   Against the wind was cleaving,
Her trembling pennant still look'd back
   To that dear isle 'twas leaving.
So loath we part from all we love,
   From all the links that bind us;
So turn our hearts, as on we rove,
   To those we've left behind us!

When, round the bowl, of vanish'd years
   We talk with joyous seeming—
With smiles that might as well be tears,
   So faint, so sad their beaming;
While memory brings us back again
   Each early tie that twined us,
O, sweet's the cup that circles then
   To those we've left behind us!

And when in other climes, we meet
   Some isle or vale enchanting,
Where all looks flowery, wild, and sweet,
   And nought but love is wanting;
We think how great had been our bliss
   If Heaven had but assign'd us
To live and die in scenes like this,
   With some we've left behind us!

As travellers oft look back at eve
　　When eastward darkly going,
To gaze upon that light they leave
　　Still faint behind them glowing,—
So, when the close of pleasure's day
　　To gloom hath near consign'd us,
We turn to catch one fading ray
　　Of joy that's left behind us.

T. MOORE

❧ 186 ❧

YOUTH AND AGE

THERE'S not a joy the world can give like that it takes
　　away
When the glow of early thought declines in feeling's dull
　　decay;
'Tis not on youth's smooth cheek the blush alone which
　　fades so fast,
But the tender bloom of heart is gone, ere youth itself be
　　past.

Then the few whose spirits float above the wreck of happi-
　　ness
Are driven o'er the shoals of guilt, or ocean of excess:
The magnet of their course is gone, or only points in vain
The shore to which their shiver'd sail shall never stretch
　　again.

Then the mortal coldness of the soul like death itself
    comes down;
It cannot feel for others' woes, it dare not dream its own;
That heavy chill has frozen o'er the fountain of our tears,
And though the eye may sparkle still, 'tis where the ice
    appears.

Though wit may flash from fluent lips, and mirth distract
    the breast,
Through midnight hours that yield no more their former
    hope of rest;
'Tis but as ivy-leaves around the ruin'd turret wreathe,
All green and wildly fresh without, but worn and grey
    beneath.

Or could I feel as I have felt, or be what I have been,
Or weep as I could once have wept o'er many a vanish'd
    scene,—
As springs in deserts found seem sweet, all brackish
    though they be,
So midst the wither'd waste of life, those tears would flow
    to me!

LORD BYRON

❧187❧

PAST AND PRESENT

I REMEMBER, I remember
The house where I was born,
The little window where the sun
Came peeping in at morn;

He never came a wink too soon
Nor brought too long a day;
But now, I often wish the night
Had borne my breath away.

I remember, I remember
The roses, red and white,
The violets, and the lily-cups—
Those flowers made of light!
The lilacs where the robin built,
And where my brother set
The laburnum on his birthday,—
The tree is living yet!

I remember, I remember
Where I was used to swing,
And thought the air must rush as fresh
To swallows on the wing;
My spirit flew in feathers then
That is so heavy now,
And summer pools could hardly cool
The fever on my brow.

I remember, I remember
The fir trees dark and high;
I used to think their slender tops
Were close against the sky:
It was a childish ignorance,
But now 'tis little joy
To know I'm farther off from Heaven
Than when I was a boy.

T. HOOD

THE LIGHT OF OTHER DAYS

OFT in the stilly night
   Ere slumber's chain has bound me,
Fond Memory brings the light
   Of other days around me:
     The smiles, the tears
     Of boyhood's years,
   The words of love then spoken;
     The eyes that shone,
     Now dimm'd and gone,
   The cheerful hearts now broken!
Thus in the stilly night
   Ere slumber's chain has bound me,
Sad Memory brings the light
   Of other days around me.

When I remember all
   The friends so link'd together
I've seen around me fall
   Like leaves in wintry weather,
     I feel like one
     Who treads alone
   Some banquet-hall deserted,
     Whose lights are fled
     Whose garlands dead,

And all but he departed!
Thus in the stilly night
 Ere slumber's chain has bound me,
Sad Memory brings the light
 Of other days around me.

T. MOORE

❧ 189 ☙

INVOCATION

RARELY, rarely, comest thou,
 Spirit of Delight!
Wherefore hast thou left me now
 Many a day and night?
Many a weary night and day
'Tis since thou art fled away.

How shall ever one like me
 Win thee back again?
With the joyous and the free
 Thou wilt scoff at pain.
Spirit false! thou hast forgot
All but those who need thee not.

As a lizard with the shade
 Of a trembling leaf,
Thou with sorrow art dismay'd;
 Even the sighs of grief
Reproach thee, that thou art not near,
And reproach thou wilt not hear.

Let me set my mornful ditty
　　To a merry measure;—
Thou wilt never come for pity,
　　Thou wilt come for pleasure;—
Pity then will cut away
Those cruel wings, and thou wilt stay.

I love all that thou lovest,
　　Spirit of Delight!
The fresh Earth in new leaves drest
　　And the starry night;
Autumn evening, and the morn
When the golden mists are born.

I love snow and all the forms
　　Of the radiant frost;
I love waves, and winds, and storms,
　　Everything almost
Which is Nature's, and may be
Untainted by man's misery.

I love tranquil solitude,
　　And such society
As is quiet, wise, and good.
　　Between thee and me
What diff'rence? but thou dost possess
The things I seek, not love them less.

I love Love—though he has wings,
　　And like light can flee,
But above all other things,
　　Spirit, I love thee—

Thou art love and life! O come!
Make once more my heart thy home!

P. B. SHELLEY

❧ 190 ❧

THE SCHOLAR

My days among the Dead are passed;
Around me I behold,
Where'er these casual eyes are cast,
The mighty minds of old:
My never-failing friends are they,
With whom I converse day by day.

With them I take delight in weal
And seek relief in woe;
And while I understand and feel
How much to them I owe,
My cheeks have often been bedew'd
With tears of thoughtful gratitude.

My thoughts are with the Dead; with them
I live in long-past years,
Their virtues love, their faults condemn,
Partake their hopes and fears,
And from their lessons seek and find
Instruction with an humble mind.

My hopes are with the Dead; anon
My place with them will be,

And I with them shall travel on
Through all Futurity;
Yet leaving here a name, I trust,
That will not perish in the dust.

R. SOUTHEY

❧ 191 ☙

THE MERMAID TAVERN

Souls of Poets dead and gone,
What Elysium have ye known,
Happy field or mossy cavern,
Choicer than the Mermaid Tavern?
Have ye tippled drink more fine
Than mine host's Canary wine?
Or are fruits of Paradise
Sweeter than those dainty pies
Of Venison? O generous food!
Drest as though bold Robin Hood
Would, with his Maid Marian,
Sup and bowse from horn and can.

I have heard that on a day
Mine host's signboard flew away
Nobody knew whither, till
An astrologer's old quill
To a sheepskin gave the story—
Said he saw you in your glory
Underneath a new-old Sign

Sipping beverage divine,
And pledging with contented smack
The Mermaid in the Zodiac!

Souls of Poets dead and gone
What Elysium have ye known—
Happy field or mossy cavern—
Choicer than the Mermaid Tavern?

J. KEATS

❧ 192 ☙

THE PRIDE OF YOUTH

Proud Maisie is in the wood,
   Walking so early;
Sweet Robin sits on the bush,
   Singing so rarely.

'Tell me, thou bonny bird,
   When shall I marry me?'
—'When six braw gentlemen
   Kirkward shall carry ye.'

'Who makes the bridal bed,
   Birdie, say truly?'
—'The grey-headed sexton
   That delves the grave duly.

'The glowworm o'er grave and stone
   Shall light thee steady;

325

The owl from the steeple sing
Welcome, proud lady.'

SIR W. SCOTT

⚜ 193 ⚜

THE BRIDGE OF SIGHS

ONE more Unfortunate
Weary of breath,
Rashly importunate,
Gone to her death!

Take her up tenderly,
Lift her with care;
Fashion'd so slenderly,
Young, and so fair!

Look at her garments
Clinging like cerements;
Whilst the wave constantly
Drips from her clothing;
Take her up instantly,
Loving, not loathing.

Touch her not scornfully;
Think of her mournfully,
Gently and humanly;
Not of the stains of her—
All that remains of her
Now is pure womanly.

Make no deep scrutiny
Into her mutiny
Rash and undutiful:
Past all dishonour,
Death has left on her
Only the beautiful.

Still, for all slips of hers,
One of Eve's family—
Wipe those poor lips of hers
Oozing so clammily.

Loop up her tresses
Escaped from the comb,
Her fair auburn tresses;
Whilst wonderment guesses
Where was her home?

Who was her father?
Who was her mother?
Had she a sister?
Had she a brother?
Or was there a dearer one
Still, and a nearer one
Yet, than all other?

Alas! for the rarity
Of Christian charity
Under the sun!
O! it was pitiful!
Near a whole city full,
Home she had none.

Sisterly, brotherly,
Fatherly, motherly
Feelings had changed:
Love, by harsh evidence,
Thrown from its eminence;
Even God's providence
Seeming estranged.

Where the lamps quiver
So far in the river,
With many a light
From window and casement,
From garret to basement,
She stood, with amazement,
Houseless by night.

The bleak wind of March
Made her tremble and shiver;
But not the dark arch,
Or the black flowing river:
Mad from life's history,
Glad to death's mystery
Swift to be hurl'd—
Anywhere, anywhere
Out of the world!

In she plunged boldly,
No matter how coldly
The rough river ran,
Over the brink of it,—
Picture it, think of it,

Dissolute Man!
Lave in it, drink of it,
Then, if you can!

Take her up tenderly,
Lift her with care;
Fashion'd so slenderly,
Young, and so fair!

Ere her limbs frigidly
Stiffen too rigidly,
Decently, kindly,
Smooth and compose them;
And her eyes, close them,
Staring so blindly!

Dreadfully staring
Thro' muddy impurity,
As when with the daring
Last look of despairing
Fix'd on futurity.

Perishing gloomily,
Spurr'd by contumely,
Cold inhumanity,
Burning insanity,
Into her rest.
—Cross her hands humbly
As if praying dumbly,
Over her breast!

Owning her weakness,

Her evil behaviour,
And leaving, with meekness,
Her sins to her Saviour!

T. HOOD

❧ 194 ❦

HESTER

WHEN maidens such as Hester die,
Their place ye may not well supply,
Though ye among a thousand try
    With vain endeavour.
A month or more hath she been dead,
Yet cannot I by force be led
To think upon the wormy bed
    And her together.

A springy motion in her gait,
A rising step, did indicate
Of pride and joy no common rate
    That flush'd her spirit:
I know not by what name beside
I shall it call: if 'twas not pride,
It was a joy to that allied
    She did inherit.

Her parents held the Quaker rule,
Which doth the human feeling cool,

But she was train'd in Nature's school,
  Nature had blest her.
A waking eye, a prying mind,
A heart that stirs, is hard to bind;
A hawk's keen sight ye cannot blind,
  Ye could not Hester.

My sprightly neighbour! gone before
To that unknown and silent shore,
Shall we not meet, as heretofore
  Some summer morning—
When from thy cheerful eyes a ray
Hath struck a bliss upon the day,
A bliss that would not go away,
  A sweet fore-warning?

C. LAMB

✣195✣

THE DEATH BED

WE watch'd her breathing thro' the night,
  Her breathing soft and low,
As in her breast the wave of life
  Kept heaving to and fro.

But when the morn came dim and sad
  And chill with early showers,
Her quiet eyelids closed—she had
  Another morn than ours.

T. HOOD

ON AN INFANT DYING AS SOON
AS BORN

I SAW where in the shroud did lurk
A curious frame of Nature's work;
A flow'ret crushéd in the bud,
A nameless piece of Babyhood,
Was in her cradle-coffin lying;
Extinct, with scarce the sense of dying:
So soon to exchange the imprisoning womb
For darker closets of the tomb!
She did but ope an eye, and put
A clear beam forth, then straight up shut
For the long dark: ne'er more to see
Through glasses of mortality.
Riddle of destiny, who can show
What thy short visit meant, or know
What thy errand here below?
Shall we say, that Nature blind
Check'd her hand, and changed her mind
Just when she had exactly wrought
A finish'd pattern without fault?
Could she flag, or could she tire,
Or lack'd she the Promethean fire
(With her nine moons' long workings sicken'd)
That should thy little limbs have quicken'd?

Limbs so firm, they seem'd to assure
Life of health, and days mature;
Woman's self in miniature!
Limbs so fair, they might supply
(Themselves now but cold imagery)
The sculptor to make Beauty by.
Or did the stern-eyed Fate descry
That babe or mother, one must die;
So in mercy left the stock
And cut the branch; to save the shock
Of young years widow'd, and the pain
When Single State comes back again
To the lone man who, reft of wife,
Thenceforward drags a maiméd life?
The economy of Heaven is dark,
And wisest clerks have miss'd the mark
Why human buds, like this, should fall
More brief than fly ephemeral
That has his day; while shrivell'd crones
Stiffen with age to stocks and stones;
And crabbéd use the conscience sears
In sinners of an hundred years.
—Mother's prattle, mother's kiss,
Baby fond, thou ne'er wilt miss:
Rites, which custom does impose,
Silver bells, and baby clothes;
Coral redder than those lips
Which pale death did late eclipse;
Music framed for infants' glee,
Whistle never tuned for thee;

Though thou want'st not, thou shalt have them,
Loving hearts were they which gave them.
Let not one be missing; nurse,
See them laid upon the hearse
Of infant slain by doom perverse.
Why should kings and nobles have
Pictured trophies to their grave,
And we, churls, to thee deny
Thy pretty toys with thee to lie—
A more harmless vanity?

C. LAMB

❧ 197 ❧

THE AFFLICTION OF MARGARET

WHERE art thou, my beloved Son,
Where art thou, worse to me than dead!
O find me, prosperous or undone!
Or if the grave be now thy bed,
Why am I ignorant of the same
That I may rest; and neither blame
Nor sorrow may attend thy name?

Seven years, alas! to have received
No tidings of an only child—
To have despair'd, have hoped, believed,
And been for evermore beguiled,—
Sometimes with thoughts of very bliss!

I catch at them, and then I miss;
Was ever darkness like to this?

He was among the prime in worth,
An object beauteous to behold;
Well born, well bred; I sent him forth
Ingenuous, innocent, and bold:
If things ensued that wanted grace
As hath been said, they were not base;
And never blush was on my face.

Ah! little doth the young one dream
When full of play and childish cares,
What power is in his wildest scream
Heard by his mother unawares!
He knows it not, he cannot guess;
Years to a mother bring distress;
But do not make her love the less.

Neglect me! no, I suffer'd long
From that ill thought; and being blind
Said 'Pride shall help me in my wrong:
Kind mother have I been, as kind
As ever breathed:' and that is true;
I've wet my path with tears like dew,
Weeping for him when no one knew.

My Son, if thou be humbled, poor,
Hopeless of honour and of gain,
O! do not dread thy mother's door;
Think not of me with grief and pain:

I now can see with better eyes;
And worldly grandeur I despise
And fortune with her gifts and lies.

Alas! the fowls of heaven have wings,
And blasts of heaven will aid their flight;
They mount—how short a voyage brings
The wanderers back to their delight!
Chains tie us down by land and sea;
And wishes, vain as mine, may be
All that is left to comfort thee.

Perhaps some dungeon hears thee groan
Maim'd, mangled by inhuman men;
Or thou upon a desert thrown
Inheritest the lion's den;
Or hast been summon'd to the deep,
Thou, thou, and all thy mates to keep
An incommunicable sleep.

I look for ghosts: but none will force
Their way to me; 'tis falsely said
That there was ever intercourse
Between the living and the dead;
For surely then I should have sight
Of him I wait for day and night
With love and longings infinite.

My apprehensions come in crowds;
I dread the rustling of the grass;
The very shadows of the clouds
Have power to shake me as they pass;

I question things, and do not find
One that will answer to my mind;
And all the world appears unkind.

Beyond participation lie
My troubles, and beyond relief:
If any chance to heave a sigh
They pity me, and not my grief.
Then come to me, my Son, or send
Some tidings that my woes may end!
I have no other earthly friend.

W. WORDSWORTH

198

TO THE SKYLARK

ETHEREAL minstrel! pilgrim of the sky!
Dost thou despise the earth where cares abound?
Or while the wings aspire, are heart and eye
Both with thy nest upon the dewy ground?
Thy nest which thou canst drop into at will,
Those quivering wings composed, that music still!

To the last point of vision, and beyond
Mount, daring warbler!—that love-prompted strain
—'Twixt thee and thine a never-failing bond—
Thrills not the less the bosom of the plain:
Yet might'st thou seem, proud privilege! to sing
All independent of the leafy Spring.

Leave to the nightingale her shady wood;
A privacy of glorious light is thine,
Whence thou dost pour upon the world a flood
Of harmony, with instinct more divine;
Type of the wise, who soar, but never roam—
True to the kindred points of Heaven and Home!

W. WORDSWORTH

🦋 199 🦋

TO A SKYLARK

HAIL to thee, blithe Spirit!
　　Bird thou never wert,
That from heaven, or near it
　　Pourest thy full heart
In profuse strains of unpremeditated art.

　　Higher still and higher
　　From the earth thou springest
Like a cloud of fire;
　　The blue deep thou wingest,
And singing still dost soar, and soaring ever singest.

　　In the golden lightning
　　Of the sunken sun
O'er which clouds are brightening,
　　Thou dost float and run,
Like an unbodied joy whose race is just begun.

338

The pale purple even
   Melts around thy flight;
Like a star of heaven
   In the broad daylight
Thou art unseen, but yet I hear thy shrill delight:

   Keen as are the arrows
      Of that silver sphere,
   Whose intense lamp narrows
      In the white dawn clear
Until we hardly see, we feel that it is there.

   All the earth and air
      With thy voice is loud,
   As, when night is bare,
      From one lonely cloud
The moon rains out her beams, and heaven is overflow'd.

   What thou art we know not;
      What is most like thee?
   From rainbow clouds there flow not
      Drops so bright to see
As from thy presence showers a rain of melody.

   Like a poet hidden
      In the light of thought,
   Singing hymns unbidden,
      Till the world is wrought
To sympathy with hopes and fears it heeded not:

   Like a high-born maiden
      In a palace tower,

Soothing her love-laden
Soul in secret hour
With music sweet as love, which overflows her bower:

Like a glow-worm golden
In a dell of dew,
Scattering unbeholden
Its aerial hue
Among the flowers and grass, which screen it from the view:

Like a rose embower'd
In its own green leaves,
By warm winds deflower'd,
Till the scent it gives
Makes faint with too much sweet these heavy-wingéd
thieves.

Sound of vernal showers
On the twinkling grass,
Rain-awaken'd flowers,
All that ever was
Joyous, and clear, and fresh, thy music doth surpass.

Teach us, sprite or bird,
What sweet thoughts are thine:
I have never heard
Praise of love or wine
That panted forth a flood of rapture so divine.

Chorus hymeneal
Or triumphal chaunt
Match'd with thine, would be all

But an empty vaunt—
A thing wherein we feel there is some hidden want.

What objects are the fountains
Of thy happy strain?
What fields, or waves, or mountains?
What shapes of sky or plain?
What love of thine own kind? what ignorance of pain?

With thy clear keen joyance
Languor cannot be:
Shadow of annoyance
Never came near thee:
Thou lovest; but ne'er knew love's sad satiety.

Waking or asleep
Thou of death must deem
Things more true and deep
Than we mortals dream,
Or how could thy notes flow in such a crystal stream?

We look before and after,
And pine for what is not:
Our sincerest laughter
With some pain is fraught;
Our sweetest songs are those that tell of saddest thought.

Yet if we could scorn
Hate, and pride, and fear;
If we were things born
Not to shed a tear,
I know not how thy joy we ever should come near.

Better than all measures
Of delightful sound,
Better than all treasures
That in books are found,
Thy skill to poet were, thou scorner of the ground!

Teach me half the gladness
That thy brain must know,
Such harmonious madness
From my lips would flow
The world should listen then, as I am listening now!

P. B. SHELLEY

❧ 200 ☙

TO THE CUCKOO

O BLITHE new-comer! I have heard,
I hear thee and rejoice:
O Cuckoo! shall I call thee bird,
Or but a wandering Voice?

While I am lying on the grass
Thy twofold shout I hear;
From hill to hill it seems to pass,
At once far off and near.

Though babbling only to the vale
Of sunshine and of flowers,
Thou bringest unto me a tale
Of visionary hours.

Thrice welcome, darling of the Spring!
Even yet thou art to me
No bird, but an invisible thing,
A voice, a mystery;

The same whom in my schoolboy days
I listen'd to; that Cry
Which made me look a thousand ways
In bush, and tree, and sky.

To seek thee did I often rove
Through woods and on the green;
And thou wert still a hope, a love;
Still long'd for, never seen!

And I can listen to thee yet;
Can lie upon the plain
And listen, till I do beget
That golden time again.

O blesséd birth! the earth we pace
Again appears to be
An unsubstantial, fairy place,
That is fit home for Thee!

W. WORDSWORTH

❧ 201 ❧

ODE TO A NIGHTINGALE

My heart aches, and a drowsy numbness pains
My sense, as though of hemlock I had drunk,

Or emptied some dull opiate to the drains
    One minute past, and Lethe-wards had sunk:
'Tis not through envy of thy happy lot,
    But being too happy in thy happiness,—
        That thou, light-wingéd Dryad of the trees,
        In some melodious plot
    Of beechen green, and shadows numberless,
        Singest of summer in full-throated ease.

O for a draught of vintage! that hath been
    Cool'd a long age in the deep-delvéd earth,
Tasting of Flora and the country-green,
    Dance, and Provençal song, and sunburnt mirth.
O for a beaker full of the warm South,
    Full of the true, the blushful Hippocrene,
        With beaded bubbles winking at the brim
        And purple-stainéd mouth;
    That I might drink, and leave the world unseen,
    And with thee fade away into the forest dim.

Fade far away, dissolve, and quite forget
    What thou among the leaves hast never known,
The weariness, the fever, and the fret
    Here, where men sit and hear each other groan;
Where palsy shakes a few, sad, last grey hairs,
    Where youth grows pale, and spectre-thin, and dies;
        Where but to think is to be full of sorrow
        And leaden-eyed despairs;
    Where Beauty cannot keep her lustrous eyes,
    Or new Love pine at them beyond tomorrow.

Away! away! for I will fly to thee,

Not charioted by Bacchus and his pards,
But on the viewless wings of Poesy,
  Though the dull brain perplexes and retards:
Already with thee! tender is the night,
  And haply the Queen-Moon is on her throne,
    Cluster'd around by all her starry Fays;
      But here there is no light
Save what from heaven is with the breezes blown
    Through verdurous glooms and winding mossy ways.

I cannot see what flowers are at my feet,
  Nor what soft incense hangs upon the boughs,
But, in embalméd darkness, guess each sweet
  Wherewith the seasonable month endows
The grass, the thicket, and the fruit-tree wild;
  White hawthorn, and the pastoral eglantine;
    Fast-fading violets cover'd up in leaves;
      And mid-May's eldest child
The coming musk-rose, full of dewy wine,
    The murmurous haunt of flies on summer eves.

Darkling I listen; and for many a time
  I have been half in love with easeful Death,
Call'd him soft names in many a muséd rhyme,
  To take into the air my quiet breath;
Now more than ever seems it rich to die,
  To cease upon the midnight with no pain,
    While thou art pouring forth thy soul abroad
      In such an ecstasy!
Still wouldst thou sing, and I have ears in vain—
  To thy high requiem become a sod.

Thou wast not born for death, immortal Bird!
　　No hungry generations tread thee down;
The voice I hear this passing night was heard
　　In ancient days by emperor and clown:
Perhaps the selfsame song that found a path
　　Through the sad heart of Ruth, when, sick for home,
　　　She stood in tears amid the alien corn;
　　　　　The same that oft-times hath
　　Charm'd magic casements, opening on the foam
　　Of perilous seas, in faery lands forlorn.

Forlorn! the very word is like a bell
　　To toll me back from thee to my sole self!
Adieu! the fancy cannot cheat so well
　　As she is famed to do, deceiving elf.
Adieu! adieu! thy plaintive anthem fades
　　Past the near meadows, over the still stream,
　　　Up the hill-side; and now 'tis buried deep
　　　　　In the next valley-glades:
　　Was it a vision, or a waking dream?
　　　Fled is that music:—do I wake or sleep?

J. KEATS

THE TYGER

Tyger! Tyger! burning bright
In the forests of the night,
What immortal hand or eye
Could frame thy fearful symmetry?

In what distant deeps or skies
Burnt the fire of thine eyes?
On what wings dare he aspire?
What the hand dare seize the fire?

And what shoulder, and what art,
Could twist the sinews of thy heart?
And when thy heart began to beat,
What dread hand? and what dread feet?

What the hammer? what the chain?
In what furnace was thy brain?
What the anvil? what dread grasp
Dare its deadly terrors clasp?

When the stars threw down their spears
And watered heaven with their tears,
Did he smile his work to see?
Did he who made the Lamb make thee?

Tyger! Tyger! burning bright
In the forests of the night,

What immortal hand or eye
Dare frame thy fearful symmetry?

W. BLAKE

❧ 203 ❧

UPON WESTMINSTER BRIDGE

Sept. 3, 1802

EARTH has not anything to show more fair:
Dull would he be of soul who could pass by
A sight so touching in its majesty:
This City now doth like a garment wear

The beauty of the morning: silent, bare,
Ships, towers, domes, theatres, and temples lie
Open unto the fields, and to the sky,
All bright and glittering in the smokeless air.

Never did sun more beautifully steep
In his first splendour valley, rock, or hill;
Ne'er saw I, never felt, a calm so deep!

The river glideth at his own sweet will:
Dear God! the very houses seem asleep;
And all that mighty heart is lying still!

W. WORDSWORTH

OZYMANDIAS OF EGYPT

I MET a traveller from an antique land
Who said: Two vast and trunkless legs of stone
Stand in the desert. Near them on the sand,
Half sunk, a shatter'd visage lies, whose frown
And wrinkled lip and sneer of cold command
Tell that its sculptor well those passions read
Which yet survive, stamp'd on these lifeless things,
The hand that mock'd them and the heart that fed;
And on the pedestal these words appear:
'My name is Ozymandias, king of kings:
Look on my works, ye Mighty, and despair!'
Nothing beside remains. Round the decay
Of that colossal wreck, boundless and bare,
The lone and level sands stretch far away.

P. B. SHELLEY

ADMONITION TO A TRAVELLER

YES, there is holy pleasure in thine eye!
—The lovely cottage in the guardian nook
Hath stirr'd thee deeply; with its own dear brook,
Its own small pasture, almost its own sky!

But covet not the abode—O do not sigh
As many do, repining while they look;
Intruders who would tear from Nature's book
This precious leaf with harsh impiety:

—Think what the home would be if it were thine,
Even thine, though few thy wants!—Roof, window, door,
The very flowers are sacred to the Poor,

The roses to the porch which they entwine:
Yea, all that now enchants thee, from the day
On which it should be touch'd would melt away!

W. WORDSWORTH

❧ 206 ❧

THE REAPER

BEHOLD her, single in the field,
Yon solitary Highland Lass!
Reaping and singing by herself;
Stop here, or gently pass!
Alone she cuts and binds the grain,
And sings a melancholy strain;
O listen! for the vale profound
Is overflowing with the sound.

No nightingale did ever chaunt
More welcome notes to weary bands
Of travellers in some shady haunt,
Among Arabian sands:

A voice so thrilling ne'er was heard
In spring-time from the cuckoo-bird
Breaking the silence of the seas
Among the farthest Hebrides.

Will no one tell me what she sings?
Perhaps the plaintive numbers flow
For old, unhappy, far-off things,
And battles long ago:
Or is it some more humble lay,
Familiar matter of today?
Some natural sorrow, loss, or pain,
That has been, and may be again!

Whate'er the theme, the maiden sang
As if her song could have no ending;
I saw her singing at her work,
And o'er the sickle bending;
I listen'd, motionless and still;
And, as I mounted up the hill,
The music in my heart I bore,
Long after it was heard no more.

W. WORDSWORTH

❧ 207 ☙

THE REVERIE OF POOR SUSAN

At the corner of Wood Street, when daylight appears,
Hangs a Thrush that sings loud, it has sung for three years:

Poor Susan has pass'd by the spot, and has heard
In the silence of morning the song of the bird.

'Tis a note of enchantment; what ails her? She sees
A mountain ascending, a vision of trees;
Bright volumes of vapour through Lothbury glide,
And a river flows on through the vale of Cheapside.

Green pastures she views in the midst of the dale
Down which she so often has tripp'd with her pail;
And a single small cottage, a nest like a dove's,
The one only dwelling on earth that she loves.

She looks, and her heart is in heaven: but they fade,
The mist and the river, the hill and the shade;
The stream will not flow, and the hill will not rise,
And the colours have all pass'd away from her eyes!

W. WORDSWORTH

❧ 208 ☙

TO A LADY, WITH A GUITAR

ARIEL to Miranda:—Take
This slave of music, for the sake
Of him, who is the slave of thee;
And teach it all the harmony
In which thou canst, and only thou,
Make the delighted spirit glow,
Till joy denies itself again
And, too intense, is turn'd to pain.

For by permission and command
Of thine own Prince Ferdinand,
Poor Ariel sends this silent token
Of more than ever can be spoken;
Your guardian spirit, Ariel, who
From life to life must still pursue
Your happiness, for thus alone
Can Ariel ever find his own.
From Prospero's enchanted cell,
As the mighty verses tell,
To the throne of Naples he
Lit you o'er the trackless sea,
Flitting on, your prow before,
Like a living meteor.
When you die, the silent Moon
In her interlunar swoon
Is not sadder in her cell
Than deserted Ariel.
When you live again on earth.
Like an unseen Star of birth
Ariel guides you o'er the sea
Of life from your nativity.
Many changes have been run
Since Ferdinand and you begun
Your course of love, and Ariel still
Has track'd your steps and served your will.
Now in humbler, happier lot,
This is all remember'd not;
And now, alas! the poor sprite is
Imprison'd for some fault of his

In a body like a grave—
From you he only dares to crave,
For his service and his sorrow
A smile to-day, a song to-morrow.

The artist who this idol wrought
To echo all harmonious thought,
Fell'd a tree, while on the steep
The woods were in their winter sleep,
Rock'd in that repose divine
On the wind-swept Apennine;
And dreaming, some of Autumn past,
And some of Spring approaching fast,
And some of April buds and showers,
And some of songs in July bowers,
And all of love; and so this tree,—
O that such our death may be!—
Died in sleep, and felt no pain,
To live in happier form again:
From which, beneath Heaven's fairest star,
The artist wrought this loved Guitar;
And taught it justly to reply
To all who question skilfully
In language gentle as thine own;
Whispering in enamour'd tone
Sweet oracles of woods and dells,
And summer winds in sylvan cells;
—For it had learnt all harmonies
Of the plains and of the skies,

Of the forests and the mountains,
And the many-voicéd fountains;
The clearest echoes of the hills,
The softest notes of falling rills,
The melodies of birds and bees,
The murmuring of summer seas,
And pattering rain, and breathing dew,
And airs of evening; and it knew
That seldom-heard mysterious sound
Which, driven on its diurnal round,
As it floats through boundless day,
Our world enkindles on its way:
—All this it knows, but will not tell
To those who cannot question well
The Spirit that inhabits it;
It talks according to the wit
Of its companions; and no more
Is heard than has been felt before
By those who tempt it to betray
These secrets of an elder day.
But, sweetly as its answers will
Flatter hands of perfect skill,
It keeps its highest holiest tone
For one beloved Friend alone.

P. B. SHELLEY

209

THE DAFFODILS

I WANDER'D lonely as a cloud
That floats on high o'er vales and hills,
When all at once I saw a crowd,
A host of golden daffodils,
Beside the lake, beneath the trees
Fluttering and dancing in the breeze.

Continuous as the stars that shine
And twinkle on the milky way,
They stretch'd in never-ending line
Along the margin of a bay:
Ten thousand saw I at a glance
Tossing their heads in sprightly dance.

The waves beside them danced, but they
Out-did the sparkling waves in glee:—
A Poet could not but be gay
In such a jocund company!
I gazed—and gazed—but little thought
What wealth the show to me had brought.

For oft, when on my couch I lie
In vacant or in pensive mood,
They flash upon that inward eye
Which is the bliss of solitude;
And then my heart with pleasure fills
And dances with the daffodils.

W. WORDSWORTH

210

TO THE DAISY

WITH little here to do or see
Of things that in the great world be,
Sweet Daisy! oft I talk to thee
    For thou art worthy,
Thou unassuming Commonplace
Of Nature, with that homely face,
And yet with something of a grace
    Which love makes for thee!

Oft on the dappled turf at ease
I sit and play with similes
Loose types of things through all degrees,
    Thoughts of thy raising;
And many a fond and idle name
I give to thee, for praise or blame
As is the humour of the game,
    While I am gazing.

A nun demure, of lowly port;
Or sprightly maiden, of Love's court,
In thy simplicity the sport
    Of all temptations;
A queen in crown of rubies drest;
A starveling in a scanty vest;
Are all, as seems to suit thee best,
    Thy appellations.

A little Cyclops, with one eye
Staring to threaten and defy,
That thought comes next—and instantly
      The freak is over.
The shape will vanish, and behold!
A silver shield with boss of gold
That spreads itself, some fairy bold
      In fight to cover.

I see thee glittering from afar—
And then thou art a pretty star,
Not quite so fair as many are
      In heaven above thee!
Yet like a star, with glittering crest,
Self-poised in air thou seem'st to rest;—
May peace come never to his nest
      Who shall reprove thee!

Sweet Flower! for by that name at last
When all my reveries are past
I call thee, and to that cleave fast,
      Sweet silent Creature!
That breath'st with me in sun and air,
Do thou, as thou art wont, repair
My heart with gladness, and a share
      Of thy meek nature!

              W. WORDSWORTH

211

ODE TO AUTUMN

SEASON of mists and mellow fruitfulness!
Close bosom-friend of the maturing sun;
Conspiring with him how to load and bless
With fruit the vines that round the thatch-eaves run;
To bend with apples the moss'd cottage-trees,
And fill all fruit with ripeness to the core;
To swell the gourd, and plump the hazel shells
With a sweet kernel; to set budding more
And still more, later flowers for the bees,
Until they think warm days will never cease;
For Summer has o'erbrimm'd their clammy cells.

Who hath not seen Thee oft amid thy store?
Sometimes whoever seeks abroad may find
Thee sitting careless on a granary floor,
Thy hair soft-lifted by the winnowing wind;
Or on a half-reap'd furrow sound asleep,
Drowsed with the fume of poppies, while thy hook
Spares the next swath and all its twinéd flowers;
And sometimes like a gleaner thou dost keep
Steady thy laden head across a brook;
Or by a cider-press, with patient look,
Thou watchest the last oozings, hours by hours.

Where are the songs of Spring? Aye, where are they?
Think not of them,—thou hast thy music too,

359

While barréd clouds bloom the soft-dying day
And touch the stubble-plains with rosy hue;
Then in a wailful choir the small gnats mourn
Among the river-sallows, borne aloft
Or sinking as the light wind lives or dies;
And full-grown lambs loud bleat from hilly bourn;
Hedge-crickets sing, and now with treble soft
The redbreast whistles from a garden-croft,
And gathering swallows twitter in the skies.

J. KEATS

❧ 212 ☙

YARROW VISITED

September, 1814

AND is this—Yarrow?—This the Stream
Of which my fancy cherish'd
So faithfully, a waking dream,
An image that hath perish'd?
O that some minstrel's harp were near
To utter notes of gladness
And chase this silence from the air,
That fills my heart with sadness!

Yet why?—a silvery current flows
With uncontroll'd meanderings;
Nor have these eyes by greener hills
Been soothed, in all my wanderings.
And, through her depths, Saint Mary's Lake

Is visibly delighted;
For not a feature of those hills
Is in the mirror slighted.

A blue sky bends o'er Yarrow Vale,
Save where that pearly whiteness
Is round the rising sun diffused,
A tender hazy brightness;
Mild dawn of promise! that excludes
All profitless dejection;
Though not unwilling here to admit
A pensive recollection.

Where was it that the famous Flower
Of Yarrow Vale lay bleeding?
His bed perchance was yon smooth mound
On which the herd is feeding:
And haply from this crystal pool,
Now peaceful as the morning,
The Water-wraith ascended thrice,
And gave his doleful warning.

Delicious is the Lay that sings
The haunts of happy lovers,
The path that leads them to the grove,
The leafy grove that covers:
And pity sanctifies the verse
That paints, by strength of sorrow,
The unconquerable strength of love;
Bear witness, rueful Yarrow!

But thou that didst appear so fair

To fond imagination,
Dost rival in the light of day
Her delicate creation:
Meek loveliness is round thee spread,
A softness still and holy:
The grace of forest charms decay'd,
And pastoral melancholy.

That region left, the vale unfolds
Rich groves of lofty stature,
With Yarrow winding through the pomp
Of cultivated nature;
And rising from those lofty groves
Behold a ruin hoary,
The shatter'd front of Newark's Towers,
Renown'd in Border story.

Fair scenes for childhood's opening bloom,
For sportive youth to stray in,
For manhood to enjoy his strength,
And age to wear away in!
Yon cottage seems a bower of bliss,
A covert for protection
Of tender thoughts, that nestle there—
The brood of chaste affection.

How sweeet on this autumnal day
The wild-wood fruits to gather,
And on my true-love's forehead plant
A crest of blooming heather!
And what if I enwreathed my own?
'Twere no offence to reason;

The sober hills thus deck their brows
To meet the wintry season.

I see—but not by sight alone,
Loved Yarrow, have I won thee;
A ray of Fancy still survives—
Her sunshine plays upon thee!
Thy ever-youthful waters keep
A course of lively pleasure;
And gladsome notes my lips can breathe
Accordant to the measure.

The vapours linger round the heights,
They melt, and soon must vanish;
One hour is theirs, nor more is mine—
Sad thought! which I would banish,
But that I know, where'er I go,
Thy genuine image, Yarrow!
Will dwell with me—to heighten joy,
And cheer my mind in sorrow.

W. WORDSWORTH

❧ 213 ❧

THE INVITATION

BEST and brightest, come away,
Fairer far than this fair day,
Which, like thee, to those in sorrow
Comes to bid a sweet good-morrow
To the rough year just awake

In its cradle on the brake.
The brightest hour of unborn Spring
Through the Winter wandering,
Found, it seems, the halcyon morn
To hoar February born;
Bending from Heaven, in azure mirth,
It kiss'd the forehead of the earth,
And smiled upon the silent sea,
And bade the frozen streams be free,
And waked to music all their fountains,
And breathed upon the frozen mountains,
And like a prophetess of May
Strew'd flowers upon the barren way,
Making the wintry world appear
Like one on whom thou smilest, dear.

Away, away, from men and towns,
To the wild wood and the downs—
To the silent wilderness
Where the soul need not repress
Its music, lest it should not find
An echo in another's mind,
While the touch of Nature's art
Harmonizes heart to heart.

Radiant Sister of the Day
Awake! arise! and come away!
To the wild woods and the plains,
To the pools where winter rains
Image all their roof of leaves,
Where the pine its garland weaves

Of sapless green, and ivy dun,
Round stems that never kiss the sun,
Where the lawns and pastures be
And the sandhills of the sea,
Where the melting hoar-frost wets
The daisy-star that never sets,
And wind-flowers and violets
Which yet join not scent to hue
Crown the pale year weak and new;
When the night is left behind
In the deep east, dim and blind,
And the blue noon is over us,
And the multitudinous
Billows murmur at our feet,
Where the earth and ocean meet,
And all things seem only one
In the universal Sun.

                                    P. B. SHELLEY

❦ 214 ❧

KUBLA KHAN

OR, A VISION IN A DREAM

A FRAGMENT

In Xanadu did Kubla Khan
A stately pleasure-dome decree:
Where Alph, the sacred river, ran

Through caverns measureless to man
    Down to a sunless sea.
So twice five miles of fertile ground
With walls and towers were girdled round:
And there were gardens bright with sinuous rills,
Where blossomed many an incense-bearing tree;
And here were forests ancient as the hills,
Enfolding sunny spots of greenery.

But oh! that deep romantic chasm which slanted
Down the green hill athwart a cedarn cover!
A savage place! as holy and enchanted
As e'er beneath a waning moon was haunted
By woman wailing for her demon-lover!
And from this chasm, with ceaseless turmoil seething,
As if this earth in fast thick pants were breathing,
A mighty fountain momently was forced:
Amid whose swift half-intermitted burst
Huge fragments vaulted like rebounding hail,
Or chaffy grain beneath the thresher's flail:
And 'mid these dancing rocks at once and ever
It flung up momently the sacred river.
Five miles meandering with a mazy motion
Through wood and dale the sacred river ran,
Then reached the caverns measureless to man,
And sank in tumult to a lifeless ocean:
And 'mid this tumult Kubla heard from far
Ancestral voices prophesying war!
    The shadow of the dome of pleasure
    Floated midway on the waves;
    Where was heard the mingled measure

From the fountain and the caves.
It was a miracle of rare device,
A sunny pleasure-dome with caves of ice!

A damsel with a dulcimer
In a vision once I saw:
It was an Abyssinian maid,
And on her dulcimer she played,
Singing of Mount Abora.
Could I revive within me
Her symphony and song,
To such a deep delight 'twould win me,
That with music loud and long,
I would build that dome in air,
That sunny dome! those caves of ice!
And all who heard should see them there,
And all should cry, Beware! Beware!
His flashing eyes, his floating hair!
Weave a circle round him thrice,
And close your eyes with holy dread,
For he on honey-dew hath fed,
And drunk the milk of Paradise.

S. T. COLERIDGE

⚘ 215 ⚘

BY THE SEA

IT is a beauteous evening, calm and free;
The holy time is quiet as a Nun

Breathless with adoration; the broad sun
Is sinking down in its tranquillity;

The gentleness of heaven is on the Sea:
Listen! the mighty Being is awake,
And doth with his eternal motion make
A sound like thunder—everlastingly.

Dear child! dear girl! that walkest with me here,
If thou appear untouch'd by solemn thought
Thy nature is not therefore less divine:

Thou liest in Abraham's bosom all the year,
And worshipp'st at the Temple's inner shrine,
God being with thee when we know it not.

W. WORDSWORTH

❧ 216 ❧

A WIDOW bird sate mourning for her Love
    Upon a wintry bough;
The frozen wind crept on above,
    The freezing stream below.

There was no leaf upon the forest bare,
    No flower upon the ground,
And little motion in the air
    Except the mill-wheel's sound.

P. B. SHELLEY

TO SLEEP

A FLOCK of sheep that leisurely pass by
One after one; the sound of rain, and bees
Murmuring; the fall of rivers, winds and seas,
Smooth fields, white sheets of water, and pure sky;

I've thought of all by turns, and still I lie
Sleepless; and soon the small birds' melodies
Must hear, first utter'd from my orchard trees,
And the first cuckoo's melancholy cry.

Even thus last night, and two nights more I lay,
And could not win thee, Sleep! by any stealth:
So do not let me wear to-night away:

Without Thee what is all the morning's wealth?
Come, blesséd barrier between day and day,
Dear mother of fresh thoughts and joyous health!

W. WORDSWORTH

❧ 218 ❧

THE SOLDIER'S DREAM

OUR bugles sang truce, for the night-cloud had lower'd,
  And the sentinel stars set their watch in the sky;

And thousands had sunk on the ground overpower'd,
  The weary to sleep, and the wounded to die.

When reposing that night on my pallet of straw
  By the wolf-scaring faggot that guarded the slain,
At the dead of the night a sweet Vision I saw;
  And thrice ere the morning I dreamt it again.

Methought from the battle-field's dreadful array
  Far, far, I had roam'd on a desolate track:
'Twas Autumn,—and sunshine arose on the way
  To the home of my fathers, that welcomed me back.

I flew to the pleasant fields traversed so oft
  In life's morning march, when my bosom was young;
I heard my own mountain-goats bleating aloft,
  And knew the sweet strain that the corn-reapers sung.

Then pledged me the wine-cup, and fondly I swore
  From my home and my weeping friends never to part;
My little ones kiss'd me a thousand times o'er,
  And my wife sobb'd aloud in her fullness of heart.

'Stay—stay with us!—rest! thou art weary and worn!'
  And fain was their war-broken soldier to stay;—
But sorrow return'd with the dawning of morn,
  And the voice in my dreaming ear melted away.

T. CAMPBELL

A POISON TREE

I WAS angry with my friend:
I told my wrath, my wrath did end.
I was angry with my foe:
I told it not, my wrath did grow.

And I watered it in fears
Night and morning with my tears,
And I sunnéd it with smiles
And with soft deceitful wiles.

And it grew both day and night,
Till it bore an apple bright,
And my foe beheld it shine,
And he knew that it was mine—

And into my garden stole
When the night had veiled the pole;
In the morning, glad, I see
My foe outstretched beneath the tree.

                              W. BLAKE

WRITTEN IN EARLY SPRING

I HEARD a thousand blended notes
While in a grove I sat reclined,
In that sweet mood when pleasant thoughts
Bring sad thoughts to the mind.

To her fair works did Nature link
The human soul that through me ran;
And much it grieved my heart to think
What Man has made of Man.

Through primrose tufts, in that sweet bower,
The periwinkle trail'd its wreaths;
And 'tis my faith that every flower
Enjoys the air it breathes.

The birds around me hopp'd and play'd,
Their thoughts I cannot measure—
But the least motion which they made
It seem'd a thrill of pleasure.

The budding twigs spread out their fan
To catch the breezy air;
And I must think, do all I can,
That there was pleasure there.

If this belief from heaven be sent,
If such be Nature's holy plan,

Have I not reason to lament
What Man has made of Man?

W. WORDSWORTH

❧ 221 ☙

RUTH: OR THE INFLUENCES OF NATURE

WHEN Ruth was left half desolate
Her father took another mate;
And Ruth, not seven years old,
A slighted child, at her own will
Went wandering over dale and hill,
In thoughtless freedom, bold.

And she had made a pipe of straw,
And music from that pipe could draw
Like sounds of winds and floods;
Had built a bower upon the green,
As if she from her birth had been
An infant of the woods.

Beneath her father's roof, alone
She seem'd to live; her thoughts her own;
Herself her own delight:
Pleased with herself, nor sad nor gay.
And, passing thus the live-long day,
She grew to woman's height.

There came a youth from Georgia's shore—

A military casque he wore
With splendid feathers drest;
He brought them from the Cherokees;
The feathers nodded in the breeze
And made a gallant crest.

From Indian blood you deem him sprung:
But no! he spake the English tongue
And bore a soldier's name;
And, when America was free
From battle and from jeopardy,
He 'cross the ocean came.

With hues of genius on his cheek,
In finest tones the youth could speak:
—While he was yet a boy
The moon, the glory of the sun,
And streams that murmur as they run
Had been his dearest joy.

He was a lovely youth! I guess
The panther in the wilderness
Was not so fair as he;
And when he chose to sport and play,
No dolphin ever was so gay
Upon the tropic sea.

Among the Indians he had fought;
And with him many tales he brought
Of pleasure and of fear;
Such tales as, told to any maid

By such a youth, in the green shade,
Were perilous to hear.

He told of girls, a happy rout!
Who quit their fold with dance and shout,
Their pleasant Indian town,
To gather strawberries all day long;
Returning with a choral song
When daylight is gone down.

He spake of plants that hourly change
Their blossoms, through a boundless range
Of intermingling hues;
With budding, fading, faded flowers,
They stand the wonder of the bowers
From morn to evening dews.

He told of the Magnolia, spread
High as a cloud, high over head!
The cypress and her spire;
—Of flowers that with one scarlet gleam
Cover a hundred leagues, and seem
To set the hills on fire.

The youth of green savannahs spake,
And many an endless, endless lake
With all its fairy crowds
Of islands, that together lie
As quietly as spots of sky
Among the evening clouds.

'How pleasant,' then he said, 'it were

A fisher or a hunter there,
In sunshine or in shade
To wander with an easy mind,
And build a household fire, and find
A home in every glade!

'What days and what bright years! Ah me!
Our life were life indeed, with thee
So pass'd in quiet bliss;
And all the while,' said he, 'to know
That we were in a world of woe,
On such an earth as this!'

And then he sometimes interwove
Fond thoughts about a father's love,
'For there,' said he, 'are spun
Around the heart such tender ties,
That our own children to our eyes
Are dearer than the sun.

'Sweet Ruth! and could you go with me
My helpmate in the woods to be,
Our shed at night to rear;
Or run, my own adopted bride,
A sylvan huntress at my side,
And drive the flying deer!

'Beloved Ruth!'—No more he said.
The wakeful Ruth at midnight shed
A solitary tear:
She thought again—and did agree

With him to sail across the sea,
And drive the flying deer.

'And now, as fitting is and right,
We in the church our faith will plight,
A husband and a wife.'
Even so they did; and I may say
That to sweet Ruth that happy day
Was more than human life.

Through dream and vision did she sink,
Delighted all the while to think
That, on those lonesome floods
And green savannahs, she should share
His board with lawful joy, and bear
His name in the wild woods.

But, as you have before been told,
This Stripling, sportive, gay, and bold,
And with his dancing crest
So beautiful, through savage lands
Had roam'd about, with vagrant bands
Of Indians in the West.

The wind, the tempest roaring high,
The tumult of a tropic sky
Might well be dangerous food
For him, a youth to whom was given
So much of earth—so much of heaven,
And such impetuous blood.

Whatever in those climes he found
Irregular in sight or sound

Did to his mind impart
A kindred impulse, seem'd allied
To his own powers, and justified
The workings of his heart.

Nor less, to feed voluptuous thought,
The beauteous forms of Nature wrought,—
Fair trees and gorgeous flowers;
The breezes their own languor lent;
The stars had feelings, which they sent
Into those favour'd bowers.

Yet, in his worst pursuits, I ween
That sometimes there did intervene
Pure hopes of high intent:
For passions link'd to forms so fair
And stately, needs must have their share
Of noble sentiment.

But ill he lived, much evil saw,
With men to whom no better law
Nor better life was known;
Deliberately and undeceived
Those wild men's vices he received,
And gave them back his own.

His genius and his moral frame
Were thus impair'd, and he became
The slave of low desires:
A man who without self-control
Would seek what the degraded soul
Unworthily admires.

378

And yet he with no feign'd delight
Had woo'd the maiden, day and night
Had loved her, night and morn:
What could he less than love a maid
Whose heart with so much nature play'd—
So kind and so forlorn?

Sometimes most earnestly he said,
'O Ruth! I have been worse than dead;
False thoughts, thoughts bold and vain
Encompass'd me on every side
When I, in confidence and pride,
Had cross'd the Atlantic main.

'Before me shone a glorious world
Fresh as a banner bright, unfurl'd
To music suddenly:
I look'd upon those hills and plains,
And seem'd as if let loose from chains
To live at liberty!

'No more of this—for now, by thee,
Dear Ruth! more happily set free,
With nobler zeal I burn;
My soul from darkness is released
Like the whole sky when to the east
The morning doth return.'

Full soon that better mind was gone;
No hope, no wish remain'd, but one,—
They stirr'd him now no more;
New objects did new pleasure give,

379

And once again he wish'd to live
As lawless as before.

Meanwhile, as thus with him it fared,
They for the voyage were prepared,
And went to the seashore:
But, when they thither came, the youth
Deserted his poor bride, and Ruth
Could never find him more.

God help thee, Ruth!—Such pains she had,
That she in half a year was mad,
And in a prison housed;
And there, with many a doleful song
Made of wild words, her cup of wrong
She fearfully caroused.

Yet sometimes milder hours she knew,
Nor wanted sun, nor rain, nor dew,
Nor pastimes of the May,
—They all were with her in her cell;
And a clear brook with cheerful knell
Did o'er the pebbles play.

When Ruth three seasons thus had lain,
There came a respite to her pain;
She from her prison fled;
But of the Vagrant none took thought;
And where it liked her best she sought
Her shelter and her bread.

Among the fields she breathed again:
The master-current of her brain

Ran permanent and free;
And, coming to the banks of Tone,
There did she rest; and dwell alone
Under the greenwood tree.

The engines of her pain, the tools
That shaped her sorrow, rocks and pools,
And airs that gently stir
The vernal leaves—she loved them still,
Nor ever tax'd them with the ill
Which had been done to her.

A barn her Winter bed supplies;
But, till the warmth of Summer skies
And Summer days is gone,
(And all do in this tale agree)
She sleeps beneath the greenwood tree,
And other home hath none.

An innocent life, yet far astray!
And Ruth will, long before her day,
Be broken down and old.
Sore aches she needs must have! but less
Of mind, than body's wretchedness,
From damp, and rain, and cold.

If she is prest by want of food
She from her dwelling in the wood
Repairs to a roadside;
And there she begs at one steep place,
Where up and down with easy pace
The horsemen-travellers ride.

That oaten pipe of hers is mute
Or thrown away: but with a flute
Her loneliness she cheers;
This flute, made of a hemlock stalk,
At evening in his homeward walk
The Quantock woodman hears.

I, too, have pass'd her on the hills
Setting her little water-mills
By spouts and fountains wild—
Such small machinery as she turn'd
Ere she had wept, ere she had mourn'd,
A young and happy child!

Farewell! and when thy days are told,
Ill-fated Ruth! in hallow'd mould
Thy corpse shall buried be;
For thee a funeral bell shall ring,
And all the congregation sing
A Christian psalm for thee.

W. WORDSWORTH

❧ 222 ☙

ODE TO THE WEST WIND

O WILD West Wind, thou breath of Autumn's being,
Thou, from whose unseen presence the leaves dead
Are driven, like ghosts from an enchanter fleeing,

Yellow, and black, and pale, and hectic red,
Pestilence-stricken multitudes: O thou
Who chariotest to their dark wintry bed
The wingéd seeds, where they lie cold and low,
Each like a corpse within its grave, until
Thine azure sister of the Spring shall blow
Her clarion o'er the dreaming earth, and fill
(Driving sweet buds like flocks to feed in air)
With living hues and odours plain and hill:
Wild Spirit, which art moving everywhere;
Destroyer and Preserver; Hear, oh hear!

Thou on whose stream, 'mid the steep sky's commotion,
Loose clouds like earth's decaying leaves are shed,
Shook from the tangled boughs of Heaven and Ocean,
Angels of rain and lightning; there are spread
On the blue surface of thine airy surge,
Like the bright hair uplifted from the head
Of some fierce Maenad, ev'n from the dim verge
Of the horizon to the zenith's height—
The locks of the approaching storm. Thou dirge
Of the dying year, to which this closing night
Will be the dome of a vast sepulchre,
Vaulted with all thy congregated might
Of vapours, from whose solid atmosphere
Black rain, and fire, and hail, will burst: oh, hear!

Thou who didst waken from his summer-dreams,
The blue Mediterranean, where he lay,
Lull'd by the coil of his crystalline streams,
Beside a pumice isle in Baiae's bay,

And saw in sleep old palaces and towers
Quivering within the wave's intenser day,
All overgrown and azure moss and flowers
So sweet, the sense faints picturing them! Thou
For whose path the Atlantic's level powers
Cleave themselves into chasms, while far below
The sea-blooms and the oozy woods which wear
The sapless foliage of the ocean, know
Thy voice, and suddenly grow grey with fear
And tremble and despoil themselves: oh, hear!

If I were a dead leaf thou mightest bear;
If I were a swift cloud to fly with thee;
A wave to pant beneath thy power, and share
The impulse of thy strength, only less free
Than Thou, O uncontrollable! If even
I were as in my boyhood, and could be
The comrade of thy wanderings over heaven,
As then, when to outstrip the skyey speed
Scarce seem'd a vision, I would ne'er have striven
As thus with thee in prayer in my sore need.
Oh, lift me as a wave, a leaf, a cloud!
I fall upon the thorns of life! I bleed!
A heavy weight of hours has chain'd and bow'd
One too like thee: tameless, and swift, and proud.

Make me thy lyre, ev'n as the forest is:
What if my leaves are falling like its own!
The tumult of thy mighty harmonies
Will take from both a deep autumnal tone,
Sweet though in sadness. Be thou, Spirit fierce,

My spirit! be thou me, impetuous one!
Drive my dead thoughts over the universe
Like wither'd leaves to quicken a new birth;
And, by the incantation of this verse,
Scatter, as from an unextinguish'd hearth
Ashes and sparks, my words among mankind!
Be through my lips to unawaken'd earth
The trumpet of a prophecy! O Wind,
If Winter comes, can Spring be far behind?

P. B. SHELLEY

❧ 223 ❧

THE World is too much with us; late and soon,
Getting and spending, we lay waste our powers;
Little we see in Nature that is ours;
We have given our hearts away, a sordid boon!

This Sea that bares her bosom to the moon,
The winds that will be howling at all hours
And are up-gather'd now like sleeping flowers,
For this, for everything, we are out of tune;

It moves us not.—Great God! I'd rather be
A Pagan suckled in a creed outworn,—
So might I, standing on this pleasant lea,

Have glimpses that would make me less forlorn;
Have sight of Proteus rising from the sea;
Or hear old Triton blow his wreathéd horn.

W. WORDSWORTH

WITHIN KING'S COLLEGE CHAPEL,
CAMBRIDGE

TAX not the royal Saint with vain expense,
With ill-match'd aims the Architect who plann'd
(Albeit labouring for a scanty band
Of white-robed Scholars only) this immense

And glorious work of fine intelligence!
—Give all thou canst; high Heaven rejects the lore
Of nicely-calculated less or more:—
So deem'd the man who fashion'd for the sense

These lofty pillars, spread that branching roof
Self-poised, and scoop'd into ten thousand cells
Where light and shade repose, where music dwells

Lingering—and wandering on as loath to die;
Like thoughts whose very sweetness yieldeth proof
That they were born for immortality.

W. WORDSWORTH

YOUTH AND AGE

VERSE, a breeze 'mid blossoms straying,
Where Hope clung feeding, like a bee—
Both were mine! Life went a-maying
    With Nature, Hope, and Poesy,
     When I was young!
When I was young?—Ah, woeful when!
Ah! for the change 'twixt Now and Then!
This breathing house not built with hands,
This body that does me grievous wrong,
O'er aery cliffs and glittering sands
How lightly then it flash'd along:
Like those trim skiffs, unknown of yore,
On winding lakes and rivers wide,
That ask no aid of sail or oar,
That fear no spite of wind or tide!
Nought cared this body for wind or weather
When Youth and I lived in't together.

Flowers are lovely; Love is flower-like;
Friendship is a sheltering tree;
O! the joys, that came down shower-like,
Of Friendship, Love, and Liberty,
        Ere I was old!
Ere I was old? Ah woeful Ere,
Which tells me, Youth's no longer here!
O Youth! for years so many and sweet

'Tis known that Thou and I were one,
I'll think it but a fond conceit—
It cannot be, that Thou art gone!
Thy vesper-bell hath not yet toll'd:—
And thou wert ay a masker bold!
What strange disguise hast now put on
To make believe that thou art gone?
I see these locks in silvery slips,
This drooping gait, this alter'd size:
But Springtide blossoms on thy lips,
And tears take sunshine from thine eyes
Life is but Thought: so think I will
That Youth and I are housemates still.

Dew-drops are the gems of morning,
But the tears of mournful eve!
Where no hope is, life's a warning
That only serves to make us grieve
      When we are old:
—That only serves to make us grieve
With oft and tedious taking-leave,
Like some poor nigh-related guest
That may not rudely be dismist,
Yet hath out-stay'd his welcome while,
And tells the jest without the smile.

S. T. COLERIDGE

THE TWO APRIL MORNINGS

WE walk'd along, while bright and red
Uprose the morning sun;
And Matthew stopp'd, he look'd, and said
'The will of God be done!'

A village schoolmaster was he,
With hair of glittering grey;
As blithe a man as you could see
On a spring holiday.

And on that morning, through the grass
And by the steaming rills
We travell'd merrily, to pass
A day among the hills.

'Our work,' said I, 'was well begun;
Then, from thy breast what thought,
Beneath so beautiful a sun,
So sad a sigh has brought?'

A second time did Matthew stop;
And fixing still his eye
Upon the eastern mountain-top,
To me he made reply:

'Yon cloud with that long purple cleft
Brings fresh into my mind

A day like this, which I have left
Full thirty years behind.

'And just above yon slope of corn
Such colours, and no other,
Were in the sky, that April morn,
Of this the very brother.

'With rod and line I sued the sport
Which that sweet season gave,
And, to the churchyard come, stopp'd short
Beside my daughter's grave.

'Nine summers had she scarcely seen,
The pride of all the vale;
And then she sang:—she would have been
A very nightingale.

'Six feet in earth my Emma lay;
And yet I loved her more—
For so it seem'd,—than till that day
I e'er had loved before.

'And turning from her grave, I met
Beside the churchyard yew
A blooming Girl, whose hair was wet
With points of morning dew.

'A basket on her head she bare;
Her brow was smooth and white:
To see a child so very fair,
It was a pure delight!

'No fountain from its rocky cave

E'er tripp'd with foot so free;
She seem'd as happy as a wave
That dances on the sea.

'There came from me a sigh of pain
Which I could ill confine;
I look'd at her, and look'd again:
And did not wish her mine!'

—Matthew is in his grave, yet now
Methinks I see him stand
As that moment, with a bough
Of wilding in his hand.

W. WORDSWORTH

❧ 227 ❧

THE FOUNTAIN

A Conversation

WE talk'd with open heart, and tongue
Affectionate and true,
A pair of friends, though I was young,
And Matthew seventy-two.

We lay beneath a spreading oak,
Beside a mossy seat;
And from the turf a fountain broke
And gurgled at our feet.

'Now, Matthew!' said I, 'let us match

This water's pleasant tune
With some old border-song, or catch
That suits a summer's noon;

'Or of the church-clock and the chimes
Sing here beneath the shade
That half-mad thing of witty rhymes
Which you last April made!'

In silence Matthew lay, and eyed
The spring beneath the tree;
And thus the dear old man replied,
The grey-hair'd man of glee:

'No check, no stay, this Streamlet fears,
How merrily it goes!
'Twill murmur on a thousand years
And flow as now it flows.

'And here, on this delightful day,
I cannot choose but think
How oft, a vigorous man, I lay
Beside this fountain's brink.

'My eyes are dim with childish tears,
My heart is idly stirr'd,
For the same sound is in my ears
Which in those days I heard.

'Thus fares it still in our decay:
And yet the wiser mind
Mourns less for what Age takes away,
Than what it leaves behind.

'The blackbird amid leafy trees,
The lark above the hill,
Let loose their carols when they please,
Are quiet when they will.

'With Nature never do they wage
A foolish strife; they see
A happy youth, and their old age
Is beautiful and free:

'But we are press'd by heavy laws;
And often, glad no more,
We wear a face of joy, because
We have been glad of yore.

'If there be one who need bemoan
His kindred laid in earth,
The household hearts that were his own,—
It is the man of mirth.

'My days, my friend, are almost gone,
My life has been approved,
And many love me; but by none
Am I enough beloved.'

'Now both himself and me he wrongs,
The man who thus complains!
I live and sing my idle songs
Upon these happy plains:

'And Matthew, for thy children dead
I'll be a son to thee!'

At this he grasp'd my hand and said,
'Alas! that cannot be.'

We rose up from the fountain-side;
And down the smooth descent
Of the green sheep-track did we glide;
And through the wood we went;

And ere we came to Leonard's Rock
He sang those witty rhymes
About the crazy old church-clock,
And the bewilder'd chimes.

W. WORDSWORTH

❧ 228 ☙

THE RIVER OF LIFE

THE more we live, more brief appear
    Our life's succeeding stages:
A day to childhood seems a year,
    And years like passing ages.

The gladsome current of our youth,
    Ere passion yet disorders,
Steals lingering like a river smooth
    Along its grassy borders.

But as the careworn cheek grows wan,
    And sorrow's shafts fly thicker,
Ye Stars, that measure life to man,
    Why seem your courses quicker?

When joys have lost their bloom and breath
    And life itself is vapid,
Why, as we reach the Falls of Death,
    Feel we its tide more rapid?

It may be strange—yet who would change
    Time's course to slower speeding,
When one by one our friends have gone
    And left our bosoms bleeding?

Heaven gives our years of fading strength
    Indemnifying fleetness;
And those of youth, a seeming length,
    Proportion'd to their sweetness.

T. CAMPBELL

❧ 229 ❧

THE HUMAN SEASONS

FOUR Seasons fill the measure of the year;
There are four seasons in the mind of Man:
He has his lusty Spring, when fancy clear
Takes in all beauty with an easy span:

He has his Summer, when luxuriously
Spring's honey'd cud of youthful thought he loves
To ruminate, and by such dreaming high
Is nearest unto heaven: quiet coves

His soul has in its Autumn, when his wings

He furleth close; contented so to look
On mists in idleness—to let fair things
Pass by unheeded as a threshold brook:—

He has his Winter too of pale misfeature,
Or else he would forgo his mortal nature.

J. KEATS

❧ 230 ❧

A LAMENT

O WORLD! O Life! O Time!
On whose last steps I climb,
   Trembling at that where I had stood before;
When will return the glory of your prime?
    No more—Oh, never more!

Out of the day and night
A joy has taken flight:
   Fresh spring, and summer, and winter hoar
Move my faint heart with grief, but with delight
    No more—Oh, never more!

P. B. SHELLEY

❧ 231 ❧

My heart leaps up when I behold
A rainbow in the sky:
So was it when my life began,

So is it now I am a man,
So be it when I shall grow old
 Or let me die!
The Child is father of the Man:
And I could wish my days to be
Bound each to each by natural piety.

W. WORDSWORTH

❧ 232 ⚘

ODE ON INTIMATIONS OF IMMORTALITY FROM RECOLLECTIONS OF EARLY CHILDHOOD

THERE was a time when meadow, grove, and stream,
The earth, and every common sight
 To me did seem
 Apparell'd in celestial light,
The glory and the freshness of a dream.
It is not now as it hath been of yore;—
 Turn wheresoe'er I may,
 By night or day,
The things which I have seen I now can see no more.

 The rainbow comes and goes,
 And lovely is the rose;
 The moon doth with delight
Look round her when the heavens are bare;
 Waters on a starry night
 Are beautiful and fair;

397

The sunshine is a glorious birth;
But yet I know, where'er I go,
That there hath past away a glory from the earth.

Now, while the birds thus sing a joyous song,
And while the young lambs bound
As to the tabor's sound,
To me alone there came a thought of grief:
A timely utterance gave that thought relief,
And I again am strong.
The cataracts blow their trumpets from the steep,—
No more shall grief of mine the season wrong:
I hear the echoes through the mountains throng,
The winds come to me from the fields of sleep,
And all the earth is gay;
Land and sea
Give themselves up to jollity,
And with the heart of May
Doth every beast keep holiday;—
Thou child of joy
Shout round me, let me hear thy shouts, thou happy
Shepherd-boy!

Ye blessèd Creatures, I have heard the call
Ye to each other make; I see
The heavens laugh with you in your jubilee;
My heart is at your festival,
My head hath its coronal,
The fullness of your bliss, I feel—I feel it all.
O evil day! if I were sullen
While Earth herself is adorning

This sweet May-morning;
And the children are culling
On every side
In a thousand valleys far and wide
Fresh flowers; while the sun shines warm,
And the babe leaps up on his mother's arm:—
I hear, I hear, with joy I hear!
—But there's a tree, of many, one,
A single field which I have look'd upon,
Both of them speak of something that is gone:
The pansy at my feet
Doth the same tale repeat:
Whither is fled the visionary gleam?
Where is it now, the glory and the dream?

Our birth is but a sleep and a forgetting;
The Soul that rises with us, our life's Star,
Hath had elsewhere its setting
And cometh from afar;
Not in entire forgetfulness,
And not in utter nakedness,
But trailing clouds of glory do we come
From God, who is our home:
Heaven lies about us in our infancy!
Shades of the prison-house begin to close
Upon the growing Boy,
But he beholds the light, and whence it flows,
He sees it in his joy;
The Youth, who daily farther from the east
Must travel, still is Nature's priest,

And by the vision splendid
Is on his way attended;
At length the Man perceives it die away,
And fade into the light of common day.

Earth fills her lap with pleasures of her own;
Yearnings she hath in her own natural kind,
And, even with something of a mother's mind
And no unworthy aim,
The homely nurse doth all she can
To make her foster-child, her inmate, Man,
Forget the glories he hath known,
And that imperial palace whence he came.

Behold the Child among his new-born blisses,
A six years' darling of a pigmy size!
See, where 'mid work of his own hand he lies,
Fretted by sallies of his mother's kisses,
With light upon him from his father's eyes!
See, at his feet, some little plan or chart,
Some fragment from his dream of human life,
Shaped by himself with newly-learnéd art;
A wedding or a festival,
A mourning or a funeral;
And this hath now his heart,
And unto this he frames his song:
Then will he fit his tongue
To dialogues of business, love, or strife;
But it will not be long
Ere this be thrown aside,
And with new joy and pride

The little actor cons another part;
Filling from time to time his 'humorous stage'
With all the Persons, down to palsied Age,
That life brings with her in her equipage;
       As if his whole vocation
       Were endless imitation.

Thou, whose exterior semblance doth belie
       Thy soul's immensity;
Thou best philosopher, who yet dost keep
Thy heritage, thou eye among the blind,
That, deaf and silent, read'st the eternal deep,
Haunted for ever by the eternal Mind,—
       Mighty Prophet! Seer blest!
       On whom those truths do rest
Which we are toiling all our lives to find,
In darkness lost, the darkness of the grave;
Thou, over whom thy Immortality
Broods like a day, a master o'er a slave,
A Presence which is not to be put by;
Thou little child, yet glorious in the might
Of heaven-born freedom on thy being's height,
Why with such earnest pains dost thou provoke
The years to bring the inevitable yoke,
Thus blindly with thy blessedness at strife?
Full soon thy soul shall have her earthly freight,
And custom lies upon thee with a weight
Heavy as frost, and deep almost as life!

       O joy! that in our embers
       Is something that doth live,

That Nature yet remembers
What was so fugitive!
The thought of our past years in me doth breed
Perpetual benediction: not indeed
   For that which is most worthy to be blest,
Delight and liberty, the simple creed
Of Childhood, whether busy or at rest,
With new-fledged hope still fluttering in his breast:—
     —Not for these I raise
     The song of thanks and praise;
    But for those obstinate questionings
    Of sense and outward things,
    Fallings from us, vanishings,
    Blank misgivings of a creature
Moving about in worlds not realized,
High instincts, before which our mortal nature
Did tremble like a guilty thing surprised:
    But for those first affections,
    Those shadowy recollections,
     Which, be they what they may,
Are yet the fountain-light of all our day,
Are yet a master-light of all our seeing;
    Uphold us—cherish—and have power to make
Our noisy years seem moments in the being
Of the eternal Silence: truths that wake,
     To perish never;
Which neither listlessness, nor mad endeavour,
     Nor man nor boy,
Nor all that is at enmity with joy,
Can utterly abolish or destroy!

Hence, in a season of calm weather
        Though inland far we be,
Our souls have sight of that immortal sea
        Which brought us hither;
        Can in a moment travel thither—
And see the children sport upon the shore,
And hear the mighty waters rolling evermore.

Then, sing, ye birds, sing, sing a joyous song!
        And let the young lambs bound
        As to the tabor's sound!
We, in thought, will join your throng
        Ye that pipe and ye that play,
        Ye that through your hearts to-day
        Feel the gladness of the May!
What though the radiance which was once so bright
Be now for ever taken from my sight,
        Though nothing can bring back the hour
Of splendour in the grass, of glory in the flower;
        We will grieve not, rather find
        Strength in what remains behind;
        In the primal sympathy
        Which having been must ever be;
        In the soothing thoughts that spring
        Out of human suffering;
        In the faith that looks through death,
In years that bring the philosophic mind.

And O, ye Fountains, Meadows, Hills, and Groves,
Forbode not any severing of our loves!
Yet in my heart of hearts I feel your might;

403

I only have relinquish'd one delight
To live beneath your more habitual sway;
I love the brooks which down their channels fret
Even more than when I tripp'd lightly as they;
The innocent brightness of a new-born day
          Is lovely yet;
The clouds that gather round the setting sun
Do take a sober colouring from an eye
That hath kept watch o'er man's mortality;
Another race hath been, and other palms are won.
Thanks to the human heart by which we live,
Thanks to its tenderness, its joys, and fears,
To me the meanest flower that blows can give
Thoughts that do often lie too deep for tears.

W. WORDSWORTH

❧ 233 ❦

Music, when soft voices die,
Vibrates in the memory—
Odours, when sweet violets sicken,
Live within the sense they quicken.

Rose leaves, when the rose is dead,
Are heap'd for the beloved's bed;
And so thy thoughts, when thou art gone,
Love itself shall slumber on.

P. B. SHELLEY

BOOK FIFTH

234

IRELAND

IRELAND never was contented . . .
Say you so? you are demented.
Ireland was contented when
All could use the sword and pen,
And when Tara rose so high
That her turrets split the sky,
And about her courts were seen
Liveried Angels robed in green,
Wearing, by Saint Patrick's bounty,
Emeralds big as half a county.

W. S. LANDOR

235

ALAS! 'tis very sad to hear,
Your and your Muse's end draws near:
I only wish, if this be true,
To lie a little way from you.
The grave is cold enough for me
Without you and your poetry.

W. S. LANDOR

236

LATELY our poets loiter'd in green lanes,
Content to catch the ballads of the plains;
I fancied I had strength enough to climb
A loftier station at no distant time,
And might securely from intrusion doze
Upon the flowers thro' which Ilissus flows.
In those pale olive grounds all voices cease,
And from afar dust fills the paths of Greece.
My slumber broken and my doublet torn,
I find the laurel also bears a thorn.

W. S. LANDOR

237

DYING SPEECH OF AN OLD PHILOSOPHER

I STROVE with none, for none was worth my strife:
   Nature I loved, and, next to Nature, Art:
I warm'd both hands before the fire of Life;
   It sinks; and I am ready to depart.

W. S. LANDOR

I AM

I AM: yet what I am none cares or knows
   My friends forsake me like a memory lost,
I am the self-consumer of my woes—
   They rise and vanish in oblivious host,
Like shadows in love's frenzied, stifled throes:—
And yet I am, and live—like vapours tost

Into the nothingness of scorn and noise,
   Into the living sea of waking dreams,
Where there is neither sense of life or joys,
   But the vast shipwreck of my life's esteems;
Even the dearest, that I love the best,
Are strange—nay, rather stranger than the rest.

I long for scenes, where man hath never trod,
   A place where woman never smiled or wept—
There to abide with my Creator, God,
   And sleep as I in childhood sweetly slept,
Untroubling, and untroubled where I lie,
The grass below—above the vaulted sky.

                          J. CLARE

A VISION

I LOST the love of heaven above,
   I spurned the lust of earth below,
I felt the sweets of fancied love,
   And hell itself my only foe.

I lost earth's joys, but felt the glow
   Of heaven's flame abound in me,
Till loveliness and I did grow
   The bard of immortality.

I loved but woman fell away,
   I hid me from her faded fame,
I snatch'd the sun's eternal ray
   And wrote till earth was but a name.

In every language upon earth,
   On every shore, o'er every sea,
I gave my name immortal birth
   And kept my spirit with the free.

August 2nd, 1844

J. CLARE

THANATOPSIS

To HIM who in the love of Nature holds
Communion with her visible forms, she speaks
A various language; for his gayer hours
She has a voice of gladness, and a smile
And eloquence of beauty, and she glides
Into his darker musings, with a mild
And healing sympathy, that steals away
Their sharpness, ere he is aware. When thoughts
Of the last bitter hour come like a blight
Over thy spirit, and sad images
Of the stern agony, and shroud, and pall,
And breathless darkness, and the narrow house,
Make thee to shudder, and grow sick at heart;—
Go forth, under the open sky, and list
To Nature's teachings, while from all around—
Earth and her waters, and the depths of air—
Comes a still voice—Yet a few days, and thee
The all-beholding sun shall see no more
In all his course; nor yet in the cold ground,
Where thy pale form was laid, with many tears,
Nor in the embrace of ocean, shall exist
Thy image. Earth, that nourished thee, shall claim
Thy growth, to be resolved to earth again,
And, lost each human trace, surrendering up
Thine individual being, shalt thou go

To mix for ever with the elements,
To be a brother to the insensible rock
And to the sluggish clod, which the rude swain
Turns with his share, and treads upon. The oak
Shall send his roots abroad, and pierce thy mould.

Yet not to thine eternal resting-place
Shalt thou retire alone, nor couldst thou wish
Couch more magnificent. Thou shalt lie down
With patriarchs of the infant world—with kings,
The powerful of the earth—the wise, the good,
Fair forms, and hoary seers of ages past,
All in one mighty sepulchre. The hills
Rock-ribbed and ancient as the sun,—the vales
Stretching in pensive quietness between;
The venerable woods—rivers that move
In majesty, and the complaining brooks
That make the meadows green; and, poured round all,
Old Ocean's gray and melancholy waste,—
Are but the solemn decorations all
Of the great tomb of man. The golden sun,
The planets, all the infinite host of heaven,
Are shining on the sad abodes of death,
Through the still lapse of ages. All that tread
The globe are but a handful to the tribes
That slumber in its bosom.—Take the wings
Of morning, pierce the Barcan wilderness,
Or lose thyself in the continuous woods
Where rolls the Oregon, and hears no sound,
Save his own dashings—yet the dead are there:
And millions in those solitudes, since first

The flight of years began, have laid them down
In their last sleep—the dead reign there alone.
So shalt thou rest, and what if thou withdraw
In silence from the living, and no friend
Take note of thy departure? All that breathe
Will share thy destiny. The gay will laugh
When thou art gone, the solemn brood of care
Plod on, and each one as before will chase
His favorite phantom; yet all these shall leave
Their mirth and their employments, and shall come
And make their bed with thee. As the long train
Of ages glide away, the sons of men,
The youth in life's green spring, and he who goes
In the full strength of years, matron and maid,
The speechless babe, and the gray-headed man—
Shall one by one be gathered to thy side,
By those, who in their turn shall follow them.

So live, that when thy summons comes to join
The innumerable caravan, which moves
To that mysterious realm, where each shall take
His chamber in the silent halls of death,
Thou go not, like the quarry-slave at night,
Scourged to his dungeon, but, sustained and smoothed
By an unfaltering trust, approach thy grave,
Like one who wraps the drapery of his couch
About him, and lies down to pleasant dreams.

W. C. BRYANT

TO A WATERFOWL

WHITHER, midst falling dew,
While glow the heavens with the last steps of day,
Far, through their rosy depths, dost thou pursue
    Thy solitary way?

    Vainly the fowler's eye
Might mark thy distant flight to do thee wrong,
As, darkly seen against the crimson sky,
    Thy figure floats along.

    Seek'st thou the plashy brink
Of weedy lake, or marge of river wide,
Or where the rocking billows rise and sink
    On the chafed ocean-side?

    There is a Power whose care
Teaches thy way along that pathless coast—
The desert and illimitable air—
    Lone wandering, but not lost.

    All day thy wings have fanned,
At that far height, the cold, thin atmosphere,
Yet stoop not, weary, to the welcome land,
    Though the dark night is near.

    And soon that toil shall end;
Soon shalt thou find a summer home, and rest,

And scream among thy fellows; reeds shall bend,
    Soon, o'er thy sheltered nest.

Thou'rt gone, the abyss of heaven
Hath swallowed up thy form; yet, on my heart
Deeply has sunk the lesson thou hast given,
    And shall not soon depart.

He who, from zone to zone,
Guides through the boundless sky thy certain flight,
In the long way that I must tread alone,
    Will lead my steps aright.

W. C. BRYANT

❧ 242 ☙

TO THE FRINGED GENTIAN

THOU blossom bright with autumn dew
And colored with the heaven's own blue,
That openest when the quiet light
Succeeds the keen and frosty night—

Thou comest not when violets lean
O'er wandering brooks and springs unseen,
Or columbines, in purple dressed,
Nod o'er the ground-bird's hidden nest.

Thou waitest late and com'st alone,
When woods are bare and birds are flown,
And frosts and shortening days portend
The aged year is near his end.

Then doth thy sweet and quiet eye
Look through its fringes to the sky,
Blue—blue—as if that sky let fall
A flower from its cerulean wall.

I would that thus, when I shall see
The hour of death draw near to me,
Hope, blossoming within my heart,
May look to heaven as I depart.

W. C. BRYANT

❧ 243 ❧

MITHRIDATES

I CANNOT spare water or wine,
 Tobacco-leaf, or poppy, or rose;
From the earth-poles to the Line,
 All between that works or grows,
Every thing is kin of mine.

Give me agates for my meat;
Give me cantharids to eat;
From air and ocean bring me foods,
From all zones and altitudes;—

From all natures, sharp and slimy,
 Salt and basalt, wild and tame:
Tree and lichen, ape, sea-lion,
 Bird, and reptile, be my game.

Ivy for my fillet band;
Blinding dog-wood in my hand;
Hemlock for my sherbet cull me,
And the prussic juice to lull me;
Swing me in the upas boughs,
Vampyre-fanned, when I carouse.

Too long shut in strait and few,
Thinly dieted on dew,
I will use the world, and sift it,
To a thousand humors shift it,
As you spin a cherry.
O doleful ghosts, and goblins merry!
O all you virtues, methods, mights,
Means, appliances, delights,
Reputed wrongs and braggart rights,
Smug routine, and things allowed,
Minorities, things under cloud!
Hither! take me, use me, fill me,
Vein and artery, though ye kill me!

R. W. EMERSON

❧ 244 ❧

THE RHODORA

ON BEING ASKED, WHENCE IS THE FLOWER?

In May, when sea-winds pierced our solitudes,
I found the fresh Rhodora in the woods,

Spreading its leafless blooms in a damp nook,
To please the desert and the sluggish brook.
The purple petals, fallen in the pool,
Made the black water with their beauty gay;
Here might the red-bird come his plumes to cool,
And court the flower that cheapens his array.
Rhodora! if the sages ask thee why
This charm is wasted on the earth and sky,
Tell them, dear, that if eyes were made for seeing,
Then Beauty is its own excuse for being:
Why thou wert there, O rival of the rose!
I never thought to ask, I never knew:
But, in my simple ignorance, suppose
The self-same Power that brought me there brought you.

R. W. EMERSON

245

ODE TO BEAUTY

WHO gave thee, O Beauty,
The keys of this breast,—
Too credulous lover
Of blest and unblest?
Say, when in lapsed ages
Thee knew I of old?
Or what was the service
For which I was sold?
When first my eyes saw thee,
I found me thy thrall,

By magical drawings,
Sweet tyrant of all!
I drank at thy fountain
False waters of thirst;
Thou intimate stranger,
Thou latest and first!
Thy dangerous glances
Make women of men;
New-born, we are melting
Into nature again.

Lavish, lavish promiser,
Nigh persuading gods to err!
Guest of million painted forms,
Which in turn thy glory warms!
The frailest leaf, the mossy bark,
The acorn's cup, the raindrop's arc,
The swinging spider's silver line,
The ruby of the drop of wine,
The shining pebble of the pond,
Thou inscribest with a bond,
In thy momentary play,
Would bankrupt nature to repay.

Ah, what avails it
To hide or to shun
Whom the Infinite One
Hath granted his throne?
The heaven high over
Is the deep's lover;
The sun and sea,

Informed by thee,
Before me run
And draw me on,
Yet fly me still,
As Fate refuses
To me the heart Fate for me chooses.
Is it that my opulent soul
Was mingled from the generous whole;
Sea-valleys and the deep of skies
Furnished several supplies;
And the sands whereof I'm made
Draw me to them, self-betrayed?

I turn the proud portfolio
Which holds the grand designs
Of Salvator, of Guercino,
And Piranesi's lines.
I hear the lofty pæans
Of the masters of the shell,
Who heard the starry music
And recount the numbers well;
Olympian bards who sung
Divine Ideas below,
Which always find us young
And always keep us so.
Oft, in streets or humblest places,
I detect far-wandered graces,
Which, from Eden wide astray,
In lowly homes have lost their way.

Thee gliding through the sea of form,

Like the lightning through the storm,
Somewhat not to be possessed,
Somewhat not to be caressed,
No feet so fleet could ever find,
No perfect form could ever bind.
Thou eternal fugitive,
Hovering over all that live,
Quick and skilful to inspire
Sweet, extravagant desire,
Starry space and lily-bell
Filling with thy roseate smell,
Wilt not give the lips to taste
Of the nectar which thou hast.

All that's good and great with thee
Works in close conspiracy;
Thou hast bribed the dark and lonely
To report thy features only,
And the cold and purple morning
Itself with thoughts of thee adorning;
The leafy dell, the city mart,
Equal trophies of thine art;
E'en the flowing azure air
Thou hast touched for my despair;
And, if I languish into dreams,
Again I meet the ardent beams.
Queen of things! I dare not die
In Being's deeps past ear and eye;
Lest there I find the same deceiver
And be the sport of Fate forever.

Dread Power, but dear! if God thou be,
Unmake me quite, or give thyself to me!
R. W. EMERSON

❧ 246 ☙

GIVE ALL TO LOVE

GIVE all to love;
Obey thy heart;
Friends, kindred, days,
Estate, good-fame,
Plans, credit, and the Muse—
Nothing refuse.

'Tis a brave master;
Let it have scope:
Follow it utterly,
Hope beyond hope:
High and more high
It dives into noon,
With wing unspent,
Untold intent;
But it is a god,
Knows its own path,
And the outlets of the sky.

It was not for the mean;
It requireth courage stout,
Souls above doubt,
Valor unbending;

Such 'twill reward—
They shall return
More than they were,
And ever ascending.

Leave all for love;
Yet, hear me, yet,
One word more thy heart behoved,
One pulse more of firm endeavor—
Keep thee today,
Tomorrow, forever,
Free as an Arab
Of thy beloved.

Cling with life to the maid;
But when the surprise,
First vague shadow of surmise
Flits across her bosom young
Of a joy apart from thee,
Free be she, fancy-free;
Nor thou detain her vesture's hem,
Nor the palest rose she flung
From her summer diadem.

Though thou loved her as thyself,
As a self of purer clay,
Though her parting dims the day,
Stealing grace from all alive;
Heartily know,
When half-gods go,
The gods arrive.

R. W. EMERSON

CONCORD HYMN

By the rude bridge that arched the flood,
  Their flag to April's breeze unfurled,
Here once the embattled farmers stood,
  And fired the shot heard round the world.

The foe long since in silence slept;
  Alike the conqueror silent sleeps;
And Time the ruined bridge has swept
  Down the dark stream that seaward creeps.

On this green bank, by this soft stream,
  We set to-day a votive stone;
That memory may their deed redeem,
  When, like our sires, our sons are gone.

Spirit, that made those heroes dare
  To die, and leave their children free,
Bid Time and Nature gently spare
  The shaft we raise to them and thee.

R. W. EMERSON

BIANCA AMONG THE NIGHTINGALES

I

THE cypress stood up like a church
    That night we felt our love would hold,
And saintly moonlight seemed to search
    And wash the whole world clean as gold;
The olives crystallized the vales'
    Broad slopes until the hills grew strong:
The fireflies and the nightingales
    Throbbed each to either, flame and song.
The nightingales, the nightingales.

II

Upon the angle of its shade
    The cypress stood, self-balanced high;
Half up, half down, as double-made,
    Along the ground, against the sky.
And *we*, too! from such soul-height went
    Such leaps of blood, so blindly driven,
We scarce knew if our nature meant
    Most passionate earth or intense heaven.
The nightingales, the nightingales.

III

We paled with love, we shook with love,
    We kissed so close we could not vow;
Till Giulio whispered, 'Sweet, above
    God's Ever guarantees this Now.'
And through his words the nightingales
    Drove straight and full their long clear call,
Like arrows through heroic mails,
    And love was awful in it all.
The nightingales, the nightingales.

IV

O cold white moonlight of the north,
    Refresh these pulses, quench this hell!
O coverture of death drawn forth
    Across this garden-chamber . . . well!
But what have nightingales to do
    In gloomy England, called the free.
(Yes, free to die in! . . .) when we two
    Are sundered, singing still to me?
And still they sing, the nightingales.

V

I think I hear him, how he cried
    'My own soul's life' between their notes.
Each man has but one soul supplied,
    And that's immortal. Though his throat's
On fire with passion now, to *her*

He can't say what to me he said!
And yet he moves her, they aver.
  The nightingales sing through my head.
The nightingales, the nightingales.

VI

He says to *her* what moves her most.
  He would not name his soul within
Her hearing,—rather pays her cost
  With praises to her lips and chin.
Man has but one soul, 'tis ordained,
  And each soul but one love, I add;
Yet souls are damned and love's profaned.
  These nightingales will sing me mad!
The nightingales, the nightingales.

I marvel how the birds can sing.
  There's little difference, in their view,
Betwixt our Tuscan trees that spring
  As vital flames into the blue,
And dull round blots of foliage meant
  Like saturated sponges here
To suck the fogs up. As content
  Is *he* too in this land, 'tis clear.
And still they sing, the nightingales.

My native Florence! dear, forgone!

I see across the Alpine ridge
How the last feast-day of Saint John
   Shot rockets from Carraia bridge.
The luminous city, tall with fire,
   Trod deep down in that river of ours,
While many a boat with lamp and choir
   Skimmed birdlike over glittering towers.
I will not hear these nightingales.

IX

I seem to float, *we* seem to float
   Down Arno's stream in festive guise;
A boat strikes flame into our boat,
   And up that lady seems to rise
As then she rose. The shock had flashed
   A vision on us! What a head,
What leaping eyeballs!—beauty dashed
   To splendour by a sudden dread.
And still they sing, the nightingales.

X

Too bold to sin, too weak to die;
   Such women are so. As for me,
I would we had drowned there, he and I,
   That moment, loving perfectly.
He had not caught her with her loosed
   Gold ringlets . . . rarer in the south . . .
Nor heard the 'Grazie tanto' bruised
   To sweetness by her English mouth.
And still they sing, the nightingales.

XI

She had not reached him at my heart
   With her fine tongue, as snakes indeed
Kill flies; nor had I, for my part,
   Yearned after, in my desperate need,
And followed him as he did her
   To coasts left bitter by the tide,
Whose very nightingales, elsewhere
   Delighting, torture and deride!
For still they sing, the nightingales.

XII

A worthless woman! mere cold clay
   As all false things are! but so fair,
She takes the breath of men away
   Who gaze upon her unaware.
I would not play her larcenous tricks
   To have her looks! She lied and stole,
And spat into my love's pure pyx
   The rank saliva of her soul.
And still they sing, the nightingales.

XIII

I would not for her white and pink,
   Though such he likes—her grace of limb,
Though such he has praised—nor yet, I think,
   For life itself, though spent with him,
Commit such sacrilege, affront

429

God's nature which is love, intrude
'Twixt two affianced souls, and hunt
    Like spiders, in the altar's wood.
I cannot bear these nightingales.

XIV

If she chose sin, some gentler guise
    She might have sinned in, so it seems:
She might have pricked out both my eyes,
    And I still seen him in my dreams!
—Or drugged me in my soup or wine,
    Nor left me angry afterward:
To die here with his hand in mine
    His breath upon me, were not hard.
(Our Lady hush these nightingales!)

XV

But set a springe for *him*, 'mio ben',
    My only good, my first last love!—
Though Christ knows well what sin is, when
    He sees some things done they must move
Himself to wonder. Let her pass.
    I think of her by night and day.
Must *I* too join her . . . out, alas! . . .
    With Giulio, in each word I say!
And evermore the nightingales!

XVI

Giulio, my Giulio!—sing they so,

And you be silent? Do I speak,
And you not hear? An arm you throw
    Round some one, and I feel so weak?
—Oh, owl-like birds! They sing for spite,
    They sing for hate, they sing for doom!
They'll sing through death who sing through
        night,
    They'll sing and stun me in the tomb—
The nightingales, the nightingales!

E. B. BROWNING

❧ 249 ❦

IF THOU must love me, let it be for naught
Except for love's sake only. Do not say
'I love her for her smile . . . her look . . . her way
Of speaking gently, . . . for a trick of thought
That falls in well with mine, and certes brought
A sense of pleasant ease on such a day'—
For these things in themselves, Belovéd, may
Be changed, or change for thee,—and love, so wrought,
May be unwrought so. Neither love me for
Thine own dear pity's wiping my cheeks dry,—
A creature might forget to weep, who bore
Thy comfort long, and lose thy love thereby!
But love me for love's sake, that evermore
Thou may'st love on, through love's eternity.

E. B. BROWNING

How do I love thee? Let me count the ways.
I love thee to the depth and breadth and height
My soul can reach, when feeling out of sight
For the ends of Being and ideal Grace.
I love thee to the level of everyday's
Most quiet need, by sun and candlelight.
I love thee freely, as men strive for Right;
I love thee purely, as they turn from Praise,
I love thee with the passion put to use
In my old griefs, and with my childhood's faith.
I love thee with a love I seemed to lose
With my lost saints,—I love thee with the breath,
Smiles, tears, of all my life!—and, if God choose,
I shall but love thee better after death.

E. B. BROWNING

THE SKELETON IN ARMOR

"SPEAK! speak! thou fearful guest!
  Who, with thy hollow breast
  Still in rude armor drest,
    Comest to daunt me!
  Wrapt not in Eastern balms,
  But with thy fleshless palms

Stretched, as if asking alms,
   Why dost thou haunt me?"

Then, from those cavernous eyes
Pale flashes seemed to rise,
As when the Northern skies
   Gleam in December;
And, like the water's flow
Under December's snow,
Came a dull voice of woe
   From the heart's chamber.

"I was a Viking old!
My deeds, though manifold,
No Skald in song has told,
   No Saga taught thee!
Take heed, that in thy verse
Thou dost the tale rehearse,
Else dread a dead man's curse;
   For this I sought thee.

"Far in the Northern Land,
By the wild Baltic's strand,
I, with my childish hand,
   Tamed the gerfalcon;
And, with my skates fast-bound,
Skimmed the half-frozen Sound,
That the poor whimpering hound
   Trembled to walk on.

"Oft to his frozen lair

Tracked I the grisly bear,
While from my path the hare
  Fled like a shadow;
Oft through the forest dark
Followed the were-wolf's bark,
Until the soaring lark
  Sang from the meadow.

"But when I older grew,
 Joining a corsair's crew,
 O'er the dark sea I flew
   With the marauders.
 Wild was the life we led;
 Many the souls that sped,
 Many the hearts that bled,
   By our stern orders.

"Many a wassail-bout
 Wore the long Winter out;
 Often our midnight shout
   Set the cocks crowing,
 As we the Berserk's tale
 Measured in cups of ale,
 Draining the oaken pail,
   Filled to o'erflowing.

"Once as I told in glee
 Tales of the stormy sea,
 Soft eyes did gaze on me,
   Burning yet tender;
 And as the white stars shine

On the dark Norway pine,
On that dark heart of mine
   Fell their soft splendor.

"I wooed the blue-eyed maid,
Yielding, yet half afraid,
And in the forest's shade
   Our vows were plighted.
Under its loosened vest
Fluttered her little breast,
Like birds within their nest
   By the hawk frighted.

"Bright in her father's hall
Shields gleamed upon the wall,
Loud sang the minstrels all,
   Chanting his glory;
When of old Hildebrand
I asked his daughter's hand,
Mute did the minstrels stand
   To hear my story.

"While the brown ale he quaffed,
Loud then the champion laughed,
And as the wind-gusts waft
   The sea-foam brightly,
So the loud laugh of scorn,
Out of those lips unshorn,
From the deep drinking-horn
   Blew the foam lightly.

"She was a Prince's child,
  I but a Viking wild,
  And though she blushed and smiled,
    I was discarded!
  Should not the dove so white
  Follow the sea-mew's flight,
  Why did they leave that night
    Her nest unguarded?

"Scarce had I put to sea,
  Bearing the maid with me,
  Fairest of all was she
    Among the Norsemen!
  When on the White sea-strand,
  Waving his armèd hand,
  Saw we old Hildebrand,
    With twenty horsemen.

"Then launched they to the blast,
  Bent like a reed each mast,
  Yet we were gaining fast,
    When the wind failed us;
  And with a sudden flaw
  Came round the gusty Skaw,
  So that our foe we saw
    Laugh as he hailed us.

"And as to catch the gale
  Round veered the flapping sail,
  'Death!' was the helmsman's hail,
    'Death without quarter!'

Mid-ships with iron keel
Struck we her ribs of steel;
Down her black hulk did reel
    Through the black water!

"As with his wings aslant,
Sails the fierce cormorant,
Seeking some rocky haunt,
    With his prey laden,—
So toward the open main,
Beating to sea again,
Through the wild hurricane,
    Bore I the maiden.

"Three weeks we westward bore,
And when the storm was o'er,
Cloud-like we saw the shore
    Stretching to leeward;
There for my lady's bower
Built I the lofty tower,
Which, to this very hour,
    Stands looking seaward.

"There lived we many years;
Time dried the maiden's tears;
She had forgot her fears,
    She was a mother;
Death closed her mild blue eyes,
Under that tower she lies;
Ne'er shall the sun arise
    On such another!

"Still grew my bosom then,
  Still as a stagnant fen!
Hateful to me were men,
  The sunlight hateful!
In the vast forest here,
Clad in my warlike gear,
Fell I upon my spear,
  Oh, death was grateful!

"Thus, seamed with many scars,
Bursting these prison bars,
Up to its native stars
  My soul ascended!
There from the flowing bowl
Deep drinks the warrior's soul,
Skoal! to the Northland! *skoal!*"
  Thus the tale ended.

H. W. LONGFELLOW

❧ 252 ☙

IN THE CHURCHYARD AT CAMBRIDGE

IN THE village churchyard she lies,
Dust is in her beautiful eyes,
  No more she breathes, nor feels, nor stirs;
At her feet and at her head
Lies a slave to attend the dead,
  But their dust is white as hers.

438

Was she, a lady of high degree,
So much in love with the vanity
    And foolish pomp of this world of ours?
Or was it Christian charity,
And lowliness and humility,
    The richest and rarest of all dowers?

Who shall tell us? No one speaks;
No color shoots into those cheeks,
    Either of anger or of pride,
At the rude question we have asked;
Nor will the mystery be unmasked
    By those who are sleeping at her side.

Hereafter?—And do you think to look
On the terrible page of that Book
    To find her failings, faults, and errors?
Ah, you will then have other cares,
In your own shortcomings and despairs,
    In your own secret sins and terrors!

H. W. LONGFELLOW

❧ 253 ☙

THE JEWISH CEMETERY AT NEWPORT

How strange it seems! These Hebrews in their graves,
    Close by the street of this fair seaport town,
Silent beside the never-silent waves,
    At rest in all this moving up and down!

The trees are white with dust, that o'er their sleep
    Wave their broad curtains in the southwind's breath,
While underneath these leafy tents they keep
    The long, mysterious Exodus of Death.

And these sepulchral stones, so old and brown,
    That pave with level flags their burial-place,
Seem like the tablets of the Law, thrown down
    And broken by Moses at the mountain's base.

The very names recorded here are strange,
    Of foreign accent, and of different climes;
Alvares and Rivera interchange
    With Abraham and Jacob of old times.

"Blessed be God, for he created Death!"
    The mourners said, "and Death is rest and peace;"
Then added, in the certainty of faith,
    "And giveth Life that nevermore shall cease."

Closed are the portals of their Synagogue,
    No Psalms of David now the silence break,
No Rabbi reads the ancient Decalogue
    In the grand dialect the Prophets spake.

Gone are the living, but the dead remain,
    And not neglected; for a hand unseen,
Scattering its bounty, like a summer rain,
    Still keeps their graves and their remembrance green.

How came they here? What burst of Christian hate,
    What persecution, merciless and blind,

Drove o'er the sea—that desert desolate—
  These Ishmaels and Hagars of mankind?

They lived in narrow streets and lanes obscure,
  Ghetto and Judenstrass, in mirk and mire;
Taught in the school of patience to endure
  The life of anguish and the death of fire.

All their lives long, with the unleavened bread
  And bitter herbs of exile and its fears,
The wasting famine of the heart they fed,
  And slaked its thirst with marah of their tears.

Anathema maranatha! was the cry
  That rang from town to town, from street to street:
At every gate the accursed Mordecai
  Was mocked and jeered, and spurned by Christian feet.

Pride and humiliation hand in hand
  Walked with them through the world where'er they went;
Trampled and beaten were they as the sand,
  And yet unshaken as the continent.

For in the background figures vague and vast
  Of patriarchs and of prophets rose sublime,
And all the great traditions of the Past
  They saw reflected in the coming time.

And thus forever with reverted look
  The mystic volume of the world they read,
Spelling it backward, like a Hebrew book,
  Till life became a Legend of the Dead.

But ah! what once has been shall be no more!
    The groaning earth in travail and in pain
Brings forth its races, but does not restore,
    And the dead nations never rise again.

H. W. LONGFELLOW

❧ 254 ☙

MY LOST YOUTH

OFTEN I think of the beautiful town
    That is seated by the sea;
Often in thought go up and down
The pleasant streets of that dear old town,
    And my youth comes back to me.
        And a verse of a Lapland song
        Is haunting my memory still:
        "A boy's will is the wind's will,
And the thoughts of youth are long, long thoughts."

I can see the shadowy lines of its trees,
    And catch, in sudden gleams,
The sheen of the far-surrounding seas,
And islands that were the Hesperides
    Of all my boyish dreams.
        And the burden of that old song,
        It murmurs and whispers still:
        "A boy's will is the wind's will,
And the thoughts of youth are long, long thoughts."

I remember the black wharves and the slips,
　　And the sea-tides tossing free;
And Spanish sailors with bearded lips,
And beauty and mystery of the ships,
　　And the magic of the sea.
　　　　And the voice of that wayward song
　　　　Is singing and saying still:
　　　　"A boy's will is the wind's will,
And the thoughts of youth are long, long thoughts."

I remember the bulwarks by the shore,
　　And the fort upon the hill;
The sunrise gun, with its hollow roar,
The drum-beat repeated o'er and o'er,
　　And the bugle wild and shrill.
　　　　And the music of that old song
　　　　Throbs in my memory still:
　　　　"A boy's will is the wind's will,
And the thoughts of youth are long, long thoughts."

I remember the sea-fight far away,
　　How it thundered o'er the tide!
And the dead captains, as they lay
In their graves, o'erlooking the tranquil bay
　　Where they in battle died.
　　　　And the sound of that mournful song
　　　　Goes through me with a thrill:
　　　　"A boy's will is the wind's will,
And the thoughts of youth are long, long thoughts."

I can see the breezy dome of groves,
    The shadows of Deering's Woods;
And the friendships old and the early loves
Come back with a Sabbath sound, as of doves
    In quiet neighborhoods.
       And the verse of that sweet old song,
       It flutters and murmurs still:
       "A boy's will is the wind's will,
And the thoughts of youth are long, long thoughts."

I remember the gleams and glooms that dart
    Across the school-boy's brain;
The song and the silence in the heart,
That in part are prophecies, and in part
    Are longings wild and vain.
       And the voice of that fitful song
       Sings on, and is never still:
       "A boy's will is the wind's will,
And the thoughts of youth are long, long thoughts."

There are things of which I may not speak;
    There are dreams that cannot die;
There are thoughts that make the strong heart weak,
And bring a pallor into the cheek,
    And a mist before the eye.
       And the words of that fatal song
       Come over me like a chill:
       "A boy's will is the wind's will,
And the thoughts of youth are long, long thoughts."

Strange to me now are the forms I meet

When I visit the dear old town;
But the native air is pure and sweet,
And the trees that o'ershadow each well-known street,
   As they balance up and down
      Are singing the beautiful song,
      Are sighing and whispering still:
      "A boy's will is the wind's will,
And the thoughts of youth are long, long thoughts."

And Deering's Woods are fresh and fair,
   And with joy that is almost pain
My heart goes back to wander there,
And among the dreams of the days that were,
   I find my lost youth again.
      And the strange and beautiful song,
      The groves are repeating it still:
      "A boy's will is the wind's will,
And the thoughts of youth are long, long thoughts."

                     H. W. LONGFELLOW

255

EVANGELINE

A TALE OF ACADIE
PRELUDE

THIS is the forest primeval. The murmuring pines and the
   hemlocks,
Bearded with moss, and in garments green, indistinct in
   the twilight,

Stand like Druids of eld, with voices sad and prophetic,
Stand like harpers hoar, with beards that rest on their
bosoms.
Loud from its rocky caverns, the deep-voiced neighboring
ocean
Speaks, and in accents disconsolate answers the wail of the
forest.

This is the forest primeval; but where are the hearts that
beneath it
Leaped like the roe, when he hears in the woodland the
voice of the huntsman?
Where is the thatch-roofed village, the home of Acadian
farmers—
Men whose lives glided on like rivers that water the wood-
lands,
Darkened by shadows of earth, but reflecting an image of
heaven?
Waste are those pleasant farms, and the farmers forever
departed!
Scattered like dust and leaves, when the mighty blasts of
October
Seize them, and whirl them aloft, and sprinkle them far
o'er the ocean.
Naught but tradition remains of the beautiful village of
Grand-Pré.

Ye who believe in affection that hopes, and endures, and
is patient,
Ye who believe in the beauty and strength of woman's
devotion,

List to the mournful tradition still sung by the pines of the
    forest;
List to a Tale of Love in Acadie, home of the happy.

I

In the Acadian land, on the shores of the Basin of Minas,
Distant, secluded, still, the little village of Grand-Pré
Lay in the fruitful valley. Vast meadows stretched to the
    eastward,
Giving the village its name, and pasture to flocks without
    number.
Dikes, that the hands of the farmers had raised with labor
    incessant,
Shut out the turbulent tides; but at stated seasons the
    flood-gates
Opened and welcomed the sea to wander at will o'er the
    meadows.
West and south there were fields of flax, and orchards and
    cornfields
Spreading afar and unfenced o'er the plain; and away to
    the northward
Blomidon rose, and the forests old, and aloft on the moun-
    tains
Sea-fogs pitched their tents, and mists from the mighty
    Atlantic
Looked on the happy valley, but ne'er from their station
    descended.
There, in the midst of its farms, reposed the Acadian
    village.

447

Strongly built were the houses, with frames of oak and of
    hemlock,
Such as the peasants of Normandy built in the reign of the
    Henries.
Thatched were the roofs, with dormer windows; and gables
    projecting
Over the basement below protected and shaded the door-
    way.
There in the tranquil evenings of summer, when brightly
    the sunset
Lighted the village street, and gilded the vanes on the
    chimneys,
Matrons and maidens sat in snow-white caps and in kirtles
Scarlet and blue and green, with distaffs spinning the golden
Flax for the gossiping looms, whose noisy shuttles within
    doors
Mingled their sound with the whir of the wheels and the
    songs of the maidens.
Solemnly down the street came the parish priest, and the
    children
Paused in their play to kiss the hand he extended to bless
    them.
Reverend walked he among them; and up rose matrons
    and maidens,
Hailing his slow approach with words of affectionate wel-
    come.
Then came the laborers home from the field, and serenely
    the sun sank
Down to his rest, and twilight prevailed. Anon from the
    belfry

448

Softly the Angelus sounded, and over the roofs of the village
Columns of pale blue smoke, like clouds of incense ascending,
Rose from a hundred hearths, the homes of peace and contentment.
Thus dwelt together in love these simple Acadian farmers—
Dwelt in the love of God and of man. Alike were they free from
Fear, that reigns with the tyrant, and envy, the vice of republics.
Neither locks had they to their doors, nor bars to their windows;
But their dwellings were open as day and the hearts of the owners;
There the richest was poor, and the poorest lived in abundance.

Somewhat apart from the village, and nearer the Basin of Minas,
Benedict Bellefontaine, the wealthiest farmer of Grand-Pré,
Dwelt on his goodly acres; and with him, directing his household,
Gentle Evangeline lived, his child, and the pride of the village.
Stalworth and stately in form was the man of seventy winters;
Hearty and hale was he, an oak that is covered with snow-flakes;

White as the snow were his locks, and his cheeks as brown
as the oak leaves.
Fair was she to behold, that maiden of seventeen summers;
Black were her eyes as the berry that grows on the thorn
by the wayside,
Black, yet how softly they gleamed beneath the brown
shade of her tresses!
Sweet was her breath as the breath of kine that feed in
the meadows.
When in the harvest heat she bore to the reapers at noon-
tide
Flagons of home brewed ale, ah! fair in sooth was the
maiden.
Fairer was she when, on Sunday morn, while the bell from
its turret
Sprinkled with holy sounds the air, as the priest with his
hyssop
Sprinkles the congregation, and scatters blessings upon
them,
Down the long street she passed, with her chaplet of beads
and her missal,
Wearing her Norman cap, and her kirtle of blue, and the
earrings
Brought in the olden time from France, and since, as an
heirloom,
Handed down from mother to child, through long generations.
But a celestial brightness—a more ethereal beauty—
Shone on her face and encircled her form, when, after
confession,

Homeward serenely she walked with God's benediction
  upon her.
When she had passed, it seemed like the ceasing of exquisite music.

Firmly builded with rafters of oak, the house of the farmer
Stood on the side of a hill commanding the sea; and a
  shady
Sycamore grew by the door, with a woodbine wreathing
  around it.
Rudely carved was the porch, with seats beneath; and a
  footpath
Led through an orchard wide, and disappeared in the
  meadow.
Under the sycamore tree were hives overhung by a pent-
  house,
Such as the traveler sees in regions remote by the road-
  side,
Built o'er a box for the poor, or the blessed image of
  Mary.
Farther down, on the slope of the hill, was the well with
  its moss-grown
Bucket, fastened with iron, and near it a trough for the
  horses.
Shielding the house from storms, on the north, were the
  barns and the farmyard.
There stood the broad-wheeled wains and the antique
  ploughs and the harrows;
There were the folds for the sheep; and there, in his fea-
  thered seraglio,

Strutted the lordly turkey, and crowed the cock, with the selfsame
Voice that in ages of old had startled the penitent Peter.
Bursting with hay were the barns, themselves a village. In each one
Far o'er the gable projected a roof of thatch; and a staircase,
Under the sheltering eaves, led up to the odorous cornloft.
There too the dovecot stood, with its meek and innocent inmates
Murmuring ever of love; while above in the variant breezes
Numberless noisy weathercocks rattled and sang of mutation.

Thus, at peace with God and the world, the farmer of Grand-Pré
Lived on his sunny farm, and Evangeline governed his household.
Many a youth, as he knelt in the church and opened his missal,
Fixed his eyes upon her as the saint of his deepest devotion;
Happy was he who might touch her hand or the hem of her garment!
Many a suitor came to her door, by the darkness befriended,
And, as he knocked and waited to hear the sounds of her footsteps,

Knew not which beat the louder, his heart or the knocker
of iron;
Or, at the joyous feast of the Patron Saint of the village,
Bolder grew, and pressed her hand in the dance as he
whispered
Hurried words of love, that seemed a part of the music.
But among all who came, young Gabriel only was wel-
come;
Gabriel Lajeunesse, the son of Basil the blacksmith,
Who was a mighty man in the village, and honored of all
men;
For since the birth of time, throughout all ages and na-
tions,
Has the craft of the smith been held in repute by the
people.
Basil was Benedict's friend. Their children from earliest
childhood
Grew up together as brother and sister; and Father
Felician,
Priest and pedagogue both in the village, had taught them
their letters
Out of the selfsame book with the hymns of the church
and the plainsong.
But when the hymn was sung, and the daily lesson com-
pleted,
Swiftly they hurried away to the forge of Basil the black-
smith.
There at the door they stood, with wondering eyes to be-
hold him

Take in his leathern lap the hoof of the horse as a play-
thing,
Nailing the shoe in its place; while near him the tire of the
cart wheel
Lay like a fiery snake, coiled round in a circle of cinders.
Oft on autumnal eves, when without in the gathering dark-
ness
Bursting with light seemed the smithy, through every
cranny and crevice,
Warm by the forge within they watched the laboring bel-
lows,
And as its panting ceased, and the sparks expired in the
ashes,
Merrily laughed, and said they were nuns going into the
chapel.
Oft on sledges in winter, as swift as the swoop of the
eagle,
Down the hillside bounding, they glided away o'er the
meadow.
Oft in the barns they climbed to the populous nests on the
rafters,
Seeking with eager eyes that wondrous stone, which the
swallow
Brings from the shore of the sea to restore the sight of its
fledglings;
Lucky was he who found that stone in the nest of the swallow!
Thus passed a few swift years, and they no longer were
children.

He was a valiant youth, and his face, like the face of the
    morning,
Gladdened the earth with its light, and ripened thought
    into action.
She was a woman now, with the heart and hopes of a
    woman.
"Sunshine of Saint Eulalie" was she called; for that was
    the sunshine
Which, as the farmers believed, would load their orchards
    with apples;
She too would bring to her husband's house delight and
    abundance,
Filling it full of love and the ruddy faces of children.

II

Now had the season returned, when the nights grow colder
    and longer,
And the retreating sun the sign of the Scorpion enters.
Birds of passage sailed through the leaden air, from the
    ice-bound,
Desolate northern bays to the shores of tropical islands.
Harvests were gathered in; and wild with the winds of
    September
Wrestled the trees of the forest, as Jacob of old with the
    angel.
All the signs foretold a winter long and inclement.
Bees, with prophetic instinct of want, had hoarded their
    honey
Till the hives overflowed; and the Indian hunters asserted

Cold would the winter be, for thick was the fur of the
foxes.
Such was the advent of autumn. Then followed that
beautiful season,
Called by the pious Acadian peasants the Summer of All-
Saints!
Filled was the air with a dreamy and magical light; and
the landscape
Lay as if new-created in all the freshness of childhood.
Peace seemed to reign upon earth, and the restless heart of
the ocean
Was for a moment consoled. All sounds were in harmony
blended.
Voices of children at play, the crowing of cocks in the
farmyards,
Whir of wings in the drowsy air, and the cooing of
pigeons,
All were subdued and low as the murmurs of love, and the
great sun
Looked with the eye of love through the golden vapors
around him;
While arrayed in its robes of russet and scarlet and
yellow,
Bright with the sheen of the dew, each glittering tree of
the forest
Flashed like the plane tree the Persian adorned with
mantles and jewels.

Now recommenced the reign of rest and affection and
stillness.

Day with its burden and heat had departed, and twilight
  descending
Brought back the evening star to the sky, and the herds to
  the homestead.
Pawing the ground they came, and resting their necks on
  each other,
And with their nostrils distended inhaling the freshness of
  evening.
Foremost, bearing the bell, Evangeline's beautiful heifer,
Proud of her snow-white hide, and the ribbon that waved
  from her collar,
Quietly paced and slow, as if conscious of human affec-
  tion.
Then came the shepherd back with his bleating flocks
  from the seaside,
Where was their favorite pasture. Behind them followed
  the watchdog,
Patient, full of importance, and grand in the pride of his
  instinct,
Walking from side to side with a lordly air, and superbly
Waving his bushy tail, and urging forward the stragglers;
Regent of flocks was he when the shepherd slept; their
  protector,
When from the forest at night, through the starry silence
  the wolves howled.
Late, with the rising moon, returned the wains from the
  marshes,
Laden with briny hay, that filled the air with its odor.
Cheerily neighed the steeds, with dew on their manes and
  their fetlocks,

While aloft on their shoulders the wooden and ponderous
    saddles,
Painted with brilliant dyes, and adorned with tassels of
    crimson,
Nodded in bright array, like hollyhocks heavy with blos-
    soms.
Patiently stood the cows meanwhile, and yielded their ud-
    ders
Unto the milkmaid's hand; whilst loud and in regular
    cadence
Into the sounding pails the foaming streamlets descended.
Lowing of cattle and peals of laughter were heard in the
    farmyard,
Echoed back by the barns. Anon they sank into stillness;
Heavily closed, with a jarring sound, the valves of the
    barn doors,
Rattled the wooden bars, and all for a season was silent.

Indoors, warm by the wide-mouthed fireplace, idly the
    farmer
Sat in his elbow chair, and watched how the flames and
    the smoke wreaths
Struggled together like foes in a burning city. Behind him,
Nodding and mocking along the wall, with gestures fan-
    tastic,
Darted his own huge shadow, and vanished away into
    darkness.
Faces, clumsily carved in oak, on the back of his armchair
Laughed in the flickering light; and the pewter plates on
    the dresser

Caught and reflected the flame, as shields of armies the sunshine.
Fragments of song the old man sang, and carols of Christmas,
Such as at home, in the olden time, his fathers before him
Sang in their Norman orchards and bright Burgundian vineyards.
Close at her father's side was the gentle Evangeline seated,
Spinning flax for the loom that stood in the corner behind her.
Silent awhile were its treadles, at rest was its diligent shuttle,
While the monotonous drone of the wheel, like the drone of a bagpipe,
Followed the old man's song, and united the fragments together.
As in a church, when the chant of the choir at intervals ceases,
Footfalls are heard in the aisles, or words of the priest at the altar,
So, in each pause of the song, with measured motion the clock clicked.

Thus as they sat, there were footsteps heard, and, suddenly lifted,
Sounded the wooden latch, and the door swung back on its hinges.
Benedict knew by the hobnailed shoes it was Basil the blacksmith,

And by her beating heart Evangeline knew who was with
him.

"Welcome!" the farmer exclaimed, as their footsteps
paused on the threshold,

"Welcome, Basil, my friend! Come, take thy place on the
settle

Close by the chimneyside, which is always empty without
thee;

Take from the shelf overhead thy pipe and the box of
tobacco;

Never so much thyself art thou as when, through the curling

Smoke of the pipe or the forge, thy friendly and jovial
face gleams

Round and red as the harvest moon through the mist of
the marshes."

Then, with a smile of content, thus answered Basil the
blacksmith,

Taking with easy air the accustomed seat by the fireside:

"Benedict Bellefontaine, thou hast ever thy jest and thy
ballad!

Ever in cheerfulest mood art thou, when others are filled
with

Gloomy forebodings of ill, and see only ruin before them.

Happy art thou, as if every day thou hadst picked up a
horseshoe."

Pausing a moment, to take the pipe that Evangeline
brought him,

And with a coal from the embers had lighted, he slowly
continued:

"Four days now are passed since the English ships at their
  anchors
Ride in the Gaspereau's mouth, with their cannon pointed
  against us.
What their design may be is unknown; but all are com-
  manded
On the morrow to meet in the church, where his Majesty's
  mandate
Will be proclaimed as law in the land. Alas! in the mean-
  time
Many surmises of evil alarm the hearts of the people."
Then made answer the farmer: "Perhaps some friendlier
  purpose
Brings these ships to our shores. Perhaps the harvests in
  England
By untimely rains or untimelier heat have been blighted,
And from our bursting barns they would feed their cattle
  and children."
"Not so thinketh the folk in the village," said warmly the
  blacksmith,
Shaking his head as in doubt; then, heaving a sigh, he
  continued:
"Louisburg is not forgotten, nor Beau Séjour, nor Port
  Royal.
Many already have fled to the forest, and lurk on its out-
  skirts,
Waiting with anxious hearts the dubious fate of tomorrow.
Arms have been taken from us, and warlike weapons of
  all kinds;

Nothing is left but the blacksmith's sledge and the scythe
  of the mower."
Then with a pleasant smile made answer the jovial farmer:
"Safer are we unarmed, in the midst of our flocks and our
  cornfields,
Safer within these peaceful dikes, besieged by the ocean,
Than our fathers in forts, besieged by the enemy's cannon.
Fear no evil, my friend, and tonight may no shadow of
  sorrow
Fall on this house and hearth; for this is the night of the
  contract.
Built are the house and the barn. The merry lads of the
  village
Strongly have built them and well; and, breaking the glebe
  round about them,
Filled the barn with hay, and the house with food for a
  twelvemonth.
René Leblanc will be here anon, with his papers and ink-
  horn.
Shall we not then be glad, and rejoice in the joy of our
  children?"
As apart by the window she stood, with her hand in her
  lover's,
Blushing Evangeline heard the words that her father had
  spoken,
And, as they died on his lips, the worthy notary entered.

III

Bent like a laboring oar, that toils in the surf of the ocean,

Bent, but not broken, by age was the form of the notary
  public;
Shocks of yellow hair, like the silken floss of the maize,
  hung
Over his shoulders; his forehead was high; and glasses
  with horn bows
Sat astride on his nose, with a look of wisdom supernal.
Father of twenty children was he, and more than a hun-
  dred
Children's children rode on his knee, and heard his great
  watch tick.
Four long years in the times of the war had he languished
  a captive,
Suffering much in an old French fort as the friend of the
  English.
Now, though warier grown, without all guile or suspicion,
Ripe in wisdom was he, but patient, and simple, and
  childlike.
He was beloved by all, and most of all by the children;
For he told them tales of the Loup-garou in the forest,
And of the goblin that came in the night to water the
  horses,
And of the white Létiche, the ghost of a child who un-
  christened
Died, and was doomed to haunt unseen the chambers of
  children;
And how on Christmas eve the oxen talked in the
  stable,
And how the fever was cured by a spider shut up in a nut-
  shell,

And of the marvelous powers of four-leaved clover and
  horseshoes,
With whatsoever else was writ in the lore of the village.
Then up rose from his seat by the fireside Basil the black-
  smith,
Knocked from his pipe the ashes, and slowly extending his
  right hand,
"Father Leblanc," he exclaimed, "thou hast heard the talk
  in the village,
And, perchance, canst tell us some news of these ships and
  their errand."
Then with modest demeanor made answer the notary
  public:
"Gossip enough have I heard, in sooth, yet am never the
  wiser;
And what their errand may be I know no better than
  others.
Yet am I not of those who imagine some evil intention
Brings them here, for we are at peace; and why then
  molest us?"
"God's name!" shouted the hasty and somewhat irascrible
  blacksmith;
"Must we in all things look for the how, and the why, and
  the wherefore?
Daily injustice is done, and might is the right of the
  strongest!"

But without heeding his warmth, continued the notary
  public:
"Man is unjust, but God is just; and finally justice

Triumphs; and well I remember a story, that often con-
soled me
When as a captive I lay in the old French fort at Port
Royal."
This was the old man's favorite tale, and he loved to re-
peat it
When his neighbors complained that any injustice was
done them.
"Once in an ancient city, whose name I no longer remem-
ber,
Raised aloft on a column, a brazen statue of Justice
Stood in the public square, upholding the scales in its left
hand,
And in its right a sword, as an emblem that justice presided
Over the laws of the land, and the hearts and homes of
the people.
Even the birds had built their nests in the scales of the
balance,
Having no fear of the sword that flashed in the sunshine
above them.
But in the course of time the laws of the land were cor-
rupted;
Might took the place of right, and the weak were oppressed,
and the mighty
Ruled with an iron rod. Then it chanced in a nobleman's
palace
That a necklace of pearls was lost, and ere long a suspicion
Fell on an orphan girl who lived as maid in the household.
She, after form of trial condemned to die on the scaffold,
Patiently met her doom at the foot of the statue of Justice.

As to her Father in heaven her innocent spirit ascended,
Lo! o'er the city a tempest rose; and the bolts of the
  thunder
Smote the statue of bronze, and hurled in wrath from its
  left hand
Down on the pavement below the clattering scales of the
  balance,
And in the hollow thereof was found the nest of a magpie,
Into whose clay-built walls the necklace of pearls was
  inwoven."
Silenced, but not convinced, when the story was ended,
  the blacksmith
Stood like a man who fain would speak, but findeth no
  language;
All his thoughts were congealed into lines on his face, as
  the vapors
Freeze in fantastic shapes on the windowpanes in the
  winter.

Then Evangeline lighted the brazen lamp on the table,
Filled, till it overflowed, the pewter tankard with home-
  brewed
Nutbrown ale, that was famed for its strength in the village
  of Grand-Pré;
While from his pocket the notary drew his papers and ink-
  horn,
Wrote with a steady hand the date and the age of the
  parties,
Naming the dower of the bride in flocks of sheep and in
  cattle.

Orderly all things proceeded, and duly and well were
  completed,
And the great seal of the law was set like a sun on the
  margin.
Then from his leathern pouch the farmer threw on the
  table
Three times the old man's fee in solid pieces of silver;
And the notary rising, and blessing the bride and bride-
  groom,
Lifted aloft the tankard of ale and drank to their welfare.
Wiping the foam from his lip, he solemnly bowed and
  departed,
While in silence the others sat and mused by the fireside,
Till Evangeline brought the draughtboard out of its corner.
Soon was the game begun. In friendly contention the old
  men
Laughed at each lucky hit, or unsuccessful maneuver,
Laughed when a man was crowned, or a breach was made
  in the king row.
Meanwhile apart, in the twilight gloom of a window's
  embrasure,
Sat the lovers and whispered together, beholding the moon
  rise
Over the pallid sea and the silvery mist of the meadows.
Silently one by one, in the infinite meadows of heaven,
Blossomed the lovely stars, the forget-me-nots of the angels.

Thus was evening passed. Anon the bell from the belfry
Rang out the hour of nine, the village curfew, and straightway

Rose the guests and departed; and silence reigned in the household.

Many a farewell word and sweet goodnight on the door-step

Lingered long in Evangeline's heart, and filled it with gladness.

Carefully then were covered the embers that glowed on the heartstones,

And on the oaken stairs resounded the tread of the farmer.

Soon with a soundless step the foot of Evangeline followed.

Up the staircase moved a luminous space in the darkness,

Lighted less by the lamp than the shining face of the maiden.

Silent she passed through the hall, and entered the door of her chamber.

Simple that chamber was, with its curtains of white and its clothespress

Ample and high, on whose spacious shelves were carefully folded

Linen and woolen stuffs, by hand of Evangeline woven.

This was the precious dower she would bring to her husband in marriage,

Better than flocks and herds, being proofs of her skill as a housewife.

Soon she extinguished her lamp, for the mellow and radiant moonlight

Streamed through the windows, and lighted the room, till the heart of the maiden

Swelled and obeyed its power, like the tremulous tides of the ocean.

Ah! she was fair, exceeding fair to behold, as she stood with
Naked snow-white feet on the gleaming floor of her chamber!
Little she dreamed that below, among the trees of the orchard,
Waited her lover and watched for the gleam of her lamp and her shadow.
Yet were her thoughts of him, and at times a feeling of sadness
Passed o'er her soul, as the sailing shade of clouds in the moonlight
Flitted across the floor and darkened the room for a moment.
And, as she gazed from the window, she saw serenely the moon pass
Forth from the folds of a cloud, and one star followed her footsteps,
As out of Abraham's tent young Ishmael wandered with Hagar.

IV

Pleasantly rose next morn the sun on the village of Grand-Pré.
Pleasantly gleamed in the soft, sweet air the Basin of Minas,
Where the ships, with their wavering shadows, were riding at anchor.
Life had long been astir in the village, and clamorous labor
Knocked with its hundred hands at the golden gates of the morning.

Now from the country around, from the farms and neighboring hamlets,
Came in their holiday dresses the blithe Acadian peasants.
Many a glad good morrow and jocund laugh from the young folk
Made the bright air brighter, as up from the numerous meadows,
Where no path could be seen but the track of wheels in the greensward,
Group after group appeared, and joined, or passed on the highway.
Long ere noon, in the village all sounds of labor were silenced.
Thronged were the streets with people; and noisy groups at the house doors
Sat in the cheerful sun, and rejoiced and gossiped together.
Every house was an inn, where all were welcomed and feasted;
For with this simple people, who lived like brothers together,
All things were held in common, and what one had was another's.
Yet under Benedict's roof hospitality seemed more abundant:
For Evangeline stood among the guests of her father;
Bright was her face with smiles, and words of welcome and gladness
Fell from her beautiful lips, and blessed the cup as she gave it.

Under the open sky, in the odorous air of the orchard,
Stript of its golden fruit, was spread the feast of betrothal.
There in the shade of the porch were the priest and the
  notary seated;
There good Benedict sat, and sturdy Basil the blacksmith.
Not far withdrawn from these, by the cider press and the
  beehives,
Michael the fiddler was placed, with the gayest of hearts
  and of waistcoats.
Shadow and light from the leaves alternately played on
  his snow-white
Hair, as it waved in the wind; and the jolly face of the
  fiddler
Glowed like a living coal when the ashes are blown from
  the embers.
Gaily the old man sang to the vibrant sound of his fiddle,
Tous les Bourgeois de Chartres, and *Le Carillon de Dun-
  kerque,*
And anon with his wooden shoes beat time to the music.
Merrily, merrily whirled the wheels of the dizzying dances
Under the orchard trees and down the path to the meadows:
Old folk and young together, and children mingled among
  them.
Fairest of all the maids was Evangeline, Benedict's
  daughter!
Noblest of all the youths was Gabriel, son of the black-
  smith!

So passed the morning away. And lo! with a summons
  sonorous

Sounded the bell from its tower, and over the meadows a
  drum beat.

Thronged ere long was the church with men. Without, in
  the churchyard,

Waited the women. They stood by the graves, and hung on
  the headstones

Garlands of autumn leaves and evergreens fresh from the
  forest.

Then came the guard from the ships, and marching proudly
  among them

Entered the sacred portal. With loud and dissonant clangor

Echoed the sound of their brazen drums from ceiling and
  casement—

Echoed a moment only, and slowly the ponderous portal

Closed, and in silence the crowd awaited the will of the
  soldiers.

Then uprose their commander, and spake from the steps
  of the altar,

Holding aloft in his hands, with its seals, the royal commission.

"You are convened this day," he said, "by his Majesty's
  orders.

Clement and kind has he been; but how you have answered his kindness

Let your own hearts reply! To my natural make and my
  temper

Painful the task is I do, which to you I know must be
  grievous.

Yet must I bow and obey, and deliver the will of our
  monarch:

Namely, that all your lands, and dwellings, and cattle of
all kinds

Forfeited be to the crown; and that you yourselves from
this province

Be transported to other lands. God grant you may dwell
there

Ever as faithful subjects, a happy and peaceable people!

Prisoners now I declare you, for such is his Majesty's
pleasure!"

As, when the air is serene in the sultry solstice of summer,

Suddenly gathers a storm, and the deadly sling of the hailstones

Beats down the farmer's corn in the field, and shatters his
windows,

Hiding the sun, and strewing the ground with thatch from
the house roofs,

Bellowing fly the herds, and seek to break their enclosures;

So on the hearts of the people descended the words of the
speaker.

Silent a moment they stood in speechless wonder, and then
rose

Louder and ever louder a wail of sorrow and anger,

And, by one impulse moved, they madly rushed to the
doorway,

Vain was the hope of escape; and cries and fierce impre-
cations

Rang through the house of prayer; and high o'er the heads
of the others

Rose, with his arms uplifted, the figure of Basil the blacksmith,

As, on a stormy sea, a spar is tossed by the billows.
Flushed was his face and distorted with passion; and wildly
   he shouted:
"Down with the tyrants of England! we never have sworn
   them allegiance!
Death to these foreign soldiers, who seize on our homes
   and our harvests!"
More he fain would have said, but the merciless hand of
   a soldier
Smote him upon the mouth, and dragged him down to the
   pavement.

In the midst of the strife and tumult of angry contention,
Lo! the door of the chancel opened, and Father Felician
Entered, with serious mien, and ascended the steps of the
   altar.
Raising his reverend hand, with a gesture he awed into
   silence
All that clamorous throng; and thus he spake to his people;
Deep were his tones and solemn; in accents measured and
   mournful
Spake he, as, after the tocsin's alarum, distinctly the clock
   strikes.
"What is this that ye do, my children? what madness has
   seized you?
Forty years of my life have I labored among you and
   taught you,
Not in word alone, but in deed, to love one another!
Is this the fruit of my toils, of my vigils and prayers and
   privations?

Have you so soon forgotten all lessons of love and forgiveness?

This is the house of the Prince of Peace, and would you
profane it

Thus with violent deeds and hearts overflowing with ha-
tred?

Lo! where the crucified Christ from His cross is gazing
upon you!

See! in those sorrowful eyes what meekness and holy compassion!

Hark! how those lips still repeat the prayer, 'O Father, forgive them!'

Let us repeat that prayer in the hour when the wicked
assail us,

Let us repeat it now, and say, 'O Father, forgive them!' "

Few were his words of rebuke, but deep in the hearts of
his people

Sank they, and sobs of contrition succeeded the passionate
outbreak,

While they repeated his prayer, and said, "O Father, forgive them!"

Then came the evening service. The tapers gleamed from
the altar;

Fervent and deep was the voice of the priest, and the
people responded,

Not with their lips alone, but their hearts; and the Ave
Maria

Sang they, and fell on their knees, and their souls, with
devotion translated,

Rose on the ardor of prayer, like Elijah ascending to
heaven.

Meanwhile had spread in the village the tidings of ill, and
on all sides,

Wandered, wailing, from house to house the women and
children.

Long at her father's door Evangeline stood, with her right
hand

Shielding her eyes from the level rays of the sun, that,
descending,

Lighted the village street with mysterious splendor, and
roofed each

Peasant's cottage with golden thatch, and emblazoned its
windows.

Long within had spread the snow-white cloth on the table;

There stood the wheaten loaf, and the honey fragrant with
wild flowers;

There stood the tankard of ale, and the cheese fresh
brought from the dairy;

And at the head of the board the great armchair of the
farmer.

Thus did Evangeline wait at her father's door, as the sunset

Threw long shadows of trees o'er the broad ambrosial
meadows.

Ah! on her spirit within a deeper shadow had fallen,

And from the fields of her soul a fragrance celestial
ascended—

Charity, meekness, love, and hope, and forgiveness, and
patience!

Then, all forgetful of self, she wandered into the village,
Cheering with looks and words the mournful hearts of the
women,
As o'er the darkening fields with lingering steps they de-
parted,
Urged by their household cares, and the weary feet of their
children.
Down sank the great red sun, and in golden, glimmering
vapors
Veiled the light of his face, like the Prophet descending
from Sinai.
Sweetly over the village the bell of the Angelus sounded.

Meanwhile, amid the gloom, by the church Evangeline
lingered.
All was silent within; and in vain at the door and the
windows
Stood she, and listened and looked, till, overcome by
emotion,
"Gabriel!" cried she aloud with tremulous voice; but no
answer
Came from the graves of the dead, nor the gloomier grave
of the living.
Slowly at length she returned to the tenantless house of
her father.
Smouldered the fire on the hearth, on the board was the
supper untasted,
Empty and drear was each room, and haunted with phantoms of terror.
Sadly echoed her step on the stair and the floor of her
chamber.

In the dead of the night she heard the disconsolate rain
   fall
Loud on the withered leaves of the sycamore tree by the
   window.
Keenly the lightning flashed; and the voice of the echoing
   thunder
Told her that God was in heaven, and governed the world
   He created!
Then she remembered the tale she had heard of the justice
   of Heaven;
Soothed was her troubled soul, and she peacefully slum-
   bered till morning.

V

Four times the sun had risen and set; and now on the
   fifth day
Cheerily called the cock to the sleeping maids of the farm-
   house.
Soon o'er the yellow fields, in silent and mournful procession,
Came from the neighboring hamlets and farms the Acadian
   women,
Driving in ponderous wains their household goods to the
   seashore,
Pausing and looking back to gaze once more on their
   dwellings,
Ere they were shut from sight by the winding road and the
   woodland.

Close at their sides their children ran, and urged on the oxen,
While in their little hands they clasped some fragments of playthings.

Thus to the Gaspereau's mouth they hurried; and there on the seabeach
Piled in confusion lay the household goods of the peasants.
All day long between the shore and the ships did the boats ply;
All day long the wains came laboring down from the village.
Late in the afternoon, when the sun was near to his setting,
Echoed far o'er the fields came the roll of drums from the churchyard.
Thither the women and children thronged. On a sudden the church doors
Opened, and forth came the guard, and marching in gloomy procession
Followed the long-imprisoned, but patient, Acadian farmers.
Even as pilgrims, who journey afar from their homes and their country,
Sing as they go, and in singing forget they are weary and wayworn,
So with songs on their lips the Acadian peasants descended
Down from the church to the shore, amid their wives and their daughters.
Foremost the young men came; and, raising together their voices,

Sang with tremulous lips a chant of the Catholic Missions:
"Sacred heart of the Saviour! O inexhaustible fountain!
Fill our hearts this day with strength and submission and
patience!"
Then the old men, as they marched, and the women that
stood by the wayside
Joined in the sacred psalm, and the birds in the sunshine
above them
Mingled their notes therewith, like voices of spirits de-
parted.

Halfway down to the shore Evangeline waited in silence,
Not overcome with grief, but strong in the hour of afflic-
tion—
Calmly and sadly she waited, until the procession ap-
proached her,
And she beheld the face of Gabriel pale with emotion.
Tears then filled her eyes, and, eagerly running to meet
him,
Clasped she his hands, and laid her head on his shoulder,
and whispered,
"Gabriel! be of good cheer! for if we love one another
Nothing, in truth, can harm us, whatever mischances may
happen!"
Smiling she spake these words; then suddenly paused, for
her father
Saw she slowly advancing. Alas! how changed was his
aspect!
Gone was the glow from his cheek, and the fire from his
eye, and his footstep

Heavier seemed with the weight of the heavy heart in his
 bosom.
But with a smile and a sigh, she clasped his neck and
 embraced him,
Speaking words of endearment where words of comfort
 availed not.
Thus to the Gaspereau's mouth moved on that mournful
 procession.

There disorder prevailed, and the tumult and stir of em-
 barking.
Busily plied the freighted boats; and in the confusion
Wives were torn from their husbands, and mothers, too
 late, saw their children
Left on the land, extending their arms, with wildest en-
 treaties.
So unto separate ships were Basil and Gabriel carried.
While in despair on the shore Evangeline stood with her
 father.
Half the task was not done when the sun went down, and
 the twilight
Deepened and darkened around; and in haste the refluent
 ocean
Fled away from the shore, and left the line of the sand-
 beach
Covered with waifs of the tide, with kelp and the slippery
 seaweed.
Farther back in the midst of the household goods and the
 wagons,
Like a gypsy camp, or a leaguer after a battle,

All escape cut off by the sea, and the sentinels near them,
Lay encamped for the night the houseless Acadian farmers.
Back to its nethermost caves retreated the bellowing ocean,
Dragging adown the beach the rattling pebbles, and leaving
Inland and far up the shore the stranded boats of the sailors.
Then, as the night descended, the herds returned from their pastures;
Sweet was the moist still air with the odor of milk from their udders;
Lowing they waited, and long, at the well-known bars of the farmyard—
Waited and looked in vain for the voice and the hand of the milkmaid.
Silence reigned in the streets; from the church no Angelus sounded,
Rose no smoke from the roofs, and gleamed no lights from the windows.

But on the shores meanwhile the evening fires had been kindled,
Built of the driftwood thrown on the sands from wrecks in the tempest.
Round them shapes of gloom and sorrowful faces were gathered,
Voices of women were heard, and of men, and the crying of children.
Onward from fire to fire, as from hearth to hearth in his parish,
Wandered the faithful priest, consoling and blessing and cheering,

Like unto shipwrecked Paul on Melita's delicate seashore.
Thus he approached the place where Evangeline sat with her father,
And in the flickering light beheld the face of the old man,
Haggard and hollow and wan, and without either thought or emotion,
E'en as the face of a clock from which the hands have been taken.
Vainly Evangeline strove with words and caresses to cheer him,
Vainly offered him food; yet he moved not, he looked not, he spake not,
But, with a vacant stare, ever gazed at the flickering fire-light.
"Benedicite!" murmured the priest in tones of compassion.
More he fain would have said, but his heart was full, and his accents
Faltered and paused on his lips, as the feet of a child on a threshold,
Hushed by the scene he beholds, and the awful presence of sorrow.
Silently, therefore, he had laid his hand on the head of the maiden,
Raising his tearful eyes to the silent stars that above them
Moved on their way, unperturbed by the wrongs and sorrows of mortals.
Then sat he down at her side, and they wept together in silence.

Suddenly rose from the south a light, as in autumn the blood-red

Moon climbs the crystal walls of heaven, and o'er the horizon
Titan-like stretches its hundred hands upon mountain and meadow,
Seizing the rocks and the rivers, and piling huge shadows together.
Broader and ever broader it gleamed on the roofs of the village,
Gleamed on the sky and the sea, and the ships that lay in the roadstead.
Columns of shining smoke uprose, and flashes of flame were
Thrust through their folds and withdrawn, like the quivering hands of a martyr.
Then as the wind seized the gleeds and the burning thatch, and, uplifting,
Whirled them aloft through the air, at once from a hundred housetops
Started the sheeted smoke with flashes of flame intermingled.

These things beheld in dismay the crowd on the shore and on shipboard.
Speechless at first they stood, then cried aloud in their anguish,
"We shall behold no more our homes in the village of Grand-Pré!"
Loud on a sudden the cocks began to crow in the farmyards,
Thinking the day had dawned; and anon the lowing of cattle

Came on the evening breeze, by the barking of dogs inter-
rupted.
Then rose a sound of dread, such as startles the sleeping
encampments
Far in the western prairies or forests that skirt the Nebraska,
When the wild horses affrighted sweep by with the speed of
the whirlwind,
Or the loud bellowing herds of buffaloes rush to the river.
Such was the sound that arose on the night, as the herds and
the horses
Broke through their folds and fences, and madly rushed o'er
the meadows.

Overwhelmed with the sight, yet speechless, the priest and
the maiden
Gazed on the scene of terror that reddened and widened
before them;
And as they turned at length to speak to their silent com-
panion,
Lo! from his seat he had fallen, and stretched abroad on
the seashore
Motionless lay his form, from which the soul had departed.
Slowly the priest lifted the lifeless head, and the maiden
Knelt at her father's side, and wailed aloud in her terror.
Then in a swoon she sank, and lay with her head on his
bosom.
Through the long night she lay in deep, oblivious slumber;
And when she woke from the trance, she beheld a multitude
near her.

Faces of friends she beheld, that were mournfully gazing
    upon her,
Pallid, with tearful eyes, and looks of saddest compassion.
Still the blaze of the burning village illumined the land-
    scape,
Reddened the sky overhead, and gleamed on the faces
    around her,
And like the day of doom it seemed to her wavering
    senses.
Then a familiar voice she heard, as it said to the people:
"Let us bury him here by the sea. When a happier season
Brings us again to our homes from the unknown land of
    our exile,
Then shall his sacred dust be piously laid in the church-
    yard."
Such were the words of the priest. And there in haste by
    the seaside,
Having the glare of the burning village for funeral torches,
But without bell or book, they buried the farmer of Grand-
    Pré.
And as the voice of the priest repeated the service of sor-
    row,
Lo! with a mournful sound like the voice of a vast congre-
    gation,
Solemnly answered the sea, and mingled its roar with the
    dirges.
'Twas the returning tide, that afar from the waste of the
    ocean,
With the first dawn of the day, came heaving and hurrying
    landward.

Then recommenced once more the stir and noise of embark-
ing;
And with the ebb of the tide the ships sailed out of the
harbor,
Leaving behind them the dead on the shore, and the village
in ruins.

PART THE SECOND

I

Many a weary year had passed since the burning of Grand-
Pré,
When on the falling tide the freighted vessels departed,
Bearing a nation, with all its household goods, into exile,
Exile without an end, and without an example in story.
Far asunder, on separate coasts, the Acadians landed;
Scattered were they, like flakes of snow, when the wind
from the northeast
Strikes aslant through the fogs that darken the Banks of
Newfoundland.
Friendless, homeless, hopeless, they wandered from city to
city,
From the cold lakes of the North to sultry Southern
savannas—
From the bleak shores of the sea to the lands where the
Father of Waters
Seizes the hills in his hands, and drags them down to the
ocean,
Deep in their sands to bury the scattered bones of the
mammoth.

Friends they sought and homes; and many, despairing, heartbroken,
Asked of the earth but a grave, and no longer a friend nor a fireside.
Written their history stands on tablets of stone in the churchyards.
Long among them was seen a maiden who waited and wandered,
Lowly and meek in spirit, and patiently suffering all things.
Fair was she and young; but, alas! before her extended,
Dreary and vast and silent, the desert of life, with its pathway
Marked by the graves of those who had sorrowed and suffered before her,
Passions long extinguished, and hopes long dead and abandoned,
As the emigrant's way o'er the Western desert is marked by
Campfires long consumed, and bones that bleach in the sunshine.
Something there was in her life incomplete, imperfect, unfinished;
As if a morning of June, with all its music and sunshine,
Suddenly paused in the sky, and, fading slowly descended
Into the east again, from whence it late had arisen.
Sometimes she lingered in towns, till, urged by the fever within her,
Urged by a restless longing, the hunger and thirst of the spirit,
She would commence again her endless search and endeavor;

Sometimes in churchyards strayed, and gazed on the crosses and tombstones,
Sat by some nameless grave, and thought that perhaps in its bosom
He was already at rest, and she longed to slumber beside him.

Sometimes a rumor, a hearsay, an inarticulate whisper,
Came with its airy hand to point and beckon her forward.
Sometimes she spake with those who had seen her beloved and known him,
But it was long ago, in some far-off place or forgotten.
"Gabriel Lajeunesse!" they said; "Oh, yes! we have seen him.
He was with Basil the blacksmith, and both have gone to the prairies;
Coureurs-des-bois are they, and famous hunters and trappers."
"Gabriel Lajeunesse!" said others; "Oh, yes! we have seen him.
He is a voyageur in the lowlands of Louisiana."
Then would they say, "Dear child! why dream and wait for him longer?
Are there not other youths as fair as Gabriel? others
Who have hearts as tender and true, and spirits as loyal?
Here is Baptiste Leblanc, the notary's son, who has loved thee
Many a tedious year; come, give him thy hand and be happy!
Thou are too fair to be left to braid Saint Catherine's tresses."

Then would Evangeline answer, serenely but sadly, "I cannot!

Whither my heart has gone, there follows my hand, and not elsewhere.

For when the heart goes before, like a lamp, and illumines the pathway,

Many things are made clear, that else lie hidden in darkness."

Thereupon the priest, her friend and father confessor,

Said, with a smile, "O daughter! thy God thus speaketh within thee!

Talk not of wasted affection, affection never was wasted;

If it enrich not the heart of another, its waters, returning

Back to their springs, like the rain, shall fill them full of refreshment;

That which the fountain sends forth returns again to the fountain.

Patience; accomplish thy labor; accomplish thy work of affection!

Sorrow and silence are strong, and patient endurance is godlike.

Therefore accomplish thy labor of love, till the heart is made godlike,

Purified, strengthened, perfected, and rendered more worthy of heaven!"

Cheered by the good man's words, Evangeline labored and waited.

Still in her heart she heard the funeral dirge of the ocean,

But with its sound there was mingled a voice that whispered, "Despair not!"

Thus did that poor soul wander in want and cheerless discomfort,
Bleeding, barefooted, over the shards and thorns of existence.
Let me essay, O Muse! to follow the wanderer's footsteps—
Not through each devious path, each changeful year of existence;
But as a traveler follows a streamlet's course through the valley:
Far from its margin at times, and seeing the gleam of its water
Here and there, in some open space, and at intervals only;
Then drawing nearer its banks, through sylvan glooms that conceal it,
Though he behold it not, he can hear its continuous murmur;
Happy, at length, if he find a spot where it reaches an outlet.

II

It was the month of May. Far down the Beautiful River,
Past the Ohio shore and past the mouth of the Wabash,
Into the golden stream of the broad and swift Mississippi,
Floated a cumbrous boat, that was rowed by Acadian boatmen.
It was a band of exiles: a raft, as it were, from the shipwrecked
Nation, scattered along the coast, now floating together,
Bound by the bonds of a common belief and a common misfortune;

Men and women and children, who, guided by hope or by
   hearsay,
Sought for their kith and their kin among the few-acred
   farmers
On the Acadian coast, and the prairies of fair Opelousas.
With them Evangeline went, and her guide, the Father
   Felician.
Onward o'er sunken sands, through a wilderness somber
   with forests,
Day after day they glided adown the turbulent river;
Night after night, by their blazing fires, encamped on its
   borders.
Now through rushing chutes, among green islands, where
   plumelike
Cotton trees nodded their shadowy crests, they swept with
   the current,
Then emerged into broad lagoons, where silvery sand bars
Lay in the stream, and along the wimpling waves of their
   margin,
Shining with snow-white plumes, large flocks of pelicans
   waded.
Level the landscape grew, and along the shores of the river,
Shaded by China trees, in the midst of luxuriant gardens,
Stood the houses of planters, with Negro cabins and dove-
   cots.
They were approaching the region where reigns perpetual
   summer,
Where through the Golden Coast, and groves of orange and
   citron,
Sweeps with majestic curve the river away to the eastward.

They, too, swerved from their course; and, entering the
    Bayou of Plaquemine,
Soon were lost in a maze of sluggish and devious waters,
Which, like a network of steel, extended in every direction.
Over their heads the towering and tenebrous boughs of the
    cypress
Met in a dusky arch, and trailing mosses in mid-air
Waved like banners that hang on the walls of ancient
    cathedrals.
Deathlike the silence seemed, and unbroken, save by the
    herons
Home to their roots in the cedar trees returning at sunset,
Or by the owl, as he greeted the moon with demoniac
    laughter.
Lovely the moonlight was as it glanced and gleamed on
    the water,
Gleamed on the columns of cypress and cedar sustaining
    the arches,
Down through whose broken vaults it fell as through chinks
    in a ruin.
Dreamlike, and indistinct, and strange were all things
    around them;
And o'er their spirits there came a feeling of wonder and
    sadness,
Strange forebodings of ill, unseen and that cannot be com-
    passed.
As, at the tramp of a horse's hoof on the turf of the prairies,
Far in advance are closed the leaves of the shrinking
    mimosa,
So, at the hoofbeats of fate, with sad forebodings of evil,

Shrinks and closes the heart, ere the stroke of doom has attained it.
But Evangeline's heart was sustained by a vision, that faintly
Floated before her eyes, and beckoned her on through the moonlight.
It was the thought of her brain that assumed the shape of a phantom.
Through those shadowy aisles had Gabriel wandered before her,
And every stroke of the oar now brought him nearer and nearer.

Then in his place, at the prow of the boat, rose one of the oarsmen,
And, as a signal sound, if others like them peradventure
Sailed on those gloomy and midnight streams, blew a blast on his bugle.
Wild through the dark colonnades and corridors leafy the blast rang,
Breaking the seal of silence and giving tongues to the forest.
Soundless above them the banners of moss just stirred to the music.
Multitudinous echoes awoke and died in the distance,
Over the watery floor, and beneath the reverberant branches;
But not a voice replied; no answer came from the darkness;
And when the echoes had ceased, like a sense of pain was the silence.
Then Evangeline slept; but the boatmen rowed through the midnight,

Silent at times, then singing familiar Canadian boat songs,
Such as they sang of old on their own Acadian rivers,
While through the night were heard the mysterious sounds
of the desert,
Far off—indistinct—as of wave or wind in the forest,
Mixed with the whoop of the crane and the roar of the
grim alligator.

Thus ere another noon they emerged from the shades; and
before them
Lay, in the golden sun, the lakes of the Atchafalaya.
Water lilies in myriads rocked on the slight undulations
Made by the passing oars, and resplendent in beauty, the
lotus
Lifted her golden crown above the heads of the boat-
men.
Faint was the air with the odorous breath of magnolia
blossoms,
And with the heat of noon; and numberless sylvan islands,
Fragrant and thickly embowered with blossoming hedges
of roses,
Near to whose shores they glided along, invited to slumber.
Soon by the fairest of these their weary oars were sus-
pended.
Under the boughs of Wachita willows, that grew by the
margin,
Safely their boat was moored; and scattered about on the
greensward,
Tired with their midnight toil, the weary travelers
slumbered.
Over them vast and high extended the cope of a cedar.

Swinging from its great arms, the trumpet flower and the
grapevine
Hung their ladder of ropes aloft like the ladder of Jacob,
On whose pendulous stairs the angels ascending, descend-
ing,
Were the swift hummingbirds, that flitted from blossom to
blossom.
Such was the vision Evangeline saw as she slumbered be-
neath it.
Filled was her heart with love, and the dawn of an opening
heaven
Lighted her soul in sleep with the glory of regions celestial.

Nearer, ever nearer, among the numberless islands,
Darted a light, swift boat, that sped away o'er the
water,
Urged on its course by the sinewy arms of hunters and
trappers.
Northward its prow was turned, to the land of the bison
and beaver.
At the helm sat a youth, with countenance thoughtful and
careworn.
Dark and neglected locks overshadowed his brow, and a
sadness
Somewhat beyond his years on his face was legibly written.
Gabriel was it, who, weary with waiting, unhappy and rest-
less,
Sought in the Western wilds oblivion of self and of sorrow.

Swiftly they glided along, close under the lee of the island,
But by the opposite bank, and behind a screen of palmettos;

So that they saw not the boat, where it lay concealed in the
  willows;
All undisturbed by the dash of their oars, and unseen, were
  the sleepers;
Angel of God was there none to awaken the slumbering
  maiden.
Swiftly they glided away, like the shade of a cloud on the
  prairie.
After the sound of their oars on the tholes had died in the
  distance,
As from a magic trance the sleepers awoke, and the maiden
Said with a sigh to the friendly priest, "O Father Felician!
Something says in my heart that near me Gabriel wanders.
Is it a foolish dream, an idle and vague superstition?
Or has an angel passed, and revealed the truth to my
  spirit?"
Then, with a blush, she added, "Alas for my credulous
  fancy!
Unto ears like thine such words as these have no mean-
  ing."
But made answer the reverend man, and he smiled as he
  answered:
"Daughter, thy words are not idle; nor are they to me with-
  out meaning,
Feeling is deep and still; and the word that floats on the
  surface
Is as the tossing buoy, that betrays where the anchor is
  hidden.
Therefore trust to thy heart, and to what the world calls
  illusions.

Gabriel truly is near thee; for not far away to the south-
ward,
On the banks of the Têche, are the towns of St. Maur and
St. Martin.
There the long-wandering bride shall be given again to her
bridegroom,
There the long-absent pastor regain his flock and his sheep-
fold.
Beautiful is the land, with its prairies and forests of fruit
trees;
Under the feet a garden of flowers, and the bluest of
heavens
Bending above, and resting its dome on the walls of the
forest.
They who dwell there have named it the Eden of Louisi-
ana."

With these words of cheer they arose and continued their
journey.
Softly the evening came. The sun from the western horizon
Like a magician extended his golden wand o'er the land-
scape;
Twinkling vapors arose; and sky and water and forest
Seemed all on fire at the touch, and melted and mingled
together.
Hanging between two skies, a cloud with edges of silver,
Floated the boat, with its dripping oars, on the motionless
water.
Filled was Evangeline's heart with inexpressible sweetness.
Touched by the magic spell, the sacred fountains of feeling

Glowed with the light of love, as the skies and waters
around her.
Then from a neighboring thicket the mockingbird, wildest
of singers,
Swinging aloft on a willowy spray that hung o'er the water,
Shook from his little throat such floods of delirious music.
That the whole air and the woods and the waves seemed
silent to listen.
Plaintive at first were the tones and sad; then soaring to
madness
Seemed they to follow or guide the revel of frenzied Bac-
chantes.
Single notes were then heard, in sorrowful, low lamenta-
tion;
Till, having gathered them all, he flung them abroad in
derision,
As when, after a storm, a gust of wind through the treetops
Shakes down the rattling rain in a crystal shower on the
branches.
With such a prelude as this, and hearts that throbbed with
emotion,
Slowly they entered the Têche, where it flows through the
green Opelousas,
And, through the amber air, above the crest of the woodland,
Saw the column of smoke that arose from a neighboring
dwelling;
Sounds of a horn they heard, and the distant lowing of
cattle.

Near to the bank of the river, o'ershadowed by oaks from
    whose branches
Garlands of Spanish moss and of mystic mistletoe flaunted,
Such as the Druids cut down with golden hatchets at yule-
    tide,
Stood, secluded and still, the house of the herdsman. A
    garden
Girded it round about with a belt of luxuriant blossoms,
Filling the air with fragrance. The house itself was of tim-
    bers
Hewn from the cypress tree, and carefully fitted together.
Large and low was the roof; and on slender columns sup-
    ported,
Rose-wreathed, vine-encircled, a broad and spacious
    veranda,
Haunt of the hummingbird and the bee, extended around
    it.
At each end of the house, amid the flowers of the garden,
Stationed the dovecots were, as love's perpetual symbol,
Scenes of endless wooing, and endless contentions of rivals.
Silence reigned o'er the place. The line of shadow and sun-
    shine
Ran near the tops of the trees; but the house itself was in
    shadow,
And from its chimney top, ascending and slowly expanding
Into the evening air, a thin blue column of smoke rose.

In the rear of the house, from the garden gate, ran a path-
  way
Through the great groves of oak to the skirts of the limit-
  less prairie,
Into whose sea of flowers the sun was slowly descending.
Full in his track of light, like ships with shadowy canvas
Hanging loose from their spars in a motionless calm in the
  tropics,
Stood a cluster of trees, with tangled cordage of grapevines.

Just where the woodlands met the flowery surf of the
  prairie,
Mounted upon his horse, with Spanish saddle and stirrups,
Sat a herdsman, arrayed in gaiters and doublet of deerskin.
Broad and brown was the face that from under the Spanish
  sombrero
Gazed on the peaceful scene, with the lordly look of its mas-
  ter.
Round about him were numberless herds of kine, that were
  grazing
Quietly in the meadows, and breathing the vapory freshness
That uprose from the river, and spread itself over the land-
  scape.
Slowly lifting the horn that hung at his side, and expanding
Fully his broad, deep chest, he blew a blast that resounded
Wildly and sweet and far, through the still damp air of the
  evening.
Suddenly out of the grass the long white horns of the
  cattle
Rose like flakes of foam on the adverse currents of ocean.

Silent a moment they gazed, then bellowing rushed o'er the
    prairie,
And the whole mass became a cloud, a shade in the dis-
    tance.
Then, as the herdsman turned to the house, through the
    gate of the garden
Saw he the forms of the priest and the maiden advancing
    to meet him.
Suddenly down from his horse he sprang in amazement, and
    forward
Pushed with extended arms and exclamations of wonder;
When they beheld his face, they recognized Basil the black-
    smith.
Hearty his welcome was, as he led his guests to the garden.
There in an arbor of roses with endless question and answer
Gave they vent to their hearts, and renewed their friendly
    embraces,
Laughing and weeping by turns, or sitting silent and
    thoughtful.
Thoughtful, for Gabriel came not; and now dark doubts
    and misgivings
Stole o'er the maiden's heart; and Basil, somewhat embar-
    rassed,
Broke the silence and said, "If you came by the Atcha-
    falaya,
How have you nowhere encountered my Gabriel's boat on
    the bayous?"
Over Evangeline's face at the words of Basil a shade
    passed.

Tears came into her eyes, and she said, with a tremulous accent,
"Gone? is Gabriel gone?" and, concealing her face on his shoulder,
All her o'erburdened heart gave way, and she wept and lamented.
Then the good Basil said—and his voice grew blithe as he said it—
"Be of good cheer, my child; it is only today he departed.
Foolish boy! he has left me alone with my herds and my horses.
Moody and restless grown, and tried and troubled, his spirit
Could no longer endure the calm of this quiet existence.
Thinking ever of thee, uncertain and sorrowful ever,
Ever silent, or speaking only of thee and his troubles,
He at length had become so tedious to men and to maidens,
Tedious even to me, that at length I bethought me, and sent him
Unto the town of Adayes to trade for mules with the Spaniards.
Thence he will follow the Indian trails to the Ozark Mountains,
Hunting for furs in the forests, on rivers trapping the beaver.
Therefore be of good cheer; we will follow the fugitive lover;
He is not far on his way, and the Fates and the streams are against him.

503

Up and away tomorrow, and through the red dew of the
morning,
We will follow him fast, and bring him back to his prison."

Then glad voices were heard, and up from the banks of the
river,
Borne aloft on his comrades' arms, came Michael the fid-
dler.
Long under Basil's roof had he lived, like a god on
Olympus,
Having no other care than dispensing music to mortals.
Far renowned was he for his silver locks and his fiddle.
"Long live Michael," they cried, "our brave Acadian min-
strel!"
As they bore him aloft in triumphal procession; and
straightway
Father Felican advanced with Evangeline, greeting the old
man
Kindly and oft, and recalling the past, while Basil, en-
raptured,
Hailed with hilarious joy his old companions and gossips,
Laughing loud and long, and embracing mothers and
daughters.
Much they marveled to see the wealth of the cidevant
blacksmith,
All his domains and his herds, and his patriarchal de-
meanor;
Much they marveled to hear his tales of the soil and the
climate,
And of the prairies, whose numberless herds were his who
would take them;

Each one thought in his heart, that he, too, would go and
   do likewise.
Thus they ascended the steps, and, crossing the breezy
   veranda,
Entered the hall of the house, where already the supper of
   Basil
Waited his late return; and they rested and feasted to-
   gether.

Over the joyous feast the sudden darkness descended.
All was silent without, and, illumining the landscape with
   silver,
Fair rose the dewy moon and the myriad stars; but within
   doors,
Brighter than these, shone the faces of friends in the glim-
   mering lamplight.
Then from his station aloft, at the head of the table, the
   herdsman
Poured forth his heart and his wine together in endless pro-
   fusion.
Lighting his pipe, that was filled with sweet Natchitoches
   tobacco,
Thus he spake to his guests, who listened, and smiled as
   they listened:
"Welcome once more, my friends, who long have been
   friendless and homeless,
Welcome once more to a home, that is better perchance
   than the old one!
Here no hungry winter congeals our blood like the rivers;
Here no stony ground provokes the wrath of the farmer;

Smoothly the ploughshare runs through the soil, as a keel
through the water;
All the year round the orange groves are in blossom; and
grass grows
More in a single night than a whole Canadian summer.
Here, too, numberless herds run wild and unclaimed in the
prairies;
Here, too, lands may be had for the asking, and forests of
timber
With a few blows of the ax are hewn and framed into
houses.
After your houses are built, and your fields are yellow with
harvests,
No King George of England shall drive you away from
your homesteads,
Burning your dwellings and barns, and stealing your farms
and your cattle."
Speaking these words, he blew a wrathful cloud from his
nostrils,
While his huge brown hand came thundering down on the
table,
So that the guests all started; and Father Felician,
astounded,
Suddenly paused, with a pinch of snuff halfway to his nos-
trils.
But the brave Basil resumed, and his words were milder
and gayer:
"Only beware of the fever, my friends, beware of the fever!
For it is not like that of our cold Acadian climate,

Cured by wearing a spider hung round one's neck in a nut-
    shell!"
Then there were voices heard at the door, and footsteps
    approaching
Sounded upon the stairs and the floor of the breezy veranda.
It was the neighboring Creoles and small Acadian planters,
Who had been summoned all to the house of Basil the
    herdsman.
Merry the meeting was of ancient comrades and neighbors:
Friend clasped friend in his arms; and they who before
    were as strangers,
Meeting in exile, became straightway as friends to each
    other,
Drawn by the gentle bond of a common country together.
But in the neighboring hall, a strain of music, proceeding
From the accordant strings of Michael's melodious fiddle,
Broke up all further speech. Away, like children delighted,
All things forgotten beside, they gave themselves to the
    maddening
Whirl of the dizzy dance, as it swept and swayed to the
    music,
Dreamlike, with beaming eyes and the rush of fluttering
    garments.

Meanwhile, apart, at the head of the hall, the priest and the
    herdsman
Sat, conversing together of past and present and future;
While Evangeline stood like one entranced, for within her
Olden memories rose, and loud in the midst of the music
Heard she the sound of the sea, and an irrepressible sadness

Came o'er her heart, and unseen she stole forth into the
  garden.
Beautiful was the night. Behind the blank wall of the
  forest,
Tipping its summit with silver, arose the moon. On the
  river
Fell here and there through the branches a tremulous gleam
  of the moonlight,
Like the sweet thoughts of love on a darkened and devious
  spirit.
Nearer and round about her, the manifold flowers of the
  garden
Poured out their souls in odors, that were their prayers and
  confessions
Unto the night, as it went its way, like a silent Carthusian.
Fuller of fragrance than they, and as heavy with shadows
  and night dews,
Hung the heart of the maiden. The calm and the magical
  moonlight
Seemed to inundate her soul with indefinable longings,
As, through the garden gate, and beneath the shade of the
  oak trees,
Passed she along the path to the edge of the measureless
  prairie.
Silent it lay, with a silvery haze upon it, and fireflies
Gleaming and floating away in mingled and infinite num-
  bers.
Over her head the stars, the thoughts of God in the
  heavens,

Shone on the eyes of man, who had ceased to marvel and
worship,
Save when a blazing comet was seen on the walls of that
temple,
As if a hand had appeared and written upon them, "Up-
harsin."
And the soul of the maiden, between the stars and the fire-
flies,
Wandered alone, and she cried, "O Gabriel! O my beloved!
Art thou so near unto me, and yet thy voice does not reach
me?
Ah! how often thy feet have trod this path to the prairie!
Ah! how often thine eyes have looked on the woodlands
around me!
Ah! how often beneath this oak, returning from labor,
Thou hast lain down to rest, and to dream of me in thy
slumbers!
When shall these eyes behold, these arms be folded about
thee?"
Loud and sudden and near the note of a whippoorwill
sounded
Like a flute in the woods; and anon, through the neigh-
boring thickets,
Farther and farther away it floated and dropped into
silence.
"Patience!" whispered the oaks from the oracular caverns
of darkness;
And, from the moonlit meadow, a sigh responded, "Tomorrow!"

509

Bright rose the sun next day; and all the flowers of the garden
Bathed his shining feet with their tears, and anointed his tresses
With the delicious balm that they bore in their vases of crystal.
"Farewell!" said the priest, as he stood at the shadowy threshold;
"See that you bring us the Prodigal Son from his fasting and famine,
And, too, the Foolish Virgin, who slept when the bridegroom was coming."
"Farewell!" answered the maiden, and smiling, with Basil descended
Down to the river's brink, where the boatmen already were waiting.
Thus beginning their journey with morning, and sunshine, and gladness,
Swiftly they followed the flight of him who was speeding before them,
Blown by the blast of fate like a dead leaf over the desert.
Not that day, nor the next, nor yet the day that succeeded,
Found they trace of his course, in lake or forest or river,
Nor, after many days, had they found him; but vague and uncertain
Rumors alone were their guides through a wild and desolate country;
Till, at the little inn of the Spanish town of Adayes,
Weary and worn, they alighted, and learned from the garrulous landlord

That on the day before, with horses and guides and companions,
Gabriel left the village, and took the road of the prairies.

IV

Far in the West there lies a desert land, where the moun-
tains
Lift, through perpetual snows, their lofty and luminous
summits.
Down from their jagged, deep ravines, where the gorge,
like a gateway,
Opens a passage rude to the wheels of the emigrant's
wagon,
Westward the Oregon flows and the Walleway and Owyhee.
Eastward with devious course, among the Windriver Moun-
tains,
Through the Sweet-water Valley precipitate leaps the
Nebraska;
And to the south, from the Fontaine-qui-bout and the
Spanish sierras,
Fretted with sands and rocks, and swept by the wind of the
desert,
Numberless torrents, with ceaseless sound, descend to the
ocean,
Like the great chords of a harp, in loud and solemn vibra-
tions.
Spreading between these streams are the wondrous, beauti-
ful prairies,
Billowy bays of grass ever rolling in shadow and sunshine,

Bright with luxuriant clusters of roses and purple
  amorphas.
Over them wandered the buffalo herds, and the elk and the
  roebuck;
Over them wandered the wolves, and herds of riderless
  horses;
Fires that blast and blight, and winds that are weary with
  travel;
Over them wander the scattered tribes of Ishmael's chil-
  dren,
Staining the desert with blood; and above their terrible
  war trails
Circles and sails aloft, on pinions majestic, the vulture,
Like the implacable soul of a chieftain slaughtered in
  battle,
By invisible stairs ascending and scaling the heavens.
Here and there rise smokes from the camps of these savage
  marauders;
Here and there rise groves from the margins of swift-run-
  ning rivers;
And the grim, taciturn bear, the anchorite monk of the
  desert,
Climbs down their dark ravines to dig for roots by the
  brookside,
And all over is the sky, the clear and crystalline heaven,
Like the protecting hand of God inverted above them.

Into this wonderful land, at the base of the Ozark Mountains,
Gabriel far had entered, with hunters and trappers behind
  him.

Day after day, with their Indian guides, the maiden and
    Basil
Followed his flying steps, and thought each day to o'ertake
    him.
Sometimes they saw, or thought they saw, the smoke of his
    campfire
Rise in the morning air from the distant plain; but at night-
    fall,
When they had reached the place, they found only embers
    and ashes.
And though their hearts were sad at times and their bodies
    were weary,
Hope still guided them on, as the magic Fata Morgana
Showed them her lakes of light, that retreated and vanished
    before them.

Once, as they sat by their evening fire, there silently entered
Into the little camp an Indian woman, whose features
Wore deep traces of sorrow, and patience as great as her
    sorrow.
She was a Shawnee woman returning home to her people,
From the far-off hunting grounds of the cruel Camanches,
Where her Canadian husband, a coureur-des-bois, had been
    murdered.
Touched were their hearts at her story, and warmest and
    friendliest welcome
Gave they, with words of cheer, and she sat and feasted
    among them
On the buffalo meat and the venison cooked on the embers.
But when their meal was done, and Basil and all his com-
    panions,

Worn with the long day's march and the chase of the deer
and the bison,
Stretched themselves on the ground, and slept where the
quivering firelight
Flashed on their swarthy cheeks, and their forms wrapped
up in their blankets,
Then at the door of Evangeline's tent she sat and repeated
Slowly, with soft low voice, and the charm of her Indian
accent,
All the tale of her love, with its pleasures, and pains, and
reverses.
Much Evangeline wept at the tale, and to know that an-
other
Hapless heart like her own had loved and been disap-
pointed.
Moved to the depths of her soul by pity and woman's
compassion,
Yet in her sorrow pleased that one who had suffered was
near her,
She in turn related her love and all its disasters.
Mute with wonder the Shawnee sat, and when she had
ended
Still was mute; but at length, as if a mysterious horror
Passed through her brain, she spake, and repeated the tale
of the Mowis;
Mowis, the bridegroom of snow, who won and wedded
a maiden,
But, when the morning came, arose and passed from the
wigwam,
Fading and melting away and dissolving into the sunshine,

514

Till she beheld him no more, though she followed far into
the forest.
Then, in those sweet, low tones, that seemed like a weird
incantation,
Told she the tale of the fair Lilinau, who was wooed by a
phantom,
That, through the pines o'er her father's lodge, in the hush
of the twilight,
Breathed like the evening wind, and whispered love to the
maiden,
Till she followed his green and waving plume through the
forest,
And nevermore returned, nor was seen again by her
people.
Silent with wonder and strange surprise, Evangeline
listened
To the soft flow of her magical words, till the region around
her
Seemed like enchanted ground, and her swarthy guest the
enchantress.
Slowly over the tops of the Ozark Mountains the moon
rose,
Lighting the little tent, and with a mysterious splendor
Touching the somber leaves, and embracing and filling the
woodland.
With a delicious sound the brook rushed by, and the
branches
Swayed and sighed overhead in scarcely audible whispers.
Filled with the thoughts of love was Evangeline's heart, but
a secret,

Subtile sense crept in of pain and indefinite terror,
As the cold, poisonous snake creeps into the nest of the
swallow.
It was no earthly fear. A breath from the region of spirits
Seemed to float in the air of night; and she felt for a
moment
That, like the Indian maid, she, too, was pursuing a
phantom.
With this thought she slept, and the fear and the phantom
had vanished.

Early upon the morrow the march was resumed, and the
Shawnee
Said, as they journeyed along: "On the western slope of
these mountains
Dwells in his little village the Black Robe chief of the Mis-
sion.
Much he teaches the people, and tells them of Mary and
Jesus.
Loud laugh their hearts with joy, and weep with pain, as
they hear him."
Then, with a sudden and secret emotion, Evangeline
answered,
"Let us go to the Mission, for there good tidings await us!"
Thither they turned their steeds; and behind a spur of the
mountains,
Just as the sun went down, they heard a murmur of voices,
And in a meadow green and broad, by the bank of a river,
Saw the tents of the Christians, the tents of the Jesuit Mis-
sion.

Under a towering oak, that stood in the midst of the village,
Knelt the Black Robe chief with his children. A crucifix fastened
High on the trunk of the tree, and overshadowed by grape-vines,
Looked with its agonized face on the multitude kneeling beneath it.
This was their rural chapel. Aloft, through the intricate arches
Of its aerial roof, arose the chant of their vespers,
Mingling its notes with the soft susurrus and sighs of the branches.
Silent, with heads uncovered, the travelers, nearer approaching,
Knelt on the swarded floor, and joined in the evening devotions.
But when the service was done, and the benediction had fallen
Forth from the hands of the priest, like seed from the hands of the sower,
Slowly the reverend man advanced to the strangers and bade them
Welcome; and when they replied, he smiled with benignant expression,
Hearing the homelike sounds of his mother tongue in the forest,
And, with words of kindness, conducted them into his wig-wam.
There upon mats and skins they reposed, and on cakes of the maize-ear

Feasted, and slaked their thirst from the water gourd of the teacher.

Soon was their story told; and the priest with solemnity answered:

"Not six suns have risen and set since Gabriel, seated
On this mat by my side, where now the maiden reposes,
Told me this same sad tale; then arose and continued his journey!"

Soft was the voice of the priest, and he spake with an accent of kindness;

But on Evangeline's heart fell his words as in winter the snowflakes

Fall into some lone nest from which the birds have departed.

"Far to the north he has gone," continued the priest; "but in autumn,
When the chase is done, will return again to the Mission."

Then Evangeline said, and her voice was meek and submissive,

"Let me remain with thee, for my soul is sad and afflicted."

So seemed it wise and well unto all; and betimes on the morrow,
Mounting his Mexican steed, with his Indian guides and companions,
Homeward Basil returned, and Evangeline stayed at the Mission.

Slowly, slowly, slowly the days succeeded each other—
Days and weeks and months; and the fields of maize that were springing

Green from the ground when a stranger she came, now
   waving about her,
Lifted their slender shafts, with leaves interlacing, and
   forming
Cloisters for mendicant crows and granaries pillaged by
   squirrels.
Then in the golden weather the maize was husked, and the
   maidens
Blushed at each blood-red ear, for that betokened a lover,
But at the crooked laughed, and called it a thief in the corn
   field.
Even the blood-red ear to Evangeline brought not her lover.
"Patience!" the priest would say; "have faith, and thy
   prayer will be answered!
Look at this vigorous plant that lifts its head from the
   meadow,
See how its leaves are turned to the north, as true as the
   magnet;
This is the compass flower, that the finger of God has
   planted
Here in the houseless wild, to direct the traveler's journey
Over the sea-like, pathless, limitless waste of the desert.
Such in the soul of man is faith. The blossoms of passion,
Gay and luxuriant flowers, are brighter and fuller of fra-
   grance,
But they beguile us, and lead us astray, and their odor is
   deadly.
Only this humble plant can guide us here, and hereafter
Crown us with asphodel flowers, that are wet with the dews
   of nepenthe."

So came the autumn and passed, and the winter—yet
  Gabriel came not;
Blossomed the opening spring, and the notes of the robin
  and bluebird
Sounded sweet upon wold and in wood, yet Gabriel came
  not.
But on the breath of the summer winds a rumor was wafted
Sweeter than song of bird, or hue or odor of blossom.
Far to the north and east, it said, in the Michigan forests,
Gabriel had his lodge by the banks of the Saginaw River.
And, with returning guides, that sought the lakes of St.
  Lawrence,
Saying a sad farewell, Evangeline went from the Mission.
When over weary ways, by long and perilous marches,
She had attained at length the depths of the Michigan
  forests,
Found she the hunter's lodge deserted and fallen to ruin!

Thus did the long sad years glide on, and in seasons and
  places
Divers and distant far was seen the wandering maiden:
Now in the Tents of Grace of the meek Moravian Missions,
Now in the noisy camps and the battlefields of the army,
Now in secluded hamlets, and towns and populous
  cities.
Like a phantom she came, and passed away unremem-
  bered.
Fair was she and young, when in hope began the long
  journey;
Faded was she and old, when in disappointment it ended.

Each succeeding year stole something away from her
  beauty,
Leaving behind it, broader and deeper, the gloom and the
  shadow.
Then there appeared and spread faint streaks of gray o'er
  her forehead,
Dawn of another life, that broke o'er her earthly horizon,
As in the eastern sky the first faint streaks of the morning.

V

In that delightful land which is washed by the Delaware's
  waters,
Guarding in sylvan shades the name of Penn the apostle,
Stands on the banks of its beautiful stream the city he
  founded.
There all the air is balm, and the peach is the emblem of
  beauty,
And the streets still re-echo the names of the trees of the
  forest,
As if they fain would appease the Dryads whose haunts they
  molested.
There from the troubled sea had Evangeline landed, an
  exile,
Finding among the children of Penn a home and a country.
There old René Leblanc had died, and when he departed,
Saw at his side only one of all his hundred descendants.
Something at least there was in the friendly streets of the
  city,
Something that spake to her heart, and made her no longer
  a stranger;

And her ear was pleased with the Thee and Thou of the
    Quakers,
For it recalled the past, the old Acadian country,
Where all men were equal, and all were brothers and sisters.
So, when the fruitless search, the disappointed endeavor,
Ended, to recommence no more upon earth, uncomplain-
    ing,
Thither, as leaves to the light, were turned her thoughts
    and her footsteps.
As from a mountain's top the rainy mists of the morning
Roll away, and afar we behold the landscape below us,
Sun-illumined, with shining rivers and cities and hamlets,
So fell the mists from her mind, and she saw the world far
    below her,
Dark no longer, but all illumined with love; and the path-
    way
Which she had climbed so far, lying smooth and fair in the
    distance.
Gabriel was not forgotten. Within her heart was his image,
Clothed in the beauty of love and youth, as last she beheld
    him,
Only more beautiful made by his deathlike silence and
    absence.
Into her thoughts of him time entered not, for it was not.
Over him years had no power; he was not changed, but
    transfigured;
He had become to her heart as one who is dead, and not
    absent;
Patience and abnegation of self, and devotion to others,
This was the lesson a life of trial and sorrow had taught her.

So was her love diffused, but, like to some odorous spices,
Suffered no waste nor loss, though filling the air with aroma.
Other hope had she none, nor wish in life, but to follow,
Meekly with reverent steps, the sacred feet of her Saviour.
Thus many years she lived as a Sister of Mercy; frequenting
Lonely and wretched roofs in the crowded lanes of the city,
Where distress and want concealed themselves from the
   sunlight,
Where disease and sorrow in garrets languished neglected.
Night after night when the world was asleep, as the watch-
   man repeated
Loud, through the gusty streets, that all was well in the city,
High at some lonely window he saw the light of her taper.
Day after day, in the gray of the dawn, as slow through the
   suburbs
Plodded the German farmer, with flowers and fruits for the
   market,
Met he that meek, pale face, returning home from its watch-
   ings.

Then it came to pass that a pestilence fell on the city,
Presaged by wondrous signs, and mostly by flocks of wild
   pigeons,
Darkening the sun in their flight, with naught in their craws
   but an acorn.
And, as the tides of the sea arise in the month of September,
Flooding some silver stream, till it spreads to a lake in the
   meadow,
So death flooded life, and o'erflowing its natural margin,
Spread to a brackish lake the silver stream of existence.

Wealth had no power to bribe, nor beauty to charm the op-
pressor;
But all perished alike beneath the scourge of his anger;
Only, alas! the poor, who had neither friends nor atten-
dants,
Crept away to die in the almshouse, home of the homeless.
Then in the suburbs it stood, in the midst of meadows and
woodlands—
Now the city surrounds it; but still, with its gateway and
wicket
Meek, in the midst of splendor its humble walls seem to
echo
Softly the words of the Lord: "The poor ye always have
with you."
Thither, by night and by day, came the Sister of Mercy. The
dying
Looked up into her face, and thought, indeed, to behold
there
Gleams of celestial light encircle her forehead with splen-
dor,
Such as the artist paints o'er the brows of saints and
apostles,
Or such as hangs by night o'er a city seen at a distance.
Unto their eyes it seemed the lamps of the city celestial,
Into whose shining gates erelong their spirits would enter.

Thus, on a Sabbath morn, through the streets, deserted and
silent,
Wending her quiet way, she entered the door of the almshouse.

Sweet on the summer air was the odor of flowers in the
garden;
And she paused on her way to gather the fairest among
them,
That the dying once more might rejoice in their fragrance
and beauty.
Then, as she mounted the stairs to the corridors, cooled by
the east wind,
Distant and soft on her ear fell the chimes from the belfry
of Christ Church,
While, intermingled with these, across the meadows were
wafted
Sounds of psalms, that were sung by the Swedes in their
church at Wicaco.
Soft as descending wings fell the calm of the hour on her
spirit:
Something within her said, "At length thy trials are ended;"
And, with light in her looks, she entered the chambers of
sickness.
Noiselessly moved about the assiduous, careful at-
tendants,
Moistening the feverish lip, and the aching brow, and in
silence
Closing the sightless eyes of the dead, and concealing their
faces,
Where on their pallets they lay, like drifts of snow by the
roadside.
Many a languid head, upraised as Evangeline entered,
Turned on its pillow of pain to gaze while she passed, for
her presence

Fell on their hearts like a ray of the sun on the walls of a
   prison.
And, as she looked around, she saw how Death, the con-
   soler,
Laying his hand upon many a heart, had healed it forever.
Many familiar forms had disappeared in the night time;
Vacant their places were, or filled already by strangers.

Suddenly, as if arrested by fear or a feeling of wonder,
Still she stood, with her colorless lips apart, while a shudder
Ran through her frame, and, forgotten, the flowerlets
   dropped from her fingers,
And from her eyes and cheeks the light and bloom of the
   morning.
Then there escaped from her lips a cry of such terrible an-
   guish
That the dying heard it, and started up from their pillows.
On the pallet before her was stretched the form of an old
   man.
Long, and thin, and gray were the locks that shaded his
   temples;
But, as he lay in the morning light, his face for a moment
Seemed to assume once more the forms of its earlier man-
   hood;
So are wont to be changed the faces of those who are dying.
Hot and red on his lips still burned the flush of the fever,
As if life, like the Hebrew, with blood had besprinkled its
   portals,
That the Angel of Death might see the sign, and pass over.
Motionless, senseless, dying, he lay, and his spirit exhausted

Seemed to be sinking down through infinite depths in the
darkness,
Darkness of slumber and death, forever sinking and sink-
ing.
Then through those realms of shade, in multiplied rever-
berations,
Heard he that cry of pain, and through the hush that suc-
ceeded
Whispered a gentle voice, in accents tender and saintlike,
"Gabriel! O my beloved!" and died away into silence.
Then he beheld, in a dream, once more the home of his
childhood;
Green Acadian meadows, with sylvan rivers among them,
Village, and mountain, and woodlands; and, walking under
their shadow,
As in the days of her youth, Evangeline rose in his vision.
Tears came into his eyes; and as slowly he lifted his eyelids,
Vanished the vision away, but Evangeline knelt by his bed-
side.
Vainly he strove to whisper her name, for the accents un-
uttered
Died on his lips, and their motion revealed what his tongue
would have spoken.
Vainly he strove to rise; and Evangeline, kneeling beside
him,
Kissed his dying lips, and laid his head on her bosom.
Sweet was the light of his eyes; but it suddenly sank into
darkness,
As when a lamp is blown out by a gust of wind at a case-
ment.

All was ended now, the hope, and the fear, and the sorrow,
All the aching of heart, the restless, unsatisfied longing,
All the dull, deep pain, and constant anguish of patience!
And, as she pressed once more the lifeless head to her
bosom,
Meekly she bowed her own, and murmured, "Father, I
thank thee!"

Still stands the forest primeval; but far away from its
shadow,
Side by side, in their nameless graves, the lovers are sleep-
ing.
Under the humble wall of the little Catholic churchyard,
In the heart of the city, they lie, unknown and unnoticed.
Daily the tides of life go ebbing and flowing beside them,
Thousands of throbbing hearts, where theirs are at rest and
forever,
Thousands of aching brains, where theirs no longer are
busy,
Thousands of toiling hands, where theirs have ceased from
their labors,
Thousands of weary feet, where theirs have completed their
journey!

Still stands the forest primeval; but under the shade of its
branches
Dwells another race, with other customs and language.
Only along the shore of the mournful and misty Atlantic
Linger a few Acadian peasants, whose fathers from exile
Wandered back to their native land to die in its bosom.
In the fisherman's cot the wheel and the loom are still busy;

Maidens still wear their Norman caps and their kirtles of
    homespun,
And by the evening fire repeat Evangeline's story,
While from its rocky caverns the deep-voiced, neighboring
    ocean
Speaks, and in accents disconsolate answers the wail of the
    forest.

H. W. LONGFELLOW

❧ 256 ❧

ICHABOD

So fallen! so lost! the light withdrawn
    Which once he wore!
The glory from his gray hairs gone
    Forevermore!

Revile him not, the Tempter hath
    A snare for all;
And pitying tears, not scorn and wrath,
    Befit his fall!

Oh, dumb be passion's stormy rage,
    When he who might
Have lighted up and led his age,
    Falls back in night.

Scorn! would the angels laugh, to mark
    A bright soul driven,

529

Fiend-goaded, down the endless dark,
    From hope and heaven!

Let not the land once proud of him
    Insult him now,
Nor brand with deeper shame his dim,
    Dishonored brow.

But let its humbled sons, instead,
    From sea to lake,
Along lament, as for the dead,
    In sadness make.

Of all we loved and honored, naught
    Save power remains;
A fallen angel's pride of thought,
    Still strong in chains.

All else is gone; from those great eyes
    The soul has fled:
When faith is lost, when honor dies,
    The man is dead!

Then, pay the reverence of old days
    To his dead fame;
Walk backward, with averted gaze,
    And hide the shame!

J. G. WHITTIER

BARBARA FRIETCHIE

Up from the meadows rich with corn,
Clear in the cool September morn,

The clustered spires of Frederick stand
Green-walled by the hills of Maryland.

Round about them orchards sweep,
Apple and peach tree fruited deep,

Fair as a garden of the Lord,
To the eyes of the famished rebel horde,

On that pleasant morn of the early fall
When Lee marched over the mountain wall—

Over the mountains, winding down,
Horse and foot into Frederick town.

Forty flags with their silver stars,
Forty flags with their crimson bars,

Flapped in the morning wind; the sun
Of noon looked down, and saw not one.

Up rose old Barbara Frietchie then,
Bowed with her fourscore years and ten;

Bravest of all in Frederick town,
She took up the flag the men hauled down;

531

In her attic-window the staff she set,
To show that one heart was loyal yet.

Up the street came the rebel tread,
Stonewall Jackson riding ahead.

Under his slouch hat left and right
He glanced: the old flag met his sight.

"Halt!"—the dust-brown ranks stood fast;
"Fire!"—out blazed the rifle-blast.

It shivered the window, pane and sash;
It rent the banner with seam and gash.

Quick, as it fell, from the broken staff
Dame Barbara snatched the silken scarf;

She leaned far out on the window-sill,
And shook it forth with a royal will.

"Shoot, if you must, this old gray head,
But spare your country's flag," she said.

A shade of sadness, a blush of shame,
Over the face of the leader came;

The nobler nature within him stirred
To life at that woman's deed and word:

"Who touches a hair of yon gray head
Dies like a dog! March on!" he said.

All day long through Frederick street
Sounded the tread of marching feet;

All day long that free flag tost
Over the heads of the rebel host.

Ever its torn folds rose and fell
On the loyal winds that loved it well;

And through the hill-gaps sunset light
Shone over it with a warm good-night.

Barbara Frietchie's work is o'er,
And the rebel rides on his raids no more.

Honor to her! and let a tear
Fall, for her sake, on Stonewall's bier.

Over Barbara Frietchie's grave,
Flag of freedom and union wave!

Peace and order and beauty draw
Round thy symbol of light and law;

And ever the stars above look down
On thy stars below in Frederick town.

J. G. WHITTIER

❧ 258 ❧

AT LAST

WHEN on my day of life the night is falling,
    And, in the winds from unsunned spaces blown,
I hear far voices out of darkness calling
    My feet to paths unknown,

Thou who hast made my home of life so pleasant,
    Leave not its tenant when its walls decay;
O Love Divine, O Helper ever present,
    Be Thou my strength and stay!

Be near me when all else is from me drifting;
    Earth, sky, home's pictures, days of shade and shine,
And kindly faces to my own uplifting
    The love which answers mine.

I have but Thee, my Father! let Thy spirit
    Be with me then to comfort and uphold;
No gate of pearl, no branch of palm I merit,
    Nor street of shining gold.

Suffice it if—my good and ill unreckoned,
    And both forgiven through Thy abounding grace—
I find myself by hands familiar beckoned
    Unto my fitting place.

Some humble door among Thy many mansions,
    Some sheltering shade where sin and striving cease,
And flows forever through heaven's green expansions
    The river of Thy peace.

There, from the music round about me stealing,
    I fain would learn the new and holy song,
And find at last, beneath Thy trees of healing,
    The life for which I long.

                                    J. G. WHITTIER

From the RUBÁIYÁT OF OMAR KHAYYÁM OF NAISHÁPÚR

67

Ah, with the Grape my fading Life provide,
And wash my Body whence the Life has died,
　　And in a Winding-sheet of Vine-leaf wrapt,
So bury me by some sweet Garden-side.

68

That ev'n my buried Ashes such a Snare
Of Perfume shall fling up into the Air,
　　As not a True Believer passing by
But shall be overtaken unaware.

69

Indeed the Idols I have loved so long
Have done my Credit in Men's Eye much wrong:
　　Have drown'd my Honour in a shallow Cup,
And sold my Reputation for a Song.

70

Indeed, indeed, Repentance oft before
I swore—but was I sober when I swore?

And then and then came Spring, and Rose-in-hand
My thread-bare Penitence apieces tore.

71

And much as Wine has play'd the Infidel,
And robb'd me of my Robe of Honour—well,
    I oft wonder what the Vintners buy
One-half so precious as the Goods they sell.

72

Alas, that Spring should vanish with the Rose!
That Youth's sweet-scented Manuscript should close!
    The Nightingale that in the Branches sang,
Ah, whence, and whither flown again, who knows!

73

Ah, Love! could thou and I with Fate conspire
To grasp this sorry Scheme of Things entire,
    Would not we shatter it to bits—and then
Re-mould it nearer to the Heart's Desire!

74

Ah, Moon of my Delight who know'st no wane,
The Moon of Heav'n is rising once again:
    How oft hereafter rising shall she look
Through this same Garden after me—in vain!

75

And when Thyself with shining Foot shall pass
Among the Guests Star-scatter'd on the Grass,
 And in thy joyous Errand reach the Spot
Where I made one—turn down an empty Glass!

TAMAM SHUD

E. FITZGERALD

❧ 260 ❦

TO HELEN

HELEN, thy beauty is to me
 Like those Nicean barks of yore,
That gently, o'er a perfumed sea,
 The weary, wayworn wanderer bore
 To his own native shore.

On desperate seas long wont to roam,
 Thy hyacinth hair, thy classic face,
Thy Naiad airs have brought me home
 To the glory that was Greece
 And the grandeur that was Rome.

Lo! in yon brilliant window-niche
 How statue-like I see thee stand!
 The agate lamp within thy hand,
Ah! Psyche, from the regions which
 Are Holy Land!

E. A. POE

THE RAVEN

ONCE upon a midnight dreary, while I pondered, weak and
weary,
Over many a quaint and curious volume of forgotten lore—
While I nodded, nearly napping, suddenly there came a tapping,
As of someone gently rapping, rapping at my chamber
door.
" 'Tis some visitor," I muttered, "tapping at my chamber
door—
    Only this and nothing more."

Ah, distinctly I remember it was in the bleak December;
And each separate dying ember wrought its ghost upon the
floor.
Eagerly I wished the morrow;—vainly I had sought to bor-
row
From my books surcease of sorrow—sorrow for the lost
Lenore—
For the rare and radiant maiden whom the angels name
Lenore—
    Nameless *here* forevermore.

And the silken, sad, uncertain rusting of each purple curtain
Thrilled me—filled me with fantastic terrors never felt before;

So that now, to still the beating of my heart, I stood repeat-
ing,
" 'Tis some visitor entreating entrance at my chamber
door—
Some late visitor entreating entrance at my chamber
door;—
This it is and nothing more."

Presently my soul grew stronger; hesitating then no longer,
"Sir," said I, "or madam, truly your forgiveness I implore;
But the fact is I was napping, and so gently you came rap-
ping,
And so faintly you came tapping, tapping at my chamber
door,
That I scarce was sure I heard you"—here I opened wide the
door;—
Darkness there and nothing more.

Deep into that darkness peering, long I stood there wonder-
ing, fearing,
Doubting, dreaming dreams no mortal ever dared to dream
before;
But the silence was unbroken, and the stillness gave no
token,
And the only word there spoken was the whispered word,
"Lenore?"
This I whispered, and an echo murmured back the word,
"Lenore!"
Merely this and nothing more.

Back into the chamber turning, all my soul within me
burning,

Soon again I heard a tapping somewhat louder than before.
"Surely," said I, "surely that is something at my window
lattice;
Let me see, then, what thereat is, and this mystery explore—
Let my heart be still a moment and this mystery explore;—
'Tis the wind and nothing more!"

Open here I flung the shutter, when, with many a flirt and
flutter,
In there stepped a stately Raven of the saintly days of yore;
Not the least obeisance made he; not a minute stopped or
stayed he;
But, with mien of lord or lady, perched above my chamber
door—
Perched upon a bust of Pallas just above my chamber
door—
Perched, and sat, and nothing more.

Then this ebony bird beguiling my sad fancy into smiling,
By the grave and stern decorum of the countenance it wore,
"Though thy crest be shorn and shaven, thou," I said, "art
sure no craven,
Ghastly grim and ancient Raven wandering from the
nightly shore—
Tell me what thy lordly name is on the night's Plutonian
shore!"
Quoth the Raven, "Nevermore."

Much I marveled this ungainly fowl to hear discourse so
plainly,
Though its answer little meaning—little relevancy bore;

For we cannot help agreeing that no living human being
Ever yet was blessed with seeing bird above his chamber
 door—
Bird or beast upon the sculptured bust above his chamber
 door,
     With such name as "Nevermore."
But the Raven, sitting lonely on the placid bust, spoke only
That one word, as if his soul in that one word he did out-
 pour.
Nothing farther then he uttered—not a feather then he
 fluttered—
Till I scarcely more than muttered, "Other friends have
 flown before—
On the morrow *he* will leave me, as my hopes have flown
 before."
     Then the bird said, "Nevermore."
Startled at the stillness broken by reply so aptly spoken,
"Doubtless," said I, "what it utters is its only stock and store
Caught from some unhappy master whom unmerciful
 disaster
Followed fast and followed faster till his songs one burden
 bore—
Till the dirges of his hope that melancholy burden bore
     Of 'Never—nevermore'."
But the Raven still beguiling my sad fancy into smiling,
Straight I wheeled a cushioned seat in front of bird and bust
 and door;
Then, upon the velvet sinking, I betook myself to linking
Fancy unto fancy, thinking what this ominous bird of
 yore—

What this grim, ungainly, ghastly, gaunt, and ominous bird
of yore
    Meant in croaking "Nevermore."

This I sat engaged in guessing, but no syllable expressing
To the fowl whose fiery eyes now burned into my bosom's
core;
This and more I sat divining, with my head at ease reclining
On the cushion's velvet lining that the lamplight gloated
o'er,
But whose velvet-violet lining with the lamplight gloating
o'er,
    She shall press, ah, nevermore!

Then, methought, the air grew denser, perfumed from an
unseen censer
Swung by seraphim whose footfalls tinkled on the tufted
floor.
"Wretch," I cried, "thy God hath lent thee—by these angels
he hath sent thee
Respite—respite and nepenthe from thy memories of
Lenore;
Quaff, oh, quaff this kind nepenthe and forget this lost
Lenore!"
    Quoth the Raven, "Nevermore."

"Prophet!" said I, "thing of evil!—prophet still, if bird or
devil!—
Whether Tempter sent, or whether tempest tossed thee here
ashore,
Desolate yet all undaunted, on this desert land enchanted—
On this home by horror haunted—tell me truly, I implore—

Is there—*is* there balm in Gilead?—tell me—tell me, I implore!"

 Quoth the Raven, "Nevermore."

"Prophet!" said I, "thing of evil—prophet still, if bird or
devil!

By that heaven that bends above us—by that God we both
adore—

Tell this soul with sorrow laden if, within the distant
Aidenn,

It shall clasp a sainted maiden whom the angels name
Lenore—

Clasp a rare and radiant maiden whom the angels name
Lenore."

 Quoth the Raven, "Nevermore."

"Be that word our sign of parting, bird or fiend!" I shrieked,
upstarting—

"Get thee back into the tempest and the night's Plutonian
shore!

Leave no black plume as a token of that lie thy soul hath
spoken!

Leave my loneliness unbroken!—quit the bust above my
door!

Take thy beak from out my heart, and take thy form from
off my door!"

 Quoth the Raven, "Nevermore."

And the Raven, never flitting, still is sitting, *still* is sitting
On the pallid bust of Pallas just above my chamber door;
And his eyes have all the seeming of a demon's that is
dreaming,

And the lamplight o'er him streaming throws his shadow on
    the floor;
And my soul from out that shadow that lies floating on the
    floor
       Shall be lifted—nevermore!

E. A. POE

❧262❧

ANNABEL LEE

IT was many and many a year ago,
    In a kingdom by the sea,
That a maiden there lived whom you may know
    By the name of Annabel Lee;—
And this maiden she lived with no other thought
    Than to love and be loved by me.

She was a child and I was a child,
    In this kingdom by the sea,
But we loved with a love that was more than love—
    I and my Annabel Lee—
With a love that the winged seraphs of Heaven
    Coveted her and me.

And this was the reason that, long ago,
    In this kingdom by the sea,
A wind blew out of a cloud, by night
    Chilling my Annabel Lee;
So that her highborn kinsmen came
    And bore her away from me,

To shut her up in a sepulchre
In this kingdom by the sea.

The angels, not half so happy in Heaven,
Went envying her and me:
Yes! that was the reason (as all men know,
In this kingdom by the sea)
That the wind came out of the cloud, chilling
And killing my Annabel Lee.

But our love it was stronger by far than the love
Of those who were older than we—
Of many far wiser than we—
And neither the angels in Heaven above
Nor the demons down under the sea,
Can ever dissever my soul from the soul
Of the beautiful Annabel Lee:—

For the moon never beams without bringing me dreams
Of the beautiful Annabel Lee;
And the stars never rise but I see the bright eyes
Of the beautiful Annabel Lee;
And so, all the night-tide, I lie down by the side
Of my darling, my darling, my life and my bride,
In her sepulchre there by the sea—
In her tomb by the sounding sea.

E. A. POE

❧ 263 ☙

THE EAGLE

FRAGMENT

HE clasps the crag with crooked hands;
Close to the sun in lonely lands,
Ring'd with the azure world, he stands.

The wrinkled sea beneath him crawls;
He watches from his mountain walls,
And like a thunderbolt he falls.

LORD TENNYSON

❧ 264 ☙

BREAK, break, break,
　On thy cold gray stones, O Sea!
And I would that my tongue could utter
　The thoughts that arise in me.

O well for the fisherman's boy,
　That he shouts with his sister at play!
O well for the sailor lad,
　That he sings in his boat on the bay!

And the stately ships go on
　To their haven under the hill;

But O for the touch of a vanish'd hand,
  And the sound of a voice that is still!

Break, break, break,
  At the foot of thy crags, O sea!
But the tender grace of a day that is dead
  Will never come back to me.

LORD TENNYSON

❧ 265 ❧

From THE PRINCESS

THE splendour falls on castle walls
  And snowy summits old in story:
The long light shakes across the lakes,
  And the wild cataract leaps in glory.
Blow, bugle, blow, set the wild echoes flying,
Blow, bugle; answer, echoes, dying, dying, dying.

O hark, O hear! how thin and clear,
  And thinner, clearer, farther going!
O sweet and far from cliff and scar
  The horns of Elfland faintly blowing!
Blow, let us hear the purple glens replying:
Blow, bugle; answer, echoes, dying, dying, dying.

O love, they die in yon rich sky,
  They faint on hill or field or river:
Our echoes roll from soul to soul,
  And grow for ever and for ever.

Blow, bugle, blow, set the wild echoes flying,
And answer, echoes, answer, dying, dying, dying.

❧ 266 ❧

Tears, idle tears, I know not what they mean,
Tears from the depth of some divine despair
Rise in the heart, and gather to the eyes,
In looking on the happy Autumn-fields,
And thinking of the days that are no more.

Fresh as the first beam glittering on a sail,
That brings our friends up from the underworld,
Sad as the last which reddens over one
That sinks with all we love below the verge;
So sad, so fresh, the days that are no more.

Ah, sad and strange as in dark summer dawns
The earliest pipe of half-awaken'd birds
To dying ears, when unto dying eyes
The casement slowly grows a glimmering square;
So sad, so strange, the days that are no more.

Dear as remember'd kisses after death,
And sweet as those by hopeless fancy feign'd
On lips that are for others; deep as love,
Deep as first love, and wild with all regret;
O Death in Life, the days that are no more.

❧ 267 ❧

Now sleeps the crimson petal, now the white;
Nor waves the cypress in the palace walk;
Nor winks the gold fin in the porphyry font:
The firefly wakens: waken thou with me.

Now droops the milkwhite peacock like a ghost,
And like a ghost she glimmers on to me.

Now lies the Earth all Danaë to the stars,
And all thy heart lies open unto me.

Now slides the silent meteor on, and leaves
A shining furrow, as thy thoughts in me.

Now folds the lily all her sweetness up,
And slips into the bosom of the lake:
So fold thyself, my dearest, thou, and slip
Into my bosom and be lost in me.

❧ 268 ❧

Come down, O maid, from yonder mountain
    height:
What pleasure lives in height (the shepherd sang)
In height and cold, the splendour of the hills?
But cease to move so near the Heavens, and cease
To glide a sunbeam by the blasted Pine,

To sit a star upon the sparkling spire;
And come, for Love is of the valley, come,
For Love is of the valley, come thou down
And find him; by the happy threshold, he,
Or hand in hand with Plenty in the maize,
Or red with spirted purple of the vats,
Or foxlike in the vine; nor cares to walk
With Death and Morning on the silver horns,
Nor wilt thou snare him in the white ravine,
Nor find him dropt upon the firths of ice,
That huddling slant in furrow-cloven falls
To roll the torrent out of dusky doors:
But follow; let the torrent dance thee down
To find him in the valley; let the wild
Lean-headed Eagles yelp alone, and leave
The monstrous ledges there to slope, and spill
Their thousand wreaths of dangling watersmoke,
That like a broken purpose waste in air:
So waste not thou; but come; for all the vales
Await thee; azure pillars of the hearth
Arise to thee: the children call, and I
Thy shepherd pipe, and sweet is every sound,
Sweeter thy voice, but every sound is sweet;
Myriads of rivulets hurrying thro' the lawn,
The moan of doves in immemorial elms,
And murmuring of innumerable bees.

LORD TENNYSON

269

TO THE REV. F. D. MAURICE

COME, when no graver cares employ,
Godfather, come and see your boy:
    Your presence will be sun in winter,
Making the little one leap for joy.

For, being of that honest few,
Who give the Fiend himself his due,
    Should eighty-thousand college-councils
Thunder 'Anathema,' friend, at you;

Should all our churchmen foam in spite
At you, so careful of the right,
    Yet one lay-heath would give you welcome
(Take it and come) to the Isle of Wight;

Where, far from noise and smoke of town,
I watch the twilight falling brown
    All round a careless-order'd garden
Close to the ridge of a noble down.

You'll have no scandal while you dine,
But honest talk and wholesome wine,
    And only hear the magpie gossip
Garrulous under a roof of pine:

For groves of pine on either hand,
To break the blast of winter, stand;

And further on, the hoary Channel
Tumbles a billow on chalk and sand;

Where, if below the milky steep
Some ship of battle slowly creep,
  And on thro' zones of light and shadow
Glimmer away to the lonely deep,

We might discuss the Northern sin
Which made a selfish war begin;
  Dispute the claims, arrange the chances;
Emperor, Ottoman, which shall win:

Or whether war's avenging rod
Shall lash all Europe into blood;
  Till you should turn to dearer matters,
Dear to the man that is dear to God;

How best to help the slender store,
How mend the dwellings, of the poor;
  How gain in life, as life advances,
Valour and charity more and more.

Come, Maurice, come: the lawn as yet
Is hoar with rime, or spongy-wet;
  But when the wreath of March has blossom'd,
Crocus, anemone, violet,

Or later, pay one visit here,
For those are few we hold as dear;
  Nor pay but one, but come for many,
Many and many a happy year.

January, 1854

LORD TENNYSON

270

From IN MEMORIAM A. H. H.

OBIIT MDCCCXXXIII

II

OLD Yew, which graspest at the stones
That name the under-lying dead,
Thy fibres net the dreamless head,
Thy roots are wrapt about the bones.

The seasons bring the flower again,
And bring the firstling to the flock;
And in the dusk of thee, the clock
Beats out the little lives of men.

O not for thee the glow, the bloom,
Who changest not in any gale,
Nor branding summer suns avail
To touch thy thousand years of gloom:

And gazing on thee, sullen tree,
Sick for thy stubborn hardihood,
I seem to fail from out my blood
And grow incorporate into thee.

VII

Dark house, by which once more I stand
Here in the long unlovely street,

Doors, where my heart was used to beat
So quickly, waiting for a hand,

A hand that can be clasp'd no more—
    Behold me, for I cannot sleep,
    And like a guilty thing I creep
At earliest morning to the door.

He is not here; but far away
    The noise of life begins again,
    And ghastly thro' the drizzling rain
On the bald street breaks the blank day.

XV

To-night the winds begin to rise
    And roar from yonder dropping day:
    The last red leaf is whirl'd away,
The rooks are blown about the skies;

The forest crack'd, the waters curl'd,
    The cattle huddled on the lea;
    And wildly dash'd on tower and tree
The sunbeam strikes along the world:

And but for fancies, which aver
    That all thy motions gently pass
    Athwart a plane of molten glass,
I scarce could brook the strain and stir

That makes the barren branches loud;
    And but for fear it is not so,

The wild unrest that lives in woe
Would dote and pore on yonder cloud

That rises upward always higher,
    And onward drags a labouring breast,
    And topples round the dreary west,
A looming bastion fringed with fire.

XIX

The Danube to the Severn gave
    The darken'd heart that beat no more;
    They laid him by the pleasant shore,
And in the hearing of the wave.

There twice a day the Severn fills;
    The salt sea-water passes by,
    And hushes half the babbling Wye,
And makes a silence in the hills.

The Wye is hush'd nor moved along,
    And hush'd my deepest grief of all,
    When fill'd with tears that cannot fall,
I brim with sorrow drowning song.

The tide flows down, the wave again
    Is vocal in its wooded walls;
    My deeper anguish also falls,
And I can speak a little then.

. . . . .

Till now the doubtful dusk reveal'd
   The knolls once more where, couch'd at ease,
   The white kine glimmer'd, and the trees
Laid their dark arms about the field:

And suck'd from out the distant gloom
   A breeze began to tremble o'er
   The large leaves of the sycamore,
And fluctuate all the still perfume,

And gathering freshlier overhead,
   Rock'd the full-foliaged elms, and swung
   The heavy-folded rose, and flung
The lilies to and fro, and said

'The dawn, the dawn,' and died away;
   And East and West, without a breath,
   Mixt their dim lights, like life and death,
To broaden into boundless day.

CI

Unwatch'd, the garden bough shall sway,
   The tender blossom flutter down,
   Unloved, that beech will gather brown,
This maple burn itself away;

Unloved, the sun-flower, shining fair,
   Ray round with flames her disk of seed,
   And many a rose-carnation feed

556

With summer spice the humming air;

Unloved, by many a sandy bar,
    The brook shall babble down the plain,
    At noon or when the lesser wain
Is twisting round the polar star;

Uncared for, gird the windy grove,
    And flood the haunts of hern and crake;
    Or into silver arrows break
The sailing moon in creek and cove;

Till from the garden and the wild
    A fresh association blow,
    And year by year the landscape grow
Familiar to the stranger's child;

As year by year the labourer tills
    His wonted glebe, or lops the glades;
    And year by year our memory fades
From all the circle of the hills.

CXIV

Now fades the last long streak of snow,
    Now burgeons every maze of quick
    About the flowering squares, and thick
By ashen roots the violets blow.

Now rings the woodland loud and long,
    The distance takes a lovelier hue,
    And drown'd in yonder living blue
The lark becomes a sightless song.

Now dance the lights on lawn and lea,
   The flocks are whiter down the vale,
   And milkier every milky sail
On winding stream or distant sea;

Where now the seamew pipes, or dives
   In yonder greening gleam, and fly
   The happy birds, that change their sky
To build and brood; that live their lives

From land to land; and in my breast
   Spring wakens too; and my regret
   Becomes an April violet,
And buds and blossoms like the rest.

LORD TENNYSON

❧ 271 ❦

TO VIRGIL

WRITTEN AT THE REQUEST OF THE
MANTUANS FOR THE NINETEENTH
CENTENARY OF VIRGIL'S DEATH

I

ROMAN VIRGIL, thou that singest
   Ilion's lofty temples robed in fire,
Ilion falling, Rome arising,
   wars, and filial faith, and Dido's pyre;

II

Landscape-lover, lord of language
    more than he that sang the Works and Days,
All the chosen coin of fancy
    flashing out from many a golden phrase;

III

Thou that singest wheat and woodland,
    tilth and vineyard, hive and horse and herd;
All the charm of all the Muses
    often flowering in a lonely word;

IV

Poet of the happy Tityrus
    piping underneath his beechen bowers;
Poet of the poet-satyr
    whom the laughing shepherd bound with flowers;

V

Chanter of the Pollio, glorying
    in the blissful years again to be,
Summers of the snakeless meadow,
    unlaborious earth and oarless sea;

VI

Thou that seëst Universal
    Nature moved by Universal Mind;

559

Thou majestic in thy sadness
    at the doubtful doom of human kind;

VII

Light among the vanish'd ages;
    star that gildest yet this phantom shore;
Golden branch amid the shadows,
    kings and realms that pass to rise no more;

VIII

Now thy Forum roars no longer,
    fallen every purple Cæsar's dome—
Tho' thine ocean-roll of rhythm
    sound for ever of Imperial Rome—

IX

Now the Rome of slaves hath perish'd,
    and the Rome of freemen holds her place,
I, from out the Northern Island
    sunder'd once from all the human race,

X

I salute thee, Mantovano,
    I that loved thee since my day began,
Wielder of the stateliest measure
    ever moulded by the lips of man.

LORD TENNYSON

OLD IRONSIDES

Ay, tear her tattered ensign down!
　　Long has it waved on high,
And many an eye has danced to see
　　That banner in the sky;
Beneath it rung the battle shout,
　　And burst the cannon's roar;—
The meteor of the ocean air
　　Shall sweep the clouds no more!

Her deck, once red with heroes' blood,
　　Where knelt the vanquished foe,
When winds were hurrying o'er the flood,
　　And waves were white below,
No more shall feel the victor's tread,
　　Or know the conquered knee;—
The harpies of the shore shall pluck
　　The eagle of the sea!

O better that her shattered hulk
　　Should sink beneath the wave;
Her thunders shook the mighty deep,
　　And there should be her grave;
Nail to the mast her holy flag,
　　Set every threadbare sail,

And give her to the god of storms,
The lightning and the gale!

O. W. HOLMES

❧ 273 ☙

THE LAST LEAF

I SAW him once before,
As he passed by the door,
 And again
The pavement stones resound,
As he totters o'er the ground
 With his cane.

They say that in his prime,
Ere the pruning-knife of Time
 Cut him down,
Not a better man was found
By the Crier on his round
 Through the town.

But now he walks the streets,
And he looks at all he meets
 Sad and wan,
And he shakes his feeble head,
That it seems as if he said,
 "They are gone."

The mossy marbles rest
On the lips that he has prest

In their bloom,
And the names he loved to hear
Have been carved for many a year
On the tomb.

My grandmamma has said—
Poor old lady, she is dead
Long ago—
That he had a Roman nose,
And his cheek was like a rose
In the snow.

But now his nose is thin,
And it rests upon his chin
Like a staff,
And a crook is in his back,
And a melancholy crack
In his laugh.

I know it is a sin
For me to sit and grin
At him here;
But the old three-cornered hat,
And the breeches, and all that,
Are so queer!

And if I should live to be
The last leaf upon the tree
In the spring,
Let them smile, as I do now,
At the old forsaken bough
Where I cling.

O. W. HOLMES

＊ 274 ＊

CONTENTMENT

"Man wants but little here below."

LITTLE I ask; my wants are few;
   I only wish a hut of stone,
(*A very plain* brown stone will do,)
   That I may call my own;—
And close at hand is such a one,
In yonder street that fronts the sun.

Plain food is quite enough for me;
   Three courses are as good as ten;—
If Nature can subsist on three,
   Thank Heaven for three. Amen!
I always thought cold victual nice;—
My *choice* would be vanilla-ice.

I care not much for gold or land;—
   Give me a mortgage here and there,—
Some good bank-stock, some note of hand,
   Or trifling railroad share,—
I only ask that Fortune send
A *little* more than I shall spend.

Honors are silly toys, I know,
   And titles are but empty names;
I would, *perhaps,* be Plenipo,—
   But only near St. James;

I'm very sure I should not care
To fill our Gubernator's chair.

Jewels are bawbles; 't is a sin
    To care for such unfruitful things;—
One good-sized diamond in a pin,—
        Some, *not so large,* in rings,—
A ruby, and a pearl, or so,
Will do for me;—I laugh at show.

My dame should dress in cheap attire;
    (Good, heavy silks are never dear;)—
I own perhaps I *might* desire
        Some shawls of true Cashmere,—
Some marrowy crapes of China silk,
Like wrinkled skins on scalded milk.

I would not have the horse I drive
    So fast that folks must stop and stare;
An easy gait—two, forty-five—
        Suits me; I do not care;—
Perhaps, for just a *single spurt,*
Some seconds less would do no hurt.

Of pictures, I should like to own
    Titians and Raphaels three or four,—
I love so much their style and tone,—
        One Turner, and no more,
(A landscape,—foreground golden dirt,—
The sunshine painted with a squirt.)

Of books but few,—some fifty score
    For daily use, and bound for wear;

The rest upon an upper floor;—
    Some *little* luxury *there*
Of red morocco's gilded gleam,
And vellum rich as country cream.

Busts, cameos, gems,—such things as these,
    Which others often show for pride,
I value for their power to please,
    And selfish churls deride;—
One Stradivarius, I confess,
Two Meerschaums, I would fain possess.

Wealth's wasteful tricks I will not learn
    Nor ape the glittering upstart fool;—
Shall not carved tables serve my turn,
    But *all* must be of buhl?
Give grasping pomp its double share,—
I ask but *one* recumbent chair.

Thus humble let me live and die,
    Nor long for Midas' golden touch;
If Heaven more generous gifts deny,
    I shall not miss them *much*,—
Too grateful for the blessing lent
Of simple tastes and mind content!

               O. W. HOLMES

THE DEACON'S MASTERPIECE

OR, THE WONDERFUL "ONE-HOSS SHAY."
A LOGICAL STORY.

HAVE you heard of the wonderful one-hoss shay,
That was built in such a logical way
It ran a hundred years to a day,
And then, of a sudden, it——ah, but stay,
I'll tell you what happened without delay,
Scaring the parson into fits,
Frightening people out of their wits,—
Have you ever heard of that, I say?

Seventeen hundred and fifty-five.
Georgius Secundus was then alive,—
Snuffy old drone from the German hive.
That was the year when Lisbon-town
Saw the earth open and gulp her down,
And Braddock's army was done so brown,
Left without a scalp to its crown.
It was on the terrible Earthquake-day
That the Deacon finished the one-hoss shay.

Now in building of chaises, I tell you what,
There is always *somewhere* a weakest spot,—
In hub, tire, felloe, in spring or thill,
In panel, or crossbar, or floor, or sill,

In screw, bolt, thoroughbrace,—lurking still,
Find it somewhere you must and will,—
Above or below, or within or without,—
And that's the reason, beyond a doubt,
That a chaise *breaks down,* but does n't *wear out.*

But the Deacon swore, (as Deacons do,
With an "I dew vum," or an "I tell *yeou,*")
He would build one shay to beat the taown
'n' the keounty 'n' all the kentry raoun';
It should be so built that it *couldn'* break daown:
—"Fur," said the Deacon, " 't's mighty plain
Thut the weakes' place mus' stan' the strain;
'n' the way t' fix it, uz I maintain, Is only jest
T' make that place uz strong uz the rest."

So the Deacon inquired of the village folk
Where he could find the strongest oak,
That could n't be split nor bent nor broke,—
That was for spokes and floor and sills;
He sent for lancewood to make the thills;
The crossbars were ash, from the straightest trees,
The panels of white-wood, that cuts like cheese,
But lasts like iron for things like these;
The hubs of logs from the "Settler's ellum,"—
Last of its timber,—they could n't sell 'em,
Never an axe had seen their chips,
And the wedges flew from between their lips,
Their blunt ends frizzled like celery-tips;
Step and prop-iron, bolt and screw,
Spring, tire, axle, and linchpin too,

Steel of the finest, bright and blue;
Thoroughbrace bison-skin, thick and wide;
Boot, top, dasher, from tough old hide
Found in the pit when the tanner died.
That was the way he "put her through."—
"There!" said the Deacon, "naow she'll dew!"

Do! I tell you, I rather guess
She was a wonder, and nothing less!
Colts grew horses, beards turned gray,
Deacon and deaconess dropped away,
Children and grandchildren—where were they?
But there stood the stout old one-hoss shay
As fresh as on Lisbon-earthquake-day!

EIGHTEEN HUNDRED;—it came and found
The Deacon's masterpiece strong and sound.
Eighteen hundred increased by ten;—
"Hahnsum kerridge" they called it then.
Eighteen hundred and twenty came;—
Running as usual; much the same.
Thirty and forty at last arrive,
And then come fifty, and FIFTY-FIVE.

Little of all we value here
Wakes on the morn of its hundredth year
Without both feeling and looking queer.
In fact, there's nothing that keeps its youth,
So far as I know, but a tree and truth.
(This is a moral that runs at large;
Take it.—You're welcome.—No extra charge.)

FIRST OF NOVEMBER,—the Earthquake-day—
There are traces of age in the one-hoss shay,
A general flavor of mild decay,
But nothing local, as one may say.
There could n't be,—for the Deacon's art
Had made it so like in every part
That there was n't a chance for one to start.
For the wheels were just as strong as the thills,
And the floor was just as strong as the sills,
And the panels just as strong as the floor,
And the whipple-tree neither less nor more,
And the back-crossbar as strong as the fore,
And spring and axle and hub *encore.*
And yet, *as a whole,* it is past a doubt
In another hour it will be *worn out!*

First of November, 'Fifty-five!
This morning the parson takes a drive.
Now, small boys, get out of the way!
Here comes the wonderful one-hoss shay,
Drawn by a rat-tailed, ewe-necked bay.
"Huddup!" said the parson.—Off went they.
The parson was working his Sunday's text,—
Had got to *fifthly,* and stopped perplexed
At what the—Moses—was coming next.
All at once the horse stood still,
Close by the meet'n'-house on the hill.
—First a shiver, and then a thrill,
Then something decidedly like a spill,—
And the parson was sitting upon a rock,

At half past nine by the meet'n'-house clock,—
Just the hour of the Earthquake shock!
—What do you think the parson found,
When he got up and stared around?
The poor old chaise in a heap or mound,
As if it had been to the mill and ground!
You see, of course, if you're not a dunce,
How it went to pieces all at once,—
All at once, and nothing first,—
Just as bubbles do when they burst.

End of the wonderful one-hoss shay.
Logic is logic. That's all I say.

O. W. HOLMES

✤ 276 ✤

UP AT A VILLA—DOWN IN THE CITY

(AS DISTINGUISHED BY AN ITALIAN PERSON OF QUALITY)

I

HAD I but plenty of money, money enough and to spare,
The house for me, no doubt, were a house in the city-
    square;
Ah, such a life, such a life, as one leads at the window
    there!

Something to see, by Bacchus, something to hear, at least!
There, the whole day long, one's life is a perfect feast;
While up at a villa one lives, I maintain it, no more than a
beast.

Well now, look at our villa! stuck like the horn of a bull
Just on a mountain-edge as bare as the creature's skull,
Save a mere shag of a bush with hardly a leaf to pull!
—I scratch my own, sometimes, to see if the hair's turned
wool.

But the city, oh the city—the square with the houses!
Why?
They are stone-faced, white as a curd, there's something to
take the eye!
Houses in four straight lines, not a single front awry;
You watch who crosses and gossips, who saunters, who
hurries by;
Green blinds, as a matter of course, to draw when the sun
gets high;
And the shops with fanciful signs which are painted prop-
erly.

What of a villa? Though winter be over in March by
    rights,
'Tis May perhaps ere the snow shall have withered well off
    the heights:
You've the brown ploughed land before, where the oxen
    steam and wheeze,
And the hills over-smoked behind by the faint grey olive-
    trees.

VI

Is it better in May, I ask you? You've summer all at once;
In a day he leaps complete with a few strong April suns.
'Mid the sharp short emerald wheat, scarce risen three
    fingers well,
The wild tulip, at end of its tube, blows out its great red
    bell
Like a thin clear bubble of blood, for the children to pick
    and sell.

VII

Is it ever hot in the square? There's a fountain to spout
    and splash!
In the shade it sings and springs; in the shine such foam-
    bows flash
On the horses with curling fish-tails, that prance and pad-
    dle and pash

Round the lady atop in her conch—fifty gazers do not
  abash,
Though all that she wears is some weeds round her waist
  in a sort of sash.

VIII

All the year long at the villa, nothing to see though you
  linger,
Except yon cypress that points like death's lean lifted fore-
  finger.
Some think fireflies pretty, when they mix i' the corn and
  mingle,
Or thrid the stinking hemp till the stalks of it seem
  a-tingle.
Late August or early September, the stunning cicala is
  shrill,
And the bees keep their tiresome whine round the resinous
  firs on the hill.
Enough of the seasons,—I spare you the months of the
  fever and chill.

IX

Ere you open your eyes in the city, the blessed church-
  bells begin:
No sooner the bells leave off than the diligence rattles in:
You get the pick of the news, and it costs you never a pin.
By-and-by there's the travelling doctor gives pills, lets
  blood, draws teeth;

574

Or the Pulcinello-trumpet breaks up the market beneath.

At the post-office such a scene-picture—the new play, piping hot!

And a notice how, only this morning, three liberal thieves
were shot.

Above it, behold the Archbishop's most fatherly of re-
bukes,

And beneath, with his crown and his lion, some little new
law of the Duke's!

Or a sonnet with flowery marge, to the Reverend Don So-
and-so

Who is Dante, Boccaccio, Petrarca, Saint Jerome and
Cicero,

'And moreover,' (the sonnet goes rhyming,) 'the skirts of
Saint Paul has reached,

'Having preached us those six Lent-lectures more unctuous
than ever he preached.'

Noon strikes,—here sweeps the procession! our Lady borne
smiling and smart

With a pink gauze gown all spangles, and seven swords
stuck in her heart!

Bang-whang-whang goes the drum, *tootle-te-tootle* the fife;

No keeping one's haunches still: it's the greatest pleasure
in life.

X

But bless you, it's dear—it's dear! fowls, wine, at double
the rate.

They have clapped a new tax upon salt, and what oil pays
    passing the gate
It's a horror to think of. And so, the villa for me, not the
    city!
Beggars can scarcely be choosers: but still—ah, the pity,
    the pity!
Look, two and two go the priests, then the monks with
    cowls and sandals,
And the penitents dressed in white shirts, a-holding the
    yellow candles;
One, he carries a flag up straight, and another a cross with
    handles,
And the Duke's guard brings up the rear, for the better
    prevention of scandals:
Bang-whang-whang goes the drum, *tootle-te-tootle* the fife.
Oh, a day in the city-square, there is no such pleasure in
    life!

R. BROWNING

❧ 277 ❧

A TOCCATA OF GALUPPI'S

I

OH Galuppi, Baldassaro, this is very sad to find!
I can hardly misconceive you; it would prove me deaf and
    blind;
But although I take your meaning, 'tis with such a heavy
    mind!

Here you come with your old music, and here's all the
　　good it brings.
What, they lived once thus at Venice where the merchants
　　were the kings,
Where Saint Mark's is, where the Doges used to wed the
　　sea with rings?

Ay, because the sea's the street there; and 'tis arched by
　　. . . what you call
. . . Shylock's bridge with houses on it, where they kept
　　the carnival:
I was never out of England—it's as if I saw it all.

Did young people take their pleasure when the sea was
　　warm in May?
Balls and masks begun at midnight, burning ever to mid-
　　day,
When they made up fresh adventures for the morrow, do
　　you say?

Was a lady such a lady, cheeks so round and lips so red,—
On her neck the small face buoyant, like a bell-flower on
　　its bed,

577

O'er the breast's superb abundance where a man might
    base his head?

VI

Well, and it was graceful of them—they'd break talk off
    and afford
—She, to bite her mask's black velvet—he, to finger on his
    sword,
While you sat and played Toccatas, stately at the clavi-
    chord?

VII

What? Those lesser thirds so plaintive, sixths diminished,
    sigh on sigh,
Told them something? Those suspensions, those solutions
    —'Must we die?'
Those commiserating sevenths—'Life might last! we can
    but try!'

VIII

'Were you happy?'—'Yes.'—'And are you still as happy?'—
    'Yes. And you?'
—'Then, more kisses!'—'Did *I* stop them, when a million
    seemed so few?'
Hark, the dominant's persistence till it must be answered
    to!

IX

So, an octave struck the answer. Oh, they praised you, I
    dare say!

578

'Brave Galuppi! that was music! good alike at grave and
  gay!
'I can always leave off talking when I hear a master play!'

X

Then they left you for their pleasure: till in due time, one
  by one,
Some with lives that came to nothing, some with deeds as
  well undone,
Death stepped tacitly and took them where they never see
  the sun.

XI

But when I sit down to reason, think to take my stand nor
  swerve,
While I triumph o'er a secret wrung from nature's close
  reserve,
In you come with your cold music till I creep thro' every
  nerve.

XII

Yes, you, like a ghostly cricket, creaking where a house
  was burned:
'Dust and ashes, dead and done with, Venice spent what
  Venice earned.
'The soul, doubtless, is immortal—where a soul can be dis-
  cerned.

XIII

'Yours for instance: you know physics, something of
    geology,
'Mathematics are your pastime; souls shall rise in their
    degree;
'Butterflies may dread extinction,—you'll not die, it cannot
    be!

XIV

'As for Venice and her people, merely born to bloom and
    drop,
'Here on earth they bore their fruitage, mirth and folly
    were the crop:
'What of soul was left, I wonder, when the kissing had to
    stop?

XV

'Dust and ashes!' So you creak it, and I want the heart to
    scold.
Dear dead women, with such hair, too—what's become of
    all the gold
Used to hang and brush their bosoms? I feel chilly and
    grown old.

R. BROWNING

MY LAST DUCHESS

FERRARA

THAT's my last Duchess painted on the wall,
Looking as if she were alive. I call
That piece a wonder, now: Frà Pandolf's hands
Worked busily a day, and there she stands.
Will't please you sit and look at her? I said
'Frà Pandolf' by design, for never read
Strangers like you that pictured countenance,
The depth and passion of its earnest glance,
But to myself they turned (since none puts by
The curtain I have drawn for you, but I)
And seemed as they would ask me, if they durst,
How such a glance came there; so, not the first
Are you to turn and ask thus. Sir, 'twas not
Her husband's presence only, called that spot
Of joy into the Duchess' cheek: perhaps
Frà Pandolf chanced to say 'Her mantle laps
'Over my lady's wrist too much,' or 'Paint
'Must never hope to reproduce the faint
'Half-flush that dies along her throat:' such stuff
Was courtesy, she thought, and cause enough
For calling up that spot of joy. She had
A heart—how shall I say?—too soon made glad,
Too easily impressed; she liked whate'er

She looked on, and her looks went everywhere.
Sir, 'twas all one! My favour at her breast,
The dropping of the daylight in the West,
The bough of cherries some officious fool
Broke in the orchard for her, the white mule
She rode with round the terrace—all and each
Would draw from her alike the approving speech,
Or blush, at least. She thanked men,—good! but thanked
Somehow—I know not how—as if she ranked
My gift of a nine-hundred-years-old name
With anybody's gift. Who'd stoop to blame
This sort of trifling? Even had you skill
In speech—(which I have not)—to make your will
Quite clear to such an one, and say, 'Just this
'Or that in you disgusts me; here you miss,
'Or there exceed the mark'—and if she let
Herself be lessoned so, nor plainly set
Her wits to yours, forsooth, and made excuse,
—E'en then would be some stooping; and I choose
Never to stoop. Oh sir, she smiled, no doubt,
Whene'er I passed her; but who passed without
Much the same smile? This grew; I gave commands;
Then all smiles stopped together. There she stands
As if alive. Will't please you rise? We'll meet
The company below, then. I repeat,
The Count your master's known munificence
Is ample warrant that no just pretence
Of mine for dowry will be disallowed;
Though his fair daughter's self, as I avowed
At starting, is my object. Nay, we'll go

Together down, sir. Notice Neptune, though,
Taming a sea-horse, thought a rarity,
Which Claus of Innsbruck cast in bronze for me!

R. BROWNING

❧ 279 ❧

CONFESSIONS

I

WHAT is he buzzing in my ears?
  'Now that I come to die,
'Do I view the world as a vale of tears?'
  Ah, reverend sir, not I!

II

What I viewed there once, what I view again
  Where the physic bottles stand
On the table's edge,—is a suburb lane,
  With a wall to my bedside hand.

III

That lane sloped, much as the bottles do,
  From a house you could descry
O'er the garden-wall: is the curtain blue
  Or green to a healthy eye?

To mine, it serves for the old June weather
    Blue above lane and wall;
And that farthest bottle labelled 'Ether'
    Is the house o'ertopping all.

At a terrace, somewhere near the stopper,
    There watched for me, one June,
A girl: I know, sir, it's improper,
    My poor mind's out of tune.

Only, there was a way . . . you crept
    Close by the side, to dodge
Eyes in the house, two eyes except:
    They styled their house 'The Lodge.'

What right had a lounger up their lane?
    But, by creeping very close,
With the good wall's help,—their eyes
        might strain
    And stretch themselves to Oes,

Yet never catch her and me together,
    As she left the attic, there,

By the rim of the bottle labelled 'Ether,'
    And stole from stair to stair,

IX

And stood by the rose-wreathed gate. Alas,
    We loved, sir—used to meet:
How sad and bad and mad it was—
    But then, how it was sweet!

R. BROWNING

❧ 280 ☙

LOVE

I ASKED of Time to tell me where was Love;
He pointed to her foot-steps on the snow,
Where first the angel lighted from above,
And bid me note the way and onward go;
Through populous streets of cities spreading wide,
By lonely cottage rising on the moor,
Where bursts from sundered cliff the struggling tide,
To where it hails the sea with answering roar,
She led me on; o'er mountain's frozen head,
Where mile on mile still stretches on the plain,
Then homeward whither first my feet she led,
I traced her path along the snow again;
But there the sun had melted from the earth
The prints where first she trod, a child of mortal birth.

J. VERY

281

THE HAND AND FOOT

THE hand and foot that stir not, they shall find
Sooner than all the rightful place to go:
Now in their motion free as roving wind,
Though first no snail so limited and slow;
I mark them full of labor all the day,
Each active motion made in perfect rest;
They cannot from their path mistaken stray,
Though 't is not theirs, yet in it they are blest;
The bird has not their hidden track found out,
The cunning fox though full of art he be;
It is the way unseen, the certain route,
Where ever bound, yet thou art ever free;
The path of Him, whose perfect law of love
Bids spheres and atoms in just order move.

J. VERY

282

MY PRAYER

GREAT God, I ask thee for no meaner pelf
Than that I may not disappoint myself;
That in my action I may soar as high
As I can now discern with this clear eye.

586

And next in value, which thy kindness lends,
That I may greatly disappoint my friends,
Howe'er they think or hope that it may be,
They may not dream how thou'st distinguished me.

That my weak hand may equal my firm faith,
And my life practise more than my tongue saith;
That my low conduct may not show,
Nor my relenting lines,
That I thy purpose did not know,
Or overrated thy designs.

H. D. THOREAU

283

SIC VITA

I AM a parcel of vain strivings tied
By a chance bond together,
Dangling this way and that, their links
Were made so loose and wide,
Methinks,
For milder weather.

A bunch of violets without their roots,
And sorrel intermixed,
Encircled by a wisp of straw
Once coiled about their shoots,
The law
By which I'm fixed.

A nosegay which Time clutched from out
  Those fair Elysian fields,
With weeds and broken stems, in haste,
  Doth make the rabble rout
    That waste
  The day he yields.

And here I bloom for a short hour unseen,
  Drinking my juices up,
With no root in the land
  To keep my branches green,
    But stand
  In a bare cup.

Some tender buds were left upon my stem
  In mimicry of life,
But ah! the children will not know
  Till time has withered them,
    The woe
  With which they're rife.

But now I see I was not plucked for naught,
  And after in life's vase
Of glass set while I might survive,
  But by a kind hand brought
    Alive
  To a strange place.

That stock thus thinned will soon redeem its hours,
  And by another year,
Such as God knows, with freer air,
  More fruits and fair flowers

Will bear,
While I droop here.

H. D. THOREAU

❧ 284 ☙

THE FALL OF THE LEAF

THANK God who seasons thus the year,
   And sometimes kindly slants his rays;
For in his winter he's most near
   And plainest seen upon the shortest days.

Who gently tempers now his heats,
   And then his harsher cold, lest we
Should surfeit on the summer's sweets,
   Or pine upon the winter's crudity.

A sober mind will walk alone,
   Apart from nature, if need be,
And only its own seasons own;
   For nature leaving its humanity.

Sometimes a late autumnal thought
   Has crossed my mind in green July,
And to its early freshness brought
   Late ripened fruits, and an autumnal sky.

· · ·

The evening of the year draws on,
   The fields a later aspect wear;

Since Summer's garishness is gone,
  Some grains of night tincture the noontide air.

Behold! the shadows of the trees
  Now circle wider 'bout their stem,
Like sentries that by slow degrees
  Perform their rounds, gently protecting them.

And as the year doth decline,
  The sun allows a scantier light;
Behind each needle of the pine
  There lurks a small auxiliar to the night.

I hear the cricket's slumbrous lay
  Around, beneath me, and on high;
It rocks the night, it soothes the day,
  And everywhere is Nature's lullaby.

But most he chirps beneath the sod,
  When he has made his winter bed;
His creak grown fainter but more broad,
  A film of autumn o'er the summer spread.

Small birds, in fleets migrating by,
  Now beat across some meadow's bay,
And as they tack and veer on high,
  With faint and hurried click beguile the way.

Far in the woods, these golden days,
  Some leaf obeys its Maker's call;
And through their hollow aisles it plays
  With delicate touch the prelude of the Fall.

Gently withdrawing from its stem,

It lightly lays itself along
Where the same hand hath pillowed them,
   Resigned to sleep upon the old year's throng.

The loneliest birch is brown and sere,
   The furthest pool is strewn with leaves,
Which float upon their watery bier,
   Where is no eye that sees, no heart that grieves.

The jay screams through the chestnut wood;
   The crisped and yellow leaves around
Are hue and texture of my mood—
   And these rough burrs my heirlooms on the ground.

The threadbare trees, so poor and thin—
   They are no wealthier than I;
But with as brave a core within
   They rear their boughs to the October sky.

Poor knights they are which bravely wait
   The charge of Winter's cavalry,
Keeping a simple Roman state,
   Discumbered of their Persian luxury.

H. D. THOREAU

❧ 285 ❧

SPECTATOR AB EXTRA

I

As I sat at the Café I said to myself,
They may talk as they please about what they call pelf,

They may sneer as they like about eating and drinking,
But help it I cannot, I cannot help thinking
   How pleasant it is to have money, heigh-ho!
   How pleasant it is to have money.

I sit at my table *en grand seigneur,*
And when I have done, throw a crust to the poor;
Not only the pleasure itself of good living,
But also the pleasure of now and then giving:
   So pleasant it is to have money, heigh-ho!
   So pleasant it is to have money.

They may talk as they please about what they call pelf,
And how one ought never to think of one's self,
How pleasures of thought surpass eating and drinking,—
My pleasure of thought is the pleasure of thinking
   How pleasant it is to have money, heigh-ho!
   How pleasant it is to have money.

A. H. CLOUGH

❧ 286 ☙

SUNTHIN' IN THE PASTORAL LINE

ONCE git a smell o' musk into a draw,
An' it clings hold like precerdents in law:
Your gra'ma'am put it there,—when, goodness knows,—
To jes' this-worldify her Sunday-clo'es;
But the old chist wun't sarve her gran'son's wife,
(For, 'thout new funnitoor, wut good in life?)

An' so ole clawfoot, from the precinks dread
O' the spare chamber, slinks into the shed,
Where, dim with dust, it fust or last subsides
To holdin' seeds an' fifty things besides;
But better days stick fast in heart an' husk,
An' all you keep in 't gits a scent o' musk.

Jes' so with poets: wut they 've airly read
Gits kind o' worked into their heart an' head,
So 's 't they can't seem to write but jest on sheers
With furrin countries or played-out ideers,
Nor hev a feelin', ef it doos n't smack
O' wut some critter chose to feel 'way back:
This makes 'em talk o' daisies, larks, an' things,
Ez though we 'd nothin' here that blows an' sings,—
(Why, I 'd give more for one live bobolink
Than a square mile o' larks in printer's ink,)—
This makes 'em think our fust o' May is May,
Which 't ain't, for all the almanicks can say.

O little city-gals, don't never go it
Blind on the word o' noospaper or poet!
They 're apt to puff, an' May-day seldom looks
Up in the country ez it doos in books;
They 're no more like than hornets'-nests an' hives,
Or printed sarmons be to holy lives.
I, with my trouses perched on cowhide boots,
Tuggin' my foundered feet out by the roots,
Hev seen ye come to fling on April's hearse
Your muslin nosegays from the milliner's,
Puzzlin' to find dry ground your queen to choose,

An' dance your throats sore in morocker shoes:
I 've seen ye an' felt proud, thet, come wut would,
Our Pilgrim stock wuz pethed with hardihood.
Pleasure doos make us Yankees kind o' winch,
Ez though 't wuz sunthin' paid for by the inch;
But yit we du contrive to worry thru,
Ef Dooty tells us thet the thing 's to du,
An' kerry a hollerday, ef we set out,
Ez stiddily ez though 't wuz a redoubt.

I, country-born an' bred, know where to find
Some blooms thet make the season suit the mind,
An' seem to metch the doubtin' bluebird's notes,—
Half-vent'rin' liverworts in furry coats,
Bloodroots, whose rolled-up leaves ef you oncurl,
Each on 'em 's cradle to a baby-pearl,—
But these are jes' Spring's pickets; sure ez sin,
The rebble frosts 'll try to drive 'em in;
For half our May 's so awfully like May n't,
't would rile a Shaker or an evrige saint;
Though I own up I like our back'ard springs
Thet kind o' haggle with their greens an' things,
An' when you 'most give up, 'uthout more words
Toss the fields full o' blossoms, leaves, an' birds;
Thet 's Northun natur', slow an' apt to doubt,
But when it *doos* git stirred, ther' 's no ginout!

Fust come the blackbirds clatt'rin' in tall trees,
An' settlin' things in windy Congresses,—
Queer politicians, though, for I 'll be skinned
Ef all on 'em don't head aginst the wind.

'fore long the trees begin to show belief,—
The maple crimsons to a coral-reef,
Then saffern swarms swing off from all the willers
So plump they look like yaller caterpillars,
Then gray hossches'nuts leetle hands unfold
Softer 'n a baby's be at three days old:
Thet 's robin-redbreast's almanick; he knows
Thet arter this there' 's only blossom-snows;
So, choosin' out a handy crotch an' spouse,
He goes to plast'rin' his adobe house.

Then seems to come a hitch,—things lag behind,
Till some fine mornin' Spring makes up her mind,
An' ez, when snow-swelled rivers cresh their dams
Heaped-up with ice thet dovetails in an' jams,
A leak comes spirtin' thru some pin-hole cleft,
Grows stronger, fercer, tears out right an' left,
Then all the waters bow themselves an' come,
Suddin, in one gret slope o' shedderin' foam,
Jes' so our Spring gits everythin' in tune
An' gives one leap from Aperl into June:
Then all comes crowdin' in; afore you think,
Young oak-leaves mist the side-hill woods with pink;
The catbird in the laylock-bush is loud;
The orchards turn to heaps o' rosy cloud;
Red-cedars blossom tu, though few folks know it,
An' look all dipt in sunshine like a poet;
The lime-trees pile their solid stacks o' shade
An' drows'ly simmer with the bees' sweet trade;
In ellum-shrouds the flashin' hangbird clings

An' for the summer vy'ge his hammock slings;
All down the loose-walled lanes in archin' bowers
The barb'ry droops its strings o' golden flowers,
Whose shrinkin' hearts the school-gals love to try
With pins,—they'll worry yourn so, boys, bimeby!
But I don't love your cat'logue style,—do you?—
Ez ef to sell off Natur' by vendoo;
One word with blood in 't 's twice ez good ez two:
'nuff sed, June's bridesman, poet o' the year,
Gladness on wings, the bobolink, is here;
Half-hid in tip-top apple-blooms he swings,
Or climbs aginst the breeze with quiverin' wings,
Or, givin' way to 't in a mock despair,
Runs down, a brook o' laughter, thru the air.

I ollus feel the sap start in my veins
In Spring, with curus heats an' prickly pains,
Thet drive me, when I git a chance, to walk
Off by myself to hev a privit talk
With a queer critter thet can't seem to 'gree
Along o' me like most folks,—Mister Me.
There' 's times when I 'm unsoshle ez a stone,
An' sort o' suffercate to be alone,—
I 'm crowded jes' to think thet folks are nigh,
An' can't bear nothin' closer than the sky;
Now the wind 's full ez shifty in the mind
Ez wut it is ou'-doors, ef I ain't blind,
An' sometimes, in the fairest sou'west weather,
My innard vane pints east for weeks together,
My natur' gits all goose-flesh, an' my sins
Come drizzlin' on my conscience sharp ez pins:

Wal, et sech times I jes' slip out o' sight
An' take it out in a fair stan'-up fight
With the one cuss I can't lay on the shelf,
The crook'dest stick in all the heap,—Myself.

'T wuz so las' Sabbath arter meetin'-time:
Findin' my feelin's would n't noways rhyme
With nobody's, but off the hendle flew
An' took things from an east-wind pint o' view,
I started off to lose me in the hills
Where the pines be, up back o' 'Siah's Mills:
Pines, ef you 're blue, are the best friends I know,
They mope an' sigh an' sheer your feelin's so,—
They hesh the ground beneath so, tu, I swan,
You half-forgit you 've gut a body on.
There' 's a small school'us' there where four roads meet,
The door-steps hollored out by little feet,
An' side-posts carved with names whose owners grew
To gret men, some on 'em, an' deacons, tu;
't ain't used no longer, coz the town hez gut
A high-school, where they teach the Lord knows wut:
Three-story larnin' 's pop'lar now; I guess
We thriv' ez wal on jes' two stories less,
For it strikes me there' 's sech a thing ez sinnin'
By overloadin' children's underpinnin':
Wal, here it wuz I larned my A B C,
An' it 's a kind o' favorite spot with me.

We 're curus critters : Now ain't jes' the minute
Thet ever fits us easy while we 're in it;
Long ez 't wuz futur', 't would be perfect bliss,—

597

Soon ez it's past, *thet* time's wuth ten o' this;
An' yit there ain't a man thet need be told
Thet Now 's the only bird lays eggs o' gold.
A knee-high lad, I used to plot an' plan
An' think 't wuz life's cap-sheaf to be a man;
Now, gittin' gray, there 's nothin' I enjoy
Like dreamin' back along into a boy:
So the ole school'us' is a place I choose
Afore all others, ef I want to muse;
I set down where I used to set, an' git
My boyhood back, an' better things with it,—
Faith, Hope, an' sunthin', ef it is n't Cherity,
It 's want o' guile, an' thet 's ez great a rerrity,—
While Fancy's cushin', free to Prince and Clown,
Makes the hard bench ez soft ez milkweed-down.

Now, 'fore I knowed, thet Sabbath arternoon
When I sot out to tramp myself in tune,
I found me in the school'us' on my seat,
Drummin' the march to No-wheres with my feet.
Thinkin' o' nothin', I 've heerd ole folks say
Is a hard kind o' dooty in its way:
It 's thinkin' everythin' you ever knew,
Or ever hearn, to make your feelin's blue.
I sot there tryin' thet on for a spell:
I thought o' the Rebellion, then o' Hell,
Which some folks tell ye now is jest a metterfor
(A the'ry, p'raps, it wun't *feel* none the better for);
I thought o' Reconstruction, wut we'd win
Patchin' our patent self-blow-up agin:
I thought ef this 'ere milkin' o' the wits,

So much a month, warn't givin' Natur' fits,—
Ef folks warn't druv, findin' their own milk fail,
To work the cow thet hez an iron tail,
An' ef idees 'thout ripenin' in the pan
Would send up cream to humor ary man:
From this to thet I let my worryin' creep,
Till finally I must ha' fell asleep.

Our lives in sleep are some like streams thet glide
'twixt flesh an' sperrit boundin' on each side,
Where both shores' shadders kind o' mix an' mingle
In sunthin' thet ain't jes' like either single;
An' when you cast off moorin's from Today,
An' down towards To-morrer drift away,
The imiges thet tengle on the stream
Make a new upside-down'ard world o' dream:
Sometimes they seem like sunrise-streaks an' warnin's
O' wut'll be in Heaven on Sabbath-mornin's,
An', mixed right in ez ef jest out o' spite,
Sunthin' thet says your supper ain't gone right.
I 'm gret on dreams, an' often when I wake,
I 've lived so much it makes my mem'ry ache,
An' can't skurce take a cat-nap in my cheer
'thout hevin' em, some good, some bad, all queer.

Now I wuz settin' where I 'd ben, it seemed,
An' ain't sure yit whether I r'ally dreamed,
Nor, ef I did, how long I might ha' slep',
When I hearn some un stompin' up the step,
An' lookin' round, ef two an' two make four,
I see a Pilgrim Father in the door.

He wore a steeple-hat, tall boots, an' spurs
With rowels to 'em big ez ches'nut-burrs,
An' his gret sword behind him sloped away
Long 'z a man's speech thet dunno wut to say.—
"Ef your name 's Biglow, an' your given-name
Hosee," sez he, "it 's arter you I came;
I 'm your gret-gran'ther multiplied by three."—
"My *wut?*" sez I.—"Your gret-gret-gret," sez he:
"You would n't ha' never ben here but for me.
Two hundred an' three years ago this May
The ship I come in sailed up Boston Bay;
I 'd been a cunnle in our Civil War,—
But wut on airth hev *you* gut up one for?
Coz we du things in England, 't ain't for you
To git a notion you can du 'em tu:
I 'm told you write in public prints: ef true,
It 's nateral you should know a thing or two."—
"Thet air 's an argymunt I can't endorse,—
't would prove, coz you wear spurs, you kep' a horse:
For brains," sez I, "wutever you may think,
Ain't boun' to cash the drafs o' pen-an'-ink,—
Though mos' folks write ez ef they hoped jes' quickenin'
The churn would argoo skim-milk into thickenin';
But skim-milk ain't a thing to change its view
O' wut it 's meant for more 'n a smoky flue.
But du pray tell me, 'fore we furder go,
How in all Natur' did you come to know
'bout our affairs," sez I, "in Kingdom-Come?"—
"Wal, I worked round at sperrit-rappin' some,
An' danced the tables till their legs wuz gone,

In hopes o' larnin' wut wuz goin' on,"
Sez he, "but mejums lie so like all-split
Thet I concluded it wuz best to quit.
But, come now, ef you wun't confess to knowin',
You 've some conjectures how the thing 's a-goin'."—
"Gran'ther," sez I, "a vane warn't never known
Nor asked to hev a jedgment of its own;
An' yit, ef 't ain't gut rusty in the jints,
It 's safe to trust its say on certin pints:
It knows the wind's opinions to a T,
An' the wind settles wut the weather 'll be."
"I never thought a scion of our stock
Could grow the wood to make a weathercock;
When I wuz younger 'n you, skurce more 'n a shaver,
No airthly wind," sez he, "could make me waver!"
(Ez he said this, he clinched his jaw an' forehead,
Hitchin' his belt to bring his sword-hilt forrard.)—
"Jes so it wuz with me," sez I, "I swow,
When _I_ wuz younger 'n wut you see me now,—
Nothin' from Adam's fall to Huldy's bonnet,
Thet I warn't full-cocked with my jedgment on it;
But now I 'm gittin' on in life, I find
It 's a sight harder to make up my mind,—
Nor I don't often try tu, when events
Will du it for me free of all expense.
The moral question 's ollus plain enough,—
It 's jes' the human-natur' side thet 's tough;
Wut 's best to think may n't puzzle me nor you,—
The pinch comes in decidin' wut to _du;_
Ef you _read_ History, all runs smooth ez grease,

601

Coz there the men ain't nothin' more 'n idees,—
But come to *make* it, ez we must to-day,
Th' idees hev arms an' legs an' stop the way:
It 's easy fixin' things in facts an' figgers,—
They can't resist, nor warn't brought up with niggers;
But come to try your the'ry on,—why, then
Your facts an' figgers change to ign'ant men
Actin' ez ugly—" —"Smite 'em hip an' thigh!"
Sez gran'ther, "and let every man-child die!
Oh for three weeks o' Crommle an' the Lord!
Up, Isr'el, to your tents an' grind the sword!"—
"Thet kind o' thing worked wal in ole Judee,
But you forgit how long it 's ben A. D.;
You think thet 's ellerkence,—I call it shoddy,
A thing," sez I, "wun't cover soul nor body;
I like the plain all-wool o' common-sense,
Thet warms ye now, an' will a twelve-month hence.
You took to follerin' where the Prophets beckoned,
An', fust you knowed on, back come Charles the Second;
Now wut I want 's to hev all *we* gain stick,
An' not to start Millennium too quick;
We hain't to punish only, but to keep,
An' the cure 's gut to go a cent'ry deep."
"Wall, milk-an'-water ain't the best o' glue,"
Sez he, "an' so you'll find afore you're thru;
Ef reshness venters sunthin', shilly-shally
Loses ez often wut 's ten times the vally.
Thet exe of ourn, when Charles's neck gut split,
Opened a gap thet ain't bridged over yit:
Slav'ry 's your Charles, the Lord hez gin the exe"—

"Our Charles," sez I, "hez gut eight million necks.
The hardest question ain't the black man's right,
The trouble is to 'mancipate the white;
One 's chained in body an' can be sot free,
But t' other 's chained in soul to an idee:
It 's a long job, but we shall worry thru it;
Ef bagnets fail, the spellin'-book must du it."
"Hosee," sez he, "I think you 're goin' to fail:
The rettlesnake ain't dangerous in the tail;
This 'ere rebellion 's nothing but the rettle,—
You 'll stomp on thet an' think you 've won the bettle;
It 's Slavery thet 's the fangs an' thinkin' head,
An' ef you want selvation, cresh it dead,—
An' cresh it suddin, or you 'll larn by waitin'
Thet Chance wun't stop to listen to debatin'!"—
"God's truth !" sez I,—"an ef *I* held the club,
An' knowed jes' where to strike,—but there's the rub!"—
"Strike soon," sez he, "or you'll be deadly ailin',—
Folks thet's afeared to fail are sure o' failin';
God hates your sneakin' creturs thet believe
He'll settle things they run away an' leave!"
He brought his foot down fercely, ez he spoke,
An' give me sech a startle thet I woke.

J. R. LOWELL

MALVERN HILL

(JULY, 1862.)

YE ELMS that wave on Malvern Hill
  In prime of morn and May,
Recall ye how McClellan's men
    Here stood at bay?
While deep within yon forest dim
    Our rigid comrades lay—
Some with the cartridge in their mouth,
Others with fixed arms lifted South—
    Invoking so
The cypress glades? Ah wilds of woe!

The spires of Richmond, late beheld
    Through rifts in musket-haze,
Were closed from view in clouds of dust
    On leaf-walled ways,
Where streamed our wagons in caravan;
And the Seven Nights and Days
Of march and fast, retreat and fight,
Pinched our grimed faces to ghastly plight—
    Does the elm wood
Recall the haggard beards of blood?

The battle-smoked flag, with stars eclipsed,

We followed (it never fell!)—
In silence husbanded our strength—
Received their yell;
Till on this slope we patient turned
With cannon ordered well;
Reverse we proved was not defeat;
But ah, the sod what thousands meet!—
Does Malvern Wood
Bethink itself, and muse and brood?

We elms of Malvern Hill
Remember every thing;
But sap the twig will fill:
Wag the world how it will,
Leaves must be green in Spring.

H. MELVILLE

❧ 288 ☙

A DIRGE FOR McPHERSON

KILLED IN FRONT OF ATLANTA
(July, 1864)

ARMS reversed and banners craped—
Muffled drums;
Snowy horses sable-draped—
McPherson comes.

But, tell us, shall we know him more,
Lost-Mountain and lone Kenesaw?

605

Brave the sword upon the pall—
    A gleam in gloom;
So a bright name lighteth all
    McPherson's doom.

Bear him through the chapel-door—
    Let priest in stole
Pace before the warrior
    Who led. Bell—toll!

Lay him down within the nave,
    The Lesson read—
Man is noble, man is brave,
    But man's—a weed.

Take him up again and wend
    Graveward, nor weep:
There's a trumpet that shall rend
    This Soldier's sleep.

Pass the ropes the coffin round,
    And let descend;
Prayer and volly—let it sound
    McPherson's end.

*True fame is his, for life is o'er—
Sarpedon of the mighty war.*

H. MELVILLE

❧ 289 ❧

ART

In placid hours well-pleased we dream
Of many a brave unbodied scheme.
But form to lend, pulsed life create,
What unlike things must meet and mate:
A flame to melt—a wind to freeze;
Sad patience—joyous energies;
Humility—yet pride and scorn;
Instinct and study; love and hate;
Audacity—reverence. These must mate,
And fuse with Jacob's mystic heart,
To wrestle with the angel—Art.

H. MELVILLE

❧ 290 ❧

SONG OF MYSELF

I

I CELEBRATE myself, and sing myself,
And what I assume you shall assume,
For every atom belonging to me as good belongs to you.

I loafe and invite my soul,
I lean and loafe at my ease observing a spear of summer
    grass.

My tongue, every atom of my blood, form'd from this soil, this air,
Born here of parents born here from parents the same, and their parents the same,
I, now thirty-seven years old in perfect health begin,
Hoping to cease not till death.

Creeds and schools in abeyance,
Retiring back a while sufficed at what they are, but never forgotten,
I harbor for good or bad, I permit to speak at every hazard,
Nature without check with original energy.

II

Houses and rooms are full of perfumes, the shelves are crowded with perfumes,
I breathe the fragrance myself and know it and like it,
The distillation would intoxicate me also, but I shall not let it.

The atmosphere is not a perfume, it has no taste of the distillation, it is odorless,
It is for my mouth forever, I am in love with it,
I will go to the bank by the wood and become undisguised and naked,
I am mad for it to be in contact with me.

The smoke of my own breath,
Echoes, ripples, buzz'd whispers, love-root, silk-thread, crotch and vine,

My respiration and inspiration, the beating of my heart,
the passing of blood and air through my lungs,
The sniff of green leaves and dry leaves, and of the shore
and dark-color'd sea-rocks, and of hay in the barn,
The sound of the belch'd words of my voice loos'd to the
eddies of the wind,
A few light kisses, a few embraces, a reaching around of
arms,
The play of shine and shade on the trees as the supple
boughs wag,
The delight alone or in the rush of the streets, or along
the fields and hill-sides,
The feeling of health, the full-noon trill, the song of me
rising from bed and meeting the sun.

Have you reckon'd a thousand acres much? have you
reckon'd the earth much?
Have you practis'd so long to learn to read?
Have you felt so proud to get at the meaning of poems?

Stop this day and night with me and you shall possess the
origin of all poems,
You shall possess the good of the earth and sun, (there
are millions of suns left,)
You shall no longer take things at second or third hand,
nor look through the eyes of the dead, nor feed on
the spectres in books,
You shall not look through my eyes either, nor take things
from me,
You shall listen to all sides and filter them from your self.

I have heard what the talkers were talking, the talk of the
    beginning and the end,
But I do not talk of the beginning or the end.

There was never any more inception than there is now,
Nor any more youth or age than there is now,
And will never be any more perfection than there is now,
Nor any more heaven or hell than there is now.

Urge and urge and urge,
Always the procreant urge of the world.

Out of the dimness opposite equals advance, always sub-
    stance and increase, always sex,
Always a knit of identity, always distinction, always a
    breed of life.

To elaborate is no avail, learn'd and unlearn'd feel that it
    is so.

Sure as the most certain sure, plump in the uprights, well
    entretied, braced in the beams,
Stout as a horse, affectionate, haughty, electrical,
I and this mystery here we stand.

Clear and sweet is my soul, and clear and sweet is all that
    is not my soul.

Lack one lacks both, and the unseen is proved by the seen,
Till that becomes unseen and receives proof in its turn.

Showing the best and dividing it from the worst age vexes age,

Knowing the perfect fitness and equanimity of things, while they discuss I am silent, and go bathe and admire myself.

Welcome is every organ and attribute of me, and of any man hearty and clean,

Not an inch nor a particle of an inch is vile, and none shall be less familiar than the rest.

I am satisfied—I see, dance, laugh, sing;

As the hugging and loving bed-fellow sleeps at my side through the night, and withdraws at the peep of the day with stealthy tread,

Leaving me baskets cover'd with white towels swelling the house with their plenty,

Shall I postpone my acceptation and realization and scream at my eyes,

That they turn from gazing after and down the road,

And forthwith cipher and show me to a cent,

Exactly the value of one and exactly the value of two, and which is ahead?

IV

Trippers and askers surround me,

People I meet, the effect upon me of my early life or the ward and city I live in, or the nation,

The latest dates, discoveries, inventions, societies, authors old and new,

My dinner, dress, associates, looks, compliments, dues,
The real or fancied indifference of some man or woman I
     love,
The sickness of one of my folks or of myself, or ill-doing
     or loss or lack of money, or depressions or exaltations,
Battles, the horrors of fratricidal war, the fever of doubt-
     ful news, the fitful events;
These come to me days and nights and go from me again,
But they are not the Me myself.

Apart from the pulling and hauling stands what I am,
Stands amused, complacent, compassionating, idle, unitary,
Looks down, is erect, or bends an arm on an impalpable
     certain rest,
Looking with side-curved head curious what will come next,
Both in and out of the game and watching and wondering
     at it.

Backward I see in my own days where I sweated through
     fog with linguists and contenders,
I have no mockings or arguments, I witness and wait.

v

I believe in you my soul, the other I am must not abase
     itself to you,
And you must not be abased to the other.

Loafe with me on the grass, loose the stop from your throat,
Not words, not music or rhyme I want, not custom or
     lecture, not even the best,
Only the lull I like, the hum of your valvèd voice.

I mind how once we lay such a transparent summer morning,
How you settled your head athwart my hips and gently
turn'd over upon me,
And parted the shirt from my bosom-bone, and plunged
your tongue to my bare-stript heart,
And reach'd till you felt my beard, and reach'd till you
held my feet.

Swiftly arose and spread around me the peace and knowl-
edge that pass all the argument of the earth,
And I know that the hand of God is the promise of my own,
And I know that the spirit of God is the brother of my
own,
And that all the men ever born are also my brothers, and
the women my sister and lovers,
And that a kelson of the creation is love,
And limitless are leaves stiff or drooping in the fields,
And brown ants in the little wells beneath them,
And mossy scabs of the worm fence, heap'd stones, elder,
mullein and poke-weed.

VI

A child said What is the grass? fetching it to me with full
hands;
How could I answer the child? I do not know what it is
any more than he.

I guess it must be the flag of my disposition, out of hope-
ful green stuff woven.

Or I guess it is the handkerchief of the Lord,
A scented gift and remembrancer designedly dropt,
Bearing the owner's name someway in the corners, that
we may see and remark, and say Whose?

Or I guess the grass is itself a child, the produced babe of
the vegetation.

Or I guess it is a uniform hieroglyphic,
And it means, Sprouting alike in broad zones and narrow
zones,
Growing among black folks as among white,
Kanuck, Tuckahoe, Congressman, Cuff, I give them the
same, I receive them the same.

And now it seems to me the beautiful uncut hair of graves.

Tenderly will I use you curling grass,
It may be you transpire from the breasts of young men,
It may be if I had known them I would have loved them,
It may be you are from old people, or from offspring taken
soon out of their mothers' laps,
And here you are the mothers' laps.

This grass is very dark to be from the white heads of old
mothers,
Darker than the colorless beards of old men,
Dark to come from under the faint red roofs of mouths.

O I perceive after all so many uttering tongues,
And I perceive they do not come from the roofs of mouths
for nothing.

I wish I could translate the hints about the dead young
    men and women,
And the hints about old men and mothers, and the off-
    spring taken soon out of their laps.

What do you think has become of the young and old men?
And what do you think has become of the women and
    children?

They are alive and well somewhere,
The smallest sprout shows there is really no death,
And if ever there was it led forward life, and does not
    wait at the end to arrest it,
And ceas'd the moment life appear'd.

All goes onward and outward, nothing collapses,
And to die is different from what any one supposed, and
    luckier.

VII

Has any one supposed it lucky to be born?
I hasten to inform him or her it is just as lucky to die, and
    I know it.

I pass death with the dying and birth with the new-wash'd
    babe, and am not contain'd between my hat and boots,
And peruse manifold objects, no two alike and every one
    good,
The earth good and the stars good, and their adjuncts all
    good.

I am not an earth nor an adjunct of an earth,

I am the mate and companion of people, all just as immortal and fathomless as myself,
(They do not know how immortal, but I know.)

Every kind for itself and its own, for me mine male and
female,
For me those that have been boys and that love women,
For me the man that is proud and feels how it stings to
be slighted,
For me the sweet-heart and the old maid, for me mothers
and the mothers of mothers,
For me lips that have smiled, eyes that have shed tears,
For me children and the begetters of children.

Undrape! you are not guilty to me, nor stale nor discarded,
I see through the broadcloth and gingham whether or no,
And am around, tenacious, acquisitive, tireless, and cannot
be shaken away.

VIII

The little one sleeps in its cradle,
I lift the gauze and look a long time, and silently brush
away flies with my hand.

The youngster and the red-faced girl turn aside up the
bushy hill,
I peeringly view them from the top.

The suicide sprawls on the bloody floor of the bedroom,
I witness the corpse with its dabbled hair, I note where
the pistol has fallen.

The blab of the pave, tires of carts, sluff of boot-soles, talk
of the promenaders,
The heavy omnibus, the driver with his interrogating
thumb, the clank of the shod horses on the granite
floor,
The snow-sleighs, clinking, shouted jokes, pelts of snow-
balls,
The hurrahs for popular favorites, the fury of rous'd mobs,
The flap of the curtain'd litter, a sick man inside borne to
the hospital,
The meeting of enemies, the sudden oath, the blows and
fall,
The excited crowd, the policeman with his star quickly
working his passage to the centre of the crowd,
The impassive stones that receive and return so many
echoes,
What groans of over-fed or half-starv'd who fall sunstruck
or in fits,
What exclamations of women taken suddenly who hurry
home and give birth to babes,
What living and buried speech is always vibrating here,
what howls restrain'd by decorum,
Arrests of criminals, slights, adulterous offers made, ac-
ceptances, rejections with convex lips,
I mind them or the show or resonance of them—I come
and I depart.

IX

The big doors of the country barn stand open and ready,

The dried grass of the harvest-time loads the slow-drawn
wagon,
The clear light plays on the brown gray and green inter-
tinged,
The armfuls are pack'd to the sagging mow.

I am there, I help, I came stretch'd atop of the load,
I felt its soft jolts, one leg reclined on the other,
I jump from the cross-beams and seize the clover and
timothy,
And roll head over heels and tangle my hair full of wisps.

X

Alone far in the wilds and mountains I hunt,
Wandering amazed at my own lightness and glee,
In the late afternoon choosing a safe spot to pass the night,
Kindling a fire and broiling the fresh-kill'd game,
Falling asleep on the gather'd leaves with my dog and gun
by my side.

The Yankee clipper is under her sky-sails, she cuts the
sparkle and scud,
My eyes settle the land, I bend at her prow or shout joyously from the deck.

The boatmen and clam-diggers arose early and stopt for
me,
I tuck'd my trouser-ends in my boots and went and had a
good time;
You should have been with us that day round the chowder-
kettle.

618

I saw the marriage of the trapper in the open air in the
  far west, the bride was a red girl,
Her father and his friends sat near cross-legged and
  dumbly smoking, they had moccasins to their feet
  and large thick blankets hanging from their shoulders,
On a bank lounged the trapper, he was drest mostly in
  skins, his luxuriant beard and curls protected his neck,
  he held his bride by the hand,
She had long eyelashes, her head was bare, her coarse
  straight locks descended upon her voluptuous limbs
  and reach'd to her feet.

The runaway slave came to my house and stopt outside,
I heard his motions crackling the twigs of the woodpile,
Through the swung half-door of the kitchen I saw him
  limpsy and weak,
And went where he sat on a log and led him in and assured
  him,
And brought water and fill'd a tub for his sweated body
  and bruis'd feet,
And gave him a room that enter'd from my own, and gave
  him some coarse clean clothes,
And remember perfectly well his revolving eyes and his
  awkwardness,
And remember putting plasters on the galls of his neck
  and ankles;
He staid with me a week before he was recuperated and
  pass'd north,
I had him sit next me at table, my fire-lock lean'd in the
  corner.

Twenty-eight young men bathe by the shore,
Twenty-eight young men and all so friendly;
Twenty-eight years of womanly life and all so lonesome.

She owns the fine house by the rise of the bank,
She hides handsome and richly drest aft the blinds of the
    window.

Which of the young men does she like the best?
Ah the homeliest of them is beautiful to her.

Where are you off to, lady? for I see you,
You splash in the water there, yet stay stock still in your
    room.

Dancing and laughing along the beach came the twenty-
    ninth bather,
The rest did not see her, but she saw them and loved them.

The beards of the young men glisten'd with wet, it ran
    from their long hair,
Little streams pass'd all over their bodies.

An unseen hand also pass'd over their bodies,
It descended tremblingly from their temples and ribs.

The young men float on their backs, their white bellies
    bulge to the sun, they do not ask who seizes fast to
    them,
They do not know who puffs and declines with pendant
    and bending arch,

They do not think whom they souse with spray.

XII

The butcher-boy puts off his killing-clothes, or sharpens
    his knife at the stall in the market,
I loiter enjoying his repartee and his shuffle and break-
    down.

Blacksmiths with grimed and hairy chests environ the
    anvil,
Each has his main-sledge, they are all out, there is a great
    heat in the fire.

From the cinder-strew'd threshold I follow their move-
    ments,
The lithe sheer of their waists plays even with their massive
    arms,
Overhand the hammers swing, overhand so slow, over-
    hand so sure,
They do not hasten, each man hits in his place.

XIII

The negro holds firmly the reins of his four horses, the
    block swags underneath on its tied-over chain,
The negro that drives the long dray of the stone-yard,
    steady and tall he stands pois'd on one leg on the
    string-piece,
His blue shirt exposes his ample neck and breast and
    loosens over his hip-band,

621

His glance is calm and commanding, he tosses the slouch
of his hat away from his forehead,
The sun falls on his crispy hair and mustache, falls on the
black of his polish'd and perfect limbs.

I behold the picturesque giant and love him, and I do not
stop there,
I go with the team also.

In me the caresser of life wherever moving, backward as
well as forward sluing,
To niches aside and junior bending, not a person or object missing,
Absorbing all to myself and for this song.

Oxen that rattle the yoke and chain or halt in the leafy
shade, what is that you express in your eyes?
It seems to me more than all the print I have read in my
life.

My tread scares the wood-drake and wood-duck on my
distant and day-long ramble,
They rise together, they slowly circle around.

I believe in those wing'd purposes,
And acknowledge red, yellow, white, playing within me,
And consider green and violet and the tufted crown inten-
tional,
And do not call the tortoise unworthy because she is not
something else,
And the jay in the woods never studied the gamut, yet
trills pretty well to me,
And the look of the bay mare shames silliness out of me.

The wild gander leads his flock through the cool night,
Ya-honk he says, and sounds it down to me like an invita-
tion,
The pest may suppose it meaningless, but I listening close,
Find its purpose and place up there toward the wintry sky.

The sharp-hoof'd moose of the north, the cat on the house-
sill, the chickadee, the prairie-dog,
The litter of the grunting sow as they tug at her teats,
The brood of the turkey-hen and she with her half-spread
wings,
I see in them and myself the same old law.

The press of my foot to the earth springs a hundred
affections,
They scorn the best I can do to relate them.

I am enamour'd of growing out-doors,
Of men that live among cattle or taste of the ocean or
woods,
Of the builders and steerers of ships and the wielders of
axes and mauls, and the drivers of horses,
I can eat and sleep with them week in and week out.

What is commonest, cheapest, nearest, easiest, is Me,
Me going in for my chances, spending for vast returns,
Adorning myself to bestow my self on the first that will
take me,
Not asking the sky to come down to my good will,
Scattering it freely forever.

The pure contralto sings in the organ loft,

The carpenter dresses his plank, the tongue of his fore-
plane whistles its wild ascending lisp,

The married and unmarried children ride home to their
Thanksgiving dinner,

The pilot seizes the king-pin, he heaves down with a strong
arm,

The mate stands braced in the whale-boat, lance and har-
poon are ready,

The duck-shooter walks by silent and cautious stretches,

The deacons are ordain'd with cross'd hands at the altar,

The spinning-girl retreats and advances to the hum of the
big wheel,

The farmer stops by the bars as he walks on a First-day
loafe and looks at the oats and rye,

The lunatic is carried at last to the asylum a confirm'd
case,

(He will never sleep any more as he did in the cot in his
mother's bed-room;)

The jour printer with gray head and gaunt jaws works at
his case,

He turns his quid of tobacco while his eyes blurr with the
manuscript;

The malform'd limbs are tied to the surgeon's table,

What is removed drops horribly in a pail;

The quadroon girl is sold at the auction-stand, the
drunkard nods by the bar-room stove,

The machinist rolls up his sleeves, the policeman travels his beat, the gate-keeper marks who pass,

The young fellow drives the express-wagon, (I love him, though I do not know him;)

The half-breed straps on his light boots to compete in the race,

The western turkey-shooting draws old and young, some lean on their rifles, some sit on logs,

Out from the crowds steps the marksman, takes his position, levels his piece;

The groups of newly-come immigrants cover the wharf or levee,

As the woolly-pates hoe in the sugar-field, the overseer views them from his saddle,

The bugle calls in the ball-room, the gentlemen run for their partners, the dancers bow to each other,

The youth lies awake in the cedar-roof'd garret and harks to the musical rain,

The Wolverine sets traps on the creek that helps fill the Huron,

The squaw wrapt in her yellow-hemm'd cloth is offering moccasins and bead-bags for sale,

The connoisseur peers along the exhibition-gallery with half-shut eyes bent sideways,

As the deck-hand makes fast the steamboat the plank is thrown for the shore-going passengers,

The young sister holds out the skein while the elder sister winds it off in a ball, and stops now and then for the knots,

The one-year wife is recovering and happy having a week
 ago borne her first child,
The clean-hair'd Yankee girl works with her sewing-ma-
 chine or in the factory or mill,
The paving-man leans on his two-handed rammer, the re-
 porter's lead flies swiftly over the note-book, the sign-
 painter is lettering with blue and gold,
The canal boy trots on the tow-path, the book-keeper
 counts at his desk, the shoemaker waxes his thread,
The conductor beats time for the band and all the per-
 formers follow him,
The child is baptized, the convert is making his first pro-
 fessions,
The regatta is spread on the bay, the race is begun, (how
 the white sails sparkle!)
The drover watching his drove sings out to them that
 would stray,
The peddler sweats with his pack on his back, (the pur-
 chaser higgling about the odd cent;)
The bride unrumples her white dress, the minute-hand of
 the clock moves slowly,
The opium-eater reclines with rigid head and just-open'd
 lips,
The prostitute draggles her shawl, her bonnet bobs on her
 tipsy and pimpled neck,
The crowd laugh at her blackguard oaths, the men jeer
 and wink to each other,
(Miserable! I do not laugh at your oaths nor jeer you;)
The President holding a cabinet council is surrounded by
 the great Secretaries,

On the piazza walk three matrons stately and friendly with
    twined arms,
The crew of the fish-smack pack repeated layers of halibut
    in the hold,
The Missourian crosses the plains toting his wares and his
    cattle,
As the fare-collector goes through the train he gives notice
    by the jingling of loose change,
The floor-men are laying the floor, the tinners are tinning
    the roof, the masons are calling for mortar,
In single file each shouldering his hod pass onward the
    laborers;
Seasons pursuing each other the indescribable crowd is
    gather'd, it is the fourth of Seven-month, (what sa-
    lutes of cannon and small arms!)
Seasons pursuing each other the plougher ploughs, the
    mower mows, and the winter-grain falls in the
    ground;
Off on the lakes the pike-fisher watches and waits by the
    hole in the frozen surface,
The stumps stand thick round the clearing, the squatter
    strikes deep with his axe,
Flatboatmen make fast towards dusk near the cotton-wood
    or pecan-trees,
Coon-seekers go through the regions of the Red river or
    through those drain'd by the Tennessee, or through
    those of the Arkansas,
Torches shine in the dark that hangs on the Chattahoo-
    chee or Altamahaw,

Patriarchs sit at supper with sons and grandsons and great-
grandsons around them,
In walls of adobie, in canvas tents, rest hunters and trap-
pers after their day's sport,
The city sleeps and the country sleeps,
The living sleep for their time, the dead sleep for their
time,
The old husband sleeps by his wife and the young husband
sleeps by his wife;
And these tend inward to me and I tend outward to them,
And such as it is to be of these more or less I am,
And of these one and all I weave the song of myself.

XVI

I am of old and young, of the foolish as much as the wise,
Regardless of others, ever regardful of others,
Maternal as well as paternal, a child as well as a man,
Stuff'd with the stuff that is coarse and stuff'd with the
stuff that is fine,
One of the Nation of many nations, the smallest the same
and the largest the same,
A Southerner soon as a Northerner, a planter nonchalant
and hospitable down by the Oconee I live,
A Yankee bound my own way ready for trade, my joints
the limberest joints on earth and the sternest joints on
earth,
A Kentuckian walking the vale of the Elkhorn in my deer-
skin leggings, a Louisianian or Georgian,
A boatman over lakes or bays or along coasts, a Hoosier,
Badger, Buckeye;

At home on Kanadian snow-shoes or up in the bush, or
with fishermen off Newfoundland,
At home in the fleet of ice-boats, sailing with the rest and
tacking,
At home on the hills of Vermont or in the woods of
Maine, or the Texan ranch,
Comrade of Californians, comrade of free North-West-
erners, (loving their big proportions,)
Comrade of raftsmen and coalmen, comrade of all who
shake hands and welcome to drink and meat,
A learner with the simplest, a teacher of the thoughtful-
lest,
A novice beginning yet experient of myriads of seasons,
Of every hue and caste am I, of every rank and religion,
A farmer, mechanic, artist, gentleman, sailor, quaker,
Prisoner, fancy-man, rowdy, lawyer, physician, priest.

I resist any thing better than my own diversity,
Breathe the air but leave plenty after me,
And am not stuck up, and am in my place.

(The moth and the fish-eggs are in their place,
The bright suns I see and the dark suns I cannot see are in
their place,
The palpable is in its place and the impalpable is in its
place.)

                          XVII

These are really the thoughts of all men in all ages and
lands, they are not original with me,

629

If they are not yours as much as mine they are nothing, or
next to nothing,
If they are not the riddle and the untying of the riddle
they are nothing,
If they are not just as close as they are distant they are
nothing.

This is the grass that grows wherever the land is and the
water is,
This the common air that bathes the globe.

XVIII

With music strong I come, with my cornets and my drums,
I play not marches for accepted victors only, I play
marches for conquer'd and slain persons.

Have you heard that it was good to gain the day?
I also say it is good to fall, battles are lost in the same
spirit in which they are won.

I beat and pound for the dead,
I blow through my embouchures my loudest and gayest
for them.

Vivas to those who have fail'd!
And to those whose war-vessels sank in the sea!
And to those themselves who sank in the sea!
And to all generals that lost engagements, and all over-
come heroes!
And the numberless unknown heroes equal to the greatest
heroes known!

XIX

This is the meal equally set, this the meat for natural hun-
  ger,
It is for the wicked just the same as the righteous, I make
  appointments with all,
I will not have a single person slighted or left away,
The kept-woman, sponger, thief, are hereby invited,
The heavy-lipp'd slave is invited, the venerealee is invited;
There shall be no difference between them and the rest.

This is the press of a bashful hand, this the float and odor
  of hair,
This the touch of my lips to yours, this the murmur of
  yearning,
This the far-off depth and height reflecting my own face,
This the thoughtful merge of myself, and the outlet again.

Do you guess I have some intricate purpose?
Well I have, for the Fourth-month showers have, and the
  mica on the side of a rock has.

Do you take it I would astonish?
Does the daylight astonish? does the early redstart twitter-
  ing through the woods?
Do I astonish more than they?

This hour I tell things in confidence,
I might not tell everybody, but I will tell you.

XX

Who goes there? hankering, gross, mystical, nude;
How is it I extract strength from the beef I eat?

What is a man anyhow? what am I? what are you?

All I mark as my own you shall offset it with your own,
Else it were time lost listening to me.

I do not snivel that snivel the world over,
That months are vacuums and the ground but wallow and
    filth.

Whimpering and truckling fold with powders for invalids,
    conformity goes to the fourth-remov'd,
I wear my hat as I please indoors or out.

Why should I pray? why should I venerate and be cere-
    monious?

Having pried through the strata, analyzed to a hair,
    counsel'd with doctors and calculated close,
I find no sweeter fat than sticks to my own bones.

In all people I see myself, none more and not one a barley-
    corn less,
And the good or bad I say of myself I say of them.

I know I am solid and sound,
To me the converging objects of the universe perpetually
    flow,
All are written to me, and I must get what the writing
    means.

I know I am deathless,
I know this orbit of mine cannot be swept by a carpenter's
　　compass,
I know I shall not pass like a child's carlacue cut with a
　　burnt stick at night.

I know I am august,
I do not trouble my spirit to vindicate itself or be under-
　　stood,
I see that the elementary laws never apologize,
(I reckon I behave no prouder than the level I plant my
　　house by, after all.)

I exist as I am, that is enough,
If no other in the world be aware I sit content,
And if each and all be aware I sit content.

One world is aware and by far the largest to me, and that
　　is myself,
And whether I come to my own to-day or in ten thousand
　　or ten million years,
I can cheerfully take it now, or with equal cheerfulness I
　　can wait.

My foothold is tenon'd and mortis'd in granite,
I laugh at what you call dissolution,
And I know the amplitude of time.

XXI

I am the poet of the Body and I am the poet of the Soul,
The pleasures of heaven are with me and the pains of hell
　　are with me,

The first I graft and increase upon myself, the latter I
translate into a new tongue.

I am the poet of the woman the same as the man,
And I say it is as great to be a woman as to be a man,
And I say there is nothing greater than the mother of men.

I chant the chant of dilation or pride,
We have had ducking and deprecating about enough,
I show that size is only development.

Have you outstript the rest? are you the President?
It is a trifle, they will more than arrive there every one,
and still pass on.

I am he that walks with the tender and growing night,
I call to the earth and sea half-held by the night.

Press close bare-bosom'd night—press close magnetic
nourishing night!
Night of south winds—night of the large few stars!
Still nodding night—mad naked summer night.

Smile O voluptuous cool-breath'd earth!
Earth of the slumbering and liquid trees!
Earth of departed sunset—earth of the mountains misty-
topt!
Earth of the vitreous pour of the full moon just tinged
with blue!
Earth of shine and dark mottling the tide of the river!
Earth of the limpid gray of clouds brighter and clearer for
my sake!

Far-swooping elbow'd earth—rich apple-blossom'd earth!
Smile, for your lover comes.

Prodigal, you have given me love—therefore I to you give
  love!
O unspeakable passionate love.

XXII

You sea! I resign myself to you also—I guess what you
  mean,
I behold from the beach your crooked inviting fingers,
I believe you refuse to go back without feeling of me,
We must have a turn together, I undress, hurry me out of
  sight of the land,
Cushion me soft, rock me in billowy drowse,
Dash me with amorous wet, I can repay you.

Sea of stretch'd ground-swells,
Sea breathing broad and convulsive breaths,
Sea of the brine of life and of unshovell'd yet always-ready
  graves,
Howler and scooper of storms, capricious and dainty sea,
I am integral with you, I too am of one phase and of all
  phases.

Partaker of influx and efflux I, extoller of hate and con-
  ciliation,
Extoller of amies and those that sleep in each others' arms.

I am he attesting sympathy,
(Shall I make my list of things in the house and skip the
  house that supports them?)

I am not the poet of goodness only, I do not decline to be
the poet of wickedness also.

What blurt is this about virtue and about vice?
Evil propels me and reform of evil propels me, I stand
indifferent,
My gait is no fault-finder's or rejecter's gait,
I moisten the roots of all that has grown.

Did you fear some scrofula out of the unflagging
pregnancy?
Did you guess the celestial laws are yet to be work'd over
and rectified?

I find one side a balance and the antipodal side a balance,
Soft doctrine as steady help as stable doctrine,
Thoughts and deeds of the present our rouse and early start.

This minute that comes to me over the past decillions,
There is no better than it and now.

What behaved well in the past or behaves well to-day is
not such a wonder,
The wonder is always and always how there can be a mean
man or an infidel.

XXIII

Endless unfolding of words of ages!
And mine a word of the modern, the word En-Masse.

A word of the faith that never balks,
Here or henceforward it is all the same to me, I accept
Time absolutely.

It alone is without flaw, it alone rounds and completes all,
That mystic baffling wonder alone completes all.

I accept Reality and dare not question it,
Materialism first and last imbuing.

Hurrah for positive science! long live exact demonstration!
Fetch stonecrop mixt with cedar and branches of lilac,
This is the lexicographer, this the chemist, this made a
  grammar of the old cartouches,
These mariners put the ship through dangerous unknown
  seas,
This is the geologist, this works with the scalpel, and this
  is a mathematician.

Gentlemen, to you the first honors always!
Your facts are useful, and yet they are not my dwelling,
I but enter by them to an area of my dwelling.

Less the reminders of properties told my words,
And more the reminders they of life untold, and of freedom and extrication,

And make short account of neuters and geldings, and favor
  men and women fully equipt,
And beat the gong of revolt, and stop with fugitives and
  them that plot and conspire.

XXIV

Walt Whitman, a kosmos, of Manhattan the son,
Turbulent, fleshy, sensual, eating, drinking and breeding,

No sentimentalist, no stander above men and women or
apart from them,
No more modest than immodest.

Unscrew the locks from the doors!
Unscrew the doors themselves from their jambs!

Whoever degrades another degrades me,
And whatever is done or said returns at last to me.

Through me the afflatus surging and surging, through me
the current and index.

I speak the pass-word primeval, I give the sign of democ-
racy,
By God! I will accept nothing which all cannot have their
counterpart of on the same terms.

Through me many long dumb voices,
Voices of the interminable generations of prisoners and
slaves,
Voices of the diseas'd and despairing and of thieves and
dwarfs,
Voices of cycles of preparation and accretion,
And of the threads that connect the stars, and of wombs
and of the father-stuff,
And of the rights of them the others are down upon,
Of the deform'd, trivial, flat, foolish, despised,
Fog in the air, beetles rolling balls of dung.

Through me forbidden voices,
Voices of sexes and lusts, voices veil'd and I remove the
veil,

Voices indecent by me clarified and transfigur'd.

I do not press my fingers across my mouth,
I keep as delicate around the bowels as around the head
    and heart,
Copulation is no more rank to me than death is.

I believe in the flesh and the appetites,
Seeing, hearing, feeling, are miracles, and each part and
    tag of me is a miracle.

Divine am I inside and out, and I make holy whatever I
    touch or am touch'd from,
The scent of these arm-pits aroma finer than prayer,
This head more than churches, bibles, and all the creeds.

If I worship one thing more than another it shall be the
    spread of my own body, or any part of it,
Translucent mould of me it shall be you!
Shaded ledges and rests it shall be you!
Firm masculine colter it shall be you!
Whatever goes to the tilth of me it shall be you!
You my rich blood! your milky stream pale strippings of
    my life!
Breast that presses against other breasts it shall be you!
My brain it shall be your occult convolutions!
Root of wash'd sweet-flag! timorous pond-snipe! nest of
    guarded duplicate eggs! it shall be you!
Mix'd tussled hay of head, beard, brawn, it shall be you!
Trickling sap of maple, fibre of manly wheat, it shall be you!
Sun so generous it shall be you!
Vapors lighting and shading my face it shall be you!

639

You sweaty brooks and dews it shall be you!
Winds whose soft-tickling genitals rub against me it shall
be you!
Broad muscular fields, branches of live oak, loving lounger
in my winding paths, it shall be you!
Hands I have taken, face I have kiss'd, mortal I have ever
touch'd, it shall be you.

I dote on myself, there is that lot of me and all so luscious,
Each moment and whatever happens thrills me with joy,
I cannot tell how my ankles bend, nor whence the cause of
my faintest wish,
Nor the cause of the friendship I emit, nor the cause of the
friendship I take again.

That I walk up my stoop, I pause to consider if it really be,
A morning-glory at my window satisfies me more than the
metaphysics of books.

To behold the day-break!
The little light fades the immense and diaphanous shadows,
The air tastes good to my palate.

Hefts of the moving world at innocent gambols silently
rising, freshly exuding,
Scooting obliquely high and low.

Something I cannot see puts upward libidinous prongs,
Seas of bright juice suffuse heaven.

The earth by the sky staid with, the daily close of their
junction,

The heav'd challenge from the east that moment over my
    head,
The mocking taunt, See then whether you shall be master!

XXV

Dazzling and tremendous how quick the sun-rise would
    kill me,
If I could not now and always send sun-rise out of me.

We also ascend dazzling and tremendous as the sun,
We found our own O my soul in the calm and cool of the
    day-break.

My voice goes after what my eyes cannot reach,
With the twirl of my tongue I encompass worlds and
    volumes of worlds.

Speech is the twin of my vision, it is unequal to measure
    itself,
It provokes me forever, it says sarcastically,
Walt you contain enough, why don't you let it out then?

Come now I will not be tantalized, you conceive too much
    of articulation,
Do you not know O speech how the buds beneath you are
    folded?
Waiting in gloom, protected by frost,
The dirt receding before my prophetical screams,
I underlying causes to balance them at last,
My knowledge my live parts, it keeping tally with the
    meaning of all things,

641

Happiness, (which whoever hears me let him or her set
   out in search of this day.)

My final merit I refuse you, I refuse putting from me what
   I really am,
Encompass worlds, but never try to encompass me,
I crowd your sleekest and best by simply looking toward
   you.

Writing and talk do not prove me,
I carry the plenum of proof and every thing else in my face,
With the hush of my lips I wholly confound the skeptic.

XXVI

Now I will do nothing but listen,
To accrue what I hear into this song, to let sounds con-
   tribute toward it.

I hear bravuras of birds, bustle of growing wheat, gossip
   of flames, clack of sticks cooking my meals,
I hear the sound I love, the sound of the human voice,
I hear all sounds running together, combined, fused or
   following,
Sounds of the city and sounds out of the city, sounds of
   the day and night,
Talkative young ones to those that like them, the loud
   laugh of work-people at their meals,
The angry base of disjointed friendship, the faint tones of
   the sick,
The judge with hands tight to the desk, his pallid lips pro-
   nouncing a death-sentence,

The heave'e'yo of stevedores unlading ships by the wharves,
the refrain of the anchor-lifters,
The ring of alarm-bells, the cry of fire, the whir of swift-
streaking engines and hose-carts with premonitory
tinkles and color'd lights,
The steam-whistle, the solid roll of the train of approaching cars,
The slow march play'd at the head of the association
marching two and two,
(They go to guard some corpse, the flag-tops are draped
with black muslin.)

I hear the violoncello, ('tis the young man's heart's com-
plaint,)
I hear the key'd cornet, it glides quickly in through my ears,
It shakes mad-sweet pangs through my belly and breast.

I hear the chorus, it is a grand opera,
Ah this indeed is music—this suits me.

A tenor large and fresh as the creation fills me,
The orbic flex of his mouth is pouring and filling me full.

I hear the train'd soprano (what work with hers is this?)
The orchestra whirls me wider than Uranus flies,
It wrenches such ardors from me I did not know I possess'd
them,
It sails me, I dab with bare feet, they are lick'd by the
indolent waves,
I am cut by bitter and angry hail, I lose my breath,
Steep'd amid honey'd morphine, my windpipe throttled in
fakes of death,

643

At length let up again to feel the puzzle of puzzles,
And that we call Being.

XXVII

To be in any form, what is that?
(Round and round we go, all of us, and ever come back
    thither,)
If nothing lay more develop'd the quahaug in its callous
    shell were enough.

Mine is no callous shell,
I have instant conductors all over me whether I pass or stop,
They seize every object and lead it harmlessly through me.

I merely stir, press, feel with my fingers, and am happy,
To touch my person to some one else's is about as much as
    I can stand.

XXVIII

Is this then a touch? quivering me to a new identity,
Flames and ether making a rush for my veins,
Treacherous tip of me reaching and crowding to help them,
My flesh and blood playing out lightning to strike what is
    hardly different from myself,
On all sides prurient provokers stiffening my limbs,
Straining the udder of my heart for its withheld drip,
Behaving licentious toward me, taking no denial,
Depriving me of my best as for a purpose,
Unbuttoning my clothes, holding me by the bare waist,

Deluding my confusion with the calm of the sunlight and
    pasture-fields,
Immodestly sliding the fellow-senses away,
They bribed to swap off with touch and go and gaze at the
    edges of me,
No consideration, no regard for my draining strength or
    my anger,
Fetching the rest of the herd around to enjoy them a while,
Then all uniting to stand on a headland and worry me.

The sentries desert every other part of me,
They have left me helpless to a red marauder,
They all come to the headland to witness and assist against
    me.

I am given up by traitors,
I talk wildly, I have lost my wits, I and nobody else am
    the greatest traitor,
I went myself first to the headland, my own hands carried
    me there.

You villain touch! what are you doing? my breath is tight
    in its throat,
Unclench your floodgates, you are too much for me.

XXIX

Blind loving wrestling touch, sheath'd hooded sharp-tooth'd
    touch!
Did it make you ache so, leaving me?

Parting track'd by arriving, perpetual payment of per-
    petual loan,

Rich showering rain, and recompense richer afterward.

Sprouts take and accumulate, stand by the curb prolific
and vital,
Landscapes projected masculine, full-sized and golden.

XXX

All truths wait in all things,
They neither hasten their own delivery nor resist it,
They do not need the obstetric forceps of the surgeon,
The insignificant is as big to me as any,
(What is less or more than a touch.)

Logic and sermons never convince,
The damp of the night drives deeper into my soul.

(Only what proves itself to every man and woman is so,
Only what nobody denies is so.)

A minute and a drop of me settle my brain,
I believe the soggy clods shall become lovers and lamps,
And a compend of compends is the meat of a man or
woman,
And a summit and flower there is the feeling they have for
each other,
And they are to branch boundlessly out of that lesson until
it becomes omnific,
And until one and all shall delight us, and we them.

XXXI

I believe a leaf of grass is no less than the journey-work of
the stars,

646

And the pismire is equally perfect, and a grain of sand,
and the egg of the wren,
And the tree-toad is a chef-d'œuvre for the highest,
And the running blackberry would adorn the parlors of
heaven,

And the narrowest hinge in my hand puts to scorn all
machinery,
And the cow crunching with depress'd head surpasses any
statue,
And a mouse is miracle enough to stagger sextillions of
infidels.

I find I incorporate gneiss, coal, long-threaded moss, fruits,
grains, esculent roots,
And am stucco'd with quadrupeds and birds all over,
And have distanced what is behind me for good reasons,
But call any thing back again when I desire it.

In vain the speeding or shyness,
In vain the plutonic rocks send their old heat against my
approach,
In vain the mastodon retreats beneath its own powder'd
bones,
In vain objects stand leagues off and assume manifold
shapes,
In vain the ocean settling in hollows and the great monsters
lying low,
In vain the buzzard houses herself with the sky,
In vain the snake slides through the creepers and logs,
In vain the elk takes to the inner passes of the woods,

In vain the razor-bill'd auk sails far north to Labrador,
I follow quickly, I ascend to the nest in the fissure of the
cliff.

XXXII

I think I could turn and live with animals, they are so
placid and self-contain'd,
I stand and look at them long and long.

They do not sweat and whine about their condition,
They do not lie awake in the dark and weep for their sins,
They do not make me sick discussing their duty to God,
Not one is dissatisfied, not one is demented with the mania
of owning things,
Not one kneels to another, nor to his kind that lived thou-
sands of years ago,
Not one is respectable or unhappy over the whole earth.

So they show their relations to me and I accept them,
They bring me tokens of myself, they evince them plainly
in their possession.

I wonder where they get those tokens,
Did I pass that way huge times ago and negligently drop
them?
Myself moving forward then and now and forever,
Gathering and showing more always and with velocity,
Infinite and omnigenous, and the like of these among them,
Not too exclusive toward the reachers of my remem-
brancers,

Picking out here one that I love, now go with him on
  brotherly terms.

A gigantic beauty of a stallion, fresh and responsive to my
  caresses,
Head high in the forehead, wide between the ears,
Limbs glossy and supple, tail dusting the ground,
Eyes full of sparkling wickedness, ears finely cut, flexibly
  moving.

His nostrils dilate as my heels embrace him,
His well-built limbs tremble with pleasure as we race
  around and return.

I but use you a minute, then I resign you, stallion,
Why do I need your paces when I myself out-gallop them?
Even as I stand or sit passing faster than you.

XXXIII

Space and Time! now I see it is true, what I guess'd at,
What I guess'd when I loaf'd on the grass,
What I guess'd while I lay alone in my bed,
And again as I walk'd the beach under the paling stars of
  the morning.

My ties and ballasts leave me, my elbows rest in sea-gaps,
I skirt sierras, my palms cover continents,
I am afoot with my vision.

By the city's quadrangular houses—in log huts, camping
  with lumbermen,

Along the ruts of the turnpike, along the dry gulch and
rivulet bed,
Weeding my onion-patch or hoeing rows of carrots and
parsnips, crossing savannas, trailing in forests,
Prospecting, gold-digging, girdling the trees of a new purchase,
Scorch'd ankle-deep by the hot sand, hauling my boat
down the shallow river,
Where the panther walks to and fro on a limb overhead,
where the buck turns furiously at the hunter,
Where the rattlesnake suns his flabby length on a rock,
where the otter is feeding on fish,
Where the alligator in his tough pimples sleeps by the
bayou,
Where the black bear is searching for roots or honey,
where the beaver pats the mud with his paddle-
shaped tail;
Over the growing sugar, over the yellow-flower'd cotton
plant, over the rice in its low moist field,
Over the sharp-peak'd farm house, with its scallop'd scum
and slender shoots from the gutters,
Over the western persimmon, over the long-leav'd corn,
over the delicate blue-flower flax,
Over the white and brown buckwheat, a hummer and
buzzer there with the rest,
Over the dusky green of the rye as it ripples and shades in
the breeze;
Scaling mountains, pulling myself cautiously up, holding
on by low scragged limbs,

Walking the path worn in the grass and beat through the
    leaves of the brush,
Where the quail is whistling betwixt the woods and the
    wheat-lot,
Where the bat flies in the Seventh-month eve, where the
    great gold-bug drops through the dark,
Where the brook puts out of the roots of the old tree and
    flows to the meadow,
Where cattle stand and shake away flies with the tremu-
    lous shuddering of their hides,
Where the cheese-cloth hangs in the kitchen, where and-
    irons straddle the hearth-slab, where cobwebs fall in
    festoons from the rafters;
Where trip-hammers crash, where the press is whirling its
    cylinders,
Wherever the human heart beats with terrible throes under
    its ribs,
Where the pear-shaped balloon is floating aloft, (floating
    in it myself and looking composedly down,)
Where the life-car is drawn on the slip-noose, where the
    heat hatches pale-green eggs in the dented sand,
Where the she-whale swims with her calf and never for-
    sakes it,
Where the steam-ship trails hind-ways its long pennant of
    smoke,
Where the fin of the shark cuts like a black chip out of the
    water,
Where the half-burn'd brig is riding on unknown currents,
Where shells grow to her slimy deck, where the dead are
    corrupting below;

Where the dense-starr'd flag is borne at the head of the
     regiments, .
Approaching Manhattan up by the long-stretching island,
Under Niagara, the cataract falling like a veil over my
     countenance,
Upon a door-step, upon the horse-block of hard wood out-
     side,
Upon the race-course, or enjoying picnics or jigs or a good
     game of base-ball,
At he-festivals, with blackguard gibes, ironical license,
     bull-dances, drinking, laughter,
At the cider-mill tasting the sweets of the brown mash,
     sucking the juice through a straw,
At apple-peelings wanting kisses for all the red fruit I find,
At musters, beach-parties, friendly bees, huskings, house-
     raisings;
Where the mocking-bird sounds his delicious gurgles,
     cackles, screams, weeps,
Where the hay-rick stands in the barn-yard, where the dry-
     stalks are scatter'd, where the brood-cow waits in the
     hovel,
Where the bull advances to do his masculine work, where
     the stud to the mare, where the cock is treading the
     hen,
Where the heifers browse, where geese nip their food with
     short jerks,
Where sun-down shadows lengthen over the limitless and
     lonesome prairie,
Where herds of buffalo make a crawling spread of the
     square miles far and near,

Where the humming-bird shimmers, where the neck of the
long-lived swan is curving and winding,
Where the laughing-gull scoots by the shore, where she
laughs her near-human laugh,
Where bee-hives range on a gray bench in the garden half
hid by the high weeds,
Where band-neck'd partridges roost in a ring on the
ground with their heads out,
Where burial coaches enter the arch'd gates of a cemetery,
Where winter wolves bark amid wastes of snow and icicled
trees,
Where the yellow-crown'd heron comes to the edge of the
marsh at night and feeds upon small crabs,
Where the splash of swimmers and divers cools the warm
noon,
Where the katy-did works her chromatic reed on the wal-
nut-tree over the well,
Through patches of citrons and cucumbers with silver-
wired leaves,
Through the salt-lick or orange glade, or under conical
firs,
Through the gymnasium, through the curtain'd saloon,
through the office or public hall;
Pleas'd with the native and pleas'd with the foreign,
pleas'd with the new and old,
Pleas'd with the homely woman as well as the handsome,
Pleas'd with the quakeress as she puts off her bonnet and
talks melodiously,
Pleas'd with the tune of the choir of the whitewash'd
church,

Pleas'd with the earnest words of the sweating Methodist preacher, impress'd seriously at the camp-meeting;

Looking in at the shop-windows of Broadway the whole forenoon, flatting the flesh of my nose on the thick plate glass,

Wandering the same afternoon with my face turn'd up to the clouds, or down a lane or along the beach,

My right and left arms round the sides of two friends, and I in the middle;

Coming home with the silent and dark-cheek'd bush-boy, (behind me he rides at the drape of the day,)

Far from the settlements studying the print of animals' feet, or the moccasin print,

By the cot in the hospital reaching lemonade to a feverish patient,

Nigh the coffin'd corpse when all is still, examining with a candle;

Voyaging to every port to dicker and adventure,

Hurrying with the modern crowd as eager and fickle as any,

Hot toward one I hate, ready in my madness to knife him,

Solitary at midnight in my back yard, my thoughts gone from me a long while,

Walking the old hills of Judæa with the beautiful gentle God by my side,

Speeding through space, speeding through heaven and the stars,

Speeding amid the seven satellites and the broad ring, and the diameter of eighty thousand miles,

Speeding with tail'd meteors, throwing fire-balls like the
     rest,
Carrying the crescent child that carries its own full mother
     in its belly,
Storming, enjoying, planning, loving, cautioning,
Backing and filling, appearing and disappearing,
I tread day and night such roads.

I visit the orchards of spheres and look at the product,
And look at quintillions ripen'd and look at quintillions
     green.

I fly those flights of a fluid and swallowing soul,
My course runs below the soundings of plummets.

I help myself to material and immaterial,
No guard can shut me off, no law prevent me.

I anchor my ship for a little while only,
My messengers continually cruise away or bring their re-
     turns to me.

I go hunting polar furs and the seal, leaping chasms with
     a pike-pointed staff, clinging to topples of brittle and
     blue.

I ascend to the foretruck,
I take my place late at night in the crow's-nest,
We sail the arctic sea, it is plenty light enough,
Through the clear atmosphere I stretch around on the
     wonderful beauty,
The enormous masses of ice pass me and I pass them, the
     scenery is plain in all directions,

The white-topt mountains show in the distance, I fling out
 my fancies toward them,
We are approaching some great battle-field in which we
 are soon to be engaged,
We pass the colossal outposts of the encampment, we pass
 with still feet and caution,
Or we are entering by the suburbs some vast and ruin'd
 city,
The blocks and fallen architecture more than all the living
 cities of the globe.

I am a free companion, I bivouac by invading watchfires,
I turn the bridegroom out of bed and stay with the bride
 myself,
I tighten her all night to my thighs and lips.

My voice is the wife's voice, the screech by the rail of the
 stairs,
They fetch my man's body up dripping and drown'd.

I understand the large hearts of heroes,
The courage of present times and all times,
How the skipper saw the crowded and rudderless wreck of
 the steam-ship, and Death chasing it up and down
 the storm,
How he knuckled tight and gave not back an inch, and
 was faithful of days and faithful of nights,
And chalk'd in large letters on a board, Be of good cheer,
 we will not desert you;
How he follow'd with them and tack'd with them three
 days and would not give it up,

How he saved the drifting company at last,

How the lank loose-gown'd women look'd when boated
from the side of their prepared graves,

How the silent old-faced infants and the lifted sick, and
the sharp-lipp'd unshaved men;

All this I swallow, it tastes good, I like it well, it becomes
mine,

I am the man, I suffer'd, I was there.

The disdain and calmness of martyrs,

The mother of old, condemn'd for a witch, burnt with dry
wood, her children gazing on,

The hounded slave that flags in the race, leans by the
fence, blowing, cover'd with sweat,

The twinges that sting like needles his legs and neck, the
murderous buckshot and the bullets,

All these I feel or am.

I am the hounded slave, I wince at the bite of the dogs,

Hell and despair are upon me, crack and again crack the
marksmen,

I clutch the rails of the fence, my gore dribs, thinn'd with
the ooze of my skin,

I fall on the weeds and stones,

The riders spur their unwilling horses, haul close,

Taunt my dizzy ears and beat me violently over the head
with whip-stocks.

Agonies are one of my changes of garments,

I do not ask the wounded person how he feels, I myself
become the wounded person,

My hurts turn livid upon me as I lean on a cane and observe.

I am the mash'd fireman with breast-bone broken,
Tumbling walls buried me in their debris,
Heat and smoke I inspired, I heard the yelling shouts of
my comrades,
I heard the distant click of their picks and shovels,
They have clear'd the beams away, they tenderly lift me
forth.

I lie in the night air in my red shirt, the pervading hush is
for my sake,
Painless after all I lie exhausted but not so unhappy,
White and beautiful are the faces around me, the heads
are bared of their fire-caps,
The kneeling crowd fades with the light of the torches.

Distant and dead resuscitate,
They show as the dial or move as the hands of me, I am
the clock myself.

I am an old artillerist, I tell of my fort's bombardment,
I am there again.

Again the long roll of the drummers,
Again the attacking cannon, mortars,
Again to my listening ears the cannon responsive.

I take part, I see and hear the whole,
The cries, curses, roar, the plaudits for well-aim'd shots,
The ambulanza slowly passing trailing its red drip,

Workmen searching after damages, making indispensable
　　repairs,
The fall of grenades through the rent roof, the fan-shaped
　　explosion,
The whizz of limbs, heads, stone, wood, iron, high in the
　　air.

Again gurgles the mouth of my dying general, he furiously
　　waves with his hand,
He gasps through the clot, Mind not me—mind—the en-
　　trenchments.

XXXIV

Now I tell what I knew in Texas in my early youth,
(I tell not the fall of Alamo,
Not one escaped to tell the fall of Alamo,
The hundred and fifty are dumb yet at Alamo,)
'Tis the tale of the murder in cold blood of four hundred
　　and twelve young men.

Retreating they had form'd in a hollow square with their
　　baggage for breastworks,
Nine hundred lives out of the surrounding enemies, nine
　　times their number, was the price they took in ad-
　　vance,
Their colonel was wounded and their ammunition gone,
They treated for an honorable capitulation, receiv'd writ-
　　ing and seal, gave up their arms and march'd back
　　prisoners of war.

They were the glory of the race of rangers,
Matchless with horse, rifle, song, supper, courtship,
Large, turbulent, generous, handsome, proud, and affec-
tionate,
Bearded, sunburnt, drest in the free costume of hunters,
Not a single one over thirty years of age.

The second First-day morning they were brought out in
squads and massacred, it was beautiful early summer,
The work commenced about five o'clock and was over by
eight.

None obey'd the command to kneel,
Some made a mad and helpless rush, some stood stark and
straight,
A few fell at once, shot in the temple or heart, the living
and dead lay together,
The maim'd and mangled dug in the dirt, the new-comers
saw them there,
Some half-kill'd attempted to crawl away,
These were despatch'd with bayonets or batter'd with the
blunts of muskets,
A youth not seventeen years old seiz'd his assassin till two
more came to release him,
The three were all torn and cover'd with the boy's blood.

At eleven o'clock began the burning of the bodies;
That is the tale of the murder of the four hundred and
twelve young men.

XXXV

Would you hear of an old-time sea-fight?

Would you learn who won by the light of the moon and
stars?

List to the yarn, as my grandmother's father the sailor
told it to me.

Our foe was no skulk in his ship I tell you, (said he,)

His was the surly English pluck, and there is no tougher or
truer, and never was, and never will be;

Along the lower'd eve he came horribly raking us.

We closed with him, the yards entangled, the cannon
touch'd,

My captain lash'd fast with his own hands.

We had receiv'd some eighteen pound shots under the
water,

On our lower-gun-deck two large pieces had burst at the
first fire, killing all around and blowing up overhead.

Fighting at sun-down, fighting at dark,

Ten o'clock at night, the full moon well up, our leaks on
the gain, and five feet of water reported,

The master-at-arms loosing the prisoners confined in the
after-hold to give them a chance for themselves.

The transit to and from the magazine is now stopt by the
sentinels,

They see so many strange faces they do not know whom
to trust.

Our frigate takes fire,

The other asks if we demand quarter?
If our colors are struck and the fighting done?

Now I laugh content, for I hear the voice of my little
captain,
We have not struck, he composedly cries, we have just begun our part of the fighting.

Only three guns are in use,
One is directed by the captain himself against the enemy's
main-mast,
Two well serv'd with grape and canister silence his mus-
ketry and clear his decks.
The tops alone second the fire of this little battery, espe-
cially the main-top,
They hold out bravely during the whole of the action.

Not a moment's cease,
The leaks gain fast on the pumps, the fire eats toward the
powder-magazine.

One of the pumps has been shot away, it is generally
thought we are sinking.

Serene stands the little captain,
He is not hurried, his voice is neither high nor low,
His eyes give more light to us than our battle-lanterns.

Toward twelve there in the beams of the moon they sur-
render to us.

XXXVI

Stretch'd and still lies the midnight,

Two great hulls motionless on the breast of the darkness,

Our vessel riddled and slowly sinking, preparations to pass to the one we have conquer'd,

The captain on the quarter-deck coldly giving his orders through a countenance white as a sheet,

Near by the corpse of the child that serv'd in the cabin,

The dead face of an old salt with long white hair and carefully curl'd whiskers,

The flames spite of all that can be done flickering aloft and below,

The husky voices of the two or three officers yet fit for duty,

Formless stacks of bodies and bodies by themselves, dabs of flesh upon the masts and spars,

Cut of cordage, dangle of rigging, slight shock of the soothe of waves,

Black and impassive guns, litter of powder-parcels, strong scent,

A few large stars overhead, silent and mournful shining,

Delicate sniffs of sea-breeze, smells of sedgy grass and fields by the shore, death-messages given in charge to survivors,

The hiss of the surgeon's knife, the gnawing teeth of his saw,

Wheeze, cluck, swash of falling blood, short wild scream, and long, dull, tapering groan,

These so, these irretrievable.

XXXVII

You laggards there on guard! look to your arms!

In at the conquer'd doors they crowd! I am possess'd!
Embody all presences outlaw'd or suffering,
See myself in prison shaped like another man,
And feel the dull unintermitted pain.

For me the keepers of convicts shoulder their carbines and
    keep watch,
It is I let out in the morning and barr'd at night.

Not a mutineer walks handcuff'd to jail but I am hand-
    cuff'd to him and walk by his side,
(I am less the jolly one there, and more the silent one with
    sweat on my twitching lips.)

Not a youngster is taken for larceny but I go up too, and
    am tried and sentenced.

Not a cholera patient lies at the last gasp but I also lie at
    the last gasp,
My face is ash-color'd, my sinews gnarl, away from me
    people retreat.

Askers embody themselves in me and I am embodied in
    them,
I project my hat, sit shame-faced, and beg.

XXXVIII

Enough! enough! enough!
Somehow I have been stunn'd. Stand back!
Give me a little time beyond my cuff'd head, slumbers,
    dreams, gaping,
I discover myself on the verge of a usual mistake.

That I could forget the mockers and insults!
That I could forget the trickling tears and the blows of the
bludgeons and hammers!
That I could look with a separate look on my own cruci-
fixion and bloody crowning.

I remember now,
I resume the overstaid fraction,
The grave of rock multiplies what has been confided to it,
or to any graves,
Corpses rise, gashes heal, fastenings roll from me.

I troop forth replenish'd with supreme power, one of an
average unending procession,
Inland and sea-coast we go, and pass all boundary lines,
Our swift ordinances on their way over the whole earth,
The blossoms we wear in our hats the growth of thousands
of years.

Eleves, I salute you! come forward!
Continue your annotations, continue your questionings.

XXXIX

The friendly and flowing savage, who is he?
Is he waiting for civilization, or past it and mastering it?

Is he some Southwesterner rais'd out-doors? is he Kanadian?
Is he from the Mississippi country? Iowa, Oregon, Cali-
fornia?
The mountains? prairie-life, bush-life? or sailor from the
sea?

Wherever he goes men and women accept and desire him,
They desire he should like them, touch them, speak to
them, stay with them.

Behavior lawless as snow-flakes, words simple as grass, un-
comb'd head, laughter, and naivetè,
Slow-stepping feet, common features, common modes and
emanations,
They descend in new forms from the tips of his fingers,
They are wafted with the odor of his body or breath, they
fly out of the glance of his eyes.

XL

Flaunt of the sunshine I need not your bask—lie over!
You light surfaces only, I force surfaces and depths also.

Earth! you seem to look for something at my hands,
Say, old top-knot, what do you want?

Man or woman, I might tell how I like you, but cannot,
And might tell what it is in me and what it is in you, but
cannot,
And might tell that pining I have, that pulse of my nights
and days.

Behold, I do not give lectures or a little charity,
When I give I give myself.

You there, impotent, loose in the knees,
Open your scarf'd chops till I blow grit within you,
Spread your palms and lift the flaps of your pockets,

I am not to be denied, I compel, I have stores plenty and
      to spare,
And any thing I have I bestow.

I do not ask who you are, that is not important to me,
You can do nothing and be nothing but what I will infold
      you.

To cotton-field drudge or cleaner of privies I lean,
On his right cheek I put the family kiss,
And in my soul I swear I never will deny him.

On women fit for conception I start bigger and nimbler
      babes,
(This day I am jetting the stuff of far more arrogant re-
      publics.)

To any one dying, thither I speed and twist the knob of
      the door,
Turn the bed-clothes toward the foot of the bed,
Let the physician and the priest go home.

I seize the descending man and raise him with resistless
      will,
O despairer, here is my neck,
By God, you shall not go down! hang your whole weight
      upon me.

I dilate you with tremendous breath, I buoy you up,
Every room of the house do I fill with an arm'd force,
Lovers of me, bafflers of graves.

Sleep—I and they keep guard all night,

Not doubt, not decease shall dare to lay finger upon you,

I have embraced you, and henceforth possess you to myself,

And when you rise in the morning you will find what I tell
you is so.

XLI

I am he bringing help for the sick as they pant on their
backs,

And for strong upright men I bring yet more needed help.

I heard what was said of the universe,

Heard it and heard it of several thousand years;

It is middling well as far as it goes—but is that all?

Magnifying and applying come I,

Outbidding at the start the old cautious hucksters,

Taking myself the exact dimensions of Jehovah,

Lithographing Kronos, Zeus his son, and Hercules his
grandson,

Buying drafts of Osiris, Isis, Belus, Brahma, Buddha,

In my portfolio placing Manito loose, Allah on a leaf, the
crucifix engraved,

With Odin and the hideous-faced Mexitli and every idol
and image,

Taking them all for what they are worth and not a cent
more,

Admitting they were alive and did the work of their days,

(They bore mites as for unfledg'd birds who have now to
  rise and fly and sing for themselves,)
Accepting the rough deific sketches to fill out better in my-
  self, bestowing them freely on each man and woman
  I see,
Discovering as much or more in a framer framing a house,
Putting higher claims for him there with his roll'd-up
  sleeves driving the mallet and chisel,
Not objecting to special revelations, considering a curl of
  smoke or a hair on the back of my hand just as
  curious as any revelation,
Lads ahold of fire-engines and hook-and-ladder ropes no
  less to me than the gods of the antique wars,
Minding their voices peal through the crash of destruction,
Their brawny limbs passing safe over charr'd laths, their
  white foreheads whole and unhurt out of the flames;
By the mechanic's wife with her babe at her nipple inter-
  ceding for every person born,
Three scythes at harvest whizzing in a row from three lusty
  angels with shirts bagg'd out at their waists,
The snag-tooth'd hostler with red hair redeeming sins past
  and to come,
Selling all he possesses, traveling on foot to fee lawyers for
  his brother and sit by him while he is tried for for-
  gery;
What was strewn in the amplest strewing the square rod
  about me, and not filling the square rod then,
The bull and the bug never worshipp'd half enough,
Dung and dirt more admirable than was dream'd,

The supernatural of no account, myself waiting my time
    to be one of the supremes,
The day getting ready for me when I shall do as much
    good as the best, and be as prodigious;
By my life-lumps! becoming already a creator,
Putting myself here and now to the ambush'd womb of the
    shadows.

XLII

A call in the midst of the crowd,
My own voice, orotund sweeping and final.

Come my children,
Come my boys and girls, my women, household and inti-
    mates,
Now the performer launches his nerve, he has pass'd his
    prelude on the reeds within.

Easily written loose-finger'd chords—I feel the thrum of
    your climax and close.

My head slues round on my neck,
Music rolls, but not from the organ,
Folks are around me, but they are no household of mine.

Ever the hard unsunk ground,
Ever the eaters and drinkers, ever the upward and down-
    ward sun, ever the air and the ceaseless tides,
Ever myself and my neighbors, refreshing, wicked, real,
Ever the old inexplicable query, ever that thorn'd thumb,
    that breath of itches and thirsts,

Ever the vexer's hoot! hoot! till we find where the sly one
    hides and bring him forth,
Ever love, ever the sobbing liquid of life,
Ever the bandage under the chin, ever the trestles of
    death.

Here and there with dimes on the eyes walking,
To feed the greed of the belly the brains liberally spoon-
    ing,
Tickets buying, taking, selling, but in to the feast never
    once going,
Many sweating, ploughing, thrashing, and then the chaff
    for payment receiving,
A few idly owning, and they the wheat continually claim-
    ing.

This is the city and I am one of the citizens,
Whatever interests the rest interests me, politics, wars,
    markets, newspapers, schools,
The mayor and councils, banks, tariffs, steamships, fac-
    tories, stocks, stores, real estate and personal estate.

The little plentiful manikins skipping around in collars
    and tail'd coats,
I am aware who they are, (they are positively not worms
    or fleas,)
I acknowledge the duplicates of myself, the weakest and
    shallowest is deathless with me,
What I do and say the same waits for them,
Every thought that flounders in me the same flounders in
    them.

I know perfectly well my own egotism,

Know my omnivorous lines and must not write any less,
And would fetch you whoever you are flush with myself.

Not words of routine this song of mine,
But abruptly to question, to leap beyond yet nearer bring;
This printed and bound book—but the printer and the
    printing-office boy?
The well-taken photographs—but your wife or friend close
    and solid in your arms?
The black ship mail'd with iron, her mighty guns in her
    turrets—but the pluck of the captain and engineers?
In the houses the dishes and fare and furniture—but the
    host and hostess, and the look out of their eyes?
The sky up there—yet here or next door, or across the
    way?
The saints and sages in history—but you yourself?
Sermons, creeds, theology—but the fathomless human
    brain,
And what is reason? and what is love? and what is life?

XLIII

I do not despise you priests, all time, the world over,
My faith is the greatest of faiths and the least of faiths,
Enclosing worship ancient and modern and all between
    ancient and modern,
Believing I shall come again upon the earth after five
    thousand years,
Waiting responses from oracles, honoring the gods, salut-
    ing the sun,

Making a fetich of the first rock or stump, powowing with
    sticks in the circle of obis,
Helping the llama or brahmin as he trims the lamps of the
    idols,
Dancing yet through the streets in a phallic procession,
    rapt and austere in the woods a gymnosophist,
Drinking mead from the skull-cup, to Shastas and Vedas
    admirant, minding the Koran,
Walking the teokallis, spotted with gore from the stone
    and knife, beating the serpent-skin drum,
Accepting the Gospels, accepting him that was crucified,
    knowing assuredly that he is divine,
To the mass kneeling or the puritan's prayer rising, or sit-
    ting patiently in a pew,
Ranting and frothing in my insane crisis, or waiting dead-
    like till my spirit arouses me,
Looking forth on pavement and land, or outside of pave-
    ment and land,
Belonging to the winders of the circuit of circuits.

One of that centripetal and centrifugal gang I turn and
    talk like a man leaving charges before a journey.

Down-hearted doubters dull and excluded,
Frivolous, sullen, moping, angry, affected, dishearten'd,
    atheistical,
I know every one of you, I know the sea of torment,
    doubt, despair and unbelief.

How the flukes splash!
How they contort rapid as lightning, with spasms and
    spouts of blood!

Be at peace bloody flukes of doubters and sullen mopers,
I take my place among you as much as among any,
The past is the push of you, me, all, precisely the same,
And what is yet untried and afterward is for you, me, all,
    precisely the same.

I do not know what is untried and afterward,
But I know it will in its turn prove sufficient, and cannot
    fail.

Each who passes is consider'd, each who stops is con-
    sider'd, not a single one can it fail.

It cannot fail the young man who died and was buried,
Nor the young woman who died and was put by his side,
Nor the little child that peep'd in at the door, and then
    drew back and was never seen again,
Nor the old man who has lived without purpose, and feels
    it with bitterness worse than gall,
Nor him in the poor house tubercled by rum and the bad
    disorder,
Nor the numberless slaughter'd and wreck'd, nor the
    brutish koboo call'd the ordure of humanity,
Nor the sacs merely floating with open mouths for food to
    slip in,
Nor any thing in the earth, or down in the oldest graves of
    the earth,
Nor any thing, in the myriads of spheres, nor the myriads
    of myriads that inhabit them,
Nor the present, nor the least wisp that is known.

XLIV

It is time to explain myself—let us stand up.

What is known I strip away,
I launch all men and women forward with me into the
Unknown.

The clock indicates the moment—but what does eternity
indicate?

We have thus far exhausted trillions of winters and summers,
There are trillions ahead, and trillions ahead of them.

Births have brought us richness and variety,
And other births will bring us richness and variety.

I do not call one greater and one smaller,
That which fills its period and place is equal to any.

Were mankind murderous or jealous upon you, my
brother, my sister?
I am sorry for you, they are not murderous or jealous
upon me,
All has been gentle with me, I keep no account with lamentation,
(What have I to do with lamentation?)

I am an acme of things accomplish'd, and I an encloser of
things to be.

My feet strike an apex of the apices of the stairs,

On every step bunches of ages, and larger bunches between the steps,
All below duly travel'd, and still I mount and mount.

Rise after rise bow the phantoms behind me,
Afar down I see the huge first Nothing, I know I was even there,
I waited unseen and always, and slept through the lethargic mist,
And took my time, and took no hurt from the fetid carbon.

Long I was hugg'd close—long and long.

Immense have been the preparations for me,
Faithful and friendly the arms that have help'd me.

Cycles ferried my cradle, rowing and rowing like cheerful boatmen,
For room to me stars kept aside in their own rings,
They sent influences to look after what was to hold me.

Before I was born out of my mother generations guided me,
My embryo has never been torpid, nothing could overlay it.

For it the nebula cohered to an orb,
The long slow strata piled to rest it on,
Vast vegetables gave it sustenance,
Monstrous sauroids transported it in their mouths and deposited it with care.

All forces have been steadily employ'd to complete and delight me,
Now on this spot I stand with my robust soul.

676

XLV

O span of youth! ever-push'd elasticity!
O manhood, balanced, florid and full.

My lovers suffocate me,
Crowding my lips, thick in the pores of my skin,
Jostling me through streets and public halls, coming naked
    to me at night,
Crying by day, Ahoy! from the rocks of the river, swing-
    ing and chirping over my head,
Calling my name from flower-beds, vines, tangled under-
    brush,
Lighting on every moment of my life,
Bussing my body with soft balsamic busses,
Noiselessly passing handfuls out of their hearts and giving
    them to be mine.

Old age superbly rising! O welcome, ineffable grace of
    dying days!
Every condition promulges not only itself, it promulges
    what grows after and out of itself,
And the dark hush promulges as much as any.

I open my scuttle at night and see the far-sprinkled systems,
And all I see, multiplied as high as I can cypher, edge but
    the rim of the farther systems.

Wider and wider they spread, expanding, always expand-
    ing,
Outward and outward and forever outward.

My sun has his sun and round him obediently wheels,

677

He joins with his partners a group of superior circuit,
And greater sets follow, making specks of the greatest
inside them.

There is no stoppage and never can be stoppage,
If I, you, and the worlds, and all beneath or upon their
surfaces, were this moment reduced back to a pallid
float, it would not avail in the long run,
We should surely bring up again where we now stand,
And surely go as much farther, and then farther and
farther.

A few quadrillions of eras, a few octillions of cubic leagues,
do not hazard the span or make it impatient,
They are but parts, anything is but a part.

See ever so far, there is limitless space outside of that,
Count ever so much, there is limitless time around that.

My rendezvous is appointed, it is certain,
The Lord will be there and wait till I come on perfect
terms,
The great Camerado, the lover true for whom I pine will
be there.

XLVI

I know I have the best of time and space, and was never
measured and never will be measured.

I tramp a perpetual journey, (come listen all!)
My signs are a rain-proof coat, good shoes, and a staff cut
from the woods,

No friend of mine takes his ease in my chair,
I have no chair, no church, no philosophy,
I lead no man to a dinner-table, library, exchange,
But each man and each woman of you I lead upon a knoll,
My left hand hooking you round the waist,
My right hand pointing to landscapes of continents and
    the public road.

Not I, not any one else can travel that road for you,
You must travel it for yourself.

It is not far, it is within reach,
Perhaps you have been on it since you were born and did
    not know,
Perhaps it is everywhere on water and on land.

Shoulder your duds dear son, and I will mine, and let us
    hasten forth,
Wonderful cities and free nations we shall fetch as we go.

If you tire, give me both burdens, and rest the chuff of
    your hand on my hip,
And in due time you shall repay the same service to me,
For after we start we never lie by again.

This day before dawn I ascended a hill and look'd at the
    crowded heaven,
And I said to my spirit, When we become the enfolders of
    those orbs, and the pleasure and knowledge of every
    thing in them, shall we be fill'd and satisfied then?
And my spirit said, No, we but level that lift to pass con-
    tinue beyond.

You are also asking me questions and I hear you,
I answer that I cannot answer, you must find out for yourself.

Sit a while dear son,
Here are biscuits to eat and here is milk to drink,
But as soon as you sleep and renew yourself in sweet
clothes, I kiss you with a good-by kiss and open the
gate for your egress hence.

Long enough have you dream'd contemptible dreams,
Now I wash the gum from your eyes,
You must habit yourself to the dazzle of the light and of
every moment of your life.

Long have you timidly waded holding a plank by the shore,
Now I will you to be a bold swimmer,
To jump off in the midst of the sea, rise again, nod to me,
shout, and laughingly dash with your hair.

XLVII

I am the teacher of athletes,
He that by me spreads a wider breast than my own proves
the width of my own,
He most honors my style who learns under it to destroy
the teacher.

The boy I love, the same becomes a man not through
derived power, but in his own right,
Wicked rather than virtuous out of conformity or fear,
Fond of his sweetheart, relishing well his steak,

Unrequited love or a slight cutting him worse than sharp
    steel cuts,
First-rate to ride, to fight, to hit the bull's eye, to sail a
    skiff, to sing a song or play on the banjo,
Preferring scars and the beard and faces pitted with small-
    pox over all latherers,
And those well-tann'd to those that keep out of the sun.

I teach straying from me, yet who can stray from me?
I follow you whoever you are from the present hour,
My words itch at your ears till you understand them.

I do not say these things for a dollar or to fill up the time
    while I wait for a boat,
(It is you talking just as much as myself, I act as the
    tongue of you,
Tied in your mouth, in mine it begins to be loosen'd.)

I swear I will never again mention love or death inside a
    house,
And I swear I will never translate myself at all, only to
    him or her who privately stays with me in the open
    air.

If you would understand me go to the heights or water-
    shore,
The nearest gnat is an explanation, and a drop or motion
    of waves a key,
The maul, the oar, the hand-saw, second my words.

No shutter'd room or school can commune with me,
But roughs and little children better than they.

The young mechanic is closest to me, he knows me well,
The woodman that takes his axe and jug with him shall take me with him all day,
The farm-boy ploughing in the field feels good at the sound of my voice,
In vessels that sail my words sail, I go with fishermen and seamen and love them.

The soldier camp'd or upon the march is mine,
On the night ere the pending battle many seek me, and I do not fail them,
On that solemn night (it may be their last) those that know me seek me.

My face rubs to the hunter's face when he lies down alone in his blanket,
The driver thinking of me does not mind the jolt of his wagon,
The young mother and old mother comprehend me,
The girl and the wife rest the needle a moment and forget where they are,
They and all would resume what I have told them.

XLVIII

I have said that the soul is not more than the body,
And I have said that the body is not more than the soul,
And nothing, not God, is greater to one than one's self is,
And whoever walks a furlong without sympathy walks to his own funeral drest in his shroud,
And I or you pocketless of a dime may purchase the pick of the earth,

And to glance with an eye or show a bean in its pod con-
   founds the learning of all times,
And there is no trade or employment but the young man
   following it may become a hero,
And there is no object so soft but it makes a hub for the
   wheel'd universe,
And I say to any man or woman, Let your soul stand cool
   and composed before a million universes.

And I say to mankind, Be not curious about God,
For I who am curious about each am not curious about
   God,
(No array of terms can say how much I am at peace about
   God and about death.)

I hear and behold God in every object, yet understand
   God not in the least,
Nor do I understand who there can be more wonderful
   than myself.

Why should I wish to see God better than this day?
I see something of God each hour of the twenty-four, and
   each moment then,
In the faces of men and women I see God, and in my own
   face in the glass,
I find letters from God dropt in the street, and every one
   is sign'd by God's name,
And I leave them where they are, for I know that where-
   soe'er I go,
Others will punctually come for ever and ever.

683

And as to you Death, and you bitter hug of mortality, it is
    idle to try to alarm me.

To his work without flinching the accoucheur comes,
I see the elder-hand pressing, receiving, supporting,
I recline by the sills of the exquisite flexible doors,
And mark the outlet, and mark the relief and escape.

And as to you Corpse I think you are good manure, but
    that does not offend me,
I smell the white roses sweet-scented and growing,
I reach to the leafy lips, I reach to the polish'd breasts of
    melons.

And as to you Life I reckon you are the leavings of many
    deaths,
(No doubt I have died myself ten thousand times before.)

I hear you whispering there O stars of heaven,
O suns—O grass of graves—O perpetual transfers and
    promotions,
If you do not say any thing how can I say any thing?

Of the turbid pool that lies in the autumn forest,
Of the moon that descends the steeps of the soughing
    twilight,
Toss, sparkles of day and dusk—toss on the black stems
    that decay in the muck
Toss to the moaning gibberish of the dry limbs.

I ascend from the moon, I ascend from the night,

I perceive that the ghastly glimmer is noonday sunbeams
 reflected,
And debouch to the steady and central from the offspring great or small.

There is that in me—I do not know what it is—but I know
 it is in me.
Wrench'd and sweaty—calm and cool then my body becomes,
I sleep—I sleep long.

I do not know it—it is without name—it is a word unsaid,
It is not in any dictionary, utterance, symbol.

Something it swings on more than the earth I swing on,
To it the creation is the friend whose embracing awakes
 me.

Perhaps I might tell more. Outlines! I plead for my brothers
 and sisters.

Do you see O my brothers and sisters?
It is not chaos or death—it is form, union, plan—it is eternal
 life—it is Happiness.

LI

The past and present wilt—I have fill'd them, emptied them,
And proceed to fill my next fold of the future.

Listener up there! what have you to confide to me?
Look in my face while I snuff the sidle of evening,

(Talk honestly, no one else hears you, and I stay only a
    minute longer.)

Do I contradict myself?
Very well then I contradict myself,
(I am large, I contain multitudes.)

I concentrate toward them that are nigh, I wait on the
    door-slab.

Who has done his day's work? who will soonest be through
    with his supper?
Who wishes to walk with me?

Will you speak before I am gone? will you prove already
    too late?

LII

The spotted hawk swoops by and accuses me, he complains
    of my gab and my loitering.

I too am not a bit tamed, I too am untranslatable,
I sound my barbaric yawp over the roofs of the world.

The last scud of day holds back for me,
It flings my likeness after the rest and true as any on the
    shadow'd wilds,
It coaxes me to the vapor and the dusk.

I depart as air, I shake my white locks at the runaway sun,
I effuse my flesh in eddies, and drift it in lacy jags.

I bequeath myself to the dirt to grow from the grass I love,
If you want me again look for me under your boot-soles.

You will hardly know who I am or what I mean,
But I shall be good health to you nevertheless,
And filter and fibre your blood.

Failing to fetch me at first keep encouraged,
Missing me one place search another,
I stop somewhere waiting for you.

W. WHITMAN

❧ 291 ❦

CROSSING BROOKLYN FERRY

I

FLOOD-TIDE below me! I see you face to face!
Clouds of the west—sun there half an hour high—I see you
    also face to face.

Crowds of men and women attired in the usual costumes,
    how curious you are to me!
On the ferry-boats the hundreds and hundreds that cross,
    returning home, are more curious to me than you
    suppose,
And you that shall cross from shore to shore years hence
    are more to me, and more in my meditations than
    you might suppose.

II

The impalpable sustenance of me from all things at all
    hours of the day,

The simple, compact, well-join'd scheme, myself disinte-
    grated, every one disintegrated yet part of the scheme,

The similitudes of the past and those of the future,

The glories strung like beads on my smallest sights and
    hearings, on the walk in the street and the passage
    over the river,

The current rushing so swiftly and swimming with me far
    away,

The others that are to follow me, the ties between me and
    them,

The certainty of others, the life, love, sight, hearing of
    others.

Others will enter the gates of the ferry and cross from
    shore to shore,

Others will watch the run of the flood-tide,

Others will see the shipping of Manhattan north and west,
    and the heights of Brooklyn to the south and east,

Others will see the islands large and small;

Fifty years hence, others will see them as they cross, the
    sun half an hour high,

A hundred years hence, or ever so many hundred years
    hence, others will see them,

Will enjoy the sunset, the pouring-in of the flood-tide, the
    falling-back to the sea of the ebb-tide.

III

It avails not, time nor place—distance avails not,
I am with you, you men and women of a generation, or
ever so many generations hence,
Just as you feel when you look on the river and sky, so I
felt,
Just as any of you is one of a living crowd, I was one of a
crowd,
Just as you are refresh'd by the gladness of the river and
the bright flow, I was refresh'd,
Just as you stand and lean on the rail, yet hurry with the
swift current, I stood yet was hurried,
Just as you look on the numberless masts of ships and the
thick-stemm'd pipes of steamboats, I look'd.

I too many and many a time cross'd the river of old,
Watched the Twelfth-month sea-gulls, saw them high in
the air floating with motionless wings, oscillating their
bodies,
Saw how the glistening yellow lit up parts of their bodies
and left the rest in strong shadow,
Saw the slow-wheeling circles and the gradual edging to-
ward the south,
Saw the reflection of the summer sky in the water,
Had my eyes dazzled by the shimmering track of beams,
Look'd at the fine centrifugal spokes of light round the
the shape of my head in the sunlit water,
Look'd on the haze on the hills southward and south-west-
ward,

Look'd on the vapor as it flew in fleeces tinged with violet,
Look'd toward the lower bay to notice the vessels arriving,
Saw their approach, saw aboard those that were near me,
Saw the white sails of schooners and sloops, saw the ships
    at anchor,
The sailors at work in the rigging or out astride the spars,
The round masts, the swinging motion of the hulls, the
    slender serpentine pennants,
The large and small steamers in motion, the pilots in their
    pilot-houses,
The white wake left by the passage, the quick tremulous
    whirl of the wheels,
The flags of all nations, the falling of them at sunset,
The scallop-edged waves in the twilight, the ladled cups,
    the frolicsome crests and glistening,
The stretch afar growing dimmer and dimmer, the gray
    walls of the granite storehouses by the docks,
On the river the shadowy group, the big steam-tug closely
    flank'd on each side by the barges, the hay-boat, the
    belated lighter,
On the neighboring shore the fires from the foundry chim-
    neys burning high and glaringly into the night,
Casting their flicker of black contrasted with wild red and
    yellow light over the tops of houses, and down into
    the clefts of streets.

IV

These and all else were to me the same as they are to you,
I loved well those cities, loved well the stately and rapid
    river,

The men and women I saw were all near to me,
Others the same—others who look back on me because I
    look'd forward to them,
(The time will come, though I stop here to-day and to-
    night.)

V

What is it then between us?
What is the count of the scores or hundreds of years be-
    tween us?

Whatever it is, it avails not—distance avails not, and place
    avails not,
I too lived, Brooklyn of ample hills was mine,
I too walk'd the streets of Manhattan island, and bathed
    in the waters around it,
I too felt the curious abrupt questionings stir within me,
In the day among crowds of people sometimes they came
    upon me,
In my walks home late at night or as I lay in my bed they
    came upon me,
I too had been struck from the float forever held in solution,
I too had receiv'd identity by my body,
That I was I knew was of my body, and what I should be
    I knew I should be of my body.

VI

It is not upon you alone the dark patches fall,
The dark threw its patches down upon me also,

The best I had done seem'd to me blank and suspicious,
My great thoughts as I supposed them, were they not in
    reality meagre?
Nor is it you alone who know what it is to be evil,
I am he who knew what it was to be evil,
I too knitted the old knot of contrariety,
Blabb'd, blush'd, resented, lied, stole, grudg'd,
Had guile, anger, lust, hot wishes I dared not speak,
Was wayward, vain, greedy, shallow, sly, cowardly, malig-
    nant,
The wolf, the snake, the hog, not wanting in me,
The cheating look, the frivolous word, the adulterous wish,
    not wanting,
Refusals, hates, postponements, meanness, laziness, none
    of these wanting,
Was one with the rest, the days and haps of the rest,
Was call'd by my nighest name by clear loud voices of
    young men as they saw me approaching or passing,
Felt their arms on my neck as I stood, or the negligent
    leaning of their flesh against me as I sat,
Saw many I loved in the street or ferry-boat or public
    assembly, yet never told them a word,
Lived the same life with the rest, the same old laughing,
    gnawing, sleeping,
Play'd the part that still looks back on the actor or actress,
The same old role, the role that is what we make it, as
    great as we like,
Or as small as we like, or both great and small.

VII

Closer yet I approach you,
What thought you have of me now, I had as much of you—
    I laid in my stores in advance,
I consider'd long and seriously of you before you were
    born.

Who was to know what should come home to me?
Who knows but I am enjoying this?
Who knows, for all the distance, but I am as good as look-
    ing at you now, for all you cannot see me?

VIII

Ah, what can ever be more stately and admirable to me
    than mast-hemm'd Manhattan?
River and sunset and scallop-edg'd waves of flood-tide?
The sea-gulls oscillating their bodies, the hay-boat in the
    twilight, and the belated lighter?

What gods can exceed these that clasp me by the hand,
    and with voices I love call me promptly and loudly
    by my·nighest name as I approach?
What is more subtle than this which ties me to the woman
    or man that looks in my face?
Which fuses me into you now, and pours my meaning into
    you?

We understand then do we not?
What I promis'd without mentioning it, have you not
    accepted?

What the study could not teach—what the preaching could
  not accomplish is accomplish'd, is it not?

IX

Flow on, river! flow with the flood-tide, and ebb with the
  ebb-tide!
Frolic on, crested and scallop-edg'd waves!
Gorgeous clouds of the sunset! drench with your splendor
  me, or the men and women generations after me!
Cross from shore to shore, countless crowds of passengers!
Stand up, tall masts of Mannahatta! stand up, beautiful
  hills of Brooklyn!
Throb, baffled and curious brain! throw out questions and
  answers!
Suspend here and everywhere, eternal float of solution!
Gaze, loving and thirsting eyes, in the house or street or
  public assembly!
Sound out, voices of young men! loudly and musically call
  me by my nighest name!
Live, old life! play the part that looks back on the actor or
  actress!
Play the old role, the role that is great or small according
  as one makes it!
Consider, you who peruse me, whether I may not in un-
  known ways be looking upon you;
Be firm, rail over the river, to support those who lean idly,
  yet haste with the hasting current;
Fly on, sea-birds! fly sideways, or wheel in large circles
  high in the air;

Receive the summer sky, you water, and faithfully hold it
    till all downcast eyes have time to take it from you!
Diverge, fine spokes of light, from the shape of my head,
    or any one's head, in the sunlit water!
Come on, ships from the lower bay! pass up or down,
    white-sail'd schooners, sloops, lighters!
Flaunt away, flags of all nations! be duly lower'd at sunset!
Burn high your fires, foundry chimneys! cast black shadows
    at nightfall! cast red and yellow light over the tops of
    the houses!
Appearances, now or henceforth, indicate what you are,
You necessary film, continue to envelop the soul,
About my body for me, and your body for you, be hung
    our divinest aromas,
Thrive, cities—bring your freight, bring your shows, ample
    and sufficient rivers,
Expand, being than which none else is perhaps more
    spiritual,
Keep your places, objects than which none else is more
    lasting.

You have waited, you always wait, you dumb, beautiful
    ministers,
We receive you with free sense at last, and are insatiate
    henceforward,
Not you any more shall be able to foil us, or withhold
    yourselves from us,
We use you, and do not cast you aside—we plant you per-
    manently within us,

We fathom you not—we love you—there is perfection in
you also,
You furnish your parts toward eternity,
Great or small, you furnish your parts toward the soul.

W. WHITMAN

292

OUT OF THE CRADLE ENDLESSLY ROCKING

OUT of the cradle endlessly rocking,
Out of the mocking-bird's throat, the musical shuttle,
Out of the Ninth-month midnight,
Over the sterile sands and the fields beyond, where the
child leaving his bed wandered alone, bareheaded,
barefoot,
Down from the showered halo,
Up from the mystic play of shadows twining and twisting
as if they were alive,
Out from the patches of briers and blackberries,
From the memories of the bird that chanted to me,
From your memories, sad brother, from the fitful risings
and fallings I heard,
From under that yellow half-moon late-risen and swollen
as if with tears,
From those beginning notes of yearning and love there in
the mist,
From the thousand responses of my heart never to cease,

From the myriad thence-aroused words,
From the word stronger and more delicious than any,
From such as now they start the scene revisiting.
As a flock, twittering, rising, or overhead passing,
Borne hither, ere all eludes me, hurriedly,
A man, yet by these tears a little boy again,
Throwing myself on the sand, confronting the waves,
I, chanter of pains and joys, uniter of here and hereafter,
Taking all hints to use them, but swiftly leaping beyond
    them,
A reminiscence sing.

Once Paumanok,
When the lilac-scent was in the air and Fifth-month grass
    was growing,
Up this seashore in some briers,
Two feathered guests from Alabama, two together,
And their nest, and four light-green eggs spotted with
    brown,
And every day the he-bird to and fro near at hand,
And every day the she-bird crouched on her nest, silent,
    with bright eyes,
And every day I, a curious boy, never too close, never
    disturbing them,
Cautiously peering, absorbing, translating.

Shine! shine! shine!
Pour down your warmth, great sun!
While we bask, we two together.

Two together!
Winds blow south, or winds blow north,

Day come white, or night come black,
Home, or rivers and mountains from home,
Singing all time, minding no time,
While we two keep together.

Till of a sudden,
Maybe killed, unknown to her mate,
One forenoon the she-bird crouched not on the nest,
Nor returned that afternoon, nor the next,
Nor ever appeared again.

And thenceforward all summer in the sound of the sea,
And at night under the full of the moon in calmer weather,
Over the hoarse surging of the sea,
Or flitting from brier to brier by day,
I saw, I heard at intervals the remaining one, the he-bird,
The solitary guest from Alabama.

Blow! blow! blow!
Blow up sea-winds along Paumanok's shore;
I wait and I wait till you blow my mate to me.

Yes, when the stars glistened,
All night long on the prong of a moss-scalloped stake,
Down almost amid the slapping waves,
Sat the lone singer wonderful causing tears.

He called on his mate,
He poured forth the meanings which I of all men know.

Yes, my brother, I know,—
The rest might not, but I have treasured every note,
For more than once dimly down to the beach gliding,

Silent, avoiding the moonbeams, blending myself with the
    shadows,
Recalling now the obscure shapes, the echoes, the sounds
    and sights after their sorts,
The white arms out in the breakers tirelessly tossing,
I, with bare feet, a child, the wind wafting my hair,
Listened long and long.

Listened to keep, to sing, now translating the notes,
Following you, my brother.

Soothe! soothe! soothe!
Close on its wave soothes the wave behind,
And again another behind embracing and lapping, every
    one close,
But my love soothes not me, not me.

Low hangs the moon, it rose late,
It is lagging—O I think it is heavy with love, with love.

O madly the sea pushes upon the land,
With love, with love.

O night! do I not see my love fluttering out among the
    breakers?
What is that little black thing I see there in the white?

Loud! loud! loud!
Loud I call to you, my love!

High and clear I shoot my voice over the waves,
Surely you must know who is here, is here,
You must know who I am, my love.

Low-hanging moon!
What is that dusky spot in your brown yellow?
O it is the shape, the shape of my mate!
O moon, do not keep her from me any longer.

Land! land! O land!
Whichever way I turn, O, I think you could give me my
*   mate back again if you only would,*
For I am almost sure I see her dimly whichever way I
*   look.*

O rising stars!
Perhaps the one I want so much will rise, will rise with
*   some of you.*

O throat! O trembling throat!
Sound clearer through the atmosphere!
Pierce the woods, the earth,
Somewhere listening to catch you must be the one I want.

Shake out carols!
Solitary here, the night's carols!
Carols of lonesome love! death's carols!
Carols under that lagging, yellow, waning moon!
O under that moon where she droops almost down into
*   the sea!*
O reckless despairing carols!

But soft! sink low!
Soft! let me just murmur,
And do you wait a moment, you husky-noised sea,

*For somewhere I believe I heard my mate responding to
    me,*
So faint, I must be still, be still to listen,
*But not altogether still, for then she might not come im-
    mediately to me.*

Hither, my love!
Here I am! here!
With this just-sustained note I announce myself to you,
This gentle call is for you, my love, for you.

Do not be decoyed elsewhere:
That is the whistle of the wind, it is not my voice,
That is the fluttering, the fluttering of the spray,
Those are the shadows of leaves.

O darkness! O in vain!
O I am very sick and sorrowful.

*O brown halo in the sky near the moon, drooping upon
    the sea!*
O troubled reflection in the sea!
O throat! O throbbing heart!
And I singing uselessly! uselessly all the night.

O past! O happy life! O songs of joy!
In the air, in the woods, over fields,
Loved! loved! loved! loved! loved!
But my mate no more, no more with me!
We two together no more.

The aria sinking,

All else continuing, the stars shining,
The winds blowing, the notes of the bird continuous echo-
ing,
With angry moans the fierce old mother incessantly moan-
ing,
On the sands of Paumanok's shore gray and rustling,
The yellow half-moon enlarged, sagging down, drooping,
the face of the sea almost touching,
The boy ecstatic, with his bare feet the waves, with his
hair the atmosphere dallying,
The love in the heart long pent, now loose, now at last
tumultuously bursting,
The aria's meaning, the ears, the soul, swiftly depositing,
The strange tears down the cheeks coursing,
The colloquy there, the trio, each uttering,
The undertone, the savage old mother incessantly crying,
To the boy's soul's questions sullenly timing, some
drown'd secret hissing,
To the outsetting bard.

Demon or bird! (said the boy's soul)
Is it indeed toward your mate you sing? or is it really to
me?
For I, that was a child, my tongue's use sleeping, now I
have heard you,
Now in a moment I know what I am for, I awake,
And already a thousand singers, a thousand songs, clearer,
louder and more sorrowful than yours,
A thousand warbling echoes have started to life within me,
never to die.

O you singers solitary, singing by yourself, projecting me,
O solitary me listening, never more shall I cease perpetuat-
ing you,
Never more shall I escape, never more the reverberations,
Never more the cries of unsatisfied love be absent from
me,
Never again leave me to be the peaceful child I was before
what there in the night,
By the sea under the yellow and sagging moon,
The messenger there aroused, the fire, the sweet hell
within,
The unknown want, the destiny of me.
O give me the clew! (it lurks in the night here some
where)
O if I am to have so much, let me have more!

A word then, (for I will conquer it)
The word final, superior to all,
Subtle, sent up—what is it?—I listen;
Are you whispering it, and have been all the time, you
sea-waves?
Is that it from your liquid rims and wet sands?
Whereto answering, the sea,
Delaying not, hurrying not,
Whispered me through the night, and very plainly before
daybreak,
Lisped to me the low and delicious word death,
And again death, death, death, death,
Hissing melodious, neither like the bird nor like my
aroused child's heart,

But edging near as privately for me, rustling at my feet,
Creeping thence steadily up to my ears and laving me
softly all over,
Death, death, death, death, death.

Which I do not forget,
But fuse the song of my dusky demon and brother,
That he sang to me in the moonlight on Paumanok's gray
beach,
With the thousand responsive songs at random,
My own songs awaked from that hour,
And with them the key, the word up from the waves,
The word of the sweetest song and all songs,
That strong and delicious word which, creeping to my
feet,
(Or like some old crone rocking the cradle, swathed in
sweet garments, bending aside)
The sea whispered me.

W. WHITMAN

❧ 293 ☙

FROM PENT-UP ACHING RIVERS

From pent-up aching rivers,
From that of myself without which I were nothing,
From what I am determin'd to make illustrious, even if I
stand sole among men,
From my own voice resonant, singing the phallus,
Singing the song of procreation,

Singing the need of superb children and therein superb
    grown people,
Singing the muscular urge and the blending,
Singing the bedfellow's song, (O resistless yearning!
O for any and each the body correlative attracting!
O for you whoever you are your correlative body! O it,
    more than all else, you delighting!)
From the hungry gnaw that eats me night and day,
From native moments, from bashful pains, singing them,
Seeking something yet unfound though I have diligently
    sought it many a long year,
Singing the true song of the soul fitful at random,
Renascent with grossest Nature or among animals,
Of that, of them and what goes with them my poems in-
    forming,
Of the smell of apples and lemons, of the pairing of birds,
Of the wet of woods, of the lapping of waves,
Of the mad pushes of waves upon the land, I them chant-
    ing,
The overture lightly sounding, the strain anticipating,
The welcome nearness, the sight of the perfect body,
The swimmer swimming naked in the bath, or motionless
    on his back lying and floating,
The female form approaching, I pensive, love-flesh trem-
    ulous aching,
The divine list for myself or you or for anyone making,
The face, the limbs, the index from head to foot, and what
    it arouses,
The mystic deliria, the madness amorous, the utter aban-
    donment,

(Hark close and still what I now whisper to you,
I love you, O you entirely possess me,
O that you and I escape from the rest and go utterly off,
free and lawless,
Two hawks in the air, two fishes swimming in the sea not
more lawless than we;)
The furious storm through me careering, I passionately
trembling,
The oath of the inseparableness of two together, of the
woman that loves me and whom I love more than my
life, that oath swearing,
(O I willingly stake all for you,
O let me be lost if it must be so!
O you and I! what is it to us what the rest do or think?
What is all else to us? only that we enjoy each other and
exhaust each other if it must be so;)
From the master, the pilot I yield the vessel to,
The general commanding me, commanding all, from him
permission taking,
From time the programme hastening, (I have loiter'd too
long as it is,)
From sex, from the warp and from the woof,
From privacy, from frequent repinings alone,
From plenty of persons near and yet the right person not
near,
From the soft sliding of hands over me and thrusting of
fingers through my hair and beard,
From the long sustain'd kiss upon the mouth or bosom,
From the close pressure that makes me or any man drunk,
fainting with excess,

From what the divine husband knows, from the work of
    fatherhood,
From exultation, victory and relief, from the bedfellow's
    embrace in the night,
From the act-poems of eyes, hands, hips and bosoms,
From the cling of the trembling arm,
From the bending curve and the clinch,
From side by side the pliant coverlet off-throwing,
From the one so unwilling to have me leave, and me just
    as unwilling to leave,
(Yet a moment O tender waiter, and I return,)
From the hour of shining stars and dropping dews,
From the night a moment I emerging flitting out,
Celebrate you act divine and you children prepared for,
And you stalwart loins.

                        W. WHITMAN

❧ 294 ❧

I SAW IN LOUISIANA A LIVE-OAK GROWING

I saw in Louisiana a live-oak growing,
All alone stood it and the moss hung down from the
    branches,
Without any companion it grew there uttering joyous
    leaves of dark green,
And its look, rude, unbending, lusty, made me think of
    myself,
But I wonder'd how it could utter joyous leaves standing

alone there without its friend near, for I knew I could
not,
And I broke off a twig with a certain number of leaves
upon it, and twined around it a little moss,
And brought it away, and I have placed it in sight in my
room,
It is not needed to remind me as of my own dear friends,
(For I believe lately I think of little else than of them,)
Yet it remains to me a curious token, it makes me think of
manly love;
For all that, and though the live-oak glistens there in
Louisiana solitary in a wide flat space,
Uttering joyous leaves all its life without a friend a lover
near,
I know very well I could not.

W. WHITMAN

❧ 295 ☙

THE WOUND-DRESSER

I

An old man bending I come among new faces,
Years looking backward resuming in answer to children,
Come tell us old man, as from young men and maidens
that love me,
(Arous'd and angry, I'd thought to beat the alarum, and
urge relentless war,

But soon my fingers fail'd me, my face droop'd and I re-
sign'd myself,
To sit by the wounded and soothe them, or silently watch
the dead;)
Years hence of these scenes, of these furious passions,
these chances,
Of unsurpass'd heroes, (was one side so brave? the other
was equally brave;)
Now be witness again, paint the mightiest armies of earth,
Of those armies so rapid so wondrous what saw you to tell
us?
What stays with you latest and deepest? of curious panics,
Of hard-fought engagements or sieges tremendous what
deepest remains?

II

O maidens and young men I love and that love me,
What you ask of my days those the strangest and sudden
your talking recalls,
Soldier alert I arrive after a long march cover'd with sweat
and dust,
In the nick of time I come, plunge in the fight, loudly
shout in the rush of successful charge,
Enter the captur'd works—yet lo, like a swift-running river
they fade,
Pass and are gone they fade—I dwell not on soldiers' perils
or soldiers' joys,
(Both I remember well—many the hardships, few the joys,
yet I was content.)

But in silence, in dreams' projections,
While the world of gain and appearance and mirth goes
    on,
So soon what is over forgotten, and waves wash the im-
    prints off the sand,
With hinged knees returning I enter the doors, (while for
    you up there,
Whoever you are, follow without noise and be of strong
    heart.)

Bearing the bandages, water and sponge,
Straight and swift to my wounded I go,
Where they lie on the ground after the battle brought in,
Where their priceless blood reddens the grass the ground,
Or to the rows of the hospital tent, or under the roof'd
    hospital,
To the long rows of cots up and down each side I return,
To each and all one after another I draw near, not one do
    I miss,
An attendant follows holding a tray, he carries a refuse
    pail,
Soon to be fill'd with clotted rags and blood, emptied, and
    fill'd again.

I onward go, I stop,
With hinged knees and steady hand to dress wounds,
I am firm with each, the pangs are sharp yet unavoidable,
One turns to me his appealing eyes—poor boy! I never
    knew you,
Yet I think I could not refuse this moment to die for you,
    if that would save you.

On, on I go, (open doors of time! open hospital doors!)
The crush'd head I dress, (poor crazed hand tear not the
bandage away,)
The neck of the cavalry-man with the bullet through and
through I examine,
Hard the breathing rattles, quite glazed already the eye,
yet life struggles hard,
(Come sweet death! be persuaded O beautiful death!
In mercy come quickly.)

From the stump of the arm, the amputated hand,
I undo the clotted lint, remove the slough, wash off the
matter and blood,
Back on his pillow the soldier bends with curv'd neck and
side-falling head,
His eyes are closed, his face is pale, he dares not look on
the bloody stump,
And has not yet look'd on it.

I dress a wound in the side, deep, deep,
But a day or two more, for see the frame all wasted and
sinking,
And the yellow-blue countenance see.

I dress the perforated shoulder, the foot with the bullet-
wound,
Cleanse the one with a gnawing and putrid gangrene, so
sickening, so offensive,
While the attendant stands behind aside me holding the
tray and pail.

I am faithful, I do not give out,
The fractur'd thigh, the knee, the wound in the abdomen,
These and more I dress with impassive hand, (yet deep in
my breast a fire, a burning flame.)

IV

Thus in silence in dreams' projections,
Returning, resuming, I thread my way through the hospi-
tals,
The hurt and wounded I pacify with soothing hand,
I sit by the restless all the dark night, some are so young,
Some suffer so much, I recall the experience sweet and
sad,
(Many a soldier's loving arms about this neck have cross'd
and rested,
Many a soldier's kiss dwells on these bearded lips.)

W. WHITMAN

❧ 296 ☙

O CAPTAIN! MY CAPTAIN!

O CAPTAIN! my Captain! our fearful trip is done,
The ship has weathered every rack, the prize we sought is
won,
The port is near, the bells I hear, the people all exulting,
While follow eyes the steady keel, the vessel grim and
daring;
But O heart! heart! heart!

712

O the bleeding drops of red.
Where on the deck my Captain lies,
Fallen cold and dead.

O Captain! my Captain! rise up and hear the bells;
Rise up—for you the flag is hung—for you the bugle trills,
For you bouquets and ribboned wreaths—for you the
shores a-crowding,
For you they call, the swaying mass, their eager faces turn-
ing;
Here Captain! dear father!
This arm beneath your head!
It is some dream that on the deck,
You've fallen cold and dead.

My Captain does not answer, his lips are pale and still,
My father does not feel my arm, he has no pulse nor will,
The ship is anchored safe and sound, its voyage closed and
done,
From fearful trip the victor ship comes in with object won;
Exult, O shores, and ring, O bells!
But I with mournful tread,
Walk the deck my Captain lies,
Fallen cold and dead.

W. WHITMAN

WHEN LILACS LAST IN THE DOORYARD BLOOM'D

I

WHEN lilacs last in the dooryard bloom'd,
And the great star early droop'd in the western sky in the
    night,
I mourn'd, and yet shall mourn with ever-returning spring.

Ever-returning spring, trinity sure to me you bring,
Lilac blooming perennial and drooping star in the west,
And thought of him I love.

II

O powerful western fallen star!
O shades of night—O moody, tearful night!
O great star disappear'd—O the black murk that hides the
    star!
O cruel hands that hold me powerless—O helpless soul of
    me!
O harsh surrounding cloud that will not free my soul.

III

In the dooryard fronting an old farm-house near the white-
    wash'd palings,

Stands the lilac-bush tall-growing with heart-shaped leaves
of rich green,
With many a pointed blossom rising delicate, with the perfume strong I love,
With every leaf a miracle—and from this bush in the dooryard,
With delicate-color'd blossoms and heart-shaped leaves of
rich green,
A sprig with its flower I break.

IV

In the swamp in secluded recesses,
A shy and hidden bird is warbling a song.

Solitary the thrush,
The hermit withdrawn to himself, avoiding the settle-
ments,
Sings by himself a song.

Song of the bleeding throat,
Death's outlet song of life, (for well dear brother I know,
If thou wast not granted to sing thou would'st surely die.)

V

Over the breast of the spring, the land, amid cities,
Amid lanes and through old woods, where lately the
violets peep'd from the ground, spotting the gray débris,
Amid the grass in the fields each side of the lanes, passing
the endless grass,

Passing the yellow-spear'd wheat, every grain from its
shroud in the dark-brown fields uprisen,
Passing the apple-tree blows of white and pink in the
orchards,
Carrying a corpse to where it shall rest in the grave,
Night and day journeys a coffin.

VI

Coffin that passes through lanes and streets,
Through day and night with the great cloud darkening the
land,
With the pomp of the inloop'd flags with the cities draped
in black,
With the show of the States themselves as of crape-veil'd
women standing,
With processions long and winding and the flambeaus of
the night,
With the countless torches lit, with the silent sea of faces
and the unbared heads,
With the waiting depot, the arriving coffin, and the somber
faces,
With dirges through the night, with the thousand voices
rising strong and solemn,
With all the mournful voices of the dirges pour'd around
the coffin,
The dim-lit churches and the shuddering organs—where
amid these you journey,
With the tolling tolling bells' perpetual clang,
Here, coffin that slowly passes,
I give you my sprig of lilac.

(Nor for you, for one alone,
Blossoms and branches green to coffins all I bring,
For fresh as the morning, thus would I chant a song for
    you O sane and sacred death.

All over bouquets of roses,
O death, I cover you over with roses and early lilies,
But mostly and now the lilac that blooms the first,
Copious I break, I break the sprigs from the bushes,
With loaded arms I come, pouring for you,
For you and the coffins all of you O death.)

O western orb sailing the heaven,
Now I know what you must have meant as a month since
    I walk'd,
As I walk'd in silence the transparent shadowy night,
As I saw you had something to tell as you bent to me
    night after night,
As you droop'd from the sky low down as if to my side,
    (while the other stars all look'd on,)
As we wander'd together the solemn night, (for some-
    thing I know not what kept me from sleep,)
As the night advanced, and I saw on the rim of the west
    how full you were of woe,
As I stood on the rising ground in the breeze in the cool
    transparent night,

As I watch'd where you pass'd and was lost in the nether-
  ward black of the night,
As my soul in its trouble dissatisfied sank, as where you
  sad orb,
Concluded, dropt in the night, and was gone.

IX

Sing on there in the swamp,
O singer bashful and tender, I hear your notes, I hear your
  call,
I hear, I come presently, I understand you,
But a moment I linger, for the lustrous star has detain'd
  me,
The star my departing comrade holds and detains me.

X

O how shall I warble myself for the dead one there I
  loved?
And how shall I deck my song for the large sweet soul that
  has gone?
And what shall my perfume be for the grave of him I
  love?

Sea-winds blown from east and west,
Blown from the Eastern sea and blown from the Western
  sea, till there on the priaries meeting,
These and with these and the breath of my chant,
I'll perfume the grave of him I love.

XI

O what shall I hang on the chamber walls?
And what shall the pictures be that I hang on the walls,
To adorn the burial-house of him I love?
Pictures of growing spring and farms and homes,
With the Fourth-month eve at sundown, and the gray
    smoke lucid and bright,
With floods of the yellow gold of the gorgeous, indolent,
    sinking sun, burning, expanding the air,
With the fresh sweet herbage under foot, and the pale
    green leaves of the trees prolific,
In the distance the flowing glaze, the breast of the river,
    with a wind-dapple here and there,
With ranging hills on the banks, with many a line against
    the sky, and shadows,
And the city at hand, with dwellings so dense, and stacks
    of chimneys,
And all the scenes of life and the workshops, and the
    workmen homeward returning.

XII

Lo, body and soul—this land,
My own Manhattan with spires, and the sparkling and
    hurrying tides, and the ships,
The varied and ample land, the South and the North in
    the light, Ohio's shores and flashing Missouri,
And ever the far-spreading prairies cover'd with grass and
    corn.

719

Lo, the most excellent sun so calm and haughty,
The violet and purple morn with just-felt breezes,
The gentle soft-born measureless light,
The miracle spreading bathing all, the fulfill'd noon,
The coming eve delicious, the welcome night and the stars,
Over my cities shining all, enveloping man and land.

XIII

Sing on, sing on you gray-brown bird,
Sing from the swamps, the recesses, pour your chant from
    the bushes,
Limitless out of the dusk, out of the cedars and pines.
Sing on dearest brother, warble your reedy song,
Loud human song, with voice of uttermost woe.

O liquid and free and tender!
O wild and loose to my soul—O wondrous singer!
You only I hear—yet the star holds me, (but will soon de-
    part,)
Yet the lilac with mastering odor holds me.

XIV

Now while I sat in the day and look'd forth,
In the close of the day with its light and the fields of
    spring, and the farmers preparing their crops,
In the large unconscious scenery of my land with its lakes
    and forests,
In the heavenly aerial beauty, (after the perturb'd winds
    and the storms,)

720

Under the arching heavens of the afternoon swift passing,
and the voices of children and women,
The many-moving sea-tides, and I saw the ships how they
sail'd,
And the summer approaching with richness, and the fields
all busy with labor,
And the infinite separate houses, how they all went on,
each with its meals and minutia of daily usages,
And the streets how their throbbings throbb'd, and the
cities pent—lo, then and there,
Falling upon them all and among them all, enveloping me
with the rest,
Appear'd the cloud, appear'd the long black trail,
And I knew death, its thought, and the sacred knowledge
of death.

Then with the knowledge of death as walking one side of
me,
And the thought of death close-walking the other side of
me,
And I in the middle as with companions, and as holding
the hands of companions,
I fled forth to the hiding receiving night that talks not,
Down to the shores of the water, the path by the swamp in
the dimness,
To the solemn shadowy cedars and ghostly pines so still.

And the singer so shy to the rest receiv'd me,
The gray-brown bird I know receiv'd us comrades three,
And he sang the carol of death, and a verse for him I love.

From deep secluded recesses,
From the fragrant cedars and the ghostly pines so still,
Came the carol of the bird.

And the charm of the carol rapt me
As I held as if by their hands my comrades in the night,
And the voice of my spirit tallied the song of the bird.

Come lovely and soothing death,
Undulate round the world, serenely arriving, arriving,
In the day, in the night, to all, to each,
Sooner or later delicate death.

Prais'd be the fathomless universe,
For life and joy, and for objects and knowledge curious,
And for love, sweet love—but praise! praise! praise!
For the sure-enwinding arms of cool-enfolding death.

Dark mother always gliding near with soft feet,
Have none chanted for thee a chant of fullest welcome?
Then I chant it for thee, I glorify thee above all,
I bring thee a song that when thou must indeed come,
    come unfalteringly.

Approach strong deliveress,
When it is so, when thou hast taken them I joyously sing
    the dead,
Lost in the loving floating ocean of thee,
Laved in the flood of thy bliss O death.

From me to thee glad serenades,
Dances for thee I propose saluting thee, adornments and
    feastings for thee,

And the sights of the open landscape and the high-spread
sky are fitting,
And life and the fields, and the huge and thoughtful night.

The night in silence under many a star,
The ocean shore and the husky whispering wave whose
voice I know,
And the soul turning to thee O vast and well-veil'd death,
And the body gratefully nestling close to thee.

Over the tree-tops I float thee a song,
Over the rising and sinking waves, over the myriad fields
and the prairies wide,
Over the dense-pack'd cities all and the teeming wharves
and ways,
I float this carol with joy, with joy to thee O death.

XV

To the tally of my soul,
Loud and strong kept up the gray-brown bird,
With pure deliberate notes spreading filling the night.

Loud in the pines and cedars dim,
Clear in the freshness moist and the swamp-perfume,
And I with my comrades there in the night.

While my sight that was bound in my eyes unclosed,
As to long panoramas of visions.

And I saw askant the armies,
I saw as in noiseless dreams hundreds of battle-flags,

Borne through the smoke of the battles and pierc'd with
    missiles I saw them,

And carried hither and yon through the smoke, and torn
    and bloody,

And at last but a few shreds left on the staffs, (and all in
    silence,)

And the staffs all splinter'd and broken.

I saw battle-corpses, myriads of them,

And the white skeletons of young men, I saw them,

I saw the débris and débris of all the slain soldiers of the
    war,

But I saw they were not as was thought,

They themselves were fully at rest, they suffer'd not,

The living remain'd and suffer'd, the mother suffer'd,

And the wife and the child and the musing comrade suf-
    fer'd,

And the armies that remain'd suffer'd.

XVI

Passing the visions, passing the night,

Passing, unloosing the hold of my comrades' hands,

Passing the song of the hermit bird and the tallying song
    of my soul,

Victorious song, death's outlet song, yet varying ever-alter-
    ing song,

As low and wailing, yet clear the notes, rising and falling,
    flooding the night,

Sadly sinking and fainting, as warning and warning, and
    yet again bursting with joy,

Covering the earth and filling the spread of the heaven,
As that powerful psalm in the night I heard from recesses,
Passing, I leave thee lilac with heart-shaped leaves,
I leave thee there in the dooryard, blooming, returning
    with spring.

I cease from my song for thee,
From my gaze on thee in the west, fronting the west, com-
    muning with thee,
O comrade lustrous with silver face in the night.

Yet each to keep and all, retrievements out of the night,
The song, the wondrous chant of the gray-brown bird,
And the tallying chant, the echo arous'd in my soul,
With the lustrous and drooping star with the countenance
    full of woe,
With the holders holding my hand nearing the call of the
    bird,
Comrades mine and I in the midst, and their memory ever
    to keep, for the dead I loved so well,
For the sweetest, wisest soul of all my days and lands—and
    this for his dear sake,
Lilac and star and bird twined with the chant of my soul,
There in the fragrant pines and the cedars dusk and dim.

W. WHITMAN

GOOD-BYE MY FANCY!

GOOD-BYE my Fancy!
Farewell dear mate, dear love!
I'm going away, I know not where,
Or to what fortune, or whether I may ever see you again,
So Good-bye my Fancy.

Now for my last—let me look back a moment;
The slower fainter ticking of the clock is in me,
Exit, nightfall, and soon the heart-thud stopping.

Long have we lived, joy'd, caress'd together;
Delightful!—now separation—Good-bye my Fancy.

Yet let me not be too hasty,
Long indeed have we lived, slept, filter'd, become really
  blended into one;
Then if we die we die together, (yes, we'll remain one,)
If we go anywhere we'll go together to meet what happens,
May-be we'll be better off and blither, and learn some-
  thing,
May-be it is yourself now really ushering me to the true
  songs, (who knows?)
May-be it is you the mortal knob really undoing, turning—
  so now finally,
Good-bye—and hail! my Fancy.

W. WHITMAN

THE QUESTION

How shall I array my love?
How should I arrange my fair?
Leave her standing white and silent
In the richness of her hair?
Motion silent, beauty bare
In the glory of her hair?
Or, for place and drapery,
Ravage land, and sack the sea?

Or from darkest summer sky,
When the white belts, riding high,
Cut the clear like ribs of pearl,
On the eastern upland's curl,
In the time of dusk and dew
Tear away a breadth of blue?
Touched from twilight's rosy bars,
With each twinkling tuft of stars,
And, shaking out the glints of gold,
Catch her softly from the cold?
Catch and lift her to the cloud,
Where to crown her, passing proud,
Gliding, glistening woods of June
Reach the rain-ring from the moon?

Or to fold her warmer wise

Let me try in garb and guise
Gathered from this mortal globe;
Roll her beauty in a robe
Of the Persian lilac stain,
Purple, dim with filigrane:
Belted in with rarer red
Than India's leaf ere figured,
Put a crown upon her head.
Then to lead her high and cold
Where, from a step of silver rolled,
A crimson floweth on the floor
Like a river riding o'er
Pearl and priceless marbles bright,
Onyx, myrrhine, marcasite,
And jasper green: nor these alone,
But the famed Phengites stone,
And leading upward to the throne.
Prop and pillar, roof and rise,
All ashake with drops and dyes
And the diamond's precious eyes;
And she, as if a sudden storm
Had fallen upon her face and form;
Diamonds like raindrops rare,
Pearls like hailstones in her hair;
In the lamplight's ruddy stream
Jewels crossed with jewels gleam
On jewels, jewel-circled there;
While round her wrists and ankles bare
Gems of jewels glimpse and gaze,
Hyacinth, rose-stone, idocrase.

Or she stealeth, soft arrayed
Like a white Haemonian maid,
Winding under cypress shade,
Cedar shade and paths of green
With porch and pillar white between:
Amaranth eyes do mine behold,
Hair like the pale marigold:
Dreamily she seems to me
Hero or Herodice!
With a sidelong motion sweet,
Thoro' flowers she draws her feet;
This way now the ripples come,
Shower myrtles, myrrh, and gum
With heliochryse and amomum.

Ah! not so, New England's flower,
Separate must her beauty be
From stars of old mythology:
Priestesses, or Crysophorae;
Nor fairy garb nor kingly dower
May fit her in her radiant hour;
Free and bold her steps must flow,
All men see her come and go;
At her feet the planet lies,
Day and night are in her eyes,
Over her the star-flag strewn:
Lo! she standeth there alone,
Pride, in her dark glances, king,
Love, her cheek rose-coloring:
In a garden all her own,

Lo, she standeth, crowned on
With rare roses, round her drawn
Texture like the webs of dawn
On the rosebeds lingering,
While my heart to her I bring;
Heart and garden all her own—
What in truth cares such a one
Though my arm could round her throw
Gleam of gods, or crowns bestow?
Or though the old gods could confer
All godlike gifts and grace on her?
The young Medusa's locks divine,
Pelops' shoulder eburnine,
Lips that drew the Ismenean bees,
Tears of the Heliades
Dropped into glimmering shells that be
About the indraught of the sea:
The river-riches of the sphere,
All that the dark sea bottoms bear,
The wide earth's green convexity,
The inexhaustible blue sky,
Hold not a prize, so proud, so high
That it could grace her, gay or grand,
By garden-gale and rosebreath fanned;
Or as tonight I saw her stand
Lovely in the meadow land
With a clover in her hand.

F. G. TUCKERMAN

A DREAM

WAS IT A dream? We sail'd, I thought we sail'd,
Martin and I, down a green Alpine stream,
Border'd, each bank, with pines; the morning sun,
On the wet umbrage of their glossy tops,
On the red pinings of their forest-floor,
Drew a warm scent abroad; behind the pines
The mountain-skirts, with all their sylvan change
Of bright-leaf'd chestnuts and moss'd walnut-trees
And the frail scarlet-berried ash, began.
Swiss chalets glitter'd on the dewy slopes,
And from some swarded shelf, high up, there came
Notes of wild pastoral music—over all
Ranged, diamond-bright, the eternal wall of snow.
Upon the mossy rocks at the stream's edge,
Back'd by the pines, a plank-built cottage stood,
Bright in the sun; the climbing gourd-plant's leaves
Muffled its walls, and on the stone-strewn roof
Lay the warm golden gourds; golden, within,
Under the eaves, peer'd rows of Indian corn.
We shot beneath the cottage with the stream.
On the brown, rude-carved balcony, two forms
Came forth—Olivia's, Marguerite! and thine.
Clad were they both in white, flowers in their breast;
Straw hats bedeck'd their heads, with ribbons blue,

Which danced, and on their shoulders, fluttering, play'd.
They saw us, they conferr'd; their bosoms heaved,
And more than mortal impulse fill'd their eyes.

Their lips moved; their white arms, waved eagerly,
Flash'd once, like falling streams; we rose, we gazed.
One moment, on the rapid's top, our boat
Hung poised—and then the darting river of Life
(Such now, methought, it was), the river of Life,
Loud thundering, bore us by; swift, swift it foam'd,
Black under cliffs it raced, round headlands shone.
Soon the plank'd cottage by the sun-warm'd pines
Faded—the moss—the rocks; us burning plains,
Bristled with cities, us the sea received.

M. ARNOLD

❧ 301 ❧

From SOHRAB AND RUSTUM

So, on the bloody sand, Sohrab lay dead;
And the great Rustum drew his horseman's cloak
Down o'er his face, and sate by his dead son.
As those black granite pillars, once high-rear'd
By Jemshid in Persepolis, to bear
His house, now 'mid their broken flights of steps
Lie prone, enormous, down the mountain side—
So in the sand lay Rustum by his son.
And night came down over the solemn waste,
And the two gazing hosts, and that sole pair,

And darken'd all; and a cold fog, with night,
Crept from the Oxus. Soon a hum arose,
As of a great assembly loosed, and fires
Began to twinkle through the fog; for now
Both armies moved to camp, and took their meal;
The Persians took it on the open sands
Southward, the Tartars by the river marge;
And Rustum and his son were left alone.
  But the majestic river floated on,
Out of the mist and hum of that low land,
Into the frosty starlight, and there moved,
Rejoicing, through the hush'd Chorasmian waste,
Under the solitary moon;—he flow'd
Right for the polar star, past Orgunjè,
Brimming, and bright, and large; then sands begin
To hem his watery march, and dam his streams,
And split his currents; that for many a league
The shorn and parcell'd Oxus strains along
Through beds of sand and matted rushy isles—
Oxus, forgetting the bright speed he had
In his high mountain-cradle in Pamere,
A foil'd circuitous wanderer—till at last
The long'd-for dash of waves is heard, and wide
His luminous home of waters opens, bright
And tranquil, from whose floor the new-bathed stars
Emerge, and shine upon the Aral Sea.

M. ARNOLD

DOVER BEACH

THE sea is calm to-night.
The tide is full, the moon lies fair
Upon the straits;—on the French coast the light
Gleams and is gone; the cliffs of England stand,
Glimmering and vast, out in the tranquil bay.
Come to the window, sweet is the night-air!
Only, from the long line of spray
Where the sea meets the moon-blanch'd land,
Listen! you hear the grating roar
Of pebbles which the waves draw back, and fling,
At their return, up the high strand,
Begin, and cease, and then again begin,
With tremulous cadence slow, and bring
The eternal note of sadness in.

Sophocles long ago
Heard it on the Ægæan, and it brought
Into his mind the turbid ebb and flow
Of human misery; we
Find also in the sound a thought,
Hearing it by this distant northern sea.

The Sea of Faith
Was once, too, at the full, and round earth's shore
Lay like the folds of a bright girdle furl'd.

But now I only hear
Its melancholy, long, withdrawing roar,
Retreating, to the breath
Of the night-wind, down the vast edges drear
And naked shingles of the world.

Ah, love, let us be true
To one another! for the world, which seems
To lie before us like a land of dreams,
So various, so beautiful, so new,
Hath really neither joy, nor love, nor light,
Nor certitude, nor peace, nor help for pain;
And we are here as on a darkling plain
Swept with confused alarms of struggle and flight,
Where ignorant armies clash by night.

M. ARNOLD

❧ 303 ❧

PALLADIUM

SET where the upper streams of Simois flow
Was the Palladium, high 'mid rock and wood;
And Hector was in Ilium, far below,
And fought, and saw it not—but there it stood!

It stood, and sun and moonshine rain'd their light
On the pure columns of its glen-built hall.
Backward and forward roll'd the waves of fight
Round Troy—but while this stood, Troy could not fall.

So, in its lovely moonlight, lives the soul.
Mountains surround it, and sweet virgin air;
Cold plashing, past it, crystal waters roll;
We visit it by moments, ah, too rare!

We shall renew the battle in the plain
To-morrow;—red with blood will Xanthus be;
Hector and Ajax will be there again,
Helen will come upon the wall to see.

Then we shall rust in shade, or shine in strife,
And fluctuate 'twixt blind hopes and blind despairs,
And fancy that we put forth all our life,
And never know how with the soul it fares.

Still doth the soul, from its lone fastness high,
Upon our life a ruling effluence send.
And when it fails, fight as we will, we die;
And while it lasts, we cannot wholly end.

M. ARNOLD

❧ 304 ❧

From THE ANGEL IN THE HOUSE

BOOK I: CANTO VIII (II)

THE REVELATION

AN idle poet, here and there,
  Looks around him; but, for all the rest,
The world, unfathomably fair,

736

Is duller than a witling's jest.
Love wakes men, once a lifetime each;
  They lift their heavy lids, and look;
And, lo, what one sweet page can teach,
  They read with joy, then shut the book.
And some give thanks, and some blaspheme,
  And most forget; but, either way,
That and the Child's unheeded dream
  Is all the light of all their day.

Book II: Canto III (II)

THE RAINBOW

A stately rainbow came and stood,
  When I was young, in High-Hurst Park;
Its bright feet lit the hill and wood
  Beyond, and cloud and sward were dark;
And I, who thought the splendour ours
  Because the place was, t'wards it flew,
And there, amidst the glittering showers,
  Gazed vainly for the glorious view.
With whatsoever's lovely, know
  It is not ours; stand off to see,
Or beauty's apparition so
  Puts on invisibility.

C. PATMORE

From TO THE UNKNOWN EROS

BOOK I: XII MAGNA EST VERITAS

HERE, in this little Bay,
Full of tumultuous life and great repose,
Where, twice a day,
The purposeless, glad ocean comes and goes,
Under high cliffs, and far from the huge town,
I sit me down.
For want of me the world's course will not fail:
When all its work is done, the lie shall rot;
The truth is great, and shall prevail,
When none cares whether it prevail or not.

BOOK I: XVI A FAREWELL

With all my will, but much against my heart,
We two now part.
My Very Dear,
Our solace is, the sad road lies so clear.
It needs no art,
With faint, averted feet
And many a tear,
In our opposed paths to persevere.
Go thou to East, I West.
We will not say

There's any hope, it is so far away.
But, O, my Best,
When the one darling of our widowhead,
The nursling Grief,
Is dead,
And no dews blur our eyes
To see the peach-bloom come in evening skies,
Perchance we may,
Where now this night is day,
And even through faith of still averted feet,
Making full circle of our banishment,
Amazed meet;
The bitter journey to the bourne so sweet
Seasoning the termless feast of our content
With tears of recognition never dry.

C. PATMORE

❧ 306 ☙

From THE HOUSE OF LIFE

Sonnet XLVI

A SUPERSCRIPTION

Look in my face; my name is Might-have-been;
  I am also called No-more, Too-late, Farewell;
  Unto thine ear I hold the dead-sea shell
Cast up thy Life's foam-fretted feet between;
Unto thine eyes the glass where that is seen

Which had Life's form and Love's, but by my spell
  Is now a shaken shadow intolerable,
Of ultimate things unuttered the frail screen.

Mark me, how still I am! But should there dart
  One moment through thy soul the soft surprise
  Of that winged Peace which lulls the breath of sighs,—
Then shalt thou see me smile, and turn apart
Thy visage to mine ambush at thy heart
  Sleepless with cold commemorative eyes.

D. G. ROSSETTI

❧ 307 ❧

SPRING

SPRING, with that nameless pathos in the air
Which dwells with all things fair,
Spring, with her golden suns and silver rain,
Is with us once again.

Out in the lonely woods the jasmine burns
Its fragrant lamps, and turns
Into a royal court with green festoons
The banks of dark lagoons.

In the deep heart of every forest tree
The blood is all aglee,
And there's a look about the leafless bowers
As if they dreamed of flowers.

Yet still on every side we trace the hand
Of Winter in the land,
Save where the maple reddens on the lawn,
Flushed by the season's dawn;

Or where like those strange semblances we find
That age to childhood bind,
The elm puts on, as if in Nature's scorn,
The brown of Autumn corn.

And yet the turf is dark, although you know
That, not a span below,
A thousand germs are groping through the gloom,
And soon will burst their tomb.

Already, here and there, on frailest stems
Appear some azure gems,
Small as might deck, upon a gala day,
The forehead of a fay.

In gardens you may note amid the dearth,
The crocus breaking earth;
And near the snowdrops tender white and green,
The violet in its screen.

But many gleams and shadows needs must pass
Along the budding grass,
And weeks go by, before the enamored South
Shall kiss the rose's mouth.

Still there's a sense of blossoms yet unborn
In the sweet airs of morn;

One almost looks to see the very street
Grow purple at his feet.

At times a fragrant breeze comes floating by,
And brings, you know not why,
A feeling as when eager crowds await
Before a palace gate.

Some wondrous pageant; and you scarce would start,
If from a beech's heart
A blue-eyed Dryad, stepping forth, should say,
"Behold me! I am May!"

H. TIMROD

308

I NEVER lost as much but twice,
And that was in the sod;
Twice have I stood a beggar
Before the door of God!

Angels, twice descending,
Reimbursed my store.
Burglar, banker, father,
I am poor once more!

E. DICKINSON

309

SUCCESS

Success is counted sweetest
By those who ne'er succeed.
To comprehend a nectar
Requires sorest need.

Not one of all the purple host
Who took the flag to-day
Can tell the definition,
So clear, of victory,

As he, defeated, dying,
On whose forbidden ear
The distant strains of triumph
Break, agonized and clear.

E. DICKINSON

❧ 310 ❧

PROBLEMS

Bring me the sunset in a cup,
Reckon the morning's flagons up,
  And say how many dew;
Tell me how far the morning leaps,
Tell me what time the weaver sleeps
  Who spun the breadths of blue!

Write me how many notes there be
In the new robin's ecstasy
   Among astonished boughs;
How many trips the tortoise makes,
How many cups the bee partakes,—
   The debauchee of dews!

Also, who laid the rainbow's piers,
Also, who leads the docile spheres
   By withes of supple blue?
Whose fingers string the stalactite,
Who counts the wampum of the night,
   To see that none is due?

Who built this little Alban house
And shut the windows down so close
   My spirit cannot see?
Who'll let me out some gala day,
With implements to fly away,
   Passing pomposity?

E. DICKINSON

❧ 311 ☙

A WOUNDED deer leaps highest,
I've heard the hunter tell;
'T is but the ecstasy of death,
And then the brake is still.

The smitten rock that gushes,

The trampled steel that springs:
A cheek is always redder
Just where the hectic stings!

Mirth is the mail of anguish,
In which it cautious arm,
Lest anybody spy the blood
And "You're hurt" exclaim!

E. DICKINSON

✿ 312 ✿

A DAY

I'LL tell you how the sun rose,—
A ribbon at a time.
The steeples swam in amethyst,
The news like squirrels ran.

The hills untied their bonnets,
The bobolinks begun.
Then I said softly to myself,
"That must have been the sun!"

. . . . . .

But how he set, I know not.
There seemed a purple stile
Which little yellow boys and girls
Were climbing all the while

Till when they reached the other side,

A dominie in gray
Put gently up the evening bars,
And led the flock away.

E. DICKINSON

❧ 313 ❧

AFTER great pain, a formal feeling comes,
The nerves sit ceremonious, like tombs,
The stiff heart questions was it he, that bore,
And yesterday, or centuries before?

The feet, mechanical, go round—
Of ground, or air, or ought—
A wooden way
Regardless grown,
A quartz contentment, like a stone.

This is the hour of lead,
Remembered, if outlived,
As freezing persons, recollect the snow—
First chill—then stupor—then the letting go.

E. DICKINSON

❧ 314 ❧

THIS is my letter to the world
That never wrote to me,
The simple news that nature told
With tender majesty.

Her message is committed
To hands I cannot see.
For love of her, sweet countrymen,
Judge tenderly of me.

E. DICKINSON

❧ 315 ☙

THE HEART asks pleasure first,
And then, excuse from pain;
And then, those little anodynes
That deaden suffering;

And then, to go to sleep;
And then, if it should be
The will of its Inquisitor,
The liberty to die.

E. DICKINSON

❧ 316 ☙

THIS quiet dust was gentlemen and ladies
And lads and girls—
Was laughter and ability sighing
And frocks and curls.

This passive place a summer's nimble mansion
Where bloom and bees

Exists an oriental circuit
Then cease, like these.

E. DICKINSON

❧ 317 ❧

I NEVER saw a moor,
I never saw the sea;
Yet know I how the heather looks,
And what a wave must be.

I never spoke with God,
Nor visited in heaven;
Yet certain am I of the spot
As if the chart were given.

E. DICKINSON

❧ 318 ❧

THE bustle in a house
The morning after death
Is solemnest of industries
Enacted upon earth,—

The sweeping up the heart,
And putting love away
We shall not want to use again
Until eternity.

E. DICKINSON

❧ 319 ❧

TELL all the Truth but tell it slant—
Success in circuit lies:
Too bright for our infirm delight
The Truth's superb surprise.
As lightning to the children eased
With explanation kind,
The Truth must dazzle gradually
Or every man be blind.

E. DICKINSON

❧ 320 ❧

NOT with a club, the Heart is broken
Nor with a stone—
A whip so small you could not see it
I've known

To lash the magic creature
Till it fell,
Yet that whip's name
Too noble then to tell.

Magnanimous as bird
By boy descried—
Singing unto the stone
Of which it died—

Shame need not crouch
In such an earth as ours.
Shame: stand erect—
The Universe is yours.

E. DICKINSON

❧ 321 ❦

THE Auctioneer of Parting
His "Going, going, gone"
Shouts even from the Crucifix,
And brings his hammer down—
He only sells the Wilderness,
The prices of Despair
Range from a single human Heart
To two—not any more.

E. DICKINSON

❧ 322 ❦

MY life closed twice before its close;
It yet remains to see
If Immortality unveil
A third event to me,

So huge, so hopeless to conceive,
As these that twice befell.
Parting is all we know of heaven,
And all we need of hell.

E. DICKINSON

SPRING QUIET

GONE were but the Winter,
  Come were but the Spring,
I would go to a covert
  Where the birds sing;

Where in the whitethorn
  Singeth a thrush,
And a robin sings
  In the holly-bush.

Full of fresh scents
  Are the budding boughs
Arching high over
  A cool green house;

Full of sweet scents,
  And whispering air
Which sayeth softly:
  'We spread no snare;

'Here dwell in safety,
  Here dwell alone,
With a clear stream
  And a mossy stone.

'Here the sun shineth
  Most shadily;

Here is heard an echo
    Of the far sea,
    Though far off it be.'

Towards May 1847

C. G. ROSSETTI

❧ 324 ❧

SONG

OH ROSES for the flush of youth,
    And laurel for the perfect prime;
But pluck an ivy branch for me
    Grown old before my time.

Oh violets for the grave of youth,
    And bay for those dead in their prime;
Give me the withered leaves I chose
    Before in the old time.

6 February 1849

C. G. ROSSETTI

❧ 325 ❧

EVE

'WHILE I sit at the door,
Sick to gaze within,
Mine eye weepeth sore

For sorrow and sin:
As a tree my sin stands
To darken all lands;
Death is the fruit it bore.

'How have Eden bowers grown
Without Adam to bend them?
How have Eden flowers blown,
Squandering their sweet breath,
Without me to tend them?
The Tree of Life was ours,
Tree twelvefold-fruited,
Most lofty tree that flowers,
Most deeply rooted:
I chose the Tree of Death.

'Hadst thou but said me nay,
Adam my brother,
I might have pined away—
I, but none other:
God might have let thee stay
Safe in our garden,
By putting me away
Beyond all pardon.

'I, Eve, sad mother
Of all who must live,
I, not another,
Plucked bitterest fruit to give
My friend, husband, lover.
O wanton eyes, run over!

Who but I should grieve?
Cain hath slain his brother:
Of all who must die mother,
Miserable Eve!'

Thus she sat weeping,
Thus Eve our mother,
Where one lay sleeping
Slain by his brother.
Greatest and least
Each piteous beast
To hear her voice
Forgot his joys
And set aside his feast.

The mouse paused in his walk
And dropped his wheaten stalk;
Grave cattle wagged their heads
In rumination;
The eagle gave a cry
From his cloud station:
Larks on thyme beds
Forbore to mount or sing;
Bees drooped upon the wing;
The raven perched on high
Forgot his ration;
The conies in their rock,
A feeble nation,
Quaked sympathetical;
The mocking-bird left off to mock;
Huge camels knelt as if

In deprecation;
The kind hart's tears were falling;
Chattered the wistful stork;
Dove-voices with a dying fall
Cooed desolation,
Answering grief by grief.

Only the serpent in the dust,
Wriggling and crawling,
Grinned an evil grin and thrust
His tongue out with its fork.

30 January 1865

C. G. ROSSETTI

326

REMEMBER

REMEMBER me when I am gone away,
   Gone far away into the silent land;
   When you can no more hold me by the hand,
Nor I half turn to go yet turning stay.
   Remember me when no more day by day
      You tell me of our future that you planned:
      Only remember me; you understand
It will be late to counsel then or pray.
Yet if you should forget me for a while
      And afterwards remember, do not grieve:
      For if the darkness and corruption leave

755

A vestige of the thoughts that once I had,
Better by far you should forget and smile
Than that you should remember and be sad.

C. G. ROSSETTI

❧ 327 ☙

CHORUS *from* ATALANTA IN CALYDON

WHEN the hounds of spring are on winter's traces,
  The mother of months in meadow or plain
Fills the shadows and windy places
  With lisp of leaves and ripple of rain;
And the brown bright nightingale amorous
Is half assuaged for Itylus,
For the Thracian ships and the foreign faces,
  The tongueless vigil, and all the pain.

Come with bows bent and with emptying of quivers,
  Maiden most perfect, lady of light,
With a noise of winds and many rivers,
  With a clamour of waters, and with might;
Bind on thy sandals, O thou most fleet,
Over the splendour and speed of thy feet;
For the faint east quickens, the wan west shivers,
  Round the feet of the day and the feet of the night.

Where shall we find her, how shall we sing to her,
  Fold our hands round her knees, and cling?
O that man's heart were as fire and could spring to her,
  Fire, or the strength of the streams that spring!

For the stars and the winds are unto her
As raiment, as songs of the harp-player;
For the risen stars and the fallen cling to her,
    And the southwest-wind and the west-wind sing.

For winter's rains and ruins are over,
    And all the season of snows and sins;
The days dividing lover and lover,
    The light that loses, the night that wins;
And time remembered is grief forgotten,
And frosts are slain and flowers begotten,
And in green underwood and cover
    Blossom by blossom the spring begins.

The full streams feed on flower of rushes,
    Ripe grasses trammel a travelling foot,
The faint fresh flame of the young year flushes
    From leaf to flower and flower to fruit;
And fruit and leaf are as gold and fire,
And the oat is heard above the lyre,
And the hoofèd heel of a satyr crushes
    The chestnut-husk at the chestnut-root.

And Pan by noon and Bacchus by night,
    Fleeter of foot than the fleet-foot kid,
Follows with dancing and fills with delight
    The Mænad and the Bassarid;
And soft as lips that laugh and hide
The laughing leaves of the trees divide,
And screen from seeing and leave in sight
    The god pursuing, the maiden hid.

The ivy falls with the Bacchanal's hair
  Over her eyebrows hiding her eyes;
The wild vine slipping down leaves bare
  Her bright breast shortening into sighs;
The wild vine slips with the weight of its leaves,
But the berried ivy catches and cleaves
To the limbs that glitter, the feet that scare
  The wolf that follows, the fawn that flies.

A. C. SWINBURNE

❧ 328 ☙

THAR'S MORE IN THE MAN THAN
THAR IS IN THE LAND

I KNOWED a man, which he lived in Jones,
Which Jones is a county of red hills and stones,
And he lived pretty much by gittin' of loans,
And his mules was nuthin' but skin and bones,
And his hogs was flat as his corn-bread pones,
And he had 'bout a thousand acres o' land.

This man—which his name it was also Jones—
He swore that he 'd leave them old red hills and stones,
Fur he couldn't make nuthin' but yallerish cotton,
And little o' *that,* and his fences was rotten,
And what little corn he had, *hit* was boughten
And dinged ef a livin' was in the land.

And the longer he swore the madder he got,

And he riz and he walked to the stable lot,
And he hollered to Tom to come thar and hitch
Fur to emigrate somewhar whar land was rich,
And to quit raisin' cock-burrs, thistles and sich,
And a wastin' ther time on the cussed land.

So him and Tom they hitched up the mules,
Pertestin' that folks was mighty big fools
That 'ud stay in Georgy ther lifetime out,
Jest scratchin' a livin' when all of 'em mought
Git places in Texas whar cotton would sprout
By the time you could plant it in the land.

And he driv by a house whar a man named Brown
Was a livin', not fur from the edge o' town,
And he bantered Brown fur to buy his place,
And said that bein' as money was skace,
And bein' as sheriffs was hard to face,
Two dollars an acre would git the land.

They closed at a dollar and fifty cents,
And Jones he bought him a waggin and tents,
And loaded his corn, and his wimmin, and truck,
And moved to Texas, which it tuck
His entire pile, with the best of luck,
To git thar and git him a little land.

But Brown moved out on the old Jones' farm,
And he rolled up his breeches and bared his arm,
And he picked all the rocks from off'n the groun',
And he rooted it up and he plowed it down,
Then he sowed his corn and his wheat in the land.

759

Five years glid by, and Brown, one day
(Which he'd got so fat that he wouldn't weigh),
Was a settin' down, sorter lazily,
To the bulliest dinner you ever see,
When one o' the children jumped on his knee
And says, "Yan's Jones, which you bought his land."

And thar was Jones, standin' out at the fence,
And he hadn't no waggin, nor mules, nor tents,
Fur he had left Texas afoot and cum
To Georgy to see if he couldn't git sum
Employment, and he was a lookin' as hum-
Ble as ef he had never owned any land.

But Brown he axed him in, and he sot
Him down to his vittles smokin' hot,
And when he had filled hisself and the floor
Brown looked at him sharp and riz and swore
That, "whether men's land was rich or poor
Thar was more in the *man* than thar was in the *land*."

S. LANIER

❧ 329 ☙

THE MARSHES OF GLYNN

GLOOMS of the live-oaks, beautiful-braided and woven
With intricate shades of the vines that myriad-cloven
  Clamber the forks of the multiform boughs,—
        Emerald twilights,—
        Virginal shy lights,

Wrought of the leaves to allure to the whisper of vows,
When lovers pace timidly down through the green colon-
    nades
Of the dim sweet woods, of the dear dark woods,
  Of the heavenly woods and glades,
That run to the radiant marginal sand-beach within
    The wide sea-marshes of Glynn;—

Beautiful glooms, soft dusks in the noon-day fire,—
Wildwood privacies, closets of lone desire,
Chamber from chamber parted with wavering arras of
    leaves,—
Cells for the passionate pleasure of prayer to the soul that
    grieves,
Pure with a sense of the passing of saints through the
    wood,
Cool for the dutiful weighing of ill with good;—

O braided dusks of the oak and woven shades of the vine,
While the riotous noon-day sun of the June-day long did
    shine
Ye held me fast in your heart and I held you fast in mine;
But now when the noon is no more, and riot is rest,
And the sun is a-wait at the ponderous gate of the West,
And the slant yellow beam down the wood-aisle doth seem
Like a lane into heaven that leads from a dream,—
Ay, now, when my soul all day hath drunken the soul of
    the oak,
And my heart is at ease from men, and the wearisome
    sound of the stroke
  Of the scythe of time and the trowel of trade is low,

And belief overmasters doubt, and I know that I know,
And my spirit is grown to a lordly great compass within,
That the length and the breadth and the sweep of the
    marshes of Glynn
Will work me no fear like the fear they have wrought me
    of yore
When length was fatigue, and when breadth was but bit-
    terness sore,
And when terror and shrinking and dreary unnamable
    pain
Drew over me out of the merciless miles of the plain,—
Oh, now, unafraid, I am fain to face
  The vast sweet visage of space.
To the edge of the wood I am drawn, I am drawn,
Where the gray beach glimmering runs, as a belt of the
    dawn,
    For a mete and a mark
      To the forest-dark:—
          So:
Affable live-oak, leaning low,—
Thus—with your favor—soft, with a reverent hand,
(Not lightly touching your person, Lord of the land!)
Bending your beauty aside, with a step I stand
On the firm-packed sand,
        Free
By a world of marsh that borders a world of sea.
  Sinuous southward and sinuous northward the shimmer-
    ing band
    Of the sand-beach fastens the fringe of the marsh to the
      folds of the land.

Inward and outward to northward and southward the
    beachlines linger and curl
As a silver-wrought garment that clings to and follows the
    firm sweet limbs of a girl.
Vanishing, swerving, evermore curving again into sight,
Softly the sand-beach wavers away to a dim gray looping
    of light.
And what if behind me to westward the wall of the woods
    stands high?
The world lies east: how ample, the marsh and the sea
    and the sky!
A league and a league of marsh-grass, waist-high, broad in
    the blade,
Green, and all of a height, and unflecked with a light or a
    shade,
Stretch leisurely off, in a pleasant plain,
To the terminal blue of the main.

Oh, what is abroad in the marsh and the terminal sea?
    Somehow my soul seems suddenly free
From the weighing of fate and the sad discussion of sin,
By the length and the breadth and the sweep of the
    marshes of Glynn.

Ye marshes, how candid and simple and nothing-with-
    holding and free
Ye publish yourselves to the sky and offer yourselves to
    the sea!
Tolerant plains, that suffer the sea and the rains and the
    sun,

763

Ye spread and span like the catholic man who hath
    mightily won
God out of knowledge and good out of infinite pain
And sight out of blindness and purity out of a stain.

As the marsh-hen secretly builds on the watery sod,
Behold I will build me a nest on the greatness of God:
I will fly in the greatness of God as the marsh-hen flies
In the freedom that fills all the space 'twixt the marsh and
    the skies:
By so many roots as the marsh-grass sends in the sod
I will heartily lay me a-hold on the greatness of God:
Oh, like to the greatness of God is the greatness within
The range of the marshes, the liberal marshes of Glynn.

And the sea lends large, as the marsh: lo, out of his plenty
    the sea
Pours fast: full soon the time of the flood-tide must be:
Look how the grace of the sea doth go
About and about through the intricate channels that flow
    Here and there,
        Everywhere,
Till his waters have flooded the uttermost creeks and the
    low-lying lanes,
And the marsh is meshed with a million veins,
That like as with rosy and silvery essences flow
  In the rose-and-silver evening glow.
      Farewell, my lord Sun!
The creeks overflow: a thousand rivulets run
'Twixt the roots of the sod; the blades of the marsh-grass
    stir;

Passeth a hurrying sound of wings that westward whirr;
Passeth, and all is still; and the currents cease to run;
And the sea and the marsh are one.

How still the plains of the waters be!
The tide is in his ecstasy.
The tide is at his highest height:
                    And it is night.

And now from the Vast of the Lord will the waters of
    sleep
Roll in on the souls of men,
But who will reveal to our waking ken
The forms that swim and the shapes that creep
                    Under the waters of sleep?
And I would I could know what swimmeth below when
    the tide comes in
On the length and the breadth of the marvellous marshes
    of Glynn.

S. LANIER

❧ 330 ☙

INVICTUS

OUT of the night that covers me,
    Black as the Pit from pole to pole,
I thank whatever gods may be
    For my unconquerable soul.

In the fell clutch of circumstance

I have not winced nor cried aloud.
Under the bludgeonings of chance
  My head is bloody, but unbowed.

Beyond this place of wrath and tears
  Looms but the Horror of the shade,
And yet the menace of the years
  Finds, and shall find, me unafraid.

It matters not how strait the gate,
  How charged with punishments the scroll,
I am the master of my fate:
  I am the captain of my soul.

W. E. HENLEY

✤ 331 ✤

THE KINGDOM OF GOD

'In no Strange Land'

O WORLD invisible, we view thee,
O world intangible, we touch thee,
O world unknowable, we know thee,
Inapprehensible, we clutch thee!

Does the fish soar to find the ocean,
The eagle plunge to find the air—
That we ask of the stars in motion
If they have rumour of thee there?

Not where the wheeling systems darken,

And our benumbed conceiving soars!—
The drift of pinions, would we hearken,
Beats at our own clay-shuttered doors.

The angels keep their ancient places;—
Turn but a stone, and start a wing!
'Tis ye, 'tis your estrangèd faces,
That miss the many-splendoured thing.

But (when so sad thou canst not sadder)
Cry;—and upon thy so sore loss
Shall shine the traffic of Jacob's ladder
Pitched betwixt Heaven and Charing Cross.

Yea, in the night, my Soul, my daughter,
Cry,—clinging Heaven by the hems;
And lo, Christ walking on the water
Not of Gennesareth, but Thames!

F. THOMPSON

✤ 332 ✤

NON SUM QUALIS ERAM BONAE SUB REGNO CYNARAE

Last night, ah, yesternight, betwixt her lips and mine
There fell thy shadow, Cynara! thy breath was shed
Upon my soul between the kisses and the wine;
And I was desolate and sick of an old passion,
    Yea, I was desolate and bowed my head:
I have been faithful to thee, Cynara! in my fashion.

767

All night upon mine heart I felt her warm heart beat,
Night-long within mine arms in love and sleep she lay;
Surely the kisses of her bought red mouth were sweet;
But I was desolate and sick of an old passion,
    When I awoke and found the dawn was gray:
I have been faithful to thee, Cynara! in my fashion.

I have forgot much, Cynara! gone with the wind,
Flung roses, roses riotously with the throng,
Dancing, to put thy pale, lost lilies out of mind;
But I was desolate and sick of an old passion,
    Yea, all the time, because the dance was long:
I have been faithful to thee, Cynara! in my fashion.

I cried for madder music and for stronger wine,
But when the feast is finished and the lamps expire,
Then falls thy shadow, Cynara! the night is thine;
And I am desolate and sick of an old passion,
    Yea hungry for the lips of my desire:
I have been faithful to thee, Cynara! in my fashion.

E. DOWSON

333

FADED PICTURES

ONLY two patient eyes to stare
Out of the canvas. All the rest—
The warm green gown, the small hands pressed
Light in the lap, the braided hair

That must have made the sweet low brow
So earnest, centuries ago,
When some one saw it change and glow—
All faded! Just the eyes burn now.

I dare say people pass and pass
Before the blistered little frame,
And dingy work without a name
Stuck in behind its square of glass.

But I, well, I left Raphael
Just to come drink these eyes of hers,
To think away the stains and blurs
And make all new again and well.

Only, for tears my head will bow,
Because there on my heart's last wall,
Scarce one tint left to tell it all,
A picture keeps its eyes, somehow.

W. V. MOODY

❧ 334 ❧

From THE BLACK RIDERS
AND OTHER LINES

I

BLACK riders came from the sea.
There was clang and clang of spear and shield,
And clash and clash of hoof and heel,
Wild shouts and the wave of hair

In the rush upon the wind:
Thus the ride of Sin.

XXIII

Places among the stars,
Soft gardens near the sun,
Keep your distant beauty;
Shed no beams upon my weak heart.
Since she is here
In a place of blackness,
Not your golden days
Nor your silver nights
Can call me to you.
Since she is here
In a place of blackness,
Here I stay and wait.

LXVII

God lay dead in heaven;
Angels sang the hymn of the end;
Purple winds went moaning,
Their wings drip-dripping
With blood
That fell upon the earth.
It, groaning thing,
Turned black and sank.
Then from the far caverns
Of dead sins
Came monsters, livid with desire.

770

They fought,
Wrangled over the world,
A morsel.
But of all sadness this was sad—
A woman's arms tried to shield
The head of a sleeping man
From the jaws of the final beast.

S. CRANE

❧ 335 ❧

From WAR IS KIND
AND OTHER LINES

I

Do NOT weep, maiden, for war is kind.
Because your lover threw wild hands toward the sky
And the affrighted steed ran on alone,
Do not weep.
War is kind.

> Hoarse, booming drums of the regiment,
> Little souls who thirst for fight,
> These men were born to drill and die.
> The unexplained glory flies above them,
> Great is the battle god, great, and his kingdom
> A field where a thousand corpses lie.

Do not weep, babe, for war is kind.
Because your father tumbled in the yellow trenches,

Raged at his breast, gulped and died,
Do not weep.
War is kind.

Swift blazing flag of the regiment,
Eagle with crest of red and gold,
These men were born to drill and die.
Point for them the virtue of slaughter,
Make plain to them the excellence of killing
And a field where a thousand corpses lie.

Mother whose heart hung humble as a button
On the bright splendid shroud of your son,
Do not weep.
War is kind.

XXI

A man said to the universe:
"Sir, I exist!"
"However," replied the universe,
"The fact has not created in me
A sense of obligation."

S. CRANE

THREE POEMS

I

A MAN adrift on a slim spar
A horizon smaller than the rim of a bottle
Tented waves rearing lashy dark points
The near whine of froth in circles.
                              God is cold.

The incessant raise and swing of the sea
And growl after growl of crest
The sinkings, green, seething, endless
The upheaval half-completed.
                              God is cold.

The seas are in the hollow of The Hand;
Oceans may be turned to a spray
Raining down through the stars
Because of a gesture of pity toward a babe.
Oceans may become grey ashes,
Die with a long moan and a roar
Amid the tumult of the fishes
And the cries of the ships,
Because The Hand beckons the mice.
A horizon smaller than a doomed assassin's cap,
Inky, surging tumults
A reeling, drunken sky and no sky

A pale hand sliding from a polished spar.

                          God is cold.

The puff of a coat imprisoning air:
A face kissing the water-death
A weary slow sway of a lost hand
And the sea, the moving sea, the sea.

                          God is cold.

II

Chant you loud of punishments,
Of the twisting of the heart's poor strings
Of the crash of the lightning's fierce revenge.

Then sing I of the supple-souled men
And the strong, strong gods
That shall meet in times hereafter
And the amaze of the gods
At the strength of the men.
—The strong, strong gods—
—And the supple-souled men—

III

A naked woman and a dead dwarf;
Poor dwarf!
Reigning with foolish kings
And dying mid bells and wine
Ending with a desperate comic palaver
While before thee and after thee

Endures the eternal clown—
—The eternal clown—
A naked woman.

S. CRANE

INDEX OF WRITERS

With Dates of Birth and Death, and First Lines
of the Poems and Titles

777

INDEX OF FIRST LINES

791

795

798